D0161403

DANNY MORRIS

ACES & WINGMEN II

VOLUME I

Men, machines and units of the United States Army Air Force, Eighth Fighter
Command and 354th Fighter Group, Ninth Air Force, 1943-5

Edited by
TOM FRISQUE

Illustrated by
STEVE FERGUSON

DISTRIBUTED BY

AVIATION SK
602 FRONT ST., BOX 97
USK, WA 99180

SBN 85435 241 4

Library of Congress #0-962308-1-3
Copyright by Aviation - USK
1989

DEDICATION

In memory of Peter E. Pompetti, fighter pilot and friend who passed away 26th April 1985 this book is respectfully dedicated.

ACKNOWLEDGEMENTS

I wish (once again) to thank the many friends and enthusiasts who responded time and time again to my many and numerous requests for their help and in particular to Tom and Donna Frisque and their son Randy whose patience and faith in my limited abilities made this history possible. Also to my good buddy Dwayne Tabatt who started it all off again. Cheers Guys.

I also wish to extend my grateful thanks to the following members of our great fraternity, Major William H. Austin, Chief, Magazines and Book Division, Arlington, Virginia, Vincent Ambrose, Willie Y. Anderson, Don Allen, Robert J. Bain, Clyde Bergman, Mrs. Herb Boelter, James D. Bradshaw, Henry W. Brown, Myron 'Moose' Becraft, Americo Boccardi, Hal Burch, Peter Burrell, Col. Don Blakeslee, Pat C. Bova, Marvin C. Biegelow, O. Kenneth Biggs, R. Vernon Blizzard, William E. Bryan, Tim Bivens, Col. William B. Bailey, Walter C. Beckham, George E. Bostwick, Frank E. Birtciel, Col. Dewey Ballard, Lloyd D. Boring, Charles E. Beck, Howell L. Broxton, Steve Blake, Robert Bland, Allen J. Chalmers, Maurice T. Coffman, H. Philip Causer, Robert C. Croker, Tony Chardella, Melvin Cernicky, McCauley Clark, Cheely H. Carter, Halsey S. Carey, William H. Courtney, Harols and Barbara Comstock, Gabe Cutri, John W. Cunnick, Ray Cresswell, Gil Cohen, Bert Connor, Sterling A. Conley, Glen W. Cox, Cleve Costley, David and Alison Campbell, O. B. Clifton, Lt. Col. John 'Wild Bill' Crump, the late Col. William C. Clark and Dolly and Bill Clark Jr. and Sharon, Rueben F. Curtis, William J. Cullerton, George A. Doersch, Joe DeShay, Gustave Dahlstrom, Mrs. James Darrell, Glenn E. Duncan, Urban L. Drew, Lee 'Dutch' Eisenhart, John E. Earnest, Ron Epstein, Jeffrey L. Ethell, Bob Eby, Ed Epp, John Franz, Royal D. Frey, Roger A. Freeman, Owen P. Farmer, Robert J. Frisch, L. Jeff French, Robert J. Farney, Wally B. Frank, Jim Frazier, Robert W. Fox, Glenn Fielding, Elmer Fiery, Edward B. Giller and Millie G., Bob Garlich, Frank J. Grenon of the P-51 Pilots Association, Gerald and Mary Graham, Martyn Gorskey, the late Gordon Hunsberger and Jane, Gordon and Vivian M. Graham, Dave Glover, Gravette, Phillip Gangemi, John Gehrig, Jimmy Goodson, Peter and Sylvia Gaskin, Jim, Elizabeth and Christie Golden, Carroll 'Hank' Henry, John Hudgens, Col. Wallace E. Hopkins, Ernest J. Hopcroft, Don Havey, Tom L. Hayes, Dave and Betty Harris, Fred Hayner, James R. Hanson, Jasper and Dottie Hargrove, Andy and Pat Height, Jack Hild, Sidney H. Hewett, Richard M. Holly, Richard C. Herbst, M/Gen. John B. Henry, Ian Hawkins, Jack Ilfrey, Robert E. Irion, Wilbert 'Weep' Juntilla, Bill Jaaskelainen, Robert E. Johnson, Robert S. Johnson, Leedom Kirk John, Ollie Joiner, Jack S. Jenkins, the late John W. Keeler and Elinor Keeler, Joseph D. Kelly, Walter Kozicki, Joe Kruzel, Dale Karger and Karen Karger Bender and family, Bob Kuhnert of the 355th Fighter Group Association, Ralph Knighton, Frank W. Klibbe, John Kirk III, Walter J. Konantz, Albert M. Koenig, John Leaf, John D. Landers, Bob Long, Dan Leftwich, Huie H. Lamb Jr., Witold and Penny Lanowski, Arthur Lombardi, Robert M. Littlefield, Ray Larnerd and Eddie Larnerd, Peter Laboranti, Chet and Mary Malarz, Henry Molter, Jay F. Marts, Arlen Mitchell, Evan Mondl, Bill Marshall, Herman Mondschein, Donald L. Mercier, Ralph E. Moore, Willie May, the late Daniel D. McKee, Joseph Mejaski, Russell T. McNally, Bert McDowell Jr., Ian Mactaggart, L. William May, John J. Murray, Phil McCullough, Kent Miller, Jerome Mau, Ian McLachlan, Jack E. McCoskey, Fred A. 'Doc' Nessler, Burton and Evelyn Newmark, Leroy 'Old Nock' Nitschke, Merle and Margareth Olmsted, Frank Q. O'Connor, Robin W. Olds, Lt. Col. Carroll W. Ofsthun, Harold L. Olson, Jack Pierce, Ernest J. Porter, Richard E. Penrose, Lewis S. Peter Jr., Russ Peasley, Bob and Betty Powell Jr., Chet Patterson, Richard F. Quinn, Herbert and Anne Rutland, Ed Richie, Russell Ross, G. Tom Rich, Col. Edwin 'Doug' Reinhardt, Art Shoemaker, James D. Smith, Martin and Louise Sheldrick, James C. Stewart, Marvin Satenstein, Kenneth J. Scott, Col. Hervey Stockman, Pamela and George Singleton and her late father Peter E. Pompetti, Curtis L. Smart, Col. Sloan, Kenny J. Soarce, Woodrow K. Salgren, Frank and Doris Stillwell, Robert C. Strobell, Paul Seldon, Charles Siemsen, Carl Sproles, Bill and Sarah Spencer, Bob and Donna Sand, Jim Starnes, Jack Thornell Jr., Eugene Timony, Glenn A. Tessmer, Harrison 'Bud' Tordoff, Jim Tudor, Anna C. Tower, Jesse L. Truett, Robert and Jane Volkman, Don Vulgamore, George and Barbara Vanden Heuval, James and Pepper Woolery, Mrs. Martha 'Roy' Webb Jr., Robert C. Wright, Ken Willard, Betty Wyatt, Glessner Weckbacher, James N. Wood Jr., Gary Weinhold, the late Horace Q. Waggoner, Herbert Watson, Lt. Gen. Benjamin J. Webster, Ernest Workman, Robert M. York, B/Gen. Charles E. Yeager, Al Zachilli, Hubert Zemke, Edmond Zellner, Stan Ziolkowski.

Danny Morris
Avely Essey
July 4, 1989

Line up of Group Commander's aircraft at Bottisham Airfield, Cambridgeshire on 31st August 1944. Colonel Harold Rau's MC-R, 44-13337 'Gentle Annie', Colonel James Mayden's PE-X, 44-14111 'Straw Boss 2', Colonel Dave Schilling's LM-S, 42-26541, Colonel John McGinn's CL-P, 44-14291 'DaQuake', Colonel Phil Tukey's PJ-T, 42-26415 'Judy' and Col Ben Rimerman's LH-E 42-28422. Behind them are J2-R, a P-38 Lightning flown in by Hub Zemke, and Colonel Fred Gray's HL-Z 'Mr Ted' of the 78th Fighter Group.

(USAF)

EDITOR'S NOTE

After many years of diligent research Danny Morris published the first edition of ``Aces & Wingmen'' in 1972. Since then he has continued to collect photos, data and personal recollections with the intent of updating the original manuscript. Now, a full seventeen years later, we are proud to offer an entirely new and revised two volume edition.

The ensuing years have seen the interest in WW II subjects increase greatly. Concurrently, the level of sophistication of the average reader has also greatly increased with the proliferation of published data from both private individuals and declassified government records. These two volumes, it is hoped, provide a balance of new and previously published material covering each of the 48 fighter squadrons.

As can be readily seen from Danny's huge acknowledgements list, this book would not have been possible without the active participation of many, many people. And so it is on this end too: First, thanks to my wife for typing, planning, talking and thinking 8th A.F. for well over one entire year. Her cooperation was indispensable. Next, to Danny himself, for collecting and patiently recording such important historical events and for placing his trust in Aviation Usk. To Lloyd Pankey, whose Continental Investment Company made our dream into a financial reality. To Brian Mulron, whose unselfish loan of an entire photo collection contributed greatly to the richness and variety of the material. To Dwayne Tabatt, whose constant encouragement, technical expertise and substantial unpublished photo collection were also essential ingredients. To Brad Diesen, who spent hour upon hour sorting through missing aircrew reports. To Steve Ferguson, who provided more than just his usual top quality art work with his timely and encouraging suggestions. And finally, to Hal Whitmore whose 356th Fighter Group P-51 graces (literally) our cover.

This September marks the 50th year since the beginning of WW II. It would be unthinkable to legitimize something that caused so much misery with the title of ``anniversary''. It is not the purpose of this work to glorify this war, or any other for that matter. What we have attempted is a grateful tribute to those brave men who so willingly sacrificed their time, talents, health - and even their very lives so that the world as we know it might not perish.

Tom Frisque
Usk, Washington
July 4, 1989

Two photos which show a Lightning of the 554th Squadron, 496th Fighter Training Group which appears to have picked up damage, probably from a pilot who was 'daisy cutting'.

Yes, training could be dangerous too. The combination of inexperienced pilots, and often over aged high performance A/C took its toll. Here, the result of engine failure, a P-47 of the 551st SQ, 495th training group at Atcham, *(Shropshire)*

Major General William Kepner with his P-47 "Buffalo Kokomo."

(Mulron)

8th Air Force Commanding Officers.
Front Row: - Colonel L. K. Callahan, B/General Edward W. Anderson, B/General Jesse Auton, Lt General Jimmy H. Doolittle, B/General Francis H. Griswold, M/General William E. Kepner, B/General Murray C. Woodbury, Colonel Robert W. Burns, Colonel Benjamin J. Webster.
Back Row: - L/Colonel Everett W. Stewart, Colonel Hubert Zemke, L/Colonel Roy B. Caviness, L/Colonel Ben Rimerman, L/Colonel James D. Mayden, Colonel David C. Schilling, L/Colonel William H. Swanson, L/Colonel Joseph B. McManus, L/Colonel Claiborn H. Kinnard, Colonel Frederick C. Gray, L/Colonel Philip E. Tukey, Colonel John B. Henry, Colonel Donald W. Graham, Colonel George W. Crowell.

(Webster)

FOREWORD

Most analysts agree that air power was a decisive factor in the outcome of the Second World War. In Europe, the achievement of the strategic air campaign is debatable, but on one aspect all eminent authorities are in accord; that the attainment and hold of air superiority over enemy territory was a major contribution to victory. Foremost in this achievement were the fighter units of the US Eighth Air Force. Initially, their mission was to protect the large day bomber formations from enemy interceptors. So successful were they in carrying out this difficult task and finding the means to push deeper and deeper into the enemy heartland, that eventually they turned to the offensive. The Luftwaffe fighters became the quarry and the American fighters the hunters. By the spring of 1944 the German fighter force was neutralized and despite massive attempts to reassert its prowess, the US fighters kept the upper hand. In this book Danny Morris once again uses his remarkable collection of photographs to depict a selection of fighter pilots and aircraft of the 8th Air Force. What is most pleasing is that his choice embraces both the very famous and the little known, thus giving a fairer view of this gallant band. Through their pictures and combat reports we meet such colorful characters as 'Ben' Drew, successful bouncer of the ME-262 jet, the irrepressible Royal Frey, himself shot down, the dedicated 'Punchy' Powell and the daring Peter Pompetti; 'Lanny' Lanowski, veteran fighter with four air forces, and many others. Aerial warriors who in their way and day contributed to the defeat of the Nazi tyranny.

Roger A. Freeman.
1989.

"Rachel H2" was a hack aircraft of the 66th Fighter Wing. The checks on the nose were made up of all the nose colours used by the fighters assigned to the wing. In the background is Fowlmere airfield, home of the 339th Fighter Group.

(via Gotts)

This Mustang was made out of several airframes hence the name "Spare Parts." Serial was 43-6623 and it was with BAD-2.
(Holmes)

'The Eagles Wrath' under the Eifel Tower in Paris after the war. This photo was taken by Herb Rutland who flew with the 356th Fighter Group. This B-17 served with the 94th Bomb Group.
(Rutland)

TABLE OF CONTENTS

Two photographs which show a line up of aircraft taken at Debden, Essex when all commanding officers or their deputies met for a conference on 23rd March 1945 to make final plans to cover the crossing of the Rhine. The code of the operation was VARSITY. In the top photo from left to right are the 4th's hack VF-4, 359th's CV-Q, 44-15717, Bob Montgomery's LC-D, 44-72519 'Gumpy,' LH-V, 44-11646 flown by Ben Rimermann, C5-Q, 44-11678 'Bobby Jean - Ah Fung Goo' flown by Irwin Dregne, a 356th Fighter Group Mustang then two unidentified aircraft.

(Wechbacher)

Below, from left to right: P-51's of the 55th (CL-P), 355th (WR-A, "Man O' War," 479th, 339th (Bill Clark's 5Q-C) and 364th (Eugene Roberts).

(Weckbacher)

GLOSSARY

Abort	To turn back from a mission due to either a mechanical fault, bad weather or illness.
Air Medal	Awarded for completing ten missions over enemy territory.
A/D	Airdrome
AAF	Army Air Force, Army Air Field
AFB	Air Force Base
B/F	Bomber Force.
Belly-in	To make a forced landing with the undercart still retracted.
Big Friends	Allied bombers.
Bird/Kite	Aircraft
Bandit	Enemy aircraft.
Blow job	Jet aircraft (ME-163, ME-262 or AR-234)
Bogies	Unidentified aircraft
Bounce	To make an attack on enemy aircraft, usually from above or a point of maximum advantage, surprise attack.
Combat Box	Defensive formation used by USAAF bombers.
DUC	Distinguished Unit Citation.
E/A	Enemy aircraft.
E.T.O.	European Theatre of Operations.
Element	Two aircraft flying as a team.
Flight	Four aircraft.
GAF	German airforce-Luftwaffe.
H.Q.	Headquarters
KIA	Killed in Action
Little Friend	Friendly fighters.
M.A.C.R.	Missing Air Crew Report
MEW	Micro Early Warning Control
MIA	Missing in Action.
M/Sgt.	Master Sargeant
OLC	Oak Leaf Cluster (a secondary award to the Air Medal, D.F.C. etc.)
POW	Prisoner of War.
Ramrod	Bomber Escort
RODEO	Fighter sweeps
Rhubarb	Ground Strafing mission.
S/E	Single engine or start engine.
Section	Eight aircraft.
S/Sgt.	Staff Sargeant
Stream	Large Formation of Bombers.
T/E	Twin Engine.
U/I	Unidentified aircraft.
VOCG	Verbal Order of Commanding General.
ZI	Zone of Interior, United States, HOME!

Ralph K. Hofer poses with Archie Chatterley's aircraft QP-G, 41-6358 'Cal or Bust.' Hofer was flying this aircraft on his first combat mission when he shot down a ME-109 over Zwolle, Holland, 8th October 1943.

Paul E. Burnett of the 334th Fighter Squadron poses with his Crew Chief Robert S. Zane and the Assistant Crew Chief Neil F. Killen. The serial number of 'Marjorie' was 44-72327.

The scoreboard of 'C Flight' 334th Fighter Squadron (ex-71st Eagle Squadron). The little parachutes indicate pilots missing in action. A total of twentyfour pilots are listed of which seven were aces.

Johnny Godfrey and Don Gentile, one of the great two man teams produced by the Army Air Force during the Second World War. These two pilots claimed a total of 66 enemy aircraft destroyed between them. Gentile was killed in a flying accident after the war and Godfrey passed away at the age of 37 on 12th June 1958 of Amyotrophic Lateral Sclerosis (ALS) Lou Gehrig's disease.

FIGHTING HIGHLIGHTS

20th February 1942

B/General Ira C. Eaker lands in England to form the 8th Air Force.

2nd May 1942

The 97th Heavy Bombardment Group is the first group to be assigned to the 8th Air Force.

10th June 1942

The 31st and 52nd Fighter Groups are assigned to the 8th Air Force.

26th July 1942

The 31st Fighter Group dispatches six Supermarine Spitfires which carry out a sweep over the Gravelines area. The first operational mission for the 8th Fighter Command.[1]

17th August 1942

The 97th Bomb Group completes its first mission.

19th August 1942

The 52nd Fighter Group completes its first mission.

14th September 1942

The 31st and 52nd Fighter Groups are transferred to the 12th Air Force. The 31st continues to operate under the 8th Fighter Command until late October 1942.

29th September 1942

The Royal Air Force releases the three 'Eagle' Squadrons to the 8th Fighter Command. The 71st, 121st and 133rd Squadrons become the 334th, 335th and 336th Fighter Squadrons and are designated the 4th Fighter Group to be based at Debden, Essex. This was the second fighter group to be activated in a theatre of war, the first being the American Volunteer Group, which became the 23rd Fighter Group.

2nd October 1942

The 4th Fighter Group completes its first mission for the 8th Fighter Command when 23 Spitfires acted as escort for a diversionary attack on St. Omer, France. The group claimed 4 enemy aircraft destroyed for no losses.

15th October 1942

The 14th Fighter Group, flying P-38 Lightnings, escort RAF Bostons to complete its first mission for the 8th Air Force.

21st October 1942

The 14th Fighter Group completed its last mission for the 8th Air Force before transferring to the 12th Air Force. Also completing its last 8th Air Force mission is the 97th Bombardment Group.

Above - 2 photos of "Miss Plainfield," the P-47 (QP-D, SER #42-7945) flown by 334th Squadron personality Lt. S. Pissanos who scored 4 of his 5 aerial victories in this A/C. Middle photo shows red bordered star and bar national markings.

Below: The P-51B assigned to Capt Herbert J. Blanchfield whose contributions to the air-war were recognized by his DFC and air medal awards. Capt Blanchfield was lost in this A/C May 9, 1944.

Also on July 26: "Lt Col Albert P Clark, Executive Officer of 31st Ftr Gp, is shot down while flying an RAF ftr on a sweep over France, thus becoming the first Eighth AF ftr pilot to be shot down in ETO. He survives and is taken prisoner by the Germans."

31st December 1942

The 8th Fighter Command claimed a total of 9 enemy aircraft destroyed for the loss of 12 of its own fighters for 1942.

10th March 1943

The first use by the 8th Fighter Command of Republic's P-47 Thunderbolt when a mixed group of 14 P-47s and 12 Spitfires of the 4th Fighter Group carried out a patrol.

8th April 1943

First all Thunderbolt mission flown when a total of 33 Jugs flew a Rodeo to Dunkirk, France. A flight of four were from the 56th Fighter Group, twelve from the 78th based at Duxford and the rest were from the 4th Fighter Group. There were no claims and no losses.

13th April 1943

First full group missions flown by the 56th and 78th Fighter Groups.

15th April 1943

Don Blakeslee knocks down the first confirmed aerial kill in a Thunderbolt. Also the first operational loss of a Thunderbolt.

29th April 1943

For the first time over 100 fighters of the 8th are sent out. A sweep over the Pas de Calais area. The 56th lost two Thunderbolts during its first encounter with the GAF. No claims were made.

28th July 1943

The 4th Fighter Group is the first to penetrate German airspace which was made possible by the use of belly tanks. The group claimed 9 enemy aircraft destroyed for the loss of Lt. Henry Ayers of the 336th Fighter Squadron who was taken prisoner.

30th July 1943

Top: The Deacon visits friends in sunny Italy. Taken by a member of the 325th Fighter Group who reported it was flown by Lt. Howard "Deacon" Hively on a shuttle mission to Russia. Serial #44-13306 is not generally recognized as one of his A/C.

(Tabatt)

Above: "Gloria III" of the 334th F. S. prior to being flown by Lt. Grover C. Siems Jr. on a shuttle mission to Russia. On the return leg of the mission, Siems was wounded and landed the A/C, QP-O, 44-13322, in Italy. Siems was then returned to the states due to the severity of his wounds.

Below: Captain Thomas E. Joyce of Ulysses, Kansas became a POW on Sept 12, 1944 when his A/C was shot down. Capt Joyce shot down two ME-109s on July 7 and shared a FW-190 on June 20.

(Holmes)

Second use of bellytanks. Gene Roberts of the 78th Fighter Group knocks down three enemy fighters for the first triple by an 8th fighter pilot. Quince Brown strafes a train and claims another first. Charles London shoots down two enemy aircraft and is the first ace of the 8th Fighter Command. All three men flew with the 78th Fighter Group. The 4th, 56th and 78th claim a total of 25 enemy fighters shot down for the loss of seven Thunderbolts.

12th August 1943
The 353rd Fighter Group completes its first mission.

17th August 1943
Famous raid on Regensburg/Schweinfurt. A total of 240 Thunderbolts claim 19 enemy aircraft destroyed for the loss of three aircraft.

19th August 1943
Jerry Johnson claims his fifth enemy aircraft to become the 56th's first ace. The previous day he had shot down three.

9th September 1943
First Mission for the 352nd Fighter Group flying out of Bodney, Norfolk.

14th September 1943
The 355th Fighter Group completes its first combat mission from Steeple Morden, Hertfordshire. One T-bolt hits a tree on take-off and crashlands.

27th September 1943
First use by the fighters of the US 108 gallon drop tank. The 6 groups claim a total of 21 aircraft destroyed for the loss of one Thunderbolt.

2nd October 1943
Colonel Hub Zemke becomes the 56th's second ace.

10th October 1943
Lt. Colonel Dave Schilling knocks down his fifth enemy fighter in four missions.

15th October 1943
The 55th Fighter Group completes its first mission. The group sent out 36 P-38 Lightnings. The 356th based at Martlesham Heath, Suffolk also flies its first combat mission. Thirty-four Thunderbolts carried out a sweep along the Dutch coast.

3rd November 1943
The 79th Fighter Squadron, 20th Fighter Group completes its first mission while flying with the 55th Fighter Group.

25th November 1943
First use of the Thunderbolt as a divebomber when the airfield at St. Omer is attacked. The 77th Fighter Squadron, 20th Fighter Group, starts operational flying with the 55th Fighter Group.

26th November 1943
Walker Mahurin is the first pilot to claim a total of 10 enemy aircraft destroyed.

Above: So you think A/C research is a snap! The following scenario is all too commonplace: This A/C was assigned to Capt. Paul M. Ellington but it had already served with the 56th Group. Ellington scored both his confirmed victories in another P-47 (42-7968, WD-U) and became a P.O.W. in a P-51B (43-7004 WD-U). Meanwhile, this P-47 was also used by different members of the 335th - F/O Joseph Goetz shared two victories with it on Feb. 22, 1944. This information from various sources, including "Escort to Berlin" and Frank Olynyk's "Credits . . . ."

Below: A quartet of 4th F.G. A/C led by Col Don Blakesley in 44-13779. Next Pierce McKennon in 44-13883, Robert Mabie in his assigned A/C 44-13564 and VF-L of the 336th.

(Mulron)

5th December 1943

The 55th Fighter Squadron, 20th Fighter Group flies its first combat mission. This is also with the 55th Fighter Group.

13th December 1943

The 359th Fighter Group based at East Wretham, Norfolk, completes its first mission when it sends out 36 Thunderbolts on a sweep in the Pas de Calais area. No hits and no misses.

20th December 1943

The 358th Fighter Group sends out 36 Thunderbolts on a sweep in the Pas de Calais area to complete its first mission. The group is exchanged later for the 9th Air Force's 357th Fighter Group which will operate the P-51 Mustang. Captain Franklyn Greene claims the first confirmed enemy aircraft for the 352nd fighter group.

28th December 1943

The 20th Fighter Group completes its first full group mission. A young Royal D. Frey celebrated two events this day, his 20th birthday and his first combat mission. A total of 36 Lightnings carried out a sweep along the Dutch coast.

1st January 1944

Lt. Colonel Don Blakeslee takes over command of the 4th Fighter Group and immediately starts pushing to get the P-51 Mustang for the group.

4th January 1944

First use of the new paddle bladed propeller is made by Thunderbolts of the 56th Fighter Group.

21st January 1944

Pilots of the 56th Fighter Group carry out their first strafing of an enemy airfield.

30th January 1944

The 352nd Fighter Group claims 38 enemy aircraft destroyed. Eighth Air Force Box Score: 55 destroyed, 16 probables and 33 damaged.

8th February 1944

Walter C. Beckham, of the 353rd Fighter Group, shoots down an ME-109 and a FW-190 for his last claims of the war. His total stands at 18 destroyed.

Major Robert A. Ackerley in his Mustang 'Rita Marie', WD-P, 44-72416. This aircraft was later renamed 'MAN-I-ACK'. After the war in Europe was over this aircraft was sold to the Swedish Air Force and given the number 26101. In 1954 it was purchased by the Nicaraguan Air Force.

Captain William J. O'Donnell of the 335th Fighter Squadron and his Mustang 'Duchess' WD-B, 44-14557. Captain O'Donnell claimed two aerial and three ground victories.

Two interesting photos of a P-51D which crashed in Holland. Eerie personal markings VERY unusual for 4th group. Obliterated serial and code letter, 3 kill MKS but no name visable on fuselage or canopy frame. Lt. Wilbur Eaton had a P-51B (43-6897 WD-U) marked with that epigramatic logo, but this is clearly a "D" model. Eaton transferred out 2/15/45. Lt. Ken Green POW south of Rotterdam 3/3/45, in A/C listed as #44-14923 "See Me Later" in MACR 12900. Suggest this was P-51D assigned to Eaton and lost by Ken Green.
(Zijlstra)

General Eisenhower gets ready to pin a medal on Don Blakeslee as Don Gentile looks on.

P-47 of the 336 F.S./4th F.G. assigned to Lt. Jack L. Raphael Aug 23, 1943. The A/C was coded VF-M, serial #41-6529. The big bird carried 2 names "Eager Beaver" - on nose w/art and "Miss Beth" just forward of canopy.

(Crow)

Crew Chief Glessner Weckbacker runs up the engine of his Thunderbolt VF-D, 41-6192. The pilot was Woodrow Sooman who named it 'Lolapaluza'. Note the checks on the inner wheel hubs. The date is 8th November 1943.

(Weckbacher)

Assistant Crew Chief John Wilson guides in his aircraft with Lt. Woodrow Sooman at the controls of VF-D, 41-6192. The emblem is of a diving eagle with a Tommy gun, but the name has yet to be applied as in photo above.

(Weckbacher)

The aircraft of Douglas P. Pederson which he named 'Mary Belle'. It was in this Mustang that, on 16th April 1945, he destroyed eight enemy aircraft on an airfield just outside of Prague, Czechoslovakia. A total of eight pilots were lost by the 4th on this day for claims of 105 enemy aircraft destroyed on the ground.

A P-51D of the 336th F.S., 4th F.G., 8th A.A.F., near Villacoublay, Paris, France, shortly after V-E Day, 1945.

(Jim Crow)

10th February 1944
The 359th claims 6 enemy aircraft destroyed for no losses.

11th February 1944
The 357th Fighter Group begins to fly combat missions.

15th February 1944
The 56th Fighter Group adopts the red nose markings on its Thunderbolts.

20th February 1944
The 56th Fighter Group uses the US 150 gallon drop tanks for the first time. They go to Leipzig, Germany and shoot down 14 enemy aircraft. For the first time over 1,000 bombers are sent out. Total claims by the fighters are 61 for the loss of 4 fighters.

21st February 1944
The fighters claim 33 destroyed for the loss of five of their own.

22nd February 1944
Eighth Air Force Box Score: 61 for the loss of 11 fighters. One of these is Walt Beckham who was shot down by flak while strafing an airfield near Bonn, Germany.

2nd March 1944
The German 'Fortress Specialist' Egon Meyer is shot down and killed by a Thunderbolt pilot.

3rd March 1944
The 364th Fighter Group based at Honington, Suffolk completes its first mission. Colonel Harold J. Rau of the 20th Fighter Group is the first 8th Air Force fighter pilot to see 'Big B' from the air.

4th March 1944
Bombers accompanied by Mustangs of the 4th Fighter Group, and led by Don Blakeslee, fly over the Nazi capital, Berlin. Forty-eight P-51s took off from Debden but many aborted. Those that remain shoot down 4 enemy aircraft for the loss of three

'Meiner Kleiner' has its engine run up by her crew chief Glessner Weckbacker on a rest day (31st August 1944). The pilot was Lt. Joe Higgins, who flew this aircraft on the 8th Air Force's first Shuttle mission to Russia 21st June - 5th July 1944. This aircraft was lost with Lt. George Klaus at the controls on 21st November 1944. Lt. Klaus ended up as a prisoner of war. Coded VF-D, 43-6942.

(Weckbacher)

Major James A. Goodson was squadron commander of the 336th from Mar 8, 1944 until his capture June 20, 1944. Thirty swasticas under canopy record both air & ground victories.

(Tabatt)

This A/C, assigned to John McFarlane, would be lost Nov 8, 1944 with Lt Edward A. Quist as pilot. McFarlane himself, would be shot down in another A/C over Denmark Mar 12, 1945.

(Mulron)

Another interesting A/C; Malcolm canopy, red name: ''Connie'', VF-C, SER #42-103602. Assigned to Lt. George C. Smith, it was also used by Fred Glover and it went on at least one Russian Shuttle mission.

(Mulron)

Don Emerson pulls in close to a bomber of the 390th Bomb Group, 3rd September 1944. Emerson was killed in action on Christmas Day 1944. At the time he was flying VF-D, 44-15054, the assigned aircraft of Lt. Edward A. Quist.

(Evans)

Col Chesley Peterson and his South African actress wife Audrey Boyes. With over 200 WWII sorties, he earned a fist full of medals and 2 swims in the ocean! He also led the first P-47 mission in the ETO. (Escort to Berlin P 195)

(Weckbacher)

As Frank Stillwell taxis out on a mission his crew chief, S/Sgt. Michael J. Cotter holds onto his headgear. This particular aircraft was presented by the children of Bloomfield High School, New Jersey who sold War Bonds. The name 'The Bengal Lancer' refers to the school's basketball team 'The Bengals'.

(USAF Photo)

A close-up of Frank and his "Lancer" D7-D, SER. #44-15134. Note the presentation panel just below name. The date is Nov 18, 1944 and he has just returned from his first mission in his new A/C - with a claim for a ME-109.

(USAF Photo)

One of half dozen aged Mustangs delivered to the 339th Fighter Group in April 1944. Until these ships arrived the group had no idea which aircraft they were to fly. They'd trained on P-39s at Rice Field, California. This one, serialled 42-103390, has a camera port just in front of the tail wheel.

(Shoemaker)

pilots. Total claims by 8th fighters were 8 destroyed, 3 probables and 4 damaged. Losses amounted to 15 fighters. It was estimated that the mission took some 2,000 tons of bombs, 19,000,000 rounds of 50 calibre bullets, 120,000 rounds of 20mm cannon shells, 163,000 gallons of oil and something like 3,400,000 gallons of petrol.

8th March 1944

The 56th Fighter Group flew two missions today and claimed over 30 aircraft destroyed to take them over the 300 destroyed mark.

15th March 1944

The 56th Fighter Group claims 24-1-10 for the loss of Lt. John Kozey who is taken POW. Bob Johnson is the leading 8th Air Force ace with 21 confirmed aerial victories.

16th March 1944

Eighth Air Force Box Score: 77 destroyed.

25th March 1944

Walker Mahurin and Gerry Johnson, of the 56th Fighter Group, are lost. Mahurin manages to evade capture but Gerry Johnson is taken POW.

30th March 1944

Eighth Air Force fighters claim 72 enemy aircraft destroyed.

5th April 1944

The 355th Fighter Group attacks several airfields in the vicinity of Munich, Germany and claimed a record number of aircraft destroyed. The attack was carried out during a heavy snowstorm and took about 40 minutes. The pilots came away with a total 51-2-81 for the loss of three Mustangs. The 358th Squadron claimed 21-1-41 to take top honours. Duane Beeson of the 4th Fighter Group was shot down by flak and taken prisoner. (The author celebrated his fourth birthday).

8th April 1944

Captain Virgil Meroney, leading ace with the 352nd Fighter group is taken POW.

15th April 1944

Major Leroy Schrieber of the 62nd Fighter Squadron, 56th Fighter Group is hit by flak over Flensburg and spins in from 700 feet.

17th April 1944

The 56th Fighter Group transfers to Boxted, Essex where it will remain until the end of the war.

24th April 1944

Edwin L. Heller of the 352nd Fighter Group deprives the Luftwaffe of seven aircraft which he destroys on the ground.

30th April 1944

The 339th Fighter Group fly their first combat mission led by Major Jack Hayes of the 357th Fighter Group. The 352nd claimed a total of 140 aircraft destroyed during April. During the same period the 4th Fighter Group claimed 207 for the loss of 24 pilots and in doing so passed the 500 destroyed mark.

7th May 1944

The 352nd hits Berlin for the first time. Bud Mahurin of the 56th Fighter Group arrives back in London after evading capture. He returns to the ZOI and later is sent to the Pacific where he adds one more aerial victory to his tally.

12th May 1944

Captain Robert J. Rankin of the 56th Fighter Group shoots down 5 enemy aircraft.

13th May 1944

The 355th Fighter Group put on seven league boots when they go to Politz, Germany, a round trip of about 1,500 miles from their home base of Steeple Morden, Herts. Captain Frank A. Cutler of the 486th Fighter Squadron, 352nd Fighter Group is killed in action while flying his aircraft PZ-P, 43-6578 'Soldiers Vote.'

14th May 1944

Captain Robert W. Adamina of the 82nd Fighter Squadron, 78th Fighter Group is the first 8th Air Force pilot to successfully ditch his Thunderbolt. Earlier he had shot down an FW-190.

19th May 1944

Eighth Air Force Box Score: 72 enemy aircraft shot down.

24th May 1944

Carl J. Luksic of the 352nd Fighter Group is taken POW. At the time he had a total of 15½ victories.

The first two-seat conversion to be carried out on a P-51D was performed by men of the 339th Fighter Group. The rear fuselage tank was removed to take a passenger seat which made the aircraft nose heavy. The code of D7-Z (bar) was kept on 44-13965 and the name 'Gruesome Twosome' painted on. This photo was taken at Duxford airfield prior to being flown on a combat mission by Huie Lamb Jr.
(USAF Photo)

The wreckage of Lt. John W. Coley's D7-V, 44-15560 of the 503rd Fighter Squadron after he bailed out over Frinton, Essex due to the engine catching fire. Needless to say his crew chief S/Sgt. Buesino was not too happy!
(Evans)

The 'Worry Bird's' story is really unique. Flown as D7-J, 44-14118 by Lt. Robert J. Frisch, of Spokane, in the 503rd Squadron in WW II. A restored example is now flown by Frisch's good friend, Jack Rose, in these same markings. The original was also flown by Lt. Jack Price, who made his only confirmed victory, a FW, on Sept 11, 1944.
(Tabatt)

The crew chief runs up D7-P, ser #44-14947, the assigned A/C of ace Lester C. Marsh who scored 4 of his 5 confirmed victories in it - including 3 FWs on Nov 26, 1944. White skull with Black Hilites, Red Arrow and Red in kill MKS.

(J. Starnes VIA/Tabatt)

The starboard side of Vern Blizzard's new Mustang also coded 5Q-O, ''Punkie II.'' In the cockpit is Jesse L. Russell (C/C) who was responsible for the painting of 'Stormy'. The A/C/C William H. Courtney was awarded the Bronze Star for keeping two Mustangs on the line. The armorer was Davis E. Hardee Jr.

(Blizzard)

Fowlmere: Lt Col. Dale Shafer, Capt. Sal Carollo and Major William E. Bryan at the celebration of the 339th's first combat anniversary, April 30, 1945. They are, respectively, the 503rd Sq. C.O., adjutant and operations officer.

(Starnes)

26th May 1944

The last group to join the 8th Air Force flew its first combat mission. The 479th Fighter Group, based at Wattisham, carried out the usual sweep along the Dutch coast.

28th May 1944

Captain Woodrow W. Anderson is killed after bailing out of his Mustang when the 'chute fails to deploy. While with the 352nd Fighter Group he had upped his total to 14½ enemy aircraft destroyed.

30th May 1944

Eighth Air Force Box Score: 58 enemy aircraft destroyed.

6th June 1944

The day finally arrives and the 8th flies 1,873 sorties. James R. Golden of the 361st Fighter Group is the last Allied fighter pilot to be lost on the day when an oil line in his Mustang B7-A, 43-6977 breaks and he is forced to step over the side. The following day he is betrayed and taken prisoner by German troops.

13th June 1944

The first V-1 lands in England.

20th June 1944

Major Jim Goodson flying his new Mustang VF-B, 44-13303 is hit while strafing Nubarndenburg A/F and has to crashland his aircraft. He evades capture for several days but the odds are against him and he is captured.

21st June 1944

The second Shuttle Mission to Russia (the first was flown by a group based in Italy) is flown by the 4th Fighter Group led by Don Blakeslee. The 486th Fighter Squadron, 352nd Fighter Group also takes part. During the flight Lt. Howell and Major Andrew of the 486th are lost. The 4th lost 4 pilots plus S/Sgt. Robert L. Gilbert who bailed out of a B-17 that was being escorted by the fighters and ended up fighting alongside Russian partisans. S/Sgt. Gilbert returned to Debden in August.

After a particularly long ride to Koln on 10th January 1945, Vernon Robert Blizzard of the 504th Fighter Squadron had to set his ship 'Punkie' down in a field on the Essex-Cambridgeshire border near Chrishall Grange, about 2 miles southeast of Fowlmere airfield.

(Blizzard)

30th June 1944

Lt. Tucker of the 5th Emergency Rescue Squadron shoots down the first V-1 to be claimed by the 8th Fighter Command.

2nd July 1944

Lt. Ralph K. Hofer is killed in action over Yugoslavia, reputedly by Erich Hartman the top German ace of WW Two.

4th July 1944

The 56th Fighter Group passes the 500 destroyed mark and George E. Bostwick claims a triple in the air when he knocks down 3 ME-109s over Conches A/D.

5th July 1944

Francis Gabreski is the top 8th Air Force ace still flying in combat.

7th July 1944

Captain Orville E. Goodman leads the 486th Fighter Squadron, 352nd Fighter Group when the squadron claims 11 enemy aircraft destroyed for no losses. Eighth Air Force Box Score: 75 aircraft destroyed.

18th July 1944

The 352nd claims 21 and George Preddy gets four of them.

19th July 1944

The 78th Fighter Group destroys 20 enemy aircraft on the ground. A B-17 crashes while buzzing the control tower at Duxford, home of the 78th and 14 men are killed.

20th July 1944

Lt. Colonel Francis Gabreski of the 56th Ftr. Grp. is taken POW.

27th July 1944

Lt. Robert Wells of the 20th Fighter Group abandons his aircraft at 28,000 feet over England, the highest bailout altitude for any member of his group.

The crew of 'The Yankee Kid III' coded 5Q-J, 42-103737. From left to right are Americo Boccardi (A/C/C), Lt. Merle Caldwell, Jimmy Taylor (C/C) and Ken Willard armorer. This aircraft was taken over by the 9th Air Force when, due to battle damage, another pilot landed on the Continent December 13, 1944.

(Willard)

Two ground crew men of the 505th Fighter Squadron outside their living quarters in Fowlmere village. On the left is Fred 'Doc' Nessler who was the crew chief on 6N-U and on the right is Henry J. Tirabasso who was also a crew chief.

(Nessler)

29th July 1944

Lt. Rex. E. Moncrieff and Lt. Louis W. Adams of the 20th attack 50 enemy aircraft and shot down three of them but have to exit in a hurry when another 50 aircraft arrive.

6th August 1944

George Preddy of the 352nd Fighter Group shoots down six enemy aircraft. The night before he won $1,000 in a crap game which he invested in War Bonds. Mustangs fly the longest mission of the war so far when they fly to Gdynia, Poland. The mission lasted over seven hours for some of the pilots.

Bill C. Routt with his aircraft 5Q-A, 44-14060 on 7th July 1944. 'FABASCA' stood for 'Fast as a bullet and slick as a cat's arse', certainly one of the most unusual nicknames ever painted. Bill Routt had previously flown a tour in the Aleutians. His crew chief was Carmen Grande.

(USAF Photo)

12th August 1944

Colonel Thomas J.J. Christian Jr. of the 361st Fighter Group is killed in his Mustang E2-C, 44-13410 'Lou IV' while divebombing the train yards at Metz. His wingman at the time was Lt. Robert J. Bain. Also lost was Lt. Merle C. Rainey in E2-C(bar), 42-106787, Lt. John E. Engstrom in E2-G(bar), 42-106778 both of whom ended up as POW's and Lt. Clarence Zieske in B7-H, 42-106942 who was killed.

17th August 1944

The 56th Fighter Group is the first group to use rockets when Dave Schiling used six in an attack on some rolling stock in the railyard at Braine-le-Comte. Four goods cars were set on fire.

25th August 1944

The 20th Fighter Group, led by Lt. Colonel John P. Randolph, destroy a total of 20 enemy aircraft on the ground and on the water.

29th August 1944

Major Joe Myers and Lt. Manford O. Croy share in the destruction of an ME-262 in the air, a first for the Thunderbolt and the 78th Fighter Group.

5th September 1944

The 56th Fighter Group destroy 10 in the air and another 69 on the ground for a new one day record for 8th Fighter Command. The 8th claimed a total of 171 destroyed of which 28 were aerial claims.

11th September 1944

The 359th Fighter Group destroy 35 enemy aircraft out of a total of 116. The 20th Fighter Group starts

Two of the men who 'kept em flying while with the 504th Fighter Squadron. On the left is Art Shoemaker (5Q-B) and Ken Willard (5Q-J) prior to setting out on a furlough to Cambridge.

(Willard)

the third Shuttle Mission to Russia led by Harold J. Rau. The group returned to Kingscliffe on 17th September 1944.

18th September 1944

A total of sixteen P-47s flown by pilots of the 56th Fighter Group are lost while on a combat mission. The highest one day loss ever suffered by an 8th Air Force fighter group. The 357th Fighter Group claims 26 enemy aircraft for the loss of two pilots.

23rd September 1944

Lt. John Muller is lost while flying John Holloway's 6N-A(bar), 44-13624 'Sniffles' of the 339th Fighter Group.

30th September 1944

Fighters of the 8th Air Force claim a total of 469 enemy aircraft destroyed in the air and on the ground.

4th October 1944

Lt. Steve Ananian of the 505th Fighter Squadron, 339th Fighter Group bails out into the North Sea while flying Chet Malarz's 6N-M, 42-106946 'Bison Bull' due to engine failure. He was picked up by ASR. This mission was Lt. Ananian's first.

6th October 1944

The 20th Fighter Group claims 40 aircraft destroyed during attacks on seaplane bases from Stettin to Lubeck.

9th October 1944

The last mission by 8th Air Force P-38s is flown by

The brakes of the Mustang were noted for causing problems and that resulted in this taxing accident to 5Q-Y, 42-106662 piloted by Dick Penrose on July 16, 1944. Note light areas on upper wing surfaces from which the invasion stripes have been removed with acetone.

(Penrose)

the 479th Fighter Group.

12th October 1944

Lt. Chuck Yeager of the 363rd Fighter Squadron, 357th Fighter Group creams 5 enemy aircraft in the air.

30th October 1944

The 479th Fighter Group had a bad day when it lost its Group Commander, Colonel Hub Zemke (J2-Z,

Personnel of 'B' Flight with a P-51D of the 504th Fighter Squadron. Front Row L to R: E. P. Ryan, John LeJune, Carmen Grande, Ron Klatzke, Robert L. Fending and Frank Riotta. Middle row: - Casil D. Henry, John Ryan, Samuel D. Terry, Howard Brent, Donovan J. Hubbard. Back row: - Virgil Fleming, Dewey Mims, Larry Carey, Bob Turner, Robert E. Johnson and Culverwell.

(Johnson)

Stretching a friendship to the utmost, Steve Ananian readies for a mission in Chet Malarz's new P-51D. Steve lost Chets "B" - and almost his own life ditching in the North Sea on his very first mission. The full story recounted in June '85, 339th Newsletter.

(C. Malarz)

44-14351), Lt. Colonel James Herron (L2-A, 44-14396) and Lt. Doug Holmes (L2-S, 44-14627), Colonel Zemke and Lt. Holmes were taken POW and Jim Herron was killed. All three men were lost due to appalling weather conditions. Other losses for the day were Lt. Francis Christensen of the 361st Fighter Group in a P-51 Coded B7-L, 43-25033 and Lt. Russell H. Jenner in IV-Y(bar), 44-13336 'Yankee Clipper' of the 359th Fighter Group. Both were killed in action.

2nd November 1944

Eighth Air Force fighters claim 134 destroyed in the air, 25 on the ground. George Preddy of the 352nd is now the leading ace still flying combat. The 328th Fighter Squadron, 352nd Fighter Group claim 28 destroyed, with 5 of them being shot down by Don Bryan in his Mustang PE-B, 44-14061 'Little One.'

18th November 1944

A total of 14 ME-262s were destroyed on the ground by the 4th and 353rd Fighter Groups.

21st November 1944

When pilot Bill Jaaskelainen was scrambled to intercept an intruder on 12th May, 1944, he went off the East to West runway at Fowlmere, Cambs. Flying as the leader was ace Jim Starnes of Wilmington, N.C. Code was 6N-U, 42-103305.

(Bill Jaaskelainen Jr.)

Captain William T. Whisner of the 352nd F/G and Claude J. Crenshaw of the 359th F/G claim five enemy aircraft each as destroyed in the air. The rest of the fighters of the 8th claim a total of 63 for the loss of 15 fighters.

22nd November 1944

Major Ray S. Wetmore and Captain Robert M. York of the 370th Fighter Squadron, 359th Fighter Group surround approximately 200 German fighters and shoot down 7 between them.

26th November 1944

Rampaging 8th fighters shoot down 110 enemy aircraft with the 339th claiming 29. Bert Stiles, an ex-bomber pilot flying with the 505th Fighter Squadron, is killed following a FW-190 in a steep dive. The German pilot was Lt. Vollert in FW-190, Wr No. 206160, who also went in.[2]

18th December 1944

A V-1 lands near Bodney, home of the 352nd Fighter Group.

19th December 1944

The only fighter group aloft was the 78th and they claimed seven destroyed for the loss of four pilots.

23rd December 1944

Lt. Colonel Dave Schilling of the 56th Fighter Group shoots down 5 enemy aircraft.

25th December 1944

George Preddy is shot down by American flak and is killed. Also shot down with him is Lt. Jim Bouchier of the 479th Fighter Group. Lt. Bouchier bailed out safely at about 1,000 feet.

26th December 1944

Eighth Air Force fighters claim 46 enemy aircraft destroyed.

1st January 1945

In a surprise attack the Luftwaffe destroy 30 US aircraft and damage another sixty-two. The RAF loose 162 and 62 more are damaged. American fighters claim 97 E/A. Total losses for the Luftwaffe are listed as 129 aircraft.

3rd January 1945

The first P-47Ms are assigned to the 56th Fighter Group. Polish ace Captain Witold Lanowski is assigned the first production model, 44-21108, HV-Z(bar).

14th January 1945

The 56th flies its first mission using the new P-47M. Fighters of the 8th shot down 155 enemy aircraft plus another 25 claimed as damaged. Twelve US fighters were lost. The 357th Fighter Group set a new aerial record when they knock down 56½ enemy aircraft in a battle over Brandenburg. Only three Mustangs were lost and seven others received battle damage. Lt. Lawrence Powell of the 505th Fighter Squadron 339 F.G. went down and was taken POW.

Stiles was flying Jim Starnes' 6N-X, 44-14113 'Tar Heel!

26th January 1945
The 361st Fighter Group under the command of X1X Tactical Air Force is aloft and shoots down 2 enemy aircraft for the loss of one Mustang.

28th January 1945
Third anniversary of the 8th Air Force.

3rd February 1945
The 62nd Fighter Squadron, 56th Fighter Group, re-equips with the P-47M Thunderbolt.

17th February 1945
The 63rd Fighter Squadron, 56th Fighter Group is equipped with the P-47M. The group has about 130 on hand.

25th February 1945
The 55th Fighter Group shoots down 7 ME-262s - A record bag for the jet fighter. The 364th claims the first AR-234 in the air.

26th February 1945
A 479th pilot strafes and destroys a captured B-17, Flying Fortress.

2nd March 1945
The 8th claims the destruction of 102½ enemy aircraft for the loss of 12 fighters.

3rd March 1945
Captain James N. Poindexter of the 353rd Fighter Group is killed shortly after takeoff from his home base at Raydon, Suffolk.

11th March 1945
Fighter ace Arthur C. Cundy of the 353rd Fighter Group is lost over the North Sea.

15th March 1945
Ray S. Wetmore of the 359th Fighter Group shoots down an ME-163 for his last claim of the war. He is the top scoring ace still in combat with the 8th Air Force.

18th March 1945
Captain Ralph Cox of the 359th Fighter Group spots Russian aircraft while on a mission near Berlin. The Russians shot down a Mustang of the 353rd Fighter Group. The 78th claim 32-1-13 for the loss of 5 Mustangs.

Oscar Kenneth Biggs taxis to his revetment after a mission in his 6N-E, 44-72449 'Imogene' which was named after his wife. The name was carried on both sides. The frame in the background was used for bore sighting the guns of the fighter aircraft.

(Biggs)

Fighter ace Jim Woolery poses with his last Mustang 6N-I, 44-72512 'Pepper'. The crew chief was Roy Myers.

(Woolery)

Richard Thieme of the 505th Fighter Squadron with his Mustang 'Boomerang'. The code was 6N-W, 44-14705.

(Thieme)

Two photos of 6N-H #44-13556, the A/C of Chris Hanseman - the 339th's first ace. C/C Clarence Shockley wrote a great article in the 339th's newsletter about this memorable young man who lost his life just a few days before his 20th birthday, strafing near Naumberg Germany, July 29, 1944. Assnt C/C Tom Collins, Armorer. Forrest Lukehart. Pictured in front of A/C is payroll clerk Paul Rodenbach.
(Tabatt)

The aircraft of ace Jay F. Marts of the 505th Fighter Squadron. The code was 6N-J (bar), 44-14239. The name 'Junior' was in red and appeared on both sides. Dave Register was the crew chief.
(Marts)

24th March 1945

The Eighth claims 53 enemy aircraft destroyed in the air. Lt. Otto 'Dittie' Jenkins buzzes his home base of Leiston, Suffolk upon returning from his last combat mission and is killed after clipping a tree.[3] Lt. Russell D. Wade of the 361st Fighter Group is killed in action in E2-T, 44-14149 'Talley's Hoosier Hobo'.

27th March 1945

The last V-1 falls on English soil.

7th April 1945

The 339th Fighter Group knocks down 10 enemy aircraft out of a total of 64 claimed by the 8th Fighter Command. JG-300 performs the first deliberate multiple ramming of B-17s and B-24s.

9th April 1945

The 361st Fighter Group returns to Little Walden, Essex.

10th April 1945

Eighth Air Force fighters claim 20 aerial victories and over 300 destroyed on the ground. The 339th claim 105-0-77, the 78th 52-0-43. Losses came to 10 fighters.

13th April 1945

The 56th destroys 95 aircraft on the ground at Eggebeck Airdrome, which takes them into the lead over the 4th with 1,000 destroyed. Lt. Randel Murphy emerges as the 'top gun' with 10 destroyed. Other fighter groups claim 189 destroyed on the ground and 220 damaged.

16th April 1945

In many attacks on enemy airfields the fighters of the 8th claimed over 700 enemy aircraft destroyed plus nearly 400 as damaged. The 4th claimed 105 for the loss of eight pilots including Sidney Woods, who was taken prisoner. The 352nd claimed 40 destroyed and the 353rd 110. The 78th took top honours with 135-0-89, the highest score ever. The 339th set a record when it became the only group to claim over a hundred destroyed twice. They claimed 118-0-39.

17th April 1945

Another day of attacks on German airfields netted 286-0-113 for the fighters plus 13 aerial victories. Total losses to enemy action amounted to 17 US fighters. One of those lost was Colonel Elwyn G. Righetti of the 55th Fighter Group who was hit by ground fire at an airfield near Dresden. He later crashlanded his fighter and was attacked and killed by German civilians. His wingman Hank Henry re-

His Mustang, G4-X, #44-63199, was called "Toolin' Fool's Revenge"

ported that Righetti had destroyed 9 enemy fighters on the ground. The 339th Fighter Group claimed 68-0-9 for the loss of two Mustangs. The 78th made their last claims for the war when they destroyed 15 on the ground with another 13 damaged.

20th April 1945
Joe Mansker of the 20th Fighter Group flew Hank Howard (H.Q.'s) on a mission to Berlin in a two seat P-51. Mansker reported Howard did O.K. at the navigation until he decided to eat a candy bar and couldn't locate where they were until they hit the coast of Holland. The 359th and 361st Fighter Groups flew their last mission.

21st April 1945
Last missions flown by the 55th, 56th and 339th Fighter Groups.

25th April 1945
Lt. Hilton Thompson of the 479th Fighter Group scores the last aerial kill for the 8th Air Force when he shoots down an AR-234, his second jet victory. Mustangs of the 78th escort RAF Lancasters to Berchtesgaden for their last mission of the war. Also completing their final missions were the 4th, 20th, 353rd, 355th, 357th, and 479th Fighter Groups.

3rd May 1945
The 352nd flew its last mission.

6th May 1945
The 364th Fighter Group carried out its last mission of the war.

7th May 1945
Major Mike Yannell led the 356th on the last mission to be flown by the 8th Fighter Command.

8th May 1945
Peace in Europe, and the 4th Fighter Group is the top USAAF fighter group of WW 2 with a total of 1,052½ enemy aircraft destroyed, 53 probables and 426 damaged.

GROUP SCORES

Group	Air	Ground	Total	Losses
4th	583½	469	1,052½	241
20th	212	237	449	132
55th	316½	268½	585	181
56th	679½	327	1,006½	128
78th	338½	358½	697	167
339th	239½	440½	680	97
352nd	519½	287	806	118
353rd	330½	414	744½	137
355th	365½	502½	868	175
356th	201	75½	276½	122
357th	609½	106½	716	128
359th	253	98	351	106
361st	226	105	331	108
364th	256½	193	449½	134
479th	155	279	434	69

Gerry Graham's first assigned aircraft 6N-T, 42-106946 'Mary Lee'. The name was in red script. The ship later became Chet Malarz's 'Bison Bull', lost October 4, 1944 by Steve Ananian on his first combat mission. Steve was picked up by the RAF Air Sea Rescue Service.
(Graham)

Gerry Graham has just shut down his engine after a combat mission and Crew Chief Roy 'Sack' Myers and his A/C/C Homer Mobley (with box) move in to get 'Mary Lee' ready for the next mission. When Graham completed his tour the aircraft was assigned to Jim Woolery who renamed it 'Pepper' after his lovely wife. On 24th March 1945 Ellis Hupp crashed this aircraft on take-off and totaled it.
(Graham)

The Mount of Lt James L. Lynch of the 505th. The name 'Jackie II' appeared on both sides. The first 'Jackie' was a P-39 in the states. The winged "B" on the tail denotes "B" flight. C/C was John Earnest. MACR #5208 dated May 29, 1944 reports his disappearance over near the Isle of Wight: James was credited with 25 confirmed victories in this A/C just 8 days prior.

ROYAL D. FREY

55TH FIGHTER SQUADRON, 20TH FIGHTER GROUP

Royal D. Frey was born in Chillicothe Ohio on December 28, 1923. As a lad, he became a keen builder of model aeroplanes, starting with rubber powered models and graduating to petrol engines in 1937 - one of the first youngsters in his home town to do so. He was also an avid reader of the exploits of WWI pilots - an early interest in aviation which persists to the present day.

Graduating from Chillicothe High School in June, 1941, Frey entered Ohio State University in September for the obligatory two years' college stipulated by the USAAF for flying cadets at that time. When the United States entered the war, the Air Force dropped the required college period and he applied to join immediately. Mental and physical tests passed, he was duly sworn in as a cadet on March 30, 1942. There followed four frustrating months waiting for an assignment. In early August he was told to report to Santa Anna, California for pre-flight training.

After three months he was sent to Fort Stockton, Texas, for primary flying on the PT-17. His basic flying training was taken at Pecos Field on the PT-13. Next to Williams Field, Phoenix, Arizona, for twin-engined fighter training on the A-17, dubbed the 'Bamboo Bomber.' Frey completed 60 hours on the type, some of which were spent under the tutelage of an RAF instructor. There followed six hours' gunnery training

Crew Chief Lewis G. Brenton of Oakland, California and his armorer check over their aircraft. They "loaned it to Frey, pictured above, so he could fly missions over occupied Europe"(!) Plane and pilot were listed MIA Feb 10, 1944. After the war, Frey visited the area where he went down and several Germans gave him items that had once belonged to him.

(Frey)

To Danny Morris – Preparing my P-38 for its next (and although not realized at the time, it's last) mission, 9 Feb 944, Wittering RAF Station, England.

Royal D. Frey
4 June 1969

in the T-6 and ten hours in the AT-9. It was reckoned that anyone who could fly the AT-9 could fly anything with wings.

Frey's class of cadets was the first to fly the P-38 prior to assignment to a group. The aircraft were L-322-61s rejected by the RAF, complete with right-hand rotating propellors, whereas USAAF P-38s had counter-rotating airscrews. The machines used by Frey and his fellow pilots also had no armour plating, guns or superchargers. At 15,000 feet and above, the aircraft were extremely slow, but speed increased appreciably at low altitude and the controls became very light. Frey flew a total ten hours in the early version of the Lightning and graduated from flying school on May 20, 1943.

With ten days' leave, he immediately headed for home, three and a half days' journey from the base. He managed about two and a half with his family before starting back to Edwards AFB. He stayed there for a month, logging 20 hours on P-38s with an OTU. He then transferred to Glendale, California and in the next month logged 80 hours Lightning time, which included air and ground gunnery, mock combat tactics and two altitude climbs, the highest being to 20,000 feet.

In August, 1943, at March Field, California, Frey was assigned to the 55th Squadron, 20th Fighter Group. The group had just received orders to make ready for overseas duty, but had no aircraft to fly. The three squadrons - 55th, 77th and 79th - were given three different routes to travel to the East Coast; the southern, through El Paso Texas, the middle, via Kansas and for the 55th, the northern route via Los Angeles, Salt Lake City, Chicago and Columbus, Ohio. Although Frey's parents were living in Columbus at that time, orders were that no-one could get off the train, as the move was secret.

Squadron personnel arrived at Camp Miles Standish in New England and Frey was made boarding officer to arrange embarkation of the group on the *Queen Elizabeth*. All told, there were about 16,000 men on the liner and they arrived at the Clyde on August 25, 1943. The 55th Squadron disembarked at about three

Tony Levier, Lockheed Representative who, in a Lightning such as this, whipped a Spitfire in a mock dogfight over Kingscliffe airfield to demonstrate to the 20th Fighter Group pilots that in the right hands a P-38 could be a deadly opponent.

o'clock in the morning and entrained for Kingscliffe, arriving in the village after travelling for two days.

The 77th, 79th and group HQ arrived earlier and had been stationed at Kingscliffe airfield but, due to lack of space, the 55th was sent to a satellite airfield at Wittering. When personnel arrived they found a permanent base, dating from WW1. About 4 pm, the Americans learned that the British personnel on the base were about to take their famous afternoon tea. Frey and his fellows had heard of this time-honoured English custom and headed for the mess to meet the officers of 141 (Night Fighter) Squadron, which was then under the command of Bob Braham, a top scoring ace.

They were invited to tea, but unfortunately the Americans ate all the crumpets they could lay their hands on, not realizing that the British were rationed. On finding out, however, they returned later with some of their own rations to make good the loss. That evening the RAF invited the 55th Squadron pilots over to the mess and after eating they adjourned to the bar and joined in some famous RAF songs, including *Digging Up Grandfather's Grave, Salome* and *Cat on the Rooftops* - a good evening was had by all.

About the middle of September, new P-38Hs began to arrive and the group was able to put in some flying

Lt. Richard O. Loehnert and C/C T/Sgt. Tom Dickerson with their A/C "California Cutie", 42-67916, KI-S. On July 7, 1944, Loehnert bagged 2 ME-109s in a big air battle defending B-24s attacking Merseburg.

Capt. Maurice R. McLary's #42-67484 bellied in at Kingscliffe due to battle damage. His second P-38, #42-67878, was also coded KI-Y. Lt. Frey flew as his wingman on a number of occasions.

Frey's first regularly assigned P-38 named "Stardust."

(Mulron)

The pretty and often seen view of Lt. Edwin E. Wasil's P-38 J-15 LO KI-0 #43-25031 "Mama's Boy."

(Mulron)

Captain Mont J. Ryan took off on a training flight when a tyre blew. The quick thinking pilot retracted the landing gear to avoid crashing into some parked Mustangs. The date was 13th June 1945 and the ship was from the 55th Fighter Squadron coded KI-X, 44-11161.

(Helden)

Capt. Harley L. Brown (6) and his P-51D, 44-11250/KI-A/Be Good - L. nose/Brownies Ballroom on L. canopy rail.

(Tabatt)

time. At the end of the month, the 55th group was moved to Nuthampstead. As the 20th and 55th were the only long-range fighter groups in the UK at that time, they were destined for the really long missions. The 20th's P-38s were transferred to the 55th group, much to the annoyance of Frey and his fellow pilots. The only consolation was that the three squadrons of the 20th had been left a couple Lightnings apiece with which to keep their hands in.

In October and November the group did nothing except ground school, aircraft identification and take some leave in London. In early December came a delivery of P-38Js. Meanwhile, two pilots had flown the 55th Squadron's first mission - Don McAuley and Tom Heatherington going along with several 77th Squadron pilots on a mission as part of the 55th group on December 1. Lt. Jack Good of the 77th Squadron was shot down by a ME 109 and became a POW.

On December 28, the 20th group received its first assignment from the 67th Fighter Wing, a sweep over the Dutch Islands. Royal Frey's first mission, flying Number 2 to McLary in Yellow Section of the 55th Squadron. Although the group was only over the Continent for approximately 13 minutes, it had marked its combat debut. Frey swept in from the south islands and flew north to the Hague and back, getting his first experience of flak, exploding 500 feet away. His next mission came on December 31. The group took off from Wittering and flew to Kingscliffe for briefing and refueling for what was to be the longest mission so far flown by Eighth Air Force pilots. The group made several attacks on German fighters but made no claims for the day.

Frey's first mission of 1944 came on January 5, when the 20th, along with the 55th and 354th groups, provided target area support to the bombers over Kiel. This is how the Group Historian recorded it:

34

The wreckage of Lt. Walter Scroback's aircraft when he made an emergency landing at Leiston, home of the 357th Fighter Group on 5th January 1945. Although he turned the engine off it kept running due to overheating and he skiddled on the ice and overturned. The code was KI-C, 44-13794. The crew chief was Floyd McCutcheon.
(Becraft)

A line-up of 55th squadron P-51s prepare for another day at the office. In the foreground is Lt. Walter Mullins in KI-S, #44-13859.

Captain Herschell F. Ezell who flew as the Bombadier in the 20th Fighter Groups 'Droop-snoot' Lightning. The serial was 42-67450 and it carried the name 'EZE Doe's It'.

Another view of 'EZE Doe's It'. At this stage of the war it had completed ten Missions. The bombadier signalled the other aircraft by flashing its lights as to when they should drop their bombs.
(Hudgens)

'Mission Number 5. January 5, 1944. Attacking Europe on a 1,000 mile front, 13 combat wings of VIII Bomber Command bombed the port and shipbuilding centre of Kiel as well as important Luftwaffe bases at Bordeaux and Tours and targets in the southern Ruhr. Bombing was visual on all targets with good to excellent results. Total claims: Bombers: 62-13-9 and fighters 33-1-10. Losses 24 bombers, 12 fighters.

'Once again the group, with the 55th Group and 354th Group, provided target area support at Kiel. Col Russel had trouble and had to return leaving Major Montgomery in command.

The 20th arrived 20 minutes early because of favourable winds and swept the Neumunster area, southwest of Kiel. The group was bounced while at 25,000 feet by 20 or more ME 109s and FW 190s. Lt Robert A. French called and reported engine trouble. A moment later he was hit by three attacking FW 190s at 15,000 feet and bailed out.

'Major Montgomery bounced one of the FW 190s chasing Lt French, but gave it two or three seconds fire from dead astern and saw strikes on the right wing near the fuselage and pieces fly off. Claim: 1 damaged FW 190.

'Lt W. B. Taylor (55th) was leading Yellow Flight when Lt French reported engine trouble. The flight started home weaving over Lt French when 20 FW 190s and ME 109s came in from the south and ten attacked from out of the sun. The flight turned into them, Lt French was shot down and Lt Taylor got a burst at a 190 that was clinging to Lt Frey's tail. Black smoke came from the 190 as it broke down and was not seen again. Lt Bisher fired at an ME 109 but two Huns got on his tail. By making a sharp turn to the left he shook them and as he rolled out of the turn he saw three Huns in front of him and took another deflection shot but makes no claim.'

A posed shot of all the pilots who came from Seattle, Washington. From left to right are Cpt. Philip L. Schollo, Lt. Frederick H. Alexander, Major Merle B. Nichols, Cpt. Harold H. Gjolme and Cpt. James

M. Garner. The aircraft was assigned to Alexander and was coded LC-M, 44-13746

(Hudgens)

'Lt Frey (55th) had quite a time. He turned into one Hun, got another on his tail, lost his hydraulic system and couldn't use his flaps. His left inter cooler was out and he could only pull 22 inches on his left engine. He tried to outclimb the 190 and flipped over twice in a spin. Another 190 came in from two o'clock high. Frey turned into him and got in a short burst as it went directly under him. He made a pass at Lt Taylor who shot the 190 off his tail.

'Lt Arthur T. Altman (55th) was hit at 21,000 feet by a direct burst of flak from Wangerooge Island. His plane nosed down and crashed in the mud. Sorry to report that he did not get out of his plane.'

On his way back to England and safety, Frey passed over Heligoland and saw a convoy of several German ships sailing close to the coast, which he reported. That night RAF Wellingtons went out and attacked the ships.

On January 24, 560 bombers were sent to Frankfurt, but were recalled. A further 56 bombers attacked Aachen, but with poor results. A total of 15 Eighth and Ninth Air Force fighter groups and 74 RAF Spitfires provided support. Frey went as Number 2 to McLary. On the way in, Captain Melvin C. Pannell of Knoxville, Tennessee, asked Frey to cover him when he had to abort with one engine out. Frey did so and, although the two pilots saw plenty of German aircraft, none bothered them. After escorting his colleague over the North Sea, Frey was so elated at getting back in one piece that he turned back to the Continent and at 10,000 feet gave a display of aerobatics to the watching Germans who, no doubt, thought he was a lunatic! Unfortunately for Frey, a 'friend' saw him and reported his Ostend air display. When he landed he was cautioned for not flying straight back to base with Pannell.

On January 29, Frey got his first kill, an ME 110, in the air. This is how he recalls the victory:

'We were escorting the bombers to Frankfurt; when we reached the target we carried right on with them. At the same time some Germans who had been attacking the "Big Friends" pulled off to the side to let the flak take over. The bombers were at about 25,000 feet with us at 28,000, with solid cloud below.

'The bombers moved on over the target. Flak came up and the cloud began to billow so you could hardly see them in it. As they came through the cloud you could see some burning and others going down in pieces. About four miles behind them the next stream was coming in. You knew they'd seen what happened and knew it would happen to them too, but they still came on!

'After making their run the bombers swung right and headed back to the west. I looked down and saw some German fighters attacking a B-24. I called McLary, my Flight Leader, and we both started down on the enemy fighters, which were ME 110s. We dropped down to the top of the clouds and McLary

The P-51 assigned to Capt Merle J. Gilbertson in which he shared the destruction of a ME-109 with Lt John P. Stark on Jan 14, 1945. P-51 D-10, #44-14822, LC-A. This A/C displayed full serials and the code "A" on both fuselage and on tail in white on black circle.

As so often happens to fighter pilots, only 10 days after a confirmed victory, Capt Carl E. Jackson found himself downed in Holland: 20 Feb 44, P-38J-10-LO, #42-67988.

(Blake)

took off after a ME 110 which had a good start on us. He bored in but as he got within range the 110 suddenly flipped over, rolled out and headed north.

'I then went all out for the ME 110. When in range I pressed the tit and fired, obtaining some hits on his fuselage. At that precise moment the gunner in the enemy ship returned my fire. I stopped shooting and closed in on him and realized I had no gunsight image. I closed still further and sighted along the nose of my ship and fired. He sparkled all over, around the cockpit area and right wing root and then rolled off to the right trailing smoke as he spun in.

'I looked round for McLary and noticed I was losing oil from my right engine. I feathered it and upon finding McLary, pulled up on his wing and saw that he too had feathered one engine. We picked up Willy Taylor and Everett Gieger of our flight and they escorted us all the way to the Channel from Frankfurt.

'On comparing notes with McLary I found that the ME 110 gunner had put some bullets in his right wing

root and fuel tank. As he had been sitting with about two inches of gas in the bottom of his cockpit he had not continued his attack for fear of a spark if he fired his guns. He was pleased that I had shot down the ME 110 that had caused him so much trouble.

On this same day, Captain Lindol F. Graham shot down three FW 190s. Total claims made by the group were 10-1-1 for the loss of Lt Robert Moss, F/O William Harper, Lt Richard Bond and Lt Robert Flynn. Bond and his wingman Flynn were lost in a collison while attacking an ME 210 at 5,000 feet.

On February 10, the 20th Group was part of the fighter escort taking the bombers to Brunswick, about 100 miles west of Berlin. To cover the bomber force there were three long-range groups; one with the heavies on the way in, one to stay with them over the target and the third providing withdrawal support. At this time the Lightnings were suffering from engine trouble: oil congealing in the extreme high altitude temperatures. This meant that the P-38 groups were lucky to maintain 60% of their ships over the target area.

The Germans began hitting the bomber stream on the Dutch-German border and were still attacking when the 20th Group took over escort duty from a P-47 group. The group had been instructed to fly line astern formations which did not make for good mutual protection. Frey's flight was down to three, as was the next one and the two joined up. Frey spotted a FW 190 at 6 o'clock high and warned his fellow pilots just as the enemy aircraft dropped down on to the Number 5 man, Lt John Lundin of New York, and fired a burst into him. The German fighter rolled over and dived as Lundin pulled up slowly, rolled over and went down, trailing smoke. He was killed in the resulting crash. Frey blamed the restricting formation for the fact that the others were unable to help him.

Delynn Anderson and his last lightning which was coded MC-A. From left to right are Cpl. R. Gray, Sgt. Cohen, Major Anderson, Cpl. Signor and Sgt. John Duffie. Anderson was killed in Korea in April 1951 in a clash with Communist fighters.

(Hudgens)

Another one for the official photographer as Cpt. Delynn E. Anderson and Crew Chief J. P. Duffie, Line Chief H. T. Piner and Cpl. G. P. Sayig look at the artwork on MC-A, 43-28404 'Kentucky Kernel'. The name 'Sherry' appears just below the air intake of the engine. This was taken around the end of April 1944.

(Hudgens)

Approaching Dummer Lake over 10/10 cloud and 10,000 feet, Frey saw a lone P-38 turning with two ME 410s. Calling the Lightning, McLary the Flight Leader, and Frey dived to help it, but they found only an ME 110 flying west.

Frey elected to give chase as it was heading in the general direction of England. He dived after the enemy aircraft and levelled out just under the cloud base. Estimating the distance, he climbed to find the 110 still well ahead. He turned back into the clouds, increased power and went on instruments. Again Frey guessed the distance and, re-emerging from cloud cover, saw his quarry about 45° above, around 200 feet above the clouds. Pulling up directly under the Zerstorer he fired. The ME 110 shed pieces of metal and started down, heavily trailing smoke. Frey climbed 'balls out' for altitude, but after three minutes his left engine blew up and the cowling started to buckle. Assuming a blown cylinder head, he feathered the engine and started home. Shortly afterwards, the cloud cover dispersed, except for scattered snow squalls and he began to dogleg from squall to squall.

Checking his aircraft over, Frey realized that the generator housed in the left engine was now useless and he was using up the batteries. He closed down all electrical equipment and in doing so lost the power to cross-feed fuel from the left wing tank to the right. Although realizing that the right tank would soon be empty, he would be able to cross-feed gas with the remaining battery power. As he flew on, he could see German aircraft taking off from various airfields, but

Captain Jack Ilfrey and his Crew Chief Dick Burgess puzzle as to how he got back after a head-on collision with a ME-109 during a dogfight May 24, 44. Ilfrey also claimed another 109 on this day. The Lightning was coded MC-O, 42-28431 and named 'Happy Jack's Go Buggy' as were all his aircraft. (Mission 78 24 May '44)

(Hudgens)

A full shot of above A/C - note squadron code erased by wartime censor.

(Blake)

From left to right are the crew of 'Happy Jack's Go Buggy' MC-I, 44-13761: Sgt. S. Brusko (Radio), Sgt. R. E. Burgess (C/C), Sgt. O. N. Heim (Arm), Cpt. Jack Ilfrey and Sgt. R. R. Miller.

(Hudgens)

they all seemed to be climbing for altitude and did not bother the lone Lightning. Just then, some flak burst under him and the right engine caught fire, whereupon he pulled up to 4,000 feet to bail out about 30 miles from the Dutch border. He rolled the side windows down, but the resultant draught sucked the fire into the cockpit. Trimming the nose Frey rolled the aircraft on to its back, releasing his safety harness. Not feeling himself falling, he looked at his feet - now above his head - and saw that they were hooked under the control yoke. He managed to kick them free, fell out at about 2,000 feet and pulled the ripcord. The crippled P-38 screamed past in an almost vertical dive and crashed near a barn. Suddenly, Frey was passing telegraph wires and he braced for a landing.

On the ground he released his harness and attempted to pass his compass and maps to nearby French slave labourers, but some approaching Germans removed them. He had landed at Ludenhausen, near Münster, and was immediately taken prisoner and questioned, subsequently being sent to Stalag Luft 1 for about 15 months until liberated by the Russians on May 1, 1945.

Frey was moved to a Lucky Strike camp in France, but after a couple of days he went AWOL and headed for England, where he spent three weeks prior to transfer back to the States for 120 days R & R.

After his leave, he went to San Antonio Texas for redistribution and then to Craig Field, Alabama. In 1946 he went to Wright Field and on August 14 he married the sister of one of his old buddies from Chillicothe. In November, he was taken off active duty and returned to Ohio State university. By taking no holidays, he was able to cram five years' college into three and a half, to obtain his Bachelors and Junior Masters degree in History.

In 1948 Frey joined the Ohio ANG and flew the P-51H and F-84C, with which the Guard was re-equipped in 1950. In February, 1951, he was recalled back to duty and flew for two years with Air Defence Command. While some of his friends went to Korea, Frey was not allowed to, due to his late date of return from Europe. Additionally, very few of his fellows had seen overseas service and therefore took priority.

He came off active duty in November, 1952 and in December returned to work at the Historical Office on classified papers for the next five years. With a Master of History degree to back his flying experience, Frey was appointed Chief of the Research Division at Wright-Patterson AFB. He was grounded in 1955 on doctor's orders and served in France. He returned to the States in August, 1962 to take up a post at the AF Museum, where he remains today.

The 3 photos on this page are all of the same P-51B, MC-L, #43-25054 but taken at different times in its life. Top: left to rt: Lt. Willard H. Lewis and crew members Sgt. Roy Robinson, Sgt. Tex Schrader and Sgt. Tony Kublin. Lewis claimed 2 109s, 1 confirmed and 1 probable in ``Hell's Belle'' (note painting between Lewis and Robinson!) on Aug 6, 1944. Middle: The next ``owner'' of 43-25054 was Lt. Keith Price who renamed it ``Beaverhead Filly'' (note changed art work too) and flew it from Sept 44 until Jan 45. Here Tex Schrader, now C/C, and armorer Tony Kublin (interesting head gear!) congratulate Price upon completion of his tour. Bottom: A full shot of MC-L when assigned to Lt. Robert M. Scott who damaged a 109 with it on Jan 14, 1945. Again it was renamed: ``Bertie's Bet - Shoot, You're Faded.'' Altogether, this valiant A/C totalled up more than 700 combat hours - a real tribute to its fine ground crew! It ended its career on August 21, 1945 with a crash landing by Lt. Don Barnard.

(Hudgins/Schrader)

Ok, wipe that smug look off your face. We know you've seen this pic before, but did you know that this machine dropped a German prop in 44 and a jet in 45? Yep, Capt. Richard P. Gatterdam got a 109 on Nov 2, 44 and Capt John K. Hollis wasted a 262 on April 10, 45.
(Bennett)

Lt. James D. Bradshaw says goodbye to his crew on completion of his tour. L to R: Sgt. J. Strickler, Bradshaw, Sgt. S. K. Ballew, Cpl. C. W. Weaver, and Sgt. L. Nelberger. A/C #44-13535, MC-A carried "Jeanie" on portside and "Full Boost!" on starboard. (Aug 44)
(Hudgens)

Lt. Dale N. Jones of the 79th Fighter Squadron with his Father who flew B-25s in combat out of England. The only known case where a father and son were actively flying combat at the same time during World War Two. The Mustang was Dale's assigned aircraft.
(Hudgens)

Combat mission list of Lt Royal D. Frey 55th Squadron, 20th Group
All Missions: Ramrod

Date:	Location
12, 28, 1943	Holland
31	Bordeaux
1, 5, 1944	Kiel
11	Halberstadt
14	Pas de Calais
24	Frankfurt
29	Frankfurt
2, 2, 1944	Triequeville
5	Orleans
8	Frankfurt
10	Brunswick

Lt Royal D. Frey was shot down on his 11th mission on February 10, 1944.

Known aircraft flown by Lt Royal D. Frey;
P-38J KI-W Serial Unknown "Stardust"
P-38J KI-W 42-67855

Confirmed claims by Lt Royal D. Frey;

Date	Claim	Air/Grd	Area
1, 29, 1944	1 ME 110	Air	Frankfurt
2, 10, 1944	1 ME 110	Air	Brunswick

Lt. Royal D. Frey with his second P-38 Lightning. Coded KI-W, 42-67855 This photo was taken on 9th February 1944 just 24 hours before he went down in it to end up a POW.
(Frey)

EDWARD B. GILLER

343RD FIGHTER SQUADRON, 55TH FIGHTER GROUP

Born in Jacksonville, Illinois on July 8, 1918, Edward Giller spent 30 years in the USAF and rose from the rank of 2nd Lieutenant to Major General.

From 1932 until 1934 Giller was a pupil of White Hall High School in White Hall, Illinois, thence he attended the Kemper Military School in Booneville, Illinois. Entering the University of Illinois, he graduated with a BS degree in Chemical Engineering in 1940. In 1941 he joined the USAAF and was ordered to report to Houston, Texas on September 29, 1941 as a flying cadet. From Houston, he was sent to Stamford, Texas, for primary flight training. Giller began basic training at the famous Randolph AFB on January 8, 1942, followed by advanced flight training at Lubbock, Texas, beginning March 1, 1942. He graduated on May 29, 1942 and was commissioned as a 2nd Lieutenant in the USAAF Reserve.

Almost immediately, he was assigned to the 55th Group at Paine Field, Everett, Washington, which comprised a HQ Squadron and the 37th, 38th and 54th Squadrons. Later, the 37th and 54th were to be replaced by the 338th and 343rd Squadrons, on March 15, 1943 and September 11, 1942 respectively.

Ed Giller was eventually assigned to the 343rd Squadron and when it moved to Portland, Oregon, he was sent to Wright Field Ohio as a test pilot. He rejoined the squadron in Olympia, Washington, in September, 1942. In December, pilots and ground crews transferred to Pendleton, Oregon and in March, 1943, they received orders to go to McCord Field, Washington. There followed a move to Camp Kilmer on August 28, 1943, prior to being sent overseas. Orders came through on September 5, 1943 and they sailed on the *Orion*, arriving in the UK on the 14th. The group was installed at AAF Station F-131, Nuthampstead in Hertfordshire.

During his time with the 343rd Squadron, Giller 'used up' four Lightnings and four Mustangs. While flying the P-38 he destroyed two German aircraft in the air, the first on November 11, 1943, escorting the 'Big Friends' on a mission to Münster, Germany. Near Breman he was with his squadron escorting the bombers when a rocket-laden JU 88 attempted to intercept. Giller and his wingman went after it. The enemy pilot saw the two P-38s heading for him, fired his rockets at the bombers and took evasive action. Giller got within range and opened up, but saw no visible results. He prepared to pull out of this line of attack when the JU 88's right engine burst into flames and it began to spin down. Satisfied, Giller climbed to rejoin the bomber stream and his squadron.

On April 16, 1944 the group transferred to AAF Sta-

Major Edward B. Giller and the ground crew of the first 'Millie G' CY-G at Nuthampstead, Hertfordshire. This was the first of four P-38s and four P-51s assigned to Giller!

(Giller)

Lightnings taxi out at Nuthampstead airfield. The last one has the code 'Z' inside of the tail fin.

(Sand)

Big Wheels of the 55th Fighter Group Headquarters at McChord Field, Washington in mid-1943 pose with '27' 43-2312 'Wabbit'. From left to right is Cpt. Richard W. Bushing (C.O. 338th F-S), Major Milton Joel (C.O. 38th FS), Major William Kelly (Grp. Eng. Off.), Lt. Col. Frank B. James (Grp. CO.), Major Jack S. Jenkins (Grp. Ops. Off.), Major George Crowell (Ex. Off., 55th F-G) and Capt. Dallas W. Webb (C.O. 343rd F-S).

tion F-159, Wormingford, Essex where it was to remain until the end of the war in Europe. In July, 1944, it began to phase-out its Lightnings with Mustangs and by the end of the month the changeover was complete. During August the group destroyed ten enemy aircraft: four ME 109s on the 10th and six JU 88s on the 24th - for the loss of 19 P-51s, of which seven pilots were known to have bailed out safely. On September 7 the group destroyed seven. Early in 1945, when enemy aircraft were getting scarce, the Group Historian described the mission for February 23 as: 'No hits, no runs, no errors, no Huns, no flak, no terrors, even the locos had hit the sack, nary a one on any track.'

On the 2nd the boys made up for the lack of opposition by destroying seven ME 262s in the air and seven single-engined aircraft on the ground. On March 3, 1945 the group claimed 12 aircraft destroyed. In the last month of the war it flew 16 missions, the last on April 21, the pilots making claims for 150 aircraft destroyed.

It was during April that Giller scored the majority of his victories. On April 9 he claimed his last aerial kill, an ME 262, near Munich. This is what he wrote about the combat:

'While we were escorting the ''Big Friends'' to Munich they flew into a small high cloud north of the city just before their IP. I pulled south at 24,000 feet to miss the cloud and stumbled across a ME 262 at 24,000 feet in a gentle right turn. I observed two P-51s chasing him, so I dropped tanks and turned left, hoping to cut him off. I lost him for a minute and was about to give up when I saw him at 20,000 feet still being followed. Having altitude I started chasing him south and east, staying the same distance - about 1,500 yards behind him. This went on for ten minutes with the E/A in a very gentle left turn and losing altitude.

'Finally we started back over the southern edge of Munich - the E/A at 1,000 feet and me at 7,000 feet.

Lt. Colonel Jack Jenkins paid regular visits to his friend Harry J. Dayhuff of the 78th Fighter Group based at Duxford. The time was October 1943. Behind is Jack's P-38 CG-J, 42-67074 'Texas Ranger'.

Lt. Col Jack Jenkins, his ''Texas Ranger'' and friends go looking for trouble.

(Mulron)

Five victory ace Gerald Brown and his P-38, #42-67028.

(Tabatt)

Harold Olson, A/C/C on CG-P, poses with the aircraft of Major John D. Landers of the 38th Fighter Squadron. The code was CG-O, 44-13823. The crew chief was Jimmy Durnin.

(Olson)

I lost him again for a minute, then discovered him making for Munich/Riem A/D. I didn't know if he was going to land or try to drag me over some flak. Going ''balls out,'' I caught him at 50 feet just over the perimeter track. He was going west to east about 100 yards to the right of the runway. I fired several bursts and observed strikes on the left wing root and fuselage. I noticed his wheels were not down and his airspeed was about 200 mph. As my speed was about 450, I overshot rapidly and pulled up. When I looked back I saw him crash land or belly-in on the field 100 yards to the right of the runway in a large cloud of dust and flying pieces. He did not burn, which was, I believe, due to the fact that he was out of fuel. The aircraft was completely wrecked.'

Ammunition expended, 1,700 rounds, including that expended on autobahn.'

SUPPORTING STATEMENT

'While flying Major Giller's wing we encountered an ME 262 and chased for about ten minutes. As it approached Munich/Riem A/D, Major Giller fired at the E/A, and many strikes were observed. I saw the ME 262 drop in and crack up in a cloud of dust and flying pieces. I confirm one ME 262 destroyed by Major Giller.'

ERNEST E. LEON
2nd Lt, Air Corps

After the destruction of the jet Giller and two flights from the 343rd Squadron went on to Brunnthal A/D and in the attack destroyed 55 enemy aircraft and claimed 23 damaged. During this encounter Ed Giller destroyed an ME 262, an HE 111 and one ME 410 as well as claiming a damaged ME 410. Others who scored that day were:

Lt Col Righetti: 6 destroyed plus 2 damaged.
Lt Maloney: 1 destroyed plus 2 damaged.
Lt Cunnick: 3 destroyed plus 2 damaged.
Lt Best: 3 destroyed.
Lt Anderson: 1 destroyed.
Lt Williams: 2 destroyed.
Lt Mirando: 2 destroyed.
Lt Staggs: 2 destroyed.
Lt McGinnis: 2 destroyed plus 1 damaged.
Lt Bachman: 1 destroyed plus 2 damaged.
Lt Achramowicz: 2 destroyed plus 1 damaged.
Lt Schendel: 2 damaged.

Capt. Cecil Watts and crew of 38th squadron P-51C ''East Side Rat.'' Recently Capt Watts told us that, contrary to popular opinion these days, the early P-51s were not generally well liked! (SER: 43-25044, CG-M)

(Tabatt)

According to MACR #10440, Capt. Earl Fryer and his P-51D-10 ''Spunktown'' were lost to groundfire over Holland on Aug 8, 1944. Here, in happier times, 44-13804 is readied for a mission.

''My Ready Steady,'' CG-A, 44-13549, and proud crew, L to R.: Captain Donald Snell, who was the C.O. of the 38th Sq, unknown, Flight Chief Heine Zeigler and Crew Chief Richard Bock.

(Bock)

Arthur Thorsen and his P-51D, 44-13747, CG-I ''Six Gun Pete.'' This a/c was lost in combat on 11-2-44.

(Tabatt)

43

Dec '43: Two 338th Sq. P-38s with a 91st Bomb Grp. B-17 in the background.

The colorful 3rd scout force aircraft of Wm. T. Searby (see profile, P 143).

Below & Below Rt.: Capt. Darrell S. Cramer, crew and P-51D CL-Z.44-14121, ``Mick #5''. Two Japanese kill Marks are from Cramer's first tour with the 347th F.G./339 F.S./13th A F: One Zero probable Feb 11, 1943 and ½ Betty confirmed Nov 1, 1943.

(Tabatt)

Those who scored in the 343rd Squadron were: Major Giller, one ME 262 destroyed in the air, plus three destroyed and one damaged on the ground.
Lt Leon: 1 destroyed plus 1 damaged.
Lt Allen: 1 destroyed.
Capt Welch: 6 destroyed plus 2 damaged.
Lt Adams: 2 destroyed plus 1 damaged.
Lt Mahany: 2 destroyed plus 1 damaged
Lt Arnold: 2 destroyed.
Capt Birtciel: 5 destroyed plus 1 damaged.
Lt Apple: 1 destroyed, plus 1 damaged.
Lt Gordon: 1 destroyed.
Lt Boring: 2 destroyed, plus 1 damaged.
Lt Geary: 2 destroyed.
Lt Gifford: 1 destroyed plus 2 damaged.
Lt Abel: 1 destroyed.
Lt Mearns: 1 ME 410 damaged.

The last of Giller's kills came on April 16, 1945, in an attack on a number of airdromes, when the group claimed a total of 52 destroyed and 26 damaged. The 38th Squadron made its attacks on Bad Aibling, Holzhirshen and Brunnthal A/Ds. The 338th Squadron also went to Brunnthal, making six passes, returning 10-0-2. Two beached BV 142s on Lake Chiem were destroyed. Giller was hit in the shoulder by a 20 mm shell fragment. At the time he was flying the seventh 'Millie G' CY-G 44-72123 and the following is an extract from his combat report, written upon his return to Wormingford:

a. Combat (Ground Attack).
b. April 16, 1945.
c. 343rd Fighter Squadron, 55th Fighter Group.
d. 1530.
e. Munich/Brunnthal Landing Ground.
f. 5/10ths, base 3,000 feet.
g. Mixed Types.
h. Total claims: 6-0-1 (Ground) - detailed below.

I. 'I was leading Tudor Squadron on the mission of April 16, 1945. We were sweeping on ahead of the bombers in the area of Brunnthal Landing Ground. I had taken the squadron down to about 3,500 feet in order to find any targets that might present themselves. This was the same area which we had attacked on April 9 and we could see the burned-out hulks of

the many aircraft which we had destroyed. However, I could see between ten and 15 assorted types of aircraft cached away in the woods along the autobahn and around Brunnthal, that we had apparently missed on the 9th.

'Since the number of targets in this area was not lucrative enough to engage the entire squadron, I released the flights to find their own targets. I broke my White flight down into elements to cover this area. My wingman, Lt Arnold, and I made our passes parallel with the autobahn, from south to north, clobbering the aircraft which were parked in the woods along either side of the road.

'My first attack was on a HE 111. I gave it a pretty good squirt and observed many strikes on it; it started to burn in a beautiful burst of flames. Parked just beyond the '111 was a ME 109. I put the pipper on it, getting a good concentration of hits. Just as I pulled up over it, a steady stream of black smoke began to belch forth from it. I had seen two other aircraft parked in this same area on the east side of the road during this first pass, so I went in again, making the same pattern from south to north.

'The first aircraft turned out to be a JU 52, parked a little farther back from the road than the first two targets. I fired at it, pretty well covering the engines; it also burst into flames. I had to make a third pass to position myself on the fourth target which I had observed. It turned out to be a JU 88. I came in on it in the same pattern from south to north, and although I observed many strikes all over the aircraft, I could not get it to burn. As I pulled up from this last pass, a 20 mm flak shell penetrated the left side of my canopy and exploded, wounding me in the left shoulder. I was dazed and bleeding rather badly, so I called my flight together and we set course for home. As a result of this stafing attack I make the following claims:
One (1) HE 111 Destroyed.
One (1) ME 109 Destroyed.
One (1) JU 52 Destroyed.
One (1) JU 88 Damaged.
Ammo expended - 660 rounds.'

SUPPORTING STATEMENT

'I was flying Major Giller's wing and followed him through on his first two passes. I saw him clobber the HE 111 and the ME 109 - they both burst into a beautiful fire. On the second pass I had gotten pretty far out to the side of him, looking for a target for myself, and did not see what he was shooting at. I confirm the HE 111 and ME 109 by Major Giller.'

GUY E. ARNOLD,
0-834931, 2nd Lt, Air Corps.

'I was flying Tudor White 2 on Major Giller's wing when he discovered about 10-15 assorted A/C cached away in the trees along the autobahn near Brunnthal

Above 2 photos Col Elwin Righetti and his ''Katydid'' CL-M, 44-14223. Note crew names on canopy frame.

The loss of Col Righetti, their group C.O., was a tough blow for the 55th. Here, a brief part of the memorial printed originally in the 3rd Air Div's weekly ''Strikes'': ''We're going to miss you, Colonel, all 29 years of your bursting energy and vitality, your eagerness and courage, your initiative and leadership that moulded us into a deadly fighting machine, whipping the Hun at every turn. We're going to miss your cheerfulness, your decisiveness, and your understanding of human nature. You spelled aggressiveness whenever you flew, and made us into one of the eagerest gangs of eager beavers.''
(Tabatt)

The personal mount of Carroll 'Hank' Henry who was Colonel Righetti's wingman on the 17th April 1945 when Righetti was shot down and later killed by German civilians. Coded CL-G, 44-63227. 'Little Trixie'.

(Henry)

Lt. Anthony L. Piscitelli of the 343rd Fighter Squadron, 55th Fighter Group. He was killed in action while flying this aircraft on 10th April 1944.

(Carey)

Lt. Russel W. Erb with his Lightning CY-H, 42-68095. This aircraft was lost in the North Sea when Erb bailed out 7th May 1944. He was picked up by the RAF Air Sea Rescue Service. Lt. Erb later transferred to the 9th Air Force.

(Birtciel)

James May of the 343rd Fighter Squadron with his Lightning CY-J, 43-28285. "The Black Hawk IV" name was in yellow.

Lt. Donald Mercier and his Crew Chief Bill Newman with their charge CY-B, 44-14384 'Lil Pearl'. This aircraft was lost 25th December 1944 with Lt Robert A. Maxwell at the controls.

(Mercier)

Landing Ground. I made the first two passes over this area with Major Giller, but was unable to find a target for myself. As we pulled up from the second pass I sighted a ME 410 stashed away under the trees and covered with branches, on the opposite, or west, side of the road. I broke off from the Major as he was starting his third pass and made my own attack on this target.

'I made my pass along the autobahn, coming in from the south. The A/C was so heavily camouflaged that it was difficult to find it, and when I did finally pick it out again I was almost on top of it and could get in only a very short burst. I saw a few strikes on it, but it did not burn; so I decided that I had better have another go at it. I pulled up and around and my pattern was the same as the first time. This time, however, I was able to catch sight of the '410 more quickly and got in a burst on it. The A/C lighted up like a Christmas tree. After I pulled up, I looked back and it was flaming beautifully. I claim:
One (1) ME 410 Destroyed.
Ammo expended - 220 rounds.'

GUY E. ARNOLD,
0-834931, 2nd Lt, Air Corps.

'I was flying Tudor White 3 and when Major Giller released us to make our own attacks on the dispersed A/C, I picked out a couple of targets south of the area that Major Giller and his wingman were working over. I made my pass 90° to them, from east to west, on an ME 110 parked under the tree on the east side of the road. I observed many strikes on the engines and wing roots of the A/C and it quickly burst into flames.

'I made another pass, this time on an ME 410, firing at it without a sight and getting only a few strikes. I pulled around and came in for another pass from west to east on another ME 410, which was parked on the west side of the road. I got numerous strikes and saw the A/C belch flames and black smoke. Major Giller then called and said that he was hit and wanted me to come out with him. I claim:
One (1) ME 110 Destroyed.
One (1) ME 410 Destroyed.
Ammo expended - 450 rounds.'

ROBERT W. WELCH,
0-705651, Capt, Air Corps.

The 343 FS/55 grp's alphabet soup: ''A'': Capt. Frank E. Birtciel's final ''Miss Velma'' now coded CY-A, 44-13350. When Frank completed his tour this A/C was next assigned to Ray Allen, who renamed it ''Merrimack.'' ''B'': The starboard side of Don Mercier's P-51. The first 3 digits of the serial have been painted over in the Sq. color and the rampant stallion is in red. ''D'': Frank Birtciel's first ''Miss Velma'' named for the future Mrs. B. The bar under the ''D'' means there was another ''D'' operational in the squadron. The serial was 44-14561 and the canopy frame was NMF. ''F'' Robert Buttke's CY-F, 44-15025. Buttke was the 55th's second ace and ended the war with 5.5 confirmed victories. ''M'' the only A/C on this page where the code doesn't show - Richard Ozinga and ''Miss Marilyn II,'' CY-M, 44-13837. Lt. Ken Mix, while flying this A/C on Dec 24, 1944, was killed in a collision with Lt. Mooney of the 357th F.G. ''P'' Lt. Gordon in his pretty ''Lady Val,'' 44-14348. ''W'': C/C Joe Miller closes up John Gehrig's CY-W, 44-14379. The A/C carried 2 names: John's ''Hiya Myrt'' appears in picture, Joe's ''Hiya Mamie,'' to starboard. The ship had previously been Marvin Satenstein's ''Pudgy.'' ''Y'': Lt. Grady Moore's ''Lil' Jan.''

A fine shot of Ed Giller's fifth 'The Millie G' coded CY-G, 44-14985. This was one of a series of publicity shots. The colours were a red rampant stallion on the rudder with olive drab and a light green stripe from the yellow and green checks that finished at the trailing edge of the flaps. On the horizontal stabilizer was the usual white stripe and above and below the wings a black ID stripe.

(Giller)

The mission on April 16 was to be the last one flown by Giller during WWII. By the time he returned to active duty, the war in Europe was over. The group suffered its greatest single loss on the day after Giller was wounded, when it lost its CO. The great strafing exponent, Lt Col Elwyn Righetti, known as 'Eager El,' was hit by light flak over an airfield south of Dresden. The report made out for the mission shows Righetti destroyed three ME 109s and no less than six other aircraft:

'Lt Col Righetti left the bombers and had flown back into the area assigned for strafing. Sighting an airdrome, he took his wingman and was crossing the airfield to check the flak, when he sighted a FW 190 coming in to land. The Colonel told his wingman to take it while he strafed some parked aircraft. He made four to six passes, and had at least seven to nine fires going, when his wingman saw him recovering from a pass, vigorously streaming coolant. Then the skipper came in on the radio . . . "WINDSOR HERE, GANG . . . HIT BAD . . . OIL PRESSURE DROPPING FAST . . . CAN'T MAKE IT OUT OF ENEMY TERRITORY . . . JUST ENOUGH AMMO LEFT FOR ONE MORE PASS . . ." he made that pass and blasted one more Hun aircraft, then levelled out on a two seven zero heading. About a minute and a half later . . . "I'VE GOT TO SET IT DOWN." Shortly thereafter, he broke the silence with . . . "TELL THE FAMILY I'M OKAY . . . BROKE MY NOSE ON LANDING . . . IT'S BEEN A HELL OF A LOT OF FUN WORKING WITH YOU, GANG . . . BE SEEING YOU A LITTLE LATER . . . " '

As his fellow pilots left the scene Righetti was seen to be surrounded by hostile Germans and it is believed he was killed by them.

The group flew its last mission four days later, on April 21, 1945. At the time it was under the command of Ben Rimerman, who was tragically killed on a training flight in a Mustang a few days after the war ended.

War's end found Giller and the rest of the group transferred to Kaufbeuren, Germany as part of the oc-

Ed Giller & the 'G' Wormingford, Essex.

(Mulron)

cupation air forces, and the move was completed by July 21, 1945. The group was undermanned until July, 1946 when it began to build up personnel for conversion to the P-80. It was during the changeover to jets that Ed Giller lost his last 'Millie G' CY-G 44-63204. When being flown by another pilot on September 14, 1945, it is believed to have suffered engine failure, the pilot making a wheels-up landing at Kaufbeuren.

In May, 1946, the group transferred to Giebelstadt, Bavaria and remained there until it was deactivated in August 1946. At the same time, the 31st Fighter Group was activated and took over the 55th Group's personnel and equipment.

While the group was at Kaufbeuren, Giller left for the States, in early February, 1946. He had 30 days leave, after which he was stationed at March Field, California. In July, 1946, he transferred to Wright Field, Ohio.

After working for two months with a technical organization he applied and was accepted for graduate education at the University of Illinois. He completed his course and obtained an MSc in Chemical Engineering and over the following years studied for and obtained a PhD in Chemical Engineering, graduating in 1950.

From 1950 to 1955 he was assigned to the Armed Forces Special Weapons Project in the Pentagon, Washington, DC, as a technical staff officer, working on the effects of nuclear weapons. He was promoted to Colonel in January, 1951. In July, 1954 he was transferred to the Air Force Special Weapons Centre at Albuquerque, New Mexico, as the Director of Research Directorate - an organization concerned with the theory and experimental aspects of nuclear weapons effects.

In July, 1959, Giller joined the Office of Aerospace Research in Washington, DC, as Assistant to the Commander, working there until June, 1964, when he went to Air Force HQ as Director of the Research Directorate. In June, 1967 he joined the Atomic Energy Commission in Germantown, Maryland.

Promoted to Major General in July, 1968, Giller is now Assistant General Manager for Military Application with the Atomic Energy Commission. He is living in Virginia with his wife, Mildred and their children, Susan Ann, Carol Elaine, Bruce Carleton, Penny Marie, and Paul Benjamin.

Giller's decorations include the Silver Star, Legion of Merit, DFC and one OLC, Air Medal with 17 OLCs, Purple Heart, DUC badge, American Campaign Medal, American Defence Service Medal, WWII Victory Medal, European-African-Middle-Eastern Campaign Medal, National Defence Service Medal and the Croix de Guerre.

Giller's ground crew during his time with the 343rd Squadron was Sgt James T. Marine and Sgt McGee, who also served as Bill Lewis's ground crew during Giller's leave in the States.

Lt. Nick P. Bebaeff and crew with their mustang, CY-Y, 44-15246 'Miss Manya'. Note Wolf's head motiff used by several 343rd F.S. pilots.

(Carey)

Below: Interesting shot of canopy showing name and kill mks on last "G". Bottom: The end of "G" at Kaufbeuren AFB, 14 Sept 45. Although A/C was being flown by another pilot, it still retained Giller's claims.

WITOLD ALEXANDER LANOWSKI

61ST FIGHTER SQUADRON, 56TH FIGHTER GROUP

Witold Lanowski is the son of Leon and Elizabeth Lach and was born in Lwow, Poland. His parents were both gifted, his father being blessed with a photographic memory and a flair for learning. He mastered several languages, held a number of directorships and obtained a Doctor of Law Degree at the famous 14th Century Zagellonian University at Krakow. Elizabeth Lach was of German extraction and noted for the beautiful carpets - or kilims - she designed. She was later to prove her loyalty to both her adopted country and her son and daugther, Irena, when she chose a labour camp rather than take German nationality. After the war she was liberated and deposited with Irena in a displaced person's camp. Later they returned to Krakow, Elizabeth harbouring the faint hope that Witold had already returned to Poland. She died in 1954, surviving her husband by several years.

From the many accounts of the participation of the Polish Air Force in World War II, the record of Witold Lanowski emerges as nothing short of amazing. To the legal mind, his military career is intriguing, principally because the events surrounding him represent a unique case history. Even today, it remains a tangled web.

Paradoxically, Lanowski's ability in the field of sport almost prevented him becoming a fighter pilot at all. By the age of 15 he was excelling at swimming, water polo, running, shooting and skiing.

Educated at High School No 11 in Lwow, Lanowski obtained his Metriculation Certificate and seemed destined for a career in architecture, a flair for which he inherited from his mother. However, his sporting prowess led to the offer of a holiday course, under military instruction, at a gliding school. Young Lanowski found it an unforgettable experience and passed the course with the grade of First Student. The flying bug had bitten hard and in the spring of 1938 he entered a course with the Air Flying Corps at Luck. A colleague on the course was Stanislaw Skalski, later to become a celebrated Battle of Britain pilot.

With a first place on the course, Lanowski attained his civilian pilot's license and September, 1935 saw his entry into the Polish Air Force Cadet College at Deblin. Skalski entered Deblin at the same time and the two men formed a friendship that was to last until the latter's return to Poland in 1947.

The Polish Air Force was quick to recognise the new student's ability on the sport's field and Lanowski began his tug of war with authority that lasts to the present day. Acceptance of the air force's plan to make

Witold Lanowski is decorated with the DFC by General Jesse Auton at Boxted, Essex. He was to later hand this award back to the U.S. Government after the war.

(Lanowski)

him their representative in national events would mean a severe curtailment of flying; he would be called upon to train for and compete in, world championships, inter-service championships, the Pentathlon and even the Olympic Games. Only his determination not to become a 'sports machine' and let his flying suffer enabled him to maintain the very high standard demanded of Deblin cadet pilots. Nevertheless, his sports career reached a peak during his time at the college. He became PAF champion in cross-country running and represented the air force in pistol shooting and skiing. He also found time for fencing, riding and the exhilarating pastime of skijoring.

The three-year cadetship began with six months' intensive army training in a special regiment, which became a model course attended by military observers and air attachés from all over the world. Lanowski did so well that his commanding officer tried to induce him to take a commission although he freely admits that he loathed the constant pressure of sport and tried hard to avoid too much effort.

Part of the Deblin course entailed daily marches of 20-25 miles - so gruelling that horses died of exhaustion. The mileage was eventually reduced, but it was hardly the best incentive for Witold to stay in the army. Flying was a much more comfortable way to serve one's country - particularly on the feet! However, those six months of training - which included the use of live ammunition on maneuvers - made Lanowski a soldier second to none.

Flying training continued on the PWS series of aircraft, including the P-14, 16, 18 and 26 and Lanowski considers himself lucky to have had an instructor who specialized in low level work. Collecting souvenirs from trees and haystacks is one way to develop nerves of steel! This nerve was to prove an asset in later years and saved Lanowski's life on more than one occasion.

The culmination of training was a fighter pilot's course at Grudziac. It included a major air to air shooting test in which the participants flew the P-7 fighter for the first time, an exciting prospect for potential combat pilots eager to prove their worth. Lanowski won, gaining the coveted title 'Best Pilot for the 1938 Promotion Year.' This proved to be doubly an honor as this year's competition included so many fine pilots who would later distinguish themselves throughout WW II.

The value of individualism instilled into Lanowski through sports training was excellent grounding for the exacting work of a fighter pilot, but it developed an equal freedom of thought and expression that revolted at the strict disciplinarianism of Deblin. He was soon regarded as a rebel by the authorities; he abhorred anything resembling dictatorship and he and his colleagues demonstrated against what they considered outdated regulations and orders by effectively applying the same rules against the college administration itself. This action resulted in complete chaos, and an almost public scandal that would have wrecked any chance of graduation for those involved.

Lanowski's posting to the 2nd Regiment, 121st Squadron, at Krakow in September, 1938 was relatively short-lived as far as flying went. He was recalled almost immediately to train for the 1939 Olympic Patrol Run - an arduous cross-country ski race by a team of an officer and three men, each carrying a 30-pound pack and a rifle, with a shooting competition at the halfway point.

More sport followed in February and March, 1939, Lanowski taking first place in a combination of three ski races; downhill, slalom and cross-country.

On his return to the squadron he resumed flying training on the P-11C. War was imminent and he was staggered to receive orders to report back to Deblin as an instructor - the air force still wanted their leading sportsman 'under their wing.' Lanowski affected 'severe stomach pains' and underwent an operation for a fictitious appendicitis. The worsening international situation prompted him to persuade a close friend, Prince Karol Radziwill, to bring his car to the hospital ward window. With an open wound which would not heal for some weeks, this remarkable man

That's no photographic trick - that's a real, live hole blasted in the side of Praeger Neyland's "Pistol Packin' Mama" by a very unfriendly 109 jock, Jan 14, 1944.

The mount of ace Evan D. McMinn taken after a take off accident. He made 5 claims between Feb 21 and May 22, 1944 - including 2 FW-190s on the latter date. Note 6 white swasticas just below and in front of canopy.

Pilots celebrate the 800th victory of the 56th Fighter Group. Left to right: Joe Carter, Don Smith, Harold Comstock, Dave Schilling, Lucian Dade, Leslie Smith and Paul Conger. These seven men destroyed 89 aircraft between them. Picture taken on April 13, 1944.
(Conger via Blake)

Lanny's two photos of friend and fellow Polish ace, Mike Gladych with a couple of his A/C. Left is "Pengie III," HV-M, 42-25836. Mike always carried a small ceramic penguin for good luck.

discharged himself. At dawn the following day the Luftwaffe attacked Poland. At home with his mother, Lanowski watched German bombs dropping on Krakow. Incendiaries and small bombs landed in the road right below their window.

The Regiment Fighter Squadrons already operating from Krakow's satellite airfields had been destroyed on the ground, a fate suffered by a high percentage of the Polish Air Force. Lanowski found Krakow a burning shambles, but his CO insisted he follow orders and report to Deblin, which he did the following morning. After some narrow escapes from air attacks he arrived by rail, the sole passenger on a platform truck behind an engine, and joined up with Bezina, the Deblin CO, some college personnel and cadets. The group began a long march to Rumania, eluded capture by Russian Cossacks and near-internment by the Rumanians. In November, 1939, the party reached Marseilles by boat and headed for Lyon Bron, the designated centre for Polish Air Force personnel. Almost immediately a state of discontent amongst the Poles necessitated the formation of a committee and Lanowski was elected one of the five whose job it was to quell a potentially explosive situation. Some months later, he was arrested by the Polish High Command for his trouble! Meanwhile, friction disappeared and training recommenced.

Lanowski himself was selected to fly with a Finnish formation designated 1/145 (Polish) Squadron. By February, 1940, he was ready to leave for Finland, but the pace of subsequent events was to keep him in France. On May 1, 1940, he received his French wings and the squadron moved to Villacoublay, taking part in the air defence of Paris and Lyons, flying the Morane 406 and Caudron 714, the latter known as 'Flying Coffins' by the pilots.

At the end of May came his sudden arrest and, with-

out trial, he was sent to prison, despite attempts to prevent it by both Polish and French senior officers and the Polish President in Exile, and former Foreign Minister, August Zaleski.

By the fall of France, Lanowski had managed to escape from the prison in Aix-en-Provence and at Marseilles, induced the captain of a British ship to hide him aboard, much to the amusement of his friends. In England, he duly presented himself in Blackpool, where the remnants of the Polish Air Force were re-

The "official" I.D. card given to Lanowski while flying with the 56th. It would've been of little value if he'd been captured!

(Lanowski)

SUBJECT: Identification of Officer

TO: Whom it may Concern.

This is to certify that Capt. WITOLD LANOWSKI, P-0711, whose signature appears below and whose picture appears on the reverse side, is on duty with the Army Air Forces of the United States of America.

Date of Birth: 8 June 1915
Color of Eyes: Hazel
Weight   : 178 lbs.
Height   : 5 ft 9 In.
Color of Hair: Lt. Brown

(Signature)

Countersigned:

VIRGIL H. DURRANCE

Lt. Joel J. Popplewell and his P-47 Thunderbolt HV-C, 42-75565. Both pilot and aircraft served with the 61st Fighter Squadron.
(Photo USAF)

forming for flying duties with the RAF. However, it was soon made clear that Lanowski's services were not required. Despite repeated attempts to join a Polish squadron, his name was always rejected, so much so that he came to anticipate it as a matter of course. Colleagues from his 'year' were back in action, but this fully qualified fighter pilot was rejected time and again, even at the height of the Battle of Britain. The death of one comrade after another did nothing to relieve Lanowski's frustration. Learning that his name had been passed to RAF Intelligence as a dangerous communist only served to harden his resolve to return to a front line squadron.

Help eventually came in the form of the Polish Consul in London, who quickly secured him a posting as an instructor, although his aggressive flying and

antics soon resulted in a move to 308 Squadron in December 1941.

His subsequent postings were; 317 (Polish) Squadron in January, 1942, Fighter Leaders School, April, 1943 and 302 Squadron as a Flight Commander in May, 1943. Promotion to the rank of Squadron Leader was denied by Polish headquarters in March, 1944 and Lanowski was offered a desk job, which he refused. Through the offices of his friend, Group Captain Brzezina, he was given a temporary posting with a group of colleagues on 'liason duties' to the US Ninth Air Force. In mid March, Lanowski joined the 355th Squadron, 354th Fighter Group at Boxted, Essex, as an Intelligence Officer.

Equipped with the new P-51B, the 354th was escorting US bombers to Germany for the first time and, although Lanowski was allowed to log Mustang flying time, he was not permitted on operations: 'My dream was to go with them to Berlin and, of course, I couldn't, because of the job I held. I couldn't stand it - I had to get back to flying.'

About this time, a group of six Polish fighter pilots were about to be attached to Francis F. Gabreski's 61st Fighter Squadron of the 56th Fighter Group, which had recently arrived at Boxted. The scheme had the two-fold purpose of being of practical value to the young pilots and a reciprocal gesture of friendship to the Polish Air Force for the training of Polish-Americans at Northolt. Lanowski recalls: 'Our special Polish Flight, incorporated into the 61st, was unique; it consisted entirely of high ranking officers who flew complementary flight positions to each other. The others were: Flight Lieutenants Janicki, Gladych, Sawicz, Andersz and Squadron Leader Rutkowski. With ``Gabby'' Gabreski's close association with the Polish Air Force in England, we were fortunate indeed to be attached to the famous ``Zemke Wolfpack.'' We brought with us our experience and, most important, our feelings - which we did not hesitate to share with the pilots of the group.'

The attachment of the Polish group to the 56th

Two photos of 10 victory ace Robert James Rankin and the wrong side of his A/C HV-H, 42-74662 ``Wicked Wackie Weegie.''
(Blake)

Above & Below: Francis Gabreski, the top American air ace in the E.T.O. with 28 confirmed victories. What makes this accomplishment even more incredible is that he spent the last 9-10 months as a P.O.W.! He was a USAF pilot at Pearl Harbor when the Japanese attacked, but spent most of the war in the E.T.O. with the 56th group's 61st Sq - first as Flt. Ldr. and later as commander. His natural leadership abilities and flying skills won the respect & admiration of his men.

ended in August, 1944, although Lanowski had been asked to remain. Both Zemke and Colonel Dave Schilling - Zemke's Deputy Commander and CO of the 62nd Squadron - suggested that he join the USAAF as a commissioned officer, equal to his rank in the RAF. He eventually accepted when he learned that the Polish High Command was still withholding his squadron command.

From May 15, 1944 to August 28, 1944, Lanowski's first operational tour consisted of 54 operations, and he was credited with three enemy A/C; two FW 190s and one ME 109. Below are copies of the reports for the three claims:

F/Lt W. Lanowski, PAF.
a. Combat (air).
b. May 22, 1944.
c. 61st Fighter Squadron, 56th Fighter Group.
d. 1205.
e. Hoperhofen A/D.

f. 7/10 thin clouds at 6,000 feet.
g. FW 190.
h. FW 190 destroyed.
i. 'I was flying Whippet No 2 when Col Gabreski sent a flight to attack a train near Rotenburg, Red flight acting as top cover. In a dive just above the clouds, I lost my leader. I turned sharply and saw a FW 190 falling in flames and the dogfight which was then taking place. I headed for it and soon sighted four FW 190s at about 5,000 feet, climbing and turning. I went after the last one and fired a short burst, but he turned too sharply for me. Looking down I saw a P-47 firing at a FW 190 with another firing and hitting him from the stern.

'I decided to help the P-47 and went after the last Focke Wulf. I fired a burst from about 4-500 yards, approximately 10° deflection, but saw no results. Closing to about 200-150 yards, still firing, I saw hits all over the fuselage. He burst into flames and went down burning. I pulled up over the clouds, joining 3 other P-47s while still keeping an eye on the remaining FW. He was at about 6,000 feet in a slow turn. He nosed over, white smoke came from his tail and he went into the deck.

'I then joined Col Gabreski. He sighted a ME 109 at about 5,000 feet and went under the clouds. I went just above them, hoping to catch the 109 coming up. But I didn't see him again. I rejoined Col Gabreski when he came up.

'Somewhere west of Linggan we sighted two ME 109s. One was at 20,000, the other diving from that altitude. Being low on gas and suspecting a trap, we proceeded home.'
I claim one FW 190 destroyed.
j. 1,080 rounds. 50 cal. API.
A/C flown HV-E P-47G.

F/Lt W. Lanowski, PAF.
a. Combat (air).
b. June 27, 1944.
c. 61st Fighter Squadron, 56th Fighter Group.
d. 2045-2050 hours.
e. La Perth airfield.
f. 7/10.
g. ME 109.
h. ME 109 destroyed.
i. 'I was flying Whippet White 2 to Col Gabreski. After we finished our dive bombing we tried to find the ME 109s which were reported by Red flight. We flew uneventfully for about half an hour between La Perth and Connantre airfields. In a turn to the left at Connantre airfield, White 3 and 4 went down to the deck on an ME 109 which they spotted.

Flying back towards La Perth A/D, the three of us, White 1, myself and Blue 4, who had joined us after losing his element leader in the clouds, assumed the action was over and prepared to withdraw. At this moment Col Gabreski spotted something on the A/D beneath us. We circled to the left, diving below the clouds. At this time I saw light ack-ack firing at me so I turned sharply to the right, with the Colonel turning left. In my turn to the right I looked down and saw three ME 109s flying 2,000 feet below us and heading in on us in an open "Y" formation. I reported these straight away and Blue 4, who was behind us, dove on them and I saw him firing. The 109s headed for cloud cover.

'The next thing I saw was a 109 smoking and the pilot bailed out. At the same time I saw another 109 which was just hitting the ground. It burned and exploded. I believe that this was the plane Col Gabreski fired on. Glancing to the right I saw another '109 ahead diving for the deck and after calling to the Colonel to join me, I started after him. After two or three minutes at full throttle on the deck I closed on the 109 and opened fire at about 300 yards from dead astern. I observed hits on his left wing and fuselage and right wing and fuselage as he attempted slight evasive action. He then crashed into the deck and as the three of us passed over him we all gave him another short burst for good measure.'

I claim one ME 109 destroyed.
I confirm one ME 109 destroyed for Lt Patterson, (Blue 4), and also confirm one ME 109 destroyed for Col Gabreski.
j. 818 rounds. 50 cal API.
A/C flown HV-M P-47D.

F/Lt W. Lanowski.
a. Combat (air).
b. July 5, 1944.
c. 61st Fighter Squadron. 56th Fighter Group.
d. 1550 Tours.
e. Conches A/D.
f. 6/10 at 5,000 feet.
g. FW 190 and ME 109.
h. ME 109 destroyed.
i. 'I was flying White 2 to Col Gabreski. West at Conches A/D. He called in something on the ground and went down to investigate. It turned out to be two ME 109s at 3,000 feet below the clouds. I followed one, the Colonel the other. He dove to the deck, pulled up and went into the clouds where I lost him. I flew southwards and between the clouds I sighted one P-47 with a white nose being chased by a FW 190. I told him to break and turn to intercept it, but lost them both in the clouds. I turned left again, still at 5,000 feet and there right in front of me at 800 yards was a ME 109. I headed for him from dead astern firing several long bursts, but he went into the clouds.'

I claim one ME 109 destroyed.
j. 258 rounds 50 cal API.
A/C flown HV-Z P-47D.

Top: Bob Johnson, Hub Zemke and Bud Mahurin with Johnson's P-47, HV-P, 42-8461, "Lucky."

Robert S. Johnson finished the war as the second highest scoring ace in the 8th A.F. But this little episode (covered in detail in his book "Thunderbolt") on June 26 almost finished him! P-47, HV-P, 41-6235.

Johnson shows off his NMF P-47, LM-Q, 42-25512.

Lanowski, Mike Gladych and Eugene Barnum at Boxted in early '45.

The ``Silver Lady'' and ground crew who serviced it when it was assigned to Lanowski in late '44: HV-Z (Bar) 42-26044. C/C Sgt. Joseph B. Gibson, Sgt. William Giles and . . . any help out there?

Although Lanowski had been with the USAAF for fifteen months, his official transfer from one air force to another was anything but smooth. The particular requirements of the US military authorities not only managed to make him technically a civilian, despite the fact that he was helping plan fighter operations and flying combat missions, at one point he officially ceased to exist at all! His situation is even more remarkable when it is considered that he was also mentioned in letters of commendation, awarded an American DFC, a Presidential Citation and Air Medals during this period 'in limbo.' In April, 1945, he was awarded the Aeronautical Badge of Senior Pilot by the 12th Wrapper Endorsement, AAF HQ, Washington.

As all his PAF/RAF documents and pay had been withdrawn, Lanowski was given the temporary rank of Captain until his transfer was completed. He still lacked any papers and at his request, the station officer prepared an identity card consisting of a photograph mounted on a small piece of cardboard with brief personal details on the reverse - the only recognizable mark of officialdom being the date stamp. As

Lanowski observes, this 'document' would have afforded him little protection had he been shot down and captured. However, the one thing that troubled him above all else was the monthly collection made for him by some of the 61st Squadron pilots. Taking the hat round for 'dollars for Lanny' was a gesture intended to see him through until his commission and pay came through, but it became a source of acute embarrassment as the months went by.

Lanowski's contribution to the 56th was mentioned by Dave Schilling at the time: 'He flew Wing, Element Leader and Flight Leader positions. On occasions, he has led the 61st Squadron and at all times has been very helpful in training new pilots and materially aided the development of techniques used by the 56th Group against the enemy.'

This praise is endorsed in an extract from a letter from Major General W. E. Kepner: 'Lanowski, by way of his previous experience, greatly aided the (56th) Group in the planning and execution of missions against the German Air Force.'

For a green pilot, it was reassuring to have an experienced Squadron Commander flying his wing, especially one reputed to have exceptional eye-sight. Lanowski was known as 'ole X-ray eyes' for his ability to pick out the enemy over great distances. He also flew wing position to Zemke and Gabreski, alternating between the two leaders. On one occasion he saved 'Gabby's' life.

The esteem Hub Zemke felt for his colleague was reflected in his insistence that 'Lanny' accompany him to the 479th Group when he became its CO. Lanowski's circumstances prevented the move, however, and it was with deep regret that he saw Zemke leave. He considered him one of the best fighter leaders he had known and a further bitter blow was to hear the Zemke had become a prisoner of war. Lanny felt partly responsible.

From October 1, 1944, until August, 1945, he flew what was to be his second tour of combat with the 56th Group. On November 18, 1944, he shot down a FW 190 during the time when he was officially a civilian.

Below is the report of the combat:

Eighth Air Force FO 1317-A
Capt W. Lanowski, PAF, Whippet Yellow 1.
a. Combat (air).
b. November 18, 1944.
c. 61st Fighter Squadron, 56th Fighter Group.
d. 1250 hours.
e. East of Hanau.
f. 10/10 cirrus overcast as 25,000 feet.
g. FW 190.
h. FW 190 destroyed (air).
i. 'I was leading Yellow Flight over the assigned target

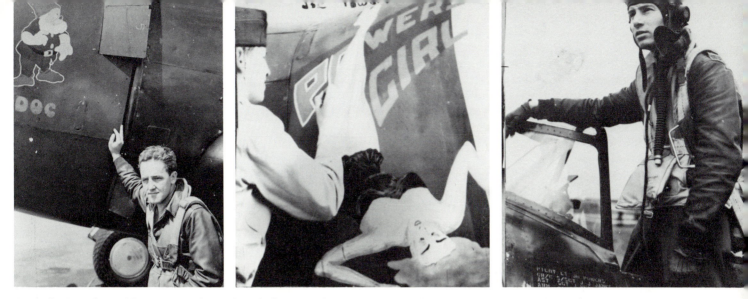

An early shot of Donald ''Doc'' Renwick during his first tour with the group. Renwick eventually rose to position of group commander in Aug '45. He made at least 1 confirmed victory in this P-47, HV-T, 4-6352.

A squadron artist puts the finishing, touches to ''Powers Girl,'' the P-47 of ace Joe Powers.

Joe and his A/C, HV-P (Bar) 4-5163.

(Conger via Blake)

having just completed dive strafing with Blue Flight on oil storage tanks with excellent results. After my second pass at the target I climbed to join Whippet Leader. At that time, at 13,000 feet, flying from northeast to southwest at one o'clock to me, I saw a formation of about 16 A/C which I presumed to be a friendly squadron but soon they dove on the tail of Whippet White Flight. I screamed ''Break - 190s!'' and combats soon ensued at about 8-9,000 feet. After a few seconds I saw one P-47 which I believe to have been flown by Lt De Mars, being attacked by two FW 190s. I saw them score hits on his A/C. He split-essed straight down and bailed out at about 5,000 feet about eight miles east of Hanau at 12.35.

'Looking round for a target I found a 190 by himself, turning, but due to the 90° deflection and 500 yard range I do not believe I scored hits. So I picked out another one in approximately the same position. Again I believe I didn't hit him. At this time I saw another 190 below me at about 4-5,000 feet, being chased by two P-47s. They didn't get him however, since he made a violent evasive break, nearly spinning in. I dove on his tail and opened fire from 200-100 yards, seeing hits all over the fuselage and cockpit. I then passed by him so close that I could see blood obscuring the hood of the cockpit. A little black smoke came out, he dove straight down, hit the ground and exploded.

I claim one FW 190 destroyed.
1,354 rounds 50 cal API.
A/C flown HV-Z 42-26044.

Lanowski's determination to keep flying missions in the face of red tape helped conceal his sorrow at the plight of his country. In his own words, it 'obliterated what I was feeling for my country's futile fight for freedom and the knowledge that I would never be able to

return to my own home, my family and my people.'

Having travelled from one department to another through England and Europe, Lanowski's papers finally reached the War Department in Washington, DC. Although Eisenhower himself had approved his commission into the USAAF, the American Secretary for War rejected it and sent notification that Witold Lanowski's services were no longer needed. The order - to take immediate effect - meant instantaneous dismissal. Within a matter of hours, Lanowski found himself on the streets of Colchester with only the clothes on his back. He bears the distinction of being the first US serviceman to have been released after the war. Unlike the others, he had never been officially demobilized.

After various approaches to the highest US military and civilian authorities for reimbursement for his time with the 56th Group, Lanowski received a minimum sum of $4,000 for his services from October 1, 1944 to August 9, 1945. It was paid in 1964, accompanied by a note that the sum was 'in full settlement of his claims for extraordinary services rendered in the United States Army Air Force during World War II.' Apart from the efforts of Lanowski himself, others took up his cause, including US correspondent Jack Anderson, through an article entitled 'The Hero We Forgot to Pay.'

Lanowski became a naturalized Briton in 1949 and and re-joined the RAF in 1950. With the rank of Sgt Pilot, he was posted to the Overseas Ferry Unit - later 167 Squadron- subsequently flying all first line fighter types acquired for home and overseas commands, from Hornets to Hunters. On his retirement, he had flown over 60 different types.

On Friday, May 3, 1955, he survived a take-off crash in Venom WE 385 at Fassburg, Germany, in which he was badly burned. He underwent several plastic surgery operations performed by G. H. Morley, Sir Archibald McIndoe's wartime assistant at East Grinstead. He resumed flying the following year and had reached Master Pilot rating by 1958. In December of that year, Lanowski left the RAF under the Premature Retirement Scheme.

While serving, Lanowski had resumed his sporting activities, competing at Bisley and the Cresta Run at St. Moritz for the RAF. He undertook the training of a group of Cadets for the Pentathlon, with some good results.

Witold Lanowski now lives in Essex with his wife, Penny, daughter Jadwiga and son Krystyn. He also has an elder son, Robin Alexander.

Lanowski flew his first RAF sortie on April 2, 1942 and until February 22, 1944 flew a total of 97 combat missions totalling 220 hours and destroyed two German aircraft. He flew a total of six hours 20 minutes with the 355th Squadron of the 354th Group and his flying hours with the 61st Squadron to August 27, 1945 were 449, of which some 22 hours were postwar.

Combat mission list of W. A. Lanowski May 21, 1944 - August 27, 1945.
Various P-51B A/C

Date	Location	Duration	Code
3, 21, 1944	Local Flight	2.20	GQ-O
25	Northolt	1.00	GQ-P
26	Local Flight	1.00	GQ-P
3, 7, 1944	Dennland	1.00	GQ-H
10	Dennland	1.00	GQ-D

List of operational sorties with the 61st Squadron of the 56th Fighter Group.
Various P-47 A/C

Pilot Russ Kyler is strapped in by his Crew Chief Van C. McGehee. Paul Shipman was the assistant crew chief and the armorer was Eugene J. Fournier. "Lorene's" overall color was a dark plum black with the red codes outlined in white.

Russ Kyler and his crew chief admire the painting on their P-47M. This cowling was transferred from their 'D' model Thunderbolt. Code and serial: HV-J, 44-21116.

The wreckage of Venom WE-385 in which Lanny crashed on take off from Fassberg May 13, 1955. Engine failure!

	Location	Duration	Code
5, 15, 1944	Local	1.40	HV-G
15	Local	1.30	HV-H
16	Local	1.30	HV-T
17	Local	0.45	HV-R
17	Local	2.00	HV-M
18	Local	2.35	HV-V
18	Local	1.05	HV-L
19	Local	1.40	HV-E
20	Local	1.20	HV-I
21	Amiens	2.55	HV-J
22	Osnabruck	4.15	HV-E
22		2.55	HV-L
23	Epernay	3.15	HV-L
24	Heligoland	4.10	HV-L
24	Local	1.00	HV-X
25		4.20	HV-N
30	Hamburg	4.20	HV-L
31	Osnabruck	4.05	HV-O
6, 3, 1944	Paris	3.40	HV-L
4	Lille	2.40	HV-N
4	Paris	3.40	HV-G
5	Dieppe	2.35	HV-G
6	Normandy	4.35	HV-G
6	Dreux	3.20	HV-O
8	Paris	3.55	HV-L
8	Paris	3.30	HV-Q

10	Harcourt	2.30	HV-L
10	Le Mans	3.50	HV-L
11	Mayenne	4.20	HV-G
12	Argentien	4.10	HV-B
13	Saumun	4.10	HV-T
14	Poix	3.10	HV-G
22	Amiens	3.20	HV-O
22	Compiegne	3.35	HV-O
23	Reims	3.20	HV-O
24	Paris	3.20	HV-P
25	Orleans	4.00	HV-F
25	S France	0.45	HV-F
27	Amiens	4.00	HV-M
27	Dungeness	0.30	HV-M
28	Coltishal	1.00	HV-M
29	Leipzig	3.55	HV-O
30	Paris	4.05	HV-H
7, 1, 1944	Local	1.15	HV-B
4	Criel	3.25	HV-Z
5		4.00	HV-Z
10	Ford	1.45	HV-P
11	Lille	3.00	HV-H
12	Mannheim	3.45	HV-U
13	Metz	4.00	HV-I
15	Orleans	4.15	HV-O
16	Saarbrucken	4.00	HV-J
19	Saarbrucken	3.15	HV-Q
21	Saarbrucken	4.00	HV-L
21	Lydd	1.00	HV-D
25	Rouen	4.15	HV-F
26	St Just en Chausse	3.30	HV-G
28	Calais	2.40	HV-O
28	Ford	1.30	HV-D
31	France	3.40	HV-V
8, 3, 1944	Strasbourg	4.50	HV-C
5	Bremen	4.15	HV-L
7	Rouen	3.25	HV-X
9	Trier	4.50	HV-Z
12	Laon	3.45	HV-H
13	Rouen	3.20	HV-T
15	Brussels	3.30	HV-X
16	Hanover	3.55	HV-X
25	Bremen	4.00	HV-X
27	Brussels	4.25	HV-G
28	Brussels	3.50	HV-G
10, 1, 1944	Wattisham	0.30	HV-O
1	Coltishall	1.00	HV-Z
2	Cross-country	2.30	HZ-Z
3	Lachen-Speyerdorf	4.30	HV-Z
5	Munster	4.30	HV-Z
6	Hamburg	5.05	HV-Z
7	Magdeburg	5.35	HV-H
12	Osnabruck	4.10	HV-Z
15	Gutersloh	4.20	HV-Z
17	Cologne	4.15	HV-Z
25	Hanover	3.50	HV-T
26	Cross-country	0.30	HV-Q
27	Cross-country	2.10	HV-Q
11, 4, 1944	Cross-country	2.00	HF-F
5	Frankfurt	5.05	HV-Z
5	Cross-country	0.20	HV-Z
6	Munster	3.40	HZ-Z
6	Cross-country	0.45	HV-Z
10	Ludwigslust	4.50	HV-J
16	Aachen	3.15	HV-Z
18	Frankfurt	4.45	HV-Z
20	Bonn	3.45	HV-Z
21	Hamburg	4.40	HV-Z

Above left and below: F/O, later Lt., Steven N. Gerick and his P-47D-5-RA, HV-O, 42-26024 "Tally Ho Chaps." Steven ended the war with at least 5 confirmed and no less than 9 damaged E/A. Note 10 symbols under cockpit!

(Tabatt)

Nice variety of 61st Squadron aircraft.

(Conger via Blake)

Lt. Sam Aggers in 42-75154 which he named "Sad Sam."

Lanowski's last assigned P-47 Thunderbolt. The aircraft is a plum black with red codes outlined in white. The Polish flag is on the cowling with a mailed fist crushing a ME-109. Lanny had a horse shoe put on just in front of the cockpit.

(Lanowski)

Date	Area	Time	Code
23	Cross-country	0.40	HV-M
12, 3, 1944	Local	0.30	HV-Z
4	Local	0.45	HV-Z
5	Local	0.45	HV-Z
8	Local	0.15	HV-Z
11	Karlsruhe	4.30	HV-S
15	Local	3.25	HV-V
	Coblenz	4.10	HV-V
29	Local	1.00	HV-V
31	Hanover	4.50	HV-V
1, 3, 1945	Frankfurt	4.15	HV-V
4	Cross-country	1.10	HV-V
7	Aachen	4.30	HV-V
10	Coblenz	4.15	HV-V
11	Cross-country	1.00	HV-V
17	Hamburg	4.35	HV-V
20	Local	1.00	HV-M
21	Local	0.20	HV-M
23	Local	1.00	HV-Z
23	Local	1.00	HV-Z
29	Local	1.00	HV-Z
2, 3, 1945	Local	1.30	HV-U
19	Local	2.00	HV-U
19	Local	2.00	HV-U
20	Local	1.00	HV-U
21	Nuremburg	5.45	HV-C
*3, 2, 1945	Local	1.00	144020
3	Local	2.00	HV-Z
* 3	Cross-country	2.15	144020
4	Cross-country	2.30	HZ-Z
4	Cross-country	2.15	HV-Z
5	Cross-country	1.30	HV-Z
5	Cross-country	1.30	HV-Z
6	Cross-country	1.45	HV-Z
* 7	Preston	2.30	144020
*3, 7	Boxted	2.00	144020
8	Local	1.30	HV-Z
9	Osnabruck	4.15	HV-Z
* 10	Cross-country	2.00	144020
12	Frankfurt	4.45	HV-Z
23	Local	1.45	HV-Z
* 31	Bovingdon	2.20	144020
4, 8, 1945	Local	1.10	HV-Z
15	Local	0.50	HV-Z
16	Munchen	5.40	HZ-Z
19	Munchen	5.10	HV-Z

*C-61 A/C Training Flight

While with the 61st Squadron Lanowski shot down four enemy aircraft:

Date	Type	Area	Aircraft details
5, 22, 1944	1 FW 190	Osnabruck	P-47G HV-E
6, 27, 1944	1 ME 109	Compiegne	P-47D HV-M
7, 5, 1944	1 ME 109	Conches	P-47D HV-Z
11, 18, 1944	1 FW 190	Frankfurt	42-26044 HV-Z

GEORGE E. BOSTWICK

63RD FIGHTER SQUADRON, 56TH FIGHTER GROUP

George Bostwick was born in Eau Claire, Wisconsin on October 19, 1919 and his family later moved to Wausaw, Wisconsin. He was educated at Ryson College from 1937-41 and obtained a BSc degree.

On June 25, 1941, he was accepted for USAAF flying training and sent to Richmond, Virginia and later Dover Field, Delaware. He graduated from flying school on October 1, 1943, and was assigned overseas combat duty. He arrived at Halesworth in early March, 1944 to fly with the 62nd Squadron of the 56th Fighter Group.

On May 11, 1944, Bostwick flew his first mission, a ramrod to Berlin. By the end of the month he had flown 13, including two more to the German capital.

The first mission for June came on the 3rd - a fighter sweep to the Paris area - and before the close of that momentous month, Bostwick had flown 37, including two on D-Day, a rodeo to Le Havre and a ramrod to the Normandy beachhead. On the 7th, he destroyed a ME 109 in the air over Grandvilliers, France.

On July 4, over Conches A/D Bostwick destroyed three ME 109s in quick succession to bring his total to four. He also managed to damage a ME 109 in the air on the same mission. The combat was recorded in the group diary:

'On July 4, 1944, Lt Bostwick was leading the second element of White Flight on a dive bombing mission, VIII Fighter Command FO No 429. In the vicinity of Conches A/D, Blue leader called in some E/A on an auxiliary A/D and positioned the flight for bombing. As he did so, ten plus ME 109s were reported at 8-10,000 feet with an additional 20 at 2,000 feet. All flights bounced and in the ensuing combat Lt Bostwick became separated from the remainder of his flight. His tachometer was out of action and his propellor, which had been causing him some trouble, began to pulsate violently.

With complete disregard for his own safety and ignoring the fact that he was alone against 20 E/A, Lt Bostwick nevertheless attacked. So determined and aggressive was his attack on the first E/A that it exploded before the pilot could get out. By this time however, eight ME 109s were on his tail and it was only through a superb display of flying skill that he was finally able to evade them and attempt to retain altitude.

'As he was climbing, he spotted two more E/A below him and attacked, destroying one. As he broke away he spotted another which he also destroyed. As a climax, while circling for altitude he attacked a fourth ME 109 which he damaged before running out of ammunition.

Lt. George E. Bostwick and his crew chief S/Sgt. Joseph A. Brennan and their ship LM-Z, 42-26280. This was taken when George was flying his first tour of combat duty.

(Bostwick)

Snackbar & relaxation room for the 62nd FS at Boxted.

Horace C. "Pappy" Craig was the first 56th Grp. pilot to complete his tour of operations - Feb 3, 1944. Note early style markings.

Bernard R. Smith smiles down from ''Sunshine,'' his P-47, UN-S, 41-6330. He scored 3 confirmed and 1 probable during the winter of 43-44.

63rd Squadron operations board, early '45.

Strikingly similar to top left photo, this is Lt. Russ Westfall.

(Mulron)

Westfall's UN-B, 42-75278, ''Anamosa'' taxies out for a mission.

Lt. Joseph L. Egan Jr's P-47 in trouble at Manston. Egan ended the war with 5 confirmed.

Pasquale A. Fares, Bostwick's armourer, on LM-Z, 42-26280 and a wingful of point fifties.

(Bostwick)

Colonel Robert B. Landry commanded the group from October 30, 1943 until January 12. 1944 while Zemke was in the U.S. The plane, 42-75109, was coded UN-W and named "Louisiana Pirate." When Landry left the plane was assigned to J. Vogt.

Major Lucian A. Dade Jr. had a big day on July 4, '44 with 2 109s confirmed and 2 damaged!

All in all Lt Bostwick destroyed three E/A during the course of this combat and damaged a fourth. For the most part of the mission, he was on his own and at a great disadvantage because of his malfunctioning aircraft.'

Two days later, on July 6, flying LM-Z 'Ugly Duckling,' Bostwick destroyed a ME 109 in the air over Beaumont, France, to become an ace.

His ground crew in the 62nd was S/Sgt Joseph A. Brennan, Crew Chief; S/Sgt A. Andy Yourick, Crew Chief and Sgt Pasquale A. Fares, Armourer.

In August Bostwick flew 18 missions and was awarded the Air Medal and Silver Star. On September 8, on his 70th mission, he destroyed three FW 190s on the ground at Euskirchen A/D. On the 10th of the month he flew the last mission of his tour, a bomber escort to Nurnberg. A day later he started back to the States for six weeks R & R.

Reassigned to the 63rd Squadron on his return to the 56th Fighter Group in January, 1945, Bostwick flew his first mission on January 10, a rodeo to Cologne. On a subsequent ramrod to Bielefeld, he attacked a ME 410 parked on Barge A/D for which he was awarded a damaged claim.

On March 25, 1945, George Bostwick became one of the few pilots to shoot down a ME 262 in the air. This is what he had to say about his jet kill:

'I was leading Daily Squadron on an escort mission in the vicinity of Hamburg. We were on the right and to the rear of our box of bombers when my Red leader called in several bogies closing rapidly on a small group of 15 bombers at about 8 o'clock to us. They were in good formation but some distance away from the rest of their box. I turned towards them just in time to see two explode.

'The ME 262s split up after their attack, most of

Two photos of ace Major Michael Jackson in his last bolt, LM-J, 44-21117. Crew names are: W.O. Noah, J.F. Price and R.E. Helwig. All of Major Jackson's 8 victories were while flying P-47s with the 56th Fighter Group's 62nd Squadron. Besides the usual ME-109s and FW-190s, Mike shot down a Ju-52, a Ju-88 and a FW-190D.

(Jackson)

A nice shot of a colorful P-47 of the 62nd F.S. with its bright red nose and yellow tail. This A/C may also have been flown by ace Joe Walter Icard, but most of his claims were recorded in 42-75040 also coded LM-I.

Lt. Charles T. McBath's P-47, UN-B, 44-21150, with P.C. Dawson puffing away contentedly alongside. Note that McBath's name is listed third on the mission board pictured on page 62 and that he also claimed a Ju-88 on page 67's strafing report.

(Jim Crow)

Wayne J. O'Conner in his first assigned P-47. He scored 1½ vics in his second A/C, also UN-O, 42-74722.

them heading roughly east. I followed until I lost sight of them and then proceeded to look over all the airfields in the area. I finally found the airdrome at Parchim and orbited it at about 12,000 feet for about 20 minutes. There were between 20-30 aircraft visible on the field. After many wide orbits, my Number 4 man called in a bogie and I directed him to lead off. This E/A was also a ME 262 and he led us back to the airdrome.

'Upon approaching the airdrome I spotted four more ME 262s milling around almost on the deck. I picked out one flying parallel to the landing strip as if he might be going to peal off to land. He did not, however, but flew straight down the runway. As he reached the end of it he passed over a second aircraft which was taking off and just breaking the ground.

'I pulled my nose through to get a shot at it but before I could the pilot apparently saw me and made a tight turn to the left. His left wing dug into the ground and the plane cart-wheeled, breaking into many pieces and strewing wreckage for some distance. I then pulled back up to the right and picked up the E/A I had originally attacked. I got in a burst from about 800 yards and 45° and observed strikes on the fuselage near the tail. It then straightened out and I fired several bursts from dead astern without effect as it was rapidly widening the gap between us. I was indicating 460 mph at this time. I fired up to my tracers and then broke off and headed out. My wingman, who had followed behind joined me shortly and a few minutes later my element joined up.

'I claim one ME 262 destroyed and one damaged in the air. A/C No 44-21160 UN-J. Ammo fired 2,060 rounds API.'

While escorting bombers to Krummel, Bostwick destroyed two ME 109s in the air and damaged an ME 262.

Captain George E. Bostwick.
a. Combat.
b. April 7, 1945.
c. 63rd Fighter Squadron, 56th Fighter Group.
d. 1220-1305.
e. S of Bremen to N of Hamburg.
f. 4-5/10 cumulus tops 8,000 ft.
g. ME 262, ME 109s.
h. Two ME 109s destroyed; one ME 262 damaged.

'I was leading 56th 'B' Group on an escort mission to Hamburg. We made rendezvous with the bombers at 11.50. At 12.20 I spotted a ME 262 diving towards the rear of a box of bombers in the vicinity of Nienburg. I turned towards him and got a short burst from about 70° and about 800 yards, scoring a few hits around the canopy. I pulled in behind him and fired another short burst without affect. I followed him for a few minutes to see that he didn't turn in towards the bombers and then I returned to escort.

One of the 8th's top scorers, Frederick J. Christensen Jr. joined the 56th in Aug 43, finishing the war with 21.5 confirmed aerial vics. "Rozzie Geth" was nickname for his girlfriend Rosamond Gethro.

'A few minutes later, Nuthouse reported E/A above the bomber formation. Spotting two contrails, I climbed to 30,000 feet to intercept and on closing recognized one of the E/A as a ME 109E. I fired a short burst from about 300 yards and observed many hits on both wing roots and fuselage. Glycol was streaming out of the A/C as I passed underneath. I looked back, saw the pilot bail out and watched him disappear without opening the 'chute (see supporting statement).

'I then picked up another contrail which I closed on, to find it was a P-51, which led me to five more ME 109s just above the target area. I was closing on one but he spotted me and split-essed from about 30,000 feet. I followed him through this maneuver but was a little too far back to fire. He went straight down at terrific speed and at 5,000-10,000 feet I saw a black object which may have been the pilot. I did not see a 'chute open, however. The plane continued in its dive and went straight into a small rectangular pond or reservoir. I flipped my dive recovery flaps and pulled out very abruptly. I blacked out and lost my vision for a few seconds and was at 12,000 feet when I regained it. I dove slightly and took a short picture of the oil slick made on the water by the enemy A/C with my wing camera.

'I then climbed to about 18,000 feet where many P-51s were in a fight with several ME 109s. I maneuvered into position three different times astern of a ME 109 but was forced to break away by P-51s coming in on my tail. This was probably due to the fact that I was the only P-47 in the fight.

I claim two ME 109s destroyed and one ME 262 damaged in the air.
j. A/C No 44-21112 UN-Z. Ammo fired 523 rounds.

API.'

SUPPORTING STATEMENT
'While flying above the bombers at 30,000 feet, I spotted Captain Bostwick closing on a ME 109. I cut him off in the turn and was very close when he fired on the E/A. Many hits were seen and coolant streamed from it. The E/A nosed down and while flying close to it I saw the pilot bail out and hit the tail assembly. The 'chute did not open.'
EUGENE W. ANDERMATT 0-2000223
1st Lt, Air Corps

On April 10, Bostwick flew a rodeo to Berlin and in an attack on Werder Airdrome, destroyed four aircraft on the ground, to bring his total to fifteen destroyed, of which seven were aerial victories and eight ground. He also damaged four more aircraft, two in the air and two on the ground. The mission was his 89th and the following extracts from his, and several other pilots' combat reports record claims totalling 15 destroyed and nine damaged on the ground.
a. Strafing.
b. April 10, 1945.
c. 63rd Fighter Squadron, 56th Fighter Group.
d. Werder Airdrome (5224n-1255).
e. 1450 to 1505 hrs.
f. CAVU.
g. FW 190, ME 109s, JU 88s, DO 217s and several U/I/T/E and S/EE/A.
h. Total claims 15-0-9 on the ground.
i. Account of combat.
'I was leading 56th 'B' Group on a sweep and escort mission in the Berlin area. We reached the city approximately fifteen minutes early, so I flew down to the

vicinity of Briest Airdrome with the intent of making a few strafing passes before leaving to make rendezvous with our bombers. I spotted an airdrome (later identified as Werder) which had five or six oil fires on it and which was being strafed by about 12 P-51s. They seemed to be getting practically no flak and there were 75/100 enemy aircraft of all types on the field, so I decided to join their pattern.

'I had 12 aircraft with me at the time, so left one flight up as top cover and took eight aircraft down to strafe, each of us making three passes on the airdrome. The P-51s changed their pattern a few times, but we did not have too much difficulty conforming to it. All three passes were made generally from northwest to southeast.

'On the first pass I destroyed a JU 88; Lt Naylor an unidentified single-engined E/A; Lt T. W. Smith a JU 88; Captain Flagg a DO 217; Lt Hoffman an unidentified twin-engined E/A and Lt V. A. Smith a JU 88. In addition to these Lt T. W. Smith damaged a JU 88 and Lt Hennessey damaged a DO 217.

'Our second pass was made almost north to south. I damaged an unidentified twin-engined E/A on the north edge of the field and then continued on across the field firing into the open end of a hangar. I scored strikes on one unidentified twin-engined E/A which burst into flames. As I pulled up the whole hangar burst into flames. I saw one other E/A in the hangar and there may have been more.

Lt Naylor destroyed a FW 190; Captain Flagg a DO 217 and a ME 109; Lt Hoffman an unidentified twin-engined E/A and Lt McBath damaged a JU 88 on this pass.

'Our third pass was made from the northwest again. I concentrated my fire on a JU 88 and a ME 109 which were parked close together. The JU 88 burned as I pulled up. Lt Naylor destroyed a ME 109 and Captain Flagg an unidentified single-engined E/A. Lt Naylor also damaged a DO 217; Captain Flagg a ME 109; Lt Hennessy a DO 217 and Lt V. A. Smith an unidentified twin-engined E/A.

'Upon pulling up from each pass I took pictures with my K-25 camera. All aircraft on the field seemed to have plenty of gasoline in them and most of them burst into flames after having been hit two or three times. The 78th Group P-51s which were strafing with us estimated in their mission summary that we had started 20-25 fires, and we were claiming 15 as destroyed. The P-51s started 10-12 fires on the field proper while we were there and were working over a dispersal area to the west of the field as we left. After our third pass we reformed and escorted our bombers out to Dümmer Lake.'

SUPPORTING STATEMENT

'I witnessed an enemy aircraft destroyed by Lt T. W. Smith on his first pass and also observed an enemy aircraft destroyed by Captain Bostwick on his first pass.'

JAMES C. NAYLOR
2nd Lt, Air Corps.

'I witnessed Captain Bostwick on our second pass clobbering a hangar loaded with enemy aircraft. It was a very good concentration of fire power and when I passed over the whole inside was blazing.

'On our third pass I witnessed Captain Bostwick destroy a JU 88. The nose and engine were covered in flames.'

CHARLES T. McBATH
2nd Lt, Air Corps.

'I witnessed the plane Captain Flagg fired on during his first pass burst into flames.

'I also witnessed Lt Hoffman on his third pass firing at an enemy aircraft parked near a hangar. As he passed over the plane it burst into flames.'

VERNON A. SMITH
2nd Lt, Air Corps.

Left: Dave Shilling in LM-S, 42-26541 and George Bostwick in LM-Z, 42-26280 ready to roll down the runway at Boxted on another escort mission over Germany.

Right: War correspondents were frequent visitors at Boxted. Here one talks to David Schilling, famous ace, and one of the driving forces in the 56th - first as 62nd Sq. Commander and later as Group C.O.

'I witnessed the destruction of a DO 217 by Captain Flagg on his third pass. The E/A burst into flames immediately after it was hit.'

THOMAS B. HENNESSY
2nd Lt, Air Corps.

Bostwick flew his last mission of the war on April 20, 1945, a ramrod to Muhldorf and on the following day the 56th Group flew its last mission of the war.

At the cessation of hostilities the Air Force sent Bostwick to college at the USAF Institute of Technology and Stanford University for four and a half years. On graduating he served in procurement, engineering and maintenance capacities, retiring from the USAF on October 31, 1963. Since then he has worked at the General Dynamics plant at Fort Worth in Texas.

A 356th group P-51 flown by Bostwick while the 56th was experiencing engine troubles with its new P-47Ms.

(Bostwick)

Confirmed claims by Major George E. Bostwick.

Date	Type	Credit	Air/Grd.	Area
6, 7, 44	1 ME 109	Des	Air	Grandvilliers Area
6, 4, 44	3 ME 109s	Des	Air	Conches Area
4	1 ME 109	Dam	Air	Conches Area
6	1 ME 109	Des	Air	Beaumont
9, 8, 44	3 FW 190s	Des	Grd	Koblenz
1, 15, 45	1 ME 410	Dam	Grd	Barge A/D
3, 25, 45	1 ME 262	Des	Air	Parchim Area
4, 7, 45	2 ME 109s	Des	Air	S of Bremen
10	2 JU 88s	Des	Grd	Werder A/D
10	1 U/I/T/E	Des	Grd	Werder A/D
10	1 U/I/T/E	Des	Grd	Werder A/D
10	1 U/I/T/E	Dam	Grd	Werder A/D

Combat mission list of Major George E. Bostwick, 63rd Squadron, 56th Fighter Group.

Mission No	Date	Location	Type of Mission
1	5, 11, 44	Berlin	Ramrod
2	12	Frankfurt	Rodeo
3	13	Tutow	Ramrod
4	19	Brunswick	Ramrod
5	20	Liege	Rodeo
6	22	Hassett	Rodeo
7	22	Munsten	Bombing
8	24	Berlin	Ramrod
9	24	Verberie	Ramrod
10	25	Nancy	Ramrod
11	27	Ludwigshafen	Ramrod
12	28	Dessau	Rodeo
13	31	Hamm	Ramrod
14	6, 3, 44	Paris	Rodeo
15	4	St Avord	Ramrod
16	6	Le Havre	Rodeo

63rd Squadron Strafing Report. Eighth AF FO 1936A April 10, 1945.

	Type		Pilot	Call sign	Pass
(1)	JU 88	Des	Capt. Bostwick	White One	1st pass
(2)	U/I/T/E	Dam	Capt. Bostwick	White One	2nd pass
(3)	U/I/T/E	Des	Capt. Bostwick	White One	2nd pass
(4)	U/I	Des	Capt. Bostwick	White One	2nd pass
(5)	ME 109	Dam	Capt. Bostwick	White One	3rd pass
(6)	JU 88	Des	Capt. Bostwick	White One	3rd pass
(7)	U/I/S/E	Des	Lt. Naylor	White Two	1st pass
(8)	FW 190	Des	Lt. Naylor	White Two	2nd pass
(9)	ME 109	Des	Lt. Naylor	White Two	3rd pass
(10)	DO 217	Dam	Lt. Naylor	White Two	3rd pass
(11)	JU 88	Dam	Lt. McBath	White Three	2nd pass
(12)	JU 88	Des	Lt. Smith, T.W.	White Four	1st pass
(13)	JU 88	Dam	Lt. Smith, T.W.	White Four	1st pass
(14)	DO 217	Des	Capt. Flagg	Blue One	1st pass
(15)	DO 217	Des	Capt. Flagg	Blue One	2nd pass
(16)	ME 109	Des	Capt. Flagg	Blue One	2nd pass
(17)	U/I	Des	Capt. Flagg	Blue One	3rd pass
(18)	ME 109	Dam	Capt. Flagg	Blue One	3rd pass
(19)	DO 217	Dam	Lt. Hennessy	Blue Two	1st pass
(20)	DO 217	Dam	Lt. Hennessy	Blue Two	3rd pass
(21)	U/I/T/E	Des	Lt. Hoffman	Blue Three	1st pass
(22)	U/I/T/E	Des	Lt. Hoffman	Blue Three	2nd pass
(23)	JU 88	Des	Lt. Smith, V.A.	Blue Four	1st pass
(24)	U/I/T/E	Dam	Lt. Smith, V.A.	Blue Four	3rd pass

Total claims: 15-0-9 on the ground.

17	6	Normandy	Ramrod
18	7	Normandy	Bombing
19	8	Dreux	Ramrod
20	10	Normandy	Bombing
21	10	Normandy	Bombing
22	10	Normandy	Bombing
23	11	Mayenne	Bombing
24	12	Paris	Rodeo
25	13	Saumun	Bombing
26	14	Poix A/D	Ramrod
27	15	Paris	Ramrod
28	17	Angers	Ramrod
29	18	Bremen	Ramrod
30	19	Pontivy	Rodeo
31	20	Lille	Rodeo
32	21	Ruhland	Ramrod
33	22	Compiegne	Bombing
34	24	Montdidier	Ramrod
35	25	Conches	Ramrod
36	29	Oschersleben	Ramrod
37	30	Joigny	Bombing
38	7, 4, 44	Conches A/D	Bombing
39	6	Paris	Bombing
40	7	Liepzig	Ramrod
41	8	Rouen	Rodeo
42	11	Munich	Ramrod
43	13	Munich	Ramrod
44	15	La Chapelle	Bombing

Mission No	Date	Location	Type of Mission
45	19	Angsburg	Ramrod
46	21	Saarbrucken	Ramrod
47	25	Rouen	Ramrod
48	26	St-Just-en-Chausse	Ramrod
49	28	Abbeville	Rodeo
50	31	France	Ramrod
51	8, 2, 44	Ameins	Bombing
52	4	Bremen	Ramrod
53	5	Nienburg	Ramrod
54	7	Albert	Bombing
55	8	St Just	Bombing
56	10	Namur	Bombing
57	10	Muizon	Bombing
58	12	Fouries	Bombing
59	13	Rouen	Bombing
60	13	Rouen	Bombing
61	15	Dümmer Lake	Rodeo
62	16	Dümmer Lake	Rodeo
63	18	Rouen	Bombing
64	23	Hamm	Bombing
65	25	Henin Lietard	Ramrod
66	26	Emmerich	Ramrod
67	27	Kaiserslautern	Bombing
68	29	Saarbrücken	Bombing
69	9, 1, 44	Eindhoven	Rodeo
70	8	Euskirchen A/D	Bombing
71	10	Nurnberg	Ramrod

Second tour of operations.

72	1, 10, 45	Laacher Lake, Koln	Rodeo
73	15	Strasbourg	Ramrod
74	16	Hanover	Rodeo
75	21	Heilbroon	Ramrod
76	29	Bielefeld	Ramrod
77	2, 6, 45	Magdeburg	Ramrod
78	9	Bielefeld	Ramrod
79	3, 2, 45	Magdeburg	Ramrod
80	4	Aschanffenburg	Ramrod
81	5	Hamburg	Rodeo
82	7	Soest	Rodeo
83	25	Hitzacher	Ramrod
84	30	Wilhelmshaven	Ramrod
85	4, 2, 45	Aalborg	Ramrod
86	4	Perleberg	Ramrod
87	5	Plauen	Ramrod

Mission No	Date	Location	Type of Mission
88	7	Krummel	Ramrod
89	10	Berlin	Rodeo
90	11	Amberg	Ramrod
91	13	Eggebeck A/D	Ramrod
92	20	Muhldorf	Ramrod

Total number of operational hours, 390 55 minutes.

B/Gen. Jesse Auton pins a medal on George with Dave Shilling and Lucian Dade in the background.

MARVIN C. BIGELOW

83RD FIGHTER SQUADRON, 78TH FIGHTER GROUP

Marvin C. Bigelow was born on August 23, 1923, at Dayton, Ohio and educated in Camden, New Jersey and Watsontown High School, Pennsylvania. He was called to active duty with the USAAF in February, 1943 and accepted for pilot training, attached to the South-East Training Command. His commission came in April, 1944 with orders to leave for England. He left the States for Liverpool on board the *Queen Mary*, arriving on October 10, 1944.

At this time, the Eighth Air Force was phasing out the Replacement Training Units (RTU) and Operational Training Units (OTU) and passing the responsibility of training to the group with which pilots were to serve, the advantage being that the novice obtained up-to-date indoctrination into combat tactics. Bigelow was attached to the 78th Group in mid-November, 1944 and assigned to the 83rd Squadron. His pre-combat training consisted of six hours 45 minutes in four 'familiarization flights' over England. His first mission came on December 4, 1944, lasting four hours 20 minutes. He scored his first kill on December 19, 1944, on a fighter sweep over France. This is how he recalls that victory:

'The morning of December 19, 1944 was cold and foggy as only an English day can be, when I rose in the dark. A glance at the 500 foot ceiling indicated that the mission I was scheduled to fly might be scrubbed but the insistent call of the operations clerks assured me it had not.

'As I walked from the barracks to the mess hall I wondered if somewhere up in that murk the bombers were forming up and anticipating that we would join them for the day's run to Germany. We went to the briefing room and were told who we were to escort,

target, landfall in and landfall out, time over target etc. and then went out to our Thunderbolts. The group was led by Major (later Lt Col) Sam Beckley of Grand Junction, Colorado, and I was in number four position on Lt Frances Harrington's wing in the third flight.

'After fastening the shoulder harness, seat belt, earphones, throat mike and oxygen mask, checking switches, gauges, control movements and quadrant settings I felt like a piece of equipment attached to the aircraft instead of vice versa. As I started the engine and lumbered down to my take-off position I glanced at the lowering ceiling and wondered if HQ were really serious in sending us out on a day like this.

'At 0810 we were all in position with cowl flaps open waiting and listening for our recall word ``Breadbasket.'' But the control tower fired a green flare to signal us to take-off, and before it reached the overcast the second line of eight Jugs began to roll (at Duxford we always took-off eight abreast). This method made for a wild take-off but there was never any

Above: Lt. Marvin C. Bigelow with his aircraft, a P-51K. The main change from the P-51D was the propeller. The 'K' used the Aeroprop and the 'D' used the Hamilton Standard. This aircraft was coded HL-L, 44-11557.

(Bigelow)

Below, left: Lt. Billy M. Madole, C/C Sgt. Erickson and the ``Skonk Hunter'' (P-47C HL-S, 41-6540).

Below, right: While flying this aircraft, Billy claimed the destruction of 2 FW-190s and damaged another 3. He called Stamps, Arkansas his hometown.

(May)

Above: We apologize for the quality of this photo but its great historical interest dictated its inclusion. This is the only photo in our files of Lt. Charles P. London's "El Jeepo" HL-B, #41-6335. On July 30, 1943, Charles downed a 109 and a 190 to become the 8th's first official ace.

Middle: Lt. Kenneth C. Allstaedt and his HL-W, #42-25552.

(Allstaedt)

Below: Col. Frederick C. Gray Jr. "Mr. Ted" and crew at Duxford July 10, '44. HL-Z, #42-25996.

(Mulron)

necessity to join up in the air. In fact on one occasion the entire group got aloft in one minute 56 seconds. On this mission, however, no sooner was I committed to getting the seven ton-plus Jug off the ground than the looked-for word "Breadbasket" sounded over the radio, but due to the distance I had travelled I carried on and got airborne.

'At 600 feet we entered the overcast and climbed in formation on instruments to 7,000 feet where we broke into a massive stretch of clear sky. Since Duxford had closed immediately after we took off due to the bad weather, the sixteen P-47s were the only aircraft aloft over England. Nowhere in England or France was there an Allied airstrip open where we could land. Major Beckley asked for and was given permission to carry out a fighter sweep over the front lines.

'The trip south was around, over, under and through clouds ranging from light grey to heavy black in colour and never once did we see the ground. The patrol was at about 10,000 feet and after about 40 minutes a ground control unit broke in and asked if we wanted a vector to 30 plus "bogies" who were to the west of us.

'We took the heading and 15 minutes later had reversed our own course to head back for friendly territory, apparently having missed the bogies, when someone screamed out, "bogies, nine o'clock high." They had the bounce on us and came down in a block formation of about 20 single-engined fighters. As the first enemy aircraft fired on us we broke into pairs and I followed my Number 1, Lt Harrington, in a break to the left into some of the enemy aircraft and they broke up their attacking formation.

'Lt Harrington got on the tail of one FW 190 and promptly fired at it. As he did so pieces broke off the enemy aircraft as it took hits the length of the fuselage. One of its wheels dropped, it rolled over smoking and went straight into the deck from about 3,000 feet - it must have been the first E/A to go down.

'We swung in a climbing turn to the left to head back into the mêlée and as we did so, Lt Harrington turned on his water injection and climbed even higher, coming out on top of the clouds where he shot down an ME 109. I turned on my water injection to follow Harrington but could not catch him so I stayed at about 9,000 feet and headed towards a gaggle of aircraft at about 10,000 feet, dead ahead.

'Banking to the left to clear my tail I glanced down and saw an enemy ship streaking eastward close to the ground. That was his mistake - he had surrendered altitude to hurry his departure from the battle. As I drove, lining him up in the sight, turning down the ring was no effort since he was not taking any evasive action and apparently had not seen me. The kill was quick because no sooner had I fired than the FW 190 disintegrated in a ball of flame.

'I pulled back on the stick to gain some altitude and joined up on Major Beckley's wing as he and two other elements circled a private battle. A single long-nose FW 190 was climbing in a tight spiral with a Jug sitting on his tail, every time the Jug pulled up to fire the recoil of the fifties would slow him down and he had to stop firing to regain his tight climbing turn. His wingman was flying close formation with him throughout the turns. Discretion surmounted valour in the cockpit of the FW and in the face of impossible odds the pilot jettisoned his canopy and jumped over the side of his ship. He must have delayed the opening of his parachute as no one saw it.

'Four other ships formed up on the Major and just then a call from a friendly ground station gave us a vector to a field that was open to us for about 30 minutes. Passing over the front we saw light flak and ground fire but held our course to the field. Within 25 minutes we passed over it at 15,000 feet and flying a pattern half on instruments, five of us landed. The major, having been more conservative with his fuel, advised the tower that he was heading back home for Duxford - we found out later that he had to make an instrument landing on a field in Northern France.

'Our haven for the next four days was to become a poor place of rest. We had landed at St Tronde. The front line had stretched and broken, and the Battle of the Bulge was raging just to the north of us. There is nothing more useless than a fighter pilot and his plane on the ground. While waiting we had only one instruction - to make sure that our Thunderbolts did not fall into German hands.

'Despite the fact that visibility was limited to 15 feet, I intended to blast straight ahead at full throttle and hope to get airborne knowing that the Jug had the characteristic of tearing itself to pieces before injuring the pilot in a crash. Fortunately this became unnecessary because on December 24, visibility was up to half a mile and after take-off we climbed and were in the clear at 5,000 feet.

'We formed up and headed north. We were forced lower and lower as the cloud ceiling began to drop and over the Channel were down to 700 feet. We landed on the coast of England at an emergency landing strip that looked a quarter of a mile wide and three miles long (probably Manston) and as the English say, "you can't miss it." We didn't on a straight in approach.

'The final leg of our journey to Duxford was made in the back of a truck and we arrived just in time for the Christmas Eve celebrations. At de-briefing we learned the total aircraft destroyed on our mission for December 19 was 13 for the loss of one Jug, and that we had broken the initial air support for the "Bulge" breakthrough.'

During his first month of combat, Bigelow flew 22 hours 30 minutes combat and managed to get two hours in on the Mustang - 20 minutes on December

Above: The Ground crew prepares Lt. Julius P. Maxwell's WZ-0, #42-74742. A typical ''Shared A/C,'' Maxwell got a 109 confirmed and another damaged on Mar 16, 1944 and exactly 2 wks. later Ernie Lang flying this A/C, shared a DO-217 kill 3 ways with Quince Brown and Lt. Abel.

Middle: The assigned Thunderbolt of Lt. Marvin Bigelow after he carried out an emergency landing when an oil line broke on take-off at Duxford. This P-47 was still with the group after the war in Europe was over. Coded HL-J(bar). 42-26591.

(Bigelow)

Below: The all red two-seat Thunderbolt of the 78th Fighter Group. The aircraft had previously been in service with the 84th Fighter Squadron. The ship crashlanded at Duxford 9th March 1945 and was back flying within a week or so. The 'WW' denotes a 'War Weary' aircraft.

(Lamb Jr.)

Above & Right: Most of the pilots of the 83rd had their first flight in a P-51 in this bird. Elmer K. Nieland is about to take her up on a training flight. Very unusual markings were fair warning!

Middle: Lt. Marvin C. Bigelow about to enter the cockpit of his Mustang HL-L, 44-11557. This was on a mission to Berlin on 26th February, 1945 - a six hour plus haul.

(Bigelow)

Below: Flight Officer Ralph E. Hamilton was hit by flak while flying this Mustang 22nd February 1945. After bailing out near Crail-shiem, Germany he was captured and spent the remaining few months of the war in a POW camp. Why this Mustang has D-Day invasion stripes painted on is a mystery as they'd been dispensed with months before, while the group was still flying Thunderbirds.

(via Bivens)

18 and one hour 40 minutes on the 30th.

The 78th Group converted to the Mustang in late December and flew its first combat mission with the type on the 29th.

Bigelow's first Mustang mission came on January 15, 1945, to Dresden and lasted five hours 30 minutes. It was not until the 29th that he obtained his second and final kill and claimed a damaged, both in the air.

His total Thunderbolt flying hours for January amounted to eight hours 45 minutes.

On March 3, 1945, Bigelow had an encounter with a ME 262, while flying an old P-51B and this is what he had to say about his only jet encounter:

'The penetration of March 3, I remember, was to be a deep one into Germany - when I saw my mount I could hardly believe it. The modifications to this aircraft were amazing. To begin with it was basically a P-51B, which was an early model to say the least. At one time the ship had been equipped with dive brakes, which had been welded shut. The razorback had been modified with a Malcolm hood which gave more room and better visibility but with a certain amount of visual distortion. This war-weary bird still carried grey paint - at least where it hadn't worn through or been chipped off - and undoubtedly had had numerous engine changes. On the other side of the ledger, she was modified to carry external tanks, and had the usual number of 50 calibers. The clouds were high and it was a beautiful day to travel.

We picked up the bomber stream on schedule and at 22,000 feet flew down the stream looking for our assigned group. There was a veritable river of aircraft headed east and all pulling contrails. I understand this was done purposely in order to let those below know the hopelessness of their situation. We found the group and began our work, "S" turning across our "Big Friends" in order to prevent their being surprised.

'On a sweeping turn to the left the entire canopy suddenly frosted over, making a quick shift to instruments necessary. I pushed the mike button, gave the reason, and said I was dropping out of formation. A mid-air collision was not a happy thought and could have led to serious injury.

'It was customary under these circumstances to leave in pairs, but then the canopy cleared at 18,000 feet and I could see the outside world, the bomber stream, contrails and my safety escort were nowhere to be seen. I was by myself and terribly lonesome. As I swivelled my neck trying to look in all directions at once, the only "familiar" sign I saw was Dummer Lake, a checkpoint used on many missions. This was no place for a small, lonesome boy so I decided to go home to Mother England and took the correct heading.

Below left: John A. Kirk III with his newly assigned Mustang coded HL-C, 44-63620. He served with the 83rd Fighter Squadron and shot down 4 enemy aircraft and claimed another six on the ground.
(Kirk III)

Right: This picture is likely to bring a smile to more than one 78 FG vet's face - the pub in Duxford!

Below right: John Kirk's "Small Boy Here" after a particularly unpleasant landing. Note reverse swastika scores beneath cockpit, also wing tip design and outlined rudder markings.
(Mulron)

'Ten minutes later I saw a stream of four boxes of B-17s headed south, dead ahead and about 2,000 feet above me. Reaching the conclusion there would be safety in numbers I started to climb to become their escort, which they apparently lacked. I soon noticed an element of aircraft fast approaching the bombers from the rear. When the lead ship of the element dove through the boxed bombers firing, about six shells from each of his wing cannon, I started to cut him off in a dive.

'When I had him in the K-14, the ME 262 was no more than half an inch. A glance at the airspeed showed an indicated 650 mph at 17,000 feet. The jet had shrunk to about a quarter inch when a second glance showed 680 mph and the Mustang finally began to complain. She was shaking herself like a wet puppy. The jet was gone completely, at what speed I could only guess as I was alone in the sky and down to 10,000 feet. I headed back to England and the mission whisky.

Later looking back at the circumstances I couldn't help wondering why or by what quirk of fate, I, who was on the winning side, would be flying that war-

weary bird while my opponent who left the scene, did so in an obviously vastly superior aircraft. That was the last mission for the Mustang I rode that day.'

On March 14, 1945, after returning from a mission to Ijmuiden, Bigelow landed at Duxford and was involved in a taxiing accident when his right brake froze. He ran into HL-K, the Mustang of Lt Don Montieth who had landed just ahead of him. This is how he recalls the incident:

'While landing my ship it had a failure of the right disc-brake and I swung to the right and into the path of "Monty." He hit the mid section of the fuselage of my ship with his right wing, his prop cut the tail controls and washed out the gear and as he circled my ship his prop also removed my left wing and his tail assembly was twisted off. My canopy shattered and just then there was a terrific explosion with me sitting right in the middle of it. My cockpit cleared first and

Two photos of the accident between Marvin and Lt. Montieth, Mar 14, 1945. (Monty's A/C HL-K, 44-15524)

I staggered out as best I could. I had first and second degree burns to my face and third degree burns to my leg from a ruptured coolant line. Lt Montieth had just a scratch on his forehead and got merry later when drinking to our good health. I spent two months in hospital and got out early so as not to be assigned to another group, but by that time the war in Europe was over.'

Bigelow attended the University of Colorado after the war, where he met Lt Leonard Olsen, who had served with the 84th Squadron of the 78th Group. Olsen said that when he was taken POW he had been attempting to pick up Lt Charles O'Brien of the 83rd Squadron, but his gear washed out and both had been captured. O'Brien was later shot while trying to escape from a train taking prisoners from Holland to Germany.

Marvin Bigelow married in June, 1946 and has since set something of a record among ex-Thunderbolt pilots - he and his wife Maxine have ten children: Nan Marie, Barry John, Michael Paul, Jeanne Sue, Mary Lee, Richard Lee, Elizabeth Louise, Stephen Mark, Patrick Terrance, and Terrie Lynn.

Combat mission list of Lt Marvin C. Bigelow, 83rd Squadron, 78th Fighter Group

Date	Type	Duration	Location
12, 4, 44	P-47D	4.20	
5	P-47D	4.25	
6	P-47D	4.45	Wilhelmshaven
10	P-47D	2.30	Coast of Europe
19	P-47D	6.30	France
1, 1, 45	P-51D	4.40	
3	P-51D	4.05	
15	P-51K	5.30	Dresden
17	P-51D	5.00	
21	P-51D	3.45	
29	P-51D	4.50	
2, 3, 45	P-51D	2.35	
14	P-51K	6.00	Berlin
20	P-51D	5.15	
23	P-51D	5.35	S Germany
26	P-51K	6.30	Berlin
28	P-51D	4.55	Denmark
3, 2, 45	P-51D	4.25	Leipzig
3	P-51B	4.25	Germany
5	P-51D	3.45	
9	P-51D	4.45	
11	P-51D	4.50	
14	P-51D	5.00	Ijmuiden

Known aircraft flown by Marvin C. Bigelow.

HL-I	42-26591	P-47
HL-BK	43-6736	P-51
HL-L	44-11557	P-51
HL-I	'Lil Max'	P-51

PETER E. POMPETTI

84TH FIGHTER SQUADRON, 78TH FIGHTER GROUP

Peter E. Pompetti was born December 27, 1920 in Woodbine, New Jersey and was educated through high school at various schools in Philadelphia, Pennsylvania. He enlisted in the United States Army Air Corps in January 1940, but didn't begin his Preflight Training until January, 1942. His Primary Training was at Jackson, Mississippi and his Basic Training at Gunter Field, near Montgomery, Alabama. He then went to Spence Field, Georgia for his Advanced Training and received his wings on November 10, 1942. For his Operational Training he was sent to Drew Field, Florida and flew P-40s for most of December.

After completing his Operational Training he was ordered overseas to England and arrived at Goxhill Airfield near Grimsby, Lincolnshire on February 15, 1943. Here he joined the 84th Squadron of the 78th Fighter Group and started to fly the seven ton "Jug." April 1st the entire group moved to Duxford, about eight miles south of Cambridge. There he was assigned a P-47 coded WZ-R 41-6393. The ground crew consisted of crew chief S/Sgt. Harry Cecil; assistant crew chief Charles Clark; armorer Charles Twohig; and radio man Raymond Polonsky. This aircraft, named "Axe the Axis," was flown by Peter on 81 of the 95 combat missions he flew before being shot down in WZ-Z (Harold Stump's ship) March 17, 1944.

The first mission Peter flew was a fighter sweep on April 17, 1943. Taking off at 1205 hours, the group flew along the coast of Belgium in the Blankenberge area. All the aircraft returned safely to Duxford at 1340 hours. Peter flew as wingman to Gene Roberts who was flying his aircraft "Spokane Chief" WZ-Z.

It was not until the 16th of May that Peter fired his guns for the first time in anger when his squadron mixed it with a gaggle of 109s and 190s over Heusen. Although he made an attack on an e/a he made no claim. On the 30th July while flying 'D' flight, led by Lt. Charles Silsby, Peter got his first confirmed claim. He recalled: "I was flying Bayland Blue Three, leading the second element in Lt. Silsby's flight. We followed the course well beyond the R/V point. We saw the bombers on our left, about nine o'clock, at approximately 24,000'. We were at 28,000', indicating 220 MPH. We made a turn to the left behind the bombers, sticking with eight ship flights close together. After making several turns behind the bombers, Lt Silsby (WZ-T) made a pass at two e/a below. This was in the neighborhood of Varseveld, Holland, at about 25,000' down to 18,000'. He took the one on the left, and I took the one on the right. Both were ME-109s. We came down in trail. They saw us and broke sharp left towards us. I took a short burst at mine to distract him. I don't think I had enough deflection. Lt. Silsby was

Above: The crew of WZ-R, 41-6393 'Darkie' (later 'Axe The Axis') pose with their Thunderbolt. Left to right are Raymond F. Polansky (Arm.), Sgt. Clark (A/C/C), Sgt. Harry Twowig (Arm), S/Sgt. Harry W. Cecil (C/C) and Peter Pompetti.

(Pompetti)

Middle: Shall we caption this as a 78 F.G./82 F.S. hack and see how many angry letters we get from ex-31st F.G. personnel? To add to the considerable pitfalls of U.S. WW II A/C identification, the code letters used by the 1st, 31st and 52nd groups were duplicated by issuing them to the 56th, 78th and 4th F.G.s respectively when the former were reassigned to N. Africa! This particular Spit V is Lt. Wooten's presentation A/C "Lima Challenger" of 31st Grp. 307 F.S. (Original 8 A.F.) at Manston, late summer, 1942.

(D. Kucera)

Below: In the early A.F. escort missions P-47s were limited in their range and the bombers took a real pounding once left w/o little friends. 41-6243 was later coded WZ-C and still used on OPs almost 1 full year after date of this photo - an exceptionally long time for an A/C of this period.

Above left: Capt. Harold E. Stump flew with the 84 FS for about a year before becoming a P.O.W. June 10, 1944. He had 2 assigned A/C: WZ-X, 41-6269, in which he downed a 109 on Sept. 27, and the pictured second A/C, WZ-M, 41-6245.

(May)

Above, Right: C/C Odis C. Cunningham adds another kill mark to Capt. John D. Irvin's P-47 D "Geronimo," sometime after the July 30, 43 mission when Irvin confirmed a 109 and a 190 and damaged another FW. (41-6357, WZ-B)

(Bivens)

Below: "Snafu" tries to live up to her name. A close look at the extensive mission list belies any "Jinx A/C" sobriquet. Both Ernie Lang and Julius Maxwell made claims in this bird.

also firing. But the E/A turned over and got away.

We got in string again and gained some altitude. While climbing to about 23,000', a FW-190, with underside all canary yellow, came up vertically between Lt. Hunt (WZ-U) and myself. Lt. Hunt was the number 2 man to Lt. Silsby. I called for them to break. They did. The FW-190 did a flip-over and started down after I committed myself for attack. I called my wingman to follow him, and he did. I fell in behind to act as cover. When the FW got too low, I called my wing man to break up, and get altitude. He did this and I then took over the lead. We had gotten down to 15,000', regaining altitude to 21,000'. Lt. Silsby and his wingman were nowhere in sight.

I started to climb with my wingman. I missed my wingman and called him - no answer. I continued to climb and found three ME-109s in vee formation at 25,000'. At their altitude I levelled off and gained on them. I started firing at the leader and the one on the

right wing broke and went down. After firing several bursts, he turned over on his back and I continued firing. He seemed to just hang there. I then broke in behind the third, who was much closer, and fired several short bursts in trail. His left wing then dropped. I continued closing up in trail, firing continuously until at approximately 50 yards range I observed smoke pouring out of his right side and wing root and pieces flying off. I believe the pilot was dead because he took no evasive action at all. I then broke up to avoid collision and started to climb for altitude. This part of the engagement must have taken place over, or near Didam, Holland.

Knowing that I was alone, I figured this to be my best bet. I started from 20,000' and got up to 32,000 full power, climbing at 190 MPH about 500 to 1,000' climb per minute. All this time I was behind the bombers. I now decided to pass them on the left. While climbing to the left of the bombers, I could see plenty of

FW-190s around me, lining up for passes at the Forts. I reported them to my squadron leader and continued climbing. The FW-190s around me did not make a pass. I levelled off at 32,000', pulled back RPM and manifold pressure and headed west. I was still deep in Holland. I continued at 32,000' on a westerly course and came out over Schouven Island. After crossing the Dutch coast, I lost altitude at 500' per minute. About 15 miles off the coast at about 28,000' I saw four to six bogies in a Luffberry to the left, north of me and west of Overflakke Island. They pointed their noses at me some distance off. I believed them to be FW-190s looking for stragglers. I then dropped my nose and easily out-distanced them. They turned inland. I continued on my way home, nothing else coming up.

The e/a seemed to be flying in pairs and fours straggling all over the sky. As we made the turn to pick up the bombers, I observed a straggler being attacked by several e/a. The bomber peeled off and went down with about six parachutes opening up. Later on, along the route another bomber was seen to break away from the formation and go down. No parachutes were observed. All along the route in and out there was flak, accurate for altitude but not position. Flak was heaviest over Germany. Some of the FW-190s had yellow tails as well as yellow undersides. The ME-109s had gun bulges outboard of the propeller arc. Four of my guns had stoppages after the first bursts. The other four guns fired all ammunition.''

The 8th Air Force Fighter Command claimed the destruction of 25 enemy aircraft for the loss of six Thunderbolts, of which two of the pilots were saved. On the 17th of August, in a dogfight southeast of Aachen, Germany, Peter shot down a ME-110 and afterwards his flight chased several enemy aircraft but were unable to engage them.

The following month on the 27th, the 78th Fighter Group was to provide cover for the bombers attacking Emden, Germany. This was the first time the Pathfinder bombers of the 482nd Bomb Group were used. At

10.15 hours enemy aircraft attacked the lead bombers and during the dogfight which followed the 78th claimed 10 enemy aircraft destroyed in the air with no losses.

Peter Pompetti (WZ-R) was flying as Harold Stump's (WZ-X) wingman and recalled. ''We made R/V with the bombers at 30,000' over the target. Enemy aircraft were lining up and attacking the bombers from all directions. Captain Stump followed the leading flights around for a while before sighting a ME-109 at 9 o'clock to us at 26,000 feet. We dove to attack. I was behind and slightly to the left of Captain Stump. We closed rapidly and the Captain fired at a range of 50 to 100 yards. He was getting strikes on the left wing but he overran before he could make the kill and had to pull up.

Above: Shortly after Peter Pompetti was taken POW his P-47 was transferred to the 4th Strategical Air Depot on 25th March 1944. During its combat career it suffered battle damage resulting in two new port wings and one new starboard wing and consequently it flew in a crab-wise fashion which the other pilots didn't like. Peter knew his aircraft and told the author he loved to fly his ship. At the time this photo was taken Peter had completed 29 missions.

(Pompetti)

Below, left & right: Major Jack Price and ''Feather Merchant II,'' WZ-Z, 42-74641. Frank Olynyk lists this A/C as WZ-A. Close inspection of the photo on page 8 of Bennett's ''Markings of the Aces'' shows evidence of recent repainting around the ''Z''. At any rate, Price made his final two confirmed victories in this A/C.

I was in a good position for a shot with about 5-15 degrees deflection at 150 yards range. I fired and saw strikes on the left wing, the cockpit and engine. The engine caught fire and was smoking heavily. The canopy and pieces from the top and bottom of the fuselage came off. I broke up and rejoined Captain Stump at 28,000 ft. While our flight was regaining altitude a 109 bounced us from down sun, singling out Captain Stump. He broke left and I took a squirt at the e/a as he went in front of me. It was a 60-70 degrees deflection shot and I didn't observe any strikes as the e/a broke away.

We reassembled our flight. Captain Stump then sighted another ME-109 at 24,000 feet and twelve o'clock to us. We dove, coming in behind and slightly below him. He didn't see us coming at all. Captain Stump pulled up and opened fire at about 250 yards. I saw him getting strikes across the left wing, cockpit and engine. Fire and smoke broke out, and the e/a blew up around the cockpit and engine. Our flight then pulled up.

At 25,000 feet a ME-109 made a bounce on Captain Stump from four o'clock. We broke left and the e/a immediately dove for the deck. A little later another 109 bounced me from three o'clock high. I was flying on Captain Stump's left wing. I broke sharply left and called to Captain Stump to get on the e/a's tail, while I led him in a Luffberry. We were now at 20,000 feet. I was indicating 180 MPH in the turn and the Hun was firing even though he was not able to turn tight enough to get proper deflection. Meanwhile Lt. Dougherty (WZ-U), flying No. 4 position, cut in front of the e/a and made a quartering pass on him. After three or four 360 degree turns, the e/a broke down with Lt. Dougherty following him. We were down to about 16,000 feet by this time so we pulled up, but Lt. Dougherty continued to chase his 109.

While climbing and heading for home, six ME-109s passed over Captain Stump. The last e/a saw him and got on his tail at 20,000 feet. The Captain broke sharply left, half rolled and went straight down. I gave the e/a several squirts at a wide deflection with plenty of lead. He immediately half rolled and then rolled back one quarter of a turn and followed Captain Stump straight down. I followed the e/a down. Captain Stump broke upwards at 15,000 feet, but the e/a

Above: Aces and Stars in front of WZ-W! Gen. Wm. Kepner, Eugene Roberts, Robert S. Johnson, Charles London and Gen. Hap Arnold.
(EBY)

Middle: Hand flying in front of Pompetti's aircraft, August 1943. Left to right is Burt Lantz, Peter Pompetti and Glenn Koontz all of the 78th Fighter Group based at Duxford in Cambridgeshire.
(Pompetti)

Below: A nice shot of Eugene Robert's 'Spokane Chief' WZ-Z, 41-6630. This was its regular parking space and to the left is the 84th squadrons hangar.
(Norman)

kept going down. I was forced to follow him a little lower because I couldn't pull out right away. I pulled up at about 12,000 feet. I formed up with Captain Stump and his No. 3 man in a vee, and headed for home.

We saw the bombers in front of us at 16-17,000 feet. One was struggling and behind him was a ME-110. Captain Stump fell in behind the e/a at 1,500 yards. The e/a turned slightly right and Captain Stump started to cut him off. The e/a then turned left, and I was now in a good position for a shot. Captain Stump called for me to take him while he and the No. 3 man covered me. I cut off the e/a in the left turn, and when he straightened out, I was slightly below with about 15 degrees deflection. I gave him several bursts and saw strikes on the left engine and cockpit. He was burning and smoking and pieces were falling off. I was very close. I cut my throttle and pulled above and slightly to the right of him. I could see everything clearly because I was about 25 feet away from him. In the rear of the long cockpit I could see two light machine guns on a swivel. I saw a yellow back cushion. There was no one in the seat, unless he was on the floor. I could see the pilot. He was hunched over the stick. I could only see his back and head, indicating that he was probably dead. He had on a 'Mae West' similar to the type worn by English pilots and a black helmet. The e/a was heading down and made no attempt to evade or get back to land. Our three ship flight then headed for home, landing at Coltishall, Norfolk for petrol.

Most of the enemy aircraft encountered were ME-109s but we did see an ME-110, one FW-190 and some JU-88s. Some of the ME-109s had bulges under the wings. Nothing new in camouflage or markings were seen. The enemy fighters numbered about 100 and were persistant in their attacks on both the bombers and our fighters. I saw two B-17s go down in the target area when we first R/V'd with them. After we joined up with the bombers they left the target area in a N-NW direction, going out to sea. All our combats took place in the general area between Emden and the area north of the Frisian Islands. I claim one ME-109 and 1 ME-110 destroyed.'' In knocking down these two aircraft Peter had used 1227 rounds of ammunition.

On the 1st of December Peter managed to damage a FW-190 in the air over Liege, Belgium and during the scrap he became separated from the rest of his flight so he started to head for England. After some time he saw a lone Messerschmitt making repeated attacks on a lone Fortress. After each attack the 109 would perform aerobatics and loops before making his next run at the Fortress. Before Peter could intervene the bomber reached some cloud cover and the ME-109 followed it into the clouds.

On the 4th of January 1944 flying in WZ-R, 41-6393 'Axe The Axis' he shot down a ME-109 and also dam-

Above: Two fine shots showing the markings changes to Colonel John D. Lander's 'Big Beautiful Doll' WZ-I, 44-72218 at Duxford. The serial number was later moved forward onto the vertical stabilizer and the entire rudder was then painted black. The name panel on the canopy was yellow with black lettering. Later, when Landers became a full Colonel, it became a red panel with white lettering. The anti-glare olive drab panel was later outlined in red.

(Bergman)

Below: The ultimate 'Doll' photo taken in the summer of 1945. Checks have been added to the wingtips and the top of the vertical stabilizer has been painted black. A total of 36 1/2 kill markings have been painted below the cockpit opening. When he left to take command of the 361st Fighter Group at Little Walden, Essex, Landers took this aircraft with him.

(Bergman)

Above: A fine shot of an 84th Fighter Squadron Mustang parked outside it's hangar at Duxford. Behind it is a Mustang of the 55th Fighter Group.

(via Rabey)

Middle: Burton Newmark tells his crew chief how it was after a combat mission. This aircraft was the second 'Lady Eve' (the first being a Thunderbolt, also WZ-K(bar). The serial of the Mustang was 44-63171. Newmark was shot down and taken prisoner after being hit by a flak train 21st February 1945.

(Newmark)

Below: Lt. Paul Ostrander made his only confirmed victory in this A/C, a 109, Mar 19, 1945.

(Tabatt)

aged another (both in the air) near Coesfield, Germany. Several pilots from the newly arrived 361st Fighter Group flew on this mission including Lt. Colonel Tommy Christian Jr.

On the 6th of February Peter got more then he bargained for while strafing in France. He had this to write upon returning to Duxford Airfield: ``I was leading the second element in Clinton Blue Flight. Lt. Bert Lentz (WZ-F) was the flight leader. Lt Macie Marlowe (WZ-O bar) was flying on my wing and Lt. R. E. Smith (HL-M), flying as a spare with the 82nd F.S. of 'B' group, joined the flight to make it a five plane flight. After R/V, Clinton Squadron (84th) was making a turn back to pick up another box of bombers when I heard Lt Barba (WZ-E) call ``Break left!''. We were being bounced.

I pushed everything forward and did a steep climbing turn to the left, looking for the enemy. I circled several times looking around, saw nothing, then started out with Lt. Marlowe. I saw some E/A diving away from the last box of bombers with P-38s after them. They were headed for an A/D about ten miles to the south of us. We went over to give them some cover.

As we were making a circle of the A/D, we saw about 20 to 30 E/A dispersed on it, also about six single engine E/A circling for a landing. There was a convenient cloud layer just at the eastern end of the field, giving us the advantage of surprise. Making a left hand turn and losing altitude, we got inland of the A/D over the clouds, lined ourselves up and went down. We went into clouds at 2,000 feet, came out at 800 feet just off the east edge of the field and lined up parallel with the one runway.

As I came down I saw two gutted hangars on my left and directly in front of me a twin engined A/C, probably a JU-88. I fired at it and saw strikes all around it, then I corrected my line of fire and saw strikes on it. I flew across the airfield on the deck, indicating about 400 MPH. I was still parallel with the runway, and could see some FW-190s parked alongside and just off the runway, but couldn't get at them so I continued ahead. I saw a twin engine E/A at the end of the field, just off the perimeter and close to the runway. I was going straight for it, fired and saw numerous strikes all over it. It was smoking heavily and I flew through the smoke as I passed over it, clearing it by several yards.

I saw a flak tower to my right just off the edge of the field. I turned into it, fired and saw strikes in the middle of it before smoke enveloped it. As I was attacking the flak tower, I saw a single engine e/a crash and burn to my left, about a mile or so off the A/D. Lt. Marlowe and I were now together. Several miles from the A/D, we saw a locomotive pulling some flat cars and coal cars. Lt. Marlowe attacked first, and hit the engine numerous times. It stopped and steam and smoke poured from front to back. I fired and since it was

Above, left: The "Decoration" on Major Jake Oberhansly's first P-47, MX-W, 41-6542. Right (L to R): Unknown, Assnt. Crew Chief Conrad Gerhardt, Crew Chief Johnnie Kovacevich and Line Chief Osno Tahja on the wing of the second "Iron Ass," MX-X, 42-7883.

(May and Watkins)

stopped, I had no trouble hitting it. I saw strikes and it continued smoking and giving out excess steam. I looked back and could see that it was pretty well shot up.

Just ahead of us was another freight train so we attacked the engine. Lt. Marlowe got strikes and I saw steam and smoke. It seemed to go faster, then when I fired and hit it, I looked back and it had slowed down, almost stopped, and smoke and steam enveloped it.

We continued out on the deck. Lt. Quince L. Brown (WZ-J) had circled the A/D with his flight while we shot it up. He called and said he was six o'clock high and for us to climb up and join him. We started up, but saw two a/c ahead so we hit the deck again. The a/c were P-47s, Lt. Wilkinson and his wingman (82 F.S.). We joined them and the four of us came out line abreast on the deck.

On the way, Lt. Marlowe and I shot at a tug, pulling about four barges, in a canal about 100 miles inland. The rest of the trip was uneventful. Crossed out over Cayeux on the deck, indicating about 280 MPH.

We were not fired on during the entire trip, including the jaunt across the A/D. The A/D had between 20 and 30 a/c - half were twin engine, the rest single engine, mostly FW-190s.

I claim One (1) Twin Engine e/a (probably HS-129) Destroyed.
One (1) Twin Engine e/a (probably JU-88) Damaged.
Two (2) Locomotives damaged.
One (1) Flak Tower damaged.
One (1) Tug damaged.
shared with Lt. Marlowe.

On Sunday March 26th, the *Sunday Graphic* (a London newspaper) showed several frames from Peter's gun camera film with the caption 'A way to spend a holiday Sunday afternoon.'

On March 11, Peter was given a written reprimand from Major General Bill Kepner for acting contrary to a secret order issued on November 30, 1943. The order forbade the strafing of civilian ground targets in enemy occupied Europe (ie Locos, tugs and barges etc.). General Kepner stated "I have considered your misconduct which occurred on February 6, 1944, when, during a mission in which you acted as a leader, you attacked a locomotive hauling flat cars in enemy occupied countries, in direct violation of orders contained in secret letter, this Headquarters, dated November 30, 1943, subject: "Targets in Enemy Occupied Countries" ' file 371.3; and in letter, Headquarters 66th Fighter Wing, dated December 7, 1943, relating to the foregoing letter.

'You are hereby reprimanded for your misconduct. It is understood that your actions resulted from an erroneous interpretation of certain instructions amending the orders contained in the above mentioned letters. In your case this particularly is no excuse, since as a leader it was your special duty to thoroughly and intelligently understand your orders; and your failure in this regard shows a lack of proper appreciation of the responsibilities imposed on you. It is realized that your action in attacking the locomotive was no doubt prompted by commendable zeal to damage the enemy war effort, and there is no desire to restrict that zeal when exhibited in the right direction; but at the same time, it will be apparent that you cannot adequately serve by any failure to understand orders or instructions issued by higher authority.

Consideration has been given to removing you entirely from flying status, but after mature reflection it is believed that such extreme action is not warranted in view of all the circumstances, and in further view of your exceptionally high and meritorious performance on all previous combat missions. However, no reoccurrence of a similar failure to appreciate your re-

Another 82nd Sq. pilot who scored well during the winter of '43-4. Manuel S. Martinez missed acedom by not finishing off a 110 on Jan 4, 1944. He flew 2 P-47s: MX-L 42-7954 and MX-M 41-8619.

(May)

Major Harry J. Dayhuff and his double-named P-47 (Hun Ram - Er/Mackie) MX-Z, 41-6618 dropped a 109 July 30, 1943. Sure would be nice if more photographers had had the foresight to include serial #s like this!

(EBY)

sponsibilities and duties will be tolerated, and any such reoccurrence will meet with very severe disciplinary measures.

It has been decided under all the circumstances that this reprimand in person from your Commanding General is a sufficient punishment, without the imposition of any fine. You will be expected to justify this decision by your future conduct and actions and by the example you set for your fellow pilots. A copy of this letter will be made part of your 201 File, and an appropriate notation will be made on your Officer's Qualification Card.

You have the right to appeal from this punishment if you deem it unjust or disproportionate to the offense. You will acknowledge receipt of this reprimand by indorsement hereon.''

Within a matter of weeks after Peter received the above reprimand the 8th Air Force was strafing anything that moved on land or water.

On February 25th he went down on the deck again to strafe an airfield just west of St. Wendel, Germany. The squadron had R/V'd with the bombers fifteen minutes early near Trier, and took them as far as the area southeast of Mannheim. Lt. Quince Brown (WZ-J) shot up a barrage balloon over Bad Kruieznach and Lt. Boyle (WZ-K bar) strafed an E/A on an airfield in Belgium. At about 1410 hours Lt. Pompetti and his wingman, Lt. Ernie Lang (WZ-S bar), hit the airfield near St. Wendel. Peter shot up two ME-109s parked close together and as he banked round a small build-

ing he saw some German officers standing by a staff car watching him. He later recounted, ''I flew parallel to them about 50-100 yards away and could see them plainly. They wore long grayish-blue leather military coats and garrison hats. The car was very dark - I would say black.

I called this off to Lt. Lang, made a sharp turn to the left and came back at them. I couldn't get a good shot because the road was lined with tall trees. They didn't run until I fired at them. Evidently they thought I was making another pass at the airdrome. I fired several bursts in their general direction and they left the car and ran into the fields on both sides of the road and threw themselves onto the ground. I don't know whether I hit either the car or the officers, due to the trees, and my closeness to the ground.'' Lt. Pompetti and Lt. Lang flew off. On the way home they flew over another airfield which had twenty or more aircraft on it which seemed to be dummies. They didn't attack. This was near Valenciennes and was reported upon their return to Duxford airfield.

The following month, on the 2nd, Peter and Ernie Lang shared in the destruction of one HS-126 and a JU-88 on the ground at Chartres A/D, France. Four days later he was down on the deck again with Lt. Luther Abel (WZ-V) when they shot-up two locos near the town of Cloppenberg, Germany. As Peter passed over the second loco he felt a bang and thought he'd been hit by some return fire so the two pilots headed for England. Upon landing at Duxford he discovered the

engine cowling and the fuselage were covered with soot. Also he found the supercharger bucket pushed up into the turbine wheel. Again on March 8, with Lt. Lang (WZ-S bar) as his No. Two, he shared in the destruction of a FW-190 at Bohmte A/D, Germany. They also took out a petrol bowser which was refueling two single engined aircraft.

The 78th Fighter Group was to provide withdrawal support for the bombers after their mission to Luneville, France on March 16th. The group attacked some aircraft on an airfield in the area of Metz, France. Peter damaged a 109 but was hit by ground fire. Upon returning to his home base his A/C, (WZ-R), 41-6393, was listed as Category 'A' and had to go into one of the main hangers for repairs.

Groundfire would also play a key role in Peter's next - and last - wartime mission. It again underscores the point made by the author about the extreme hazards encountered in the ground attack role. As WZ-R, Peter's assigned A/C, was still being repaired he was assigned Harold Stump's (WZ-Z), 42-74641.

Peter recalled, ``It was a murky day, fog and haze over England and the continent. We were ordered to 'stand down' that morning. However, after lunch word came from 8th Fighter Command that we could send a few aircraft out, manned by volunteers to look for 'targets of opportunity'. Weather was stinko but eight of us wanted some excitement so off we went into the murk, two flights of four aircraft. We took off at 1430 hours.

Arriving over France we split up into pairs. Ernie Lang (WZ-S bar) and I were together, turned south then west, letting down to the deck with eyes open. In short order, I found a train parked in a small town (headed west of course), loaded with tanks and a command jeep . . . probably *10 large tanks!* I didn't shoot as this same morning I'd endorsed back to the 8th Air Force Command my acceptance of the 'letter of reprimand', my punishment for earlier strafing of trains in the Low Countries. However, I did switch over to camera only and took footage of the 'fat' target. I was furious with myself that I wasn't able to strafe that train. Officers must obey orders and I was fearful of losing my wings as mentioned in the reprimand.

We continued westerly under hazy, cloudy skies with perhaps a mile forward visibility at low speed (about 210 MPH). Suddenly I saw an aerodrome directly ahead with an aircraft parked at 12 o'clock to me. I applied some throttle but speed didn't pick up appreciably as I was 'ground hugging' and the distance ahead was minimal. I opened fire, followed immediately by Lang. Just to the left of the parked aircraft, alongside a perimeter road, was a light gun position . . . probably twin 303s. He opened fire and hit me in the lower left side of the engine area.

Almost immediately dense smoke enveloped me.

Above: As Peter Pompetti pulls up over a LeO 451 he is snapped by the gun camera of Ernie Lang, his wingman. Seconds later Pompetti bailed out of WZ-Z, 42-74641 and was taken prisoner. A large section of this aircraft is still in the possession of the people who helped Pompetti hide from German soldiers.

(Pompetti)

Middle: The house at Villeteneuse, Paris on which Peter's WZ-Z crashed - amazingly, no one was injured! By the time this photo was taken, most of the wreckage had been carted off by the Germans, but note tail wheel and stabilizer. This photo was taken at great risk by locals in defiance of German authorities.

Below: Peter Pompetti and a piece of WZ-Z which a Frenchman had kept in his garden since 17th March 1944. Villeteneuse, Paris, France. 1984.

(Pompetti)

Left: The heavy end of the batting order: A/C #1 is MX-S in which both Lt. Allen Rosenblum and Major Joe Myers had confirmed victories. A/C #2 is J. W. Wilkinson's distinctive razor-back "MISS BEHAVE." A/C #3 is MX-W in which Lt. Manford O. Croy Jr. downed 2 109s on Nov 26, 1944!

Right: Detail shot of cartoon character "Sweet Pea" from "Popeye" on Lt. Wilkes' P-47, 41-6246.

(May)

The heat was intense! This is it! I couldn't see the ground or the instruments, I pulled back on the stick, disconnected the radio leads, oxygen and the seat belt and prepared to leave the aircraft. When I felt I was high enough, I released the canopy and went over the left side cleanly. The 'chute opened without a jar. Being very close to the ground, I hit going backwards and tumbled. I'd landed in a congested area, touching down within inches of a railroad track - but I wasn't hurt! I took off my 'chute and winter flying boots over my 'Mclarens of London' jodphurs (not good for running). I ran over to an alleyway close by, probably 100 to 200 feet away and off I went. Lots of French women passed me intent on the 'chute I'd left behind, yards and yards of pure silk. They smiled and gave the 'V' sign in passing. Almost immediately a man pedalled a bicycle past me and said in English "Follow me." He stayed a safe distance ahead as I ran up an alley, crossed streets, went up some other streets to other alleys until we arrived at a quarry. Progressing into the quarry he pointed down to a large hole for me to hide in and kept going. I stayed hidden and alone until about 1730 hours when a young lad, aged about 12, brought me a loaf of bread and a bottle of wine. I broke a piece off and gave him back the rest. I drank some wine and returned this to him also. This was the smartest thing I did all day as the Germans didn't know I'd been helped when I was captured later; ie no evidence.

About 1845 hours I could hear a German Wehrmacht search party coming. I had been seen bailing out just off the aerodrome so the Paris garrison was called out. The area was cordoned off and the soldiers systematically searched for me. The soldiers passed by the hole and didn't see me. The last one however, came back for a closer look (it was dusk) and saw me. He pointed his rifle downwards, then fired a shot in the air. They gathered around and took me out of the hole. Giving three loud cheers they marched me out of the quarry to a street lined with houses (village of Pierrefitte). We waited until a staff car with two Wehrmacht officers arrived and I was taken to H.Q.s.

I was interrogated very briefly by a German in civilian clothes, probably SS. He asked very little. Some soldiers talked to me informally and gave me cheese, bread and wine while I waited for the interrogator. Shortly, I was taken to a medieval type dungeon and there I spent the night. Next morning I was taken to the front gate guard-house and kept under heavy guard until about 5:00 PM (Saturday). Next I was taken in a closed van to the Paris railway station and put on the 6:00 PM or so train to Frankfurt, again well guarded.

We arrived at the outskirts of Frankfurt about dawn but the RAF had just departed, having bombed Frankfurt heavily. Not being able to get into the main station we off loaded outside the city. Along with my three guards, I walked thru the ruined city to the railroad station commuter train to Oberuressel, Dulag Luft, the interrogation centre for aircrew (RAF & USAF).

I was interrogated that afternoon (Sunday). And again about the 3rd day, I was asked the usual questions ie; name, rank and serial number, the serial number of the aircraft I was shot down in, type of aircraft I was flying, and what group I was in. I said, "Now look Mr. Scharff, you know I was shot down right in front of all your German troops. The airplane fell just a very short distance away from the airfield and your people knew what it was. I'm sure they saw the big bold letters on it, you don't need this information from me!

That's what I told him. Then after a couple general comments he asked; 'Are you Jewish?' That really took me by surprise. I was blondish with bright sparkling blue eyes and he had my dog tags. When I regained my composure, I replied: 'I said you know my name is Pompetti and you know I'm Italian. You have my dog tags and can see my religion is Roman Catholic. That would preclude me from being Jewish.' Thus ended the questions for that day. I was interrogated at least once a week for the 28 days I was kept in solitary.

The room in which I was kept had a small blacked out window and no amenities. I was not able to wash, brush my teeth or shave during that period. No baths! Same food every day; two slices of black bread in the morning with a glass of ersatz tea, same in the evening. At lunch they brought a bowl, actually just a flat dish, of ersatz potatoe soup ... no body or consistancy. I survived but slimmed down, needless to say. Finally after locating me in one of his dossiers on the 78th Fighter Group, Hans Scharff, the interrogator, decided to let me go. He never asked me any questions of importance and then, being a 1st Lt. with no security clearance, I really didn't know anything of any importance anyway. I was never physically abused - except once while awaiting the staff car outside the quarry. A soldier, NCO, came up and jabbed a Luger into my belly hard, very hard! Needless to say, it hurt! I read him the riot act in English, which he didn't understand, but which made the French men and women standing around smile.

After being released from the Interrogation Center, a group of us were put into freight cars bound for Berlin (Stalag Luft 1). We were given some Red Cross parcels to share and sustain us for the several days until reaching our permanent camp, that haven on the Baltic, Barth. At first, life was a little easier with more food - not in great quantities - but at least we could survive. But the last 2 or 3 months of the war were awfully lean for us; the Germans couldn't transport food, or anything for that matter, with the fighters and bombers overhead day and night. Russian troops overran our camp on the 1st of May, the German guards having deserted us about midnight. I stayed with the Russians for two weeks until being flown to France May 15. From there I went to Duxford, stayed a week and then on to London for three more weeks awaiting space on a ship to the States. I arrived in the USA about the 22nd of June 1945."

Peter stayed in the service until July 31, 1960 when he retired with the rank of Lt. Colonel. He was married to Mary Seibert May 29, 1949. True to Air Force tradition, she was given away by the base commander, Colonel Robert L. Scott, the author of "God is my Co-pilot." They had three children, Pamela, Annamary and Peter Jr. After retiring from the Air Force he worked for the CAB and FAA until January 1976. Peter lived in retirement in Fort Worth, Texas. He died on April 16, 1985 and is buried at Arlington National Cemetery.

Mission list of Peter E. Pompetti

Date	F.O.	Type	Duration
17- 4-43	1	Sweep	1.45
21- 4-43	2	Rodeo	1.30
3- 5-43	28	Sweep	1.20
4- 5-43	10	Support	1.30
13- 5-43	17	Support	1.45
14- 5-43	18	Sweep	1.45
15- 5-43	19	Sweep	1.45
16- 5-43	20	Sweep	1.40
16- 5-43	21	Sweep	1.30
17- 5-43	22	Sweep	2.04
18- 5-43	23	Escort	1.42
19- 5-43	24	Escort	1.30
20- 5-43	25	Sweep	1.35
21- 5-43	26	Sweep	1.35
27- 5-43	30	Sweep	1.40
28- 5-43	32	Diversion	1.23
29- 5-43	33	Ramrod	1.40
7- 6-43	38	Sweep	1.26
10- 6-43	40	Sweep	1.50
11- 6-43	41	Sweep	1.45
13- 6-43	45	Sweep	1.45
22- 6-43	52	Sweep	1.40
24- 6-43	54	Sweep	1.26

Left: Ben Mayo's MX-X, 42-26671 taken on D-Day June 6, 1944 prior to the name being painted on. He claimed his first victory the following day when he shot down a ME-109. Crew Chief Jim Tudor, Assnt. Crew Chief A. F. Christenson and Armorer Bob Thout.

(via Glover)

Right: Ben Mayo in his Jug MX-X, 42-26671. The name was in yellow and outlined in red. The two victory marks were red with a black swastika. Fellow ace Norman 'Doug' Munson was killed in this aircraft on the first mission of his second tour while strafing Mannhiem airfield 19th July 1944.

(Tudor)

The 78th lined up at Duxford, June '45. Second A/C is Huie Lamb's MX-V, #44-11631 "Etta Jeane II."

Date	F.O.	Type	Hrs.
25- 6-43	56	Sweep	1.35
28- 6-43	58	Escort	1.45
1- 7-43		ASR*	2.00
2- 7-43	62	Sweep	5.35
4- 7-43	64	Ramrod	1.25
9- 7-43	67	Sweep	1.38
10- 7-43	68	Escort	1.33
16- 7-43	73	Sweep	1.30
25- 7-43	78	Sweep	1.50
28- 7-43	83	Withdrawal	2.25
28- 7-43	84	Escort	1.40
29- 7-43	86	Sweep	1.33
30- 7-43	87	Withdrawal	2.30
12- 8-43	98	Withdrawal	1.39
15- 8-43	104	Penetration	1.49
16- 8-43	105	Penetration	2.27
17- 8-43	106	Penetration	2.18
27- 8-43	116	Escort	1.38
2- 9-43	120	Support	5.02
3- 9-43	122	Sweep	1.38
7- 9-43	126	Support	1.49
22- 9-43	138B	Sweep	1.53
23- 9-43	140	Escort	2.20
27- 9-43	146	Escort	2.30
4-10-43	150	Escort	2.35
8-10-43	151	Escort	2.35
20-10-43	163	Penetration	3.01
24-10-43	166	Escort	2.27
3-11-43	168	Escort	2.55
5-11-43	170/B	Penetration	2.17
10-11-43	175	Escort	2.16
13-11-43	180	Withdrawal	2.11
19-11-43	184	Withdrawal	2.00
25-11-43	190	Escort	1.40
29-11-43	192	Withdrawal	2.38
30-11-43	193	Withdrawal	2.40
1-12-43	194	Penetration	2.40
13-12-43	199	Withdrawal	2.40
20-12-43	204	Penetration	2.35
22-12-43	207	Penetration	2.40
24-12-43	209	Support	3.05
30-12-43	210	Support	3.09
31-12-43	211	Support	2.57
4- 1-44	212	Support	3.08
5- 1-44	213	Penetration	3.55
7- 1-44	215	Penetration	2.51
11- 1-44	216	Withdrawal	1.36
14- 1-44	217	Escort	2.34
21- 1-45	221	Support	2.53
28- 1-44	225	Support	2.32
29- 1-44	226	Penetration	2.07
30- 1-44	227	Withdrawal	2.59
31- 1-44	44/66F/W	Escort	2.15
3- 2-44	233	Escort	3.10
4- 2-44	234	Withdrawal	2.55
5- 2-44	235	Target	3.19
6- 2-44	236	Support	3.08
8- 2-44	237	Withdrawal	3.04
10- 2-44	239	Support	3.10
11- 2-44	240	Withdrawal	3.03
13- 2-44	242	Support	2.02
21- 2-44	246	Penetration	3.00
24- 2-44	250	Withdrawal	2.55
25- 2-44	251	Penetration	3.52
2- 3-44	258	Target	2.47
3- 3-44	259	Withdrawal	3.50
5- 3-44	261	Withdrawal	3.15
6- 3-44	262	Withdrawal	3.05
8- 3-44	263	Withdrawal	3.33
15- 3-44	269	Withdrawal	3.58
16- 3-44	270	Withdrawal	3.49
17- 3-44	F.O.50	"Jackpot"	1.00

All missions flown with P-47D, WZ-R, #41-6393 except: F.O. 22: WZ-T, F.O. 23: WZ-E, F.O. 38: WZ-I, F.O. 62: WZ-D, F.O. 116: WZ-H, F.O. 120: WZ-J, F.O. 233: WZ-S, F.O. 234: WZ-Y, F.O. 235: WZ-O, F.O. 236: WZ-X, F.O. 263: WZ-N, and F.O. 50: WZ-Z.

Claims list of Lt. Peter E. Pompetti

Date	Claim	Result	Location
30- 7-43	1 ME-109	Des.	Air.
17- 8-43	1 ME-110	Des.	Air.
29- 9-43	1 ME-109	Des.	Air.
	1 ME-110	Des.	Air.
1-12-43	1 FW-190	Dam.	Air.
4- 1-44	1 ME-109	Des.	Air.
	1 FW-109	Dam.	Air.
14- 1-44	1 ME-109	Dam.	Air.
5- 2-44	1 FW-190	Dam.	Air.
6- 2-44	1 JU-88	Dam.	Grd.
	1 HS-129	Des.	Air.
	2 Locos	Dam.	Grd.(w/ Lt. Marlowe).
	1 Flak Twr.	Dam.	Grd.(w/ Lt. Marlowe).
	1 Tug	Dam.	Wtr.(w/ Lt. Marlowe).
25- 2-44	2 ME-109s	Dam.	Grd.
2- 3-44	1 JU-52	Des.	Grd.(w/ Lt. Lang).
	1 HS-126	Des.	Grd.
6- 3-44	2 Locos	Dam.	Grd.(w/ Lt. Abel).
8- 3-44	1 FW-190	P/Des.	Grd. (w/ Lt. Lang).
	1 Gas truck	Des.	Grd.
13- 3-44	1 E/A	Dam.	Grd. (w/ Lt. Lang).
16- 3-44	1 ME-109	Des.	Air. (w/ Lt. Lang).
	1 ME-109	Dam.	Grd.
	1 Hangar	Dam.	Grd.
17- 3-44	1 HE-111	Des.	Grd. (w/ Lt. Lang).

ROBERT H. POWELL, JR.

328TH FIGHTER SQUADRON, 352ND FIGHTER GROUP

Robert H. Powell, Jr. was born on November 21, 1920 in Wilcoe, West Virginia. From 1929 to 1942 he attended West Virginia State University. After the war he returned and obtained a B.S. in Journalism in 1947. Prior to his return to college he married Betty Wiley. They have three children, Robert Wiley, Linda Louise, and Betsy Lynne. Since obtaining his B.S. Bob has worked as a photographer/feature writer on the *World News,* Roanoke, Virginia.

In January, 1948 he started work for the Norfolk and Western Railway but on January 5th, 1950 he was recalled to active duty and once again flew the P-51 Mustang. He was under the command of John C. Meyer who had flown with him in England with the 352nd Fighter Group. During this time he and the other pilots went through an intensive six weeks flying course at Nellis AFB, Nevada which consisted of ground support and skip-bombing missions. Later he was transferred to Wright-Patterson AFB, Ohio and in August, 1955 he resigned his commission with the rank of Captain and returned to the Norfolk and Western Railway as advertising manager. Later in 1956 he joined McGraw-Hill Publishing Company in Atlanta, Georgia as District Advertising Manager and was with the company for a total of four years before he left to join Technical Publishing Company Dun-Donnelly Publishing as the Regional Manager. Bob was still with them in 1986.

During the past few years Bob has been extremely active in the Eighth Air Force Historical Society and from that the Eighth Air Force Memorial Museum Foundation. His first love, however, is the 352nd Fighter Group Association, with over 600 members and associates, and was for a time its president. Also he is editor for the *Bluenoser,* 352nd Fighter Group Newsletter, and a member of the P-47 Thunderbolt Pilots Association. Bob and his lovely wife Betty now live in Atlanta, Georgia.

In January, 1942 Bob went to Pikeville, Kentucky where he took an Aviation Cadet examination. Within two months he was sworn in and in April 1942 was ordered to report to Santa Ana, California to begin his Basic Training. Next he went to Miraloma Flight Academy for Primary Training which he completed by the end of August. From there he went to Gardner Field, near Bakersfield, California, and on 4th January 1943 he was commissioned as a 2nd Lieutenant at Luke Field, just outside of Phoenix, Arizona. Two days later he was assigned to the 338th Fighter Group based at Dale Mabry Field, Tallahassee, Florida where he completed his Operational Training with the P-47 Thunderbolt.

The 3rd April 1943 saw him on his way to England

Bob Powell with his second P-51B Mustang which carried the code PE-P, 42-106914. An outline of West Virginia is shown in reference to Bob's home state. Note six Maltese Cross style 'kill' markings under the cockpit.

(Powell Jr.)

aboard the 'Avent Pasteur' which docked at Liverpool the 22nd. He was posted to the 12th Combat Replacement Depot at Atcham, Shropshire, the Operational Training Unit for the Thunderbolt. Along with him were two men with whom he had done much of his training, Frederick Windmeyer and Charles W. Reed. When Bob was posted to the 352nd Fighter Group at Bodney, Norfolk both Reed and Windmeyer were posted to the 56th Fighter Group. While at Atcham the pilots got an opportunity to fly Spitfire Mk Vs and this was about the only single-engined fighter that fitted Bob well due to his being on the short side.

On July 1, 1943 the 352nd Fighter Group, that Bob was to serve with, embarked on the "Queen Elizabeth" with approximately 23,000 troops aboard. By the 8th the liner had docked at Grenock, Scotland and a fourteen hour train ride followed which ended at

The P-47 of Capt. Franklin N. Greene who made the first confirmed victory, a 109F, for the 486th on Dec 20, 1943. PZ-I, 42-2509. We had this photo scanned in hopes that you'd still be able to read the nice crew panel.

Above, left: Fred A. Yochim in the cockpit of his Thunderbolt named 'Desiree Y' after his wife. Code was PE-V, 42-8434.

(Powell Jr.)

Above, right: Bob's first warhorse, shared with Lt. James L. Laing. On the port side Laing put the name 'Jamie Mi Boy.' Bob had his insignia painted by Sgt. Marinello who painted most of the insignias in the 328th. Note centre slung belly tank, the 'Babies' that helped win the air war in Europe.

(Powell Jr.)

Watton Station, about 3 miles to the east of Station 141, Bodney, Norfolk. The 352nd consisted of three squadrons, the 328th, 486th and 487th. By the end of the war the group had destroyed a total of 776 1/2 enemy aircraft and produced a total of 54 aces. The group also produced more pilots who shot down 5 or more enemy aircraft in one mission than any other 8th Air Force fighter group, namely, Carl J. Luksic, George E. Preddy, Donald S. Bryan and William T. Whisner . . . but this was all in the future.

Meanwhile Bob had a very good friend, Lt. Fred Yochim, who encouraged Major Everett W. Stewart (C.O. 328th) to get Bob into the squadron. Bob recalls, ``Fred Yochim was my best friend and the one who requested Major Stewart to send for me at Atcham. Fred and I went through a lot together before he was shot down about Easter 1944 and ended up a prisoner. A super guy and a super pilot, he later continued his Air Force career playing a significant role in the development of the cameras used in U-2s in the Cuban Missile Crisis. He retired from the Air Force after many years

Lt. Col. Luther H. Richmond on the wing of his ``Sweetie.'' PZ-R, 42-8412.

(Tabatt)

service. I treasure his memory.''

The group began flying operations on 14th September, 1943 and had flown quite a few by the time Bob joined them in November. On the 11th, Bob flew his first operational sortie as a Spotter over the North Sea in PE-M. This was in conjunction with Air Sea Rescue and he logged 2 hours and 18 minutes. After some two weeks he finally got a combat mission when he took part in a Ramrod to Bremen, Germany, which lasted just over two and one half hours.

On 22nd December, his sixth mission - a ramrod to Munster/Osnabruck, he made his first contact with the Luftwaffe. The group was part of the escort, which amounted to over 500 fighters, and when the battle was over they claimed a total of six enemy aircraft destroyed for the loss of one pilot. Bob recalls: ``On my first encounter with the enemy, I was flying with Major Stewart. Stu liked to fly his fledgling pilots on his wing for a few missions to ensure that they (1) survived and (2) knew how to handle themselves before turning them over to one of the Flight Leaders. At the time Stu, himself, had not actually engaged the enemy as the group had just come on operations. I was one of the replacement pilots assigned to the group prior to them going into combat. I had actually arrived in England before the group and had gone through the training programme at Atcham. There were a great many of us who did this and established outstanding records with the 56th and 78th Fighter Groups.

Anyway, we were returning from a mission escorting over 600 bombers to Munster-Osnabruck on 22nd December 1943 and the trip, so far, had been uneventful. Since this was my first mission on the ``Old Man's'' wing (Stewart was 5 years older than Bob), I was literally patting myself on the back for having flown in almost perfect position as his wingman. As I checked the sky to the right and then to the left for enemy aircraft, I panicked as I discovered Stu had totally disappeared in those few seconds! Looking about frantically, I saw him below me in an inverted (Split-S) dive. Quickly, I flipped my P-47 over to follow him down while I mentally chastised myself for not holding position better. Pulling out on his level, I jockeyed my throttle back and fish-tailed to keep from over running him, relieved that I had gotten back into position so quickly and, hopefully, without Stu noticing.

To my surprise, I saw that he was firing his guns! In front of him was a German aircraft and he was knocking pieces off it. Almost at the same second, I saw another just like it right in front of me. I'd been so intent on getting back on Stu's wing that I hadn't seen them and Stu had been so quick off the mark that he'd forgotten to call out. Without even looking through the reticle on my gunsight, I squeezed the trigger and saw hits all over the enemy aircraft. Stu and I had our first claims.

Landing back at Bodney, the Major and I were hugging each other and jumping around excitedly when he asked 'What the hell were they, Punchy?' For the life of me, with more than a year of aircraft recognition training, I realized that I didn't know what they were. 'Dammed if I know,' I said, 'all I saw were those big black crosses all over them.' It wasn't until later, with the help of the other pilots, that we realized they were in fact ME-110s. This was later confirmed by our gun camera films. The official report was more brief and to the point.

Putting six flights (24 aircraft) into the air, the squadron led by Major Stewart made landfall 8 miles north of Ijmuiden, penetrated to Weitsmorshen and returned home via Ijmuiden. Box score for the afternoon was 3-0-2: 3 ME-110s destroyed in the vicinity of Zwolle; one shared by Major Stewart and Lt. Powell, and one each by Lt. Coleman and Lt. Horne. In addition Major Stewart damaged a ME-210 and Lt. Powell damaged a ME-110. Red Flight encountered a FW-190 in the area of Furstenau. Red Flight consisted of Major Stewart, Lts. Powell, Coleman, and Horne.

At about this time Bob was assigned his first Thunderbolt, PE-K, 42-8657. He shared it with Lt. James Laing who had the name 'Jamie Mi Boy' painted on the port side. Bob got Sgt. Ignatzio Marinello to paint the legend 'The West 'By Gawd' Virginian' on the starboard side. The crew were S/Sgt. James Loughrey, Sgt. Frank C. Ruvo and Cpl. Clinton A. Hayes. By the end of 1943 Bob had completed a total of nine combat sorties plus the ASR spotter mission and had a total of just over 28 hours under his belt.

On 4th January 1944 Bob flew as White Two in PE-N, 42-8515. The group was part of the fighter screen to nearly 1,000 bombers which attacked targets at Kiel and Munster, Germany. Four days later on the 5th, Bob, along with Major Stewart and Lt. John B. Coleman Jr. (Stewart and Coleman also became aces), shot down an HE-177. This was the bomber type Hitler had boasted would one day bomb New York. Bob recalls "Of course, one of my big thrills was the opportunity to get in on the victory over the first HE-177 shot down by USAAF pilots."

"I was flying Turndown Yellow Two escorting the bombers at about 21,000 feet when Major Everett Stewart, Yellow leader, spotted a large enemy aircraft at about 10 o'clock above us. We started up after the enemy aircraft, identifying it as an HE-177. When the enemy pilot spotted us he started down in a steep

Bob poses with the rest of his flight. From left to right front row: James L. Laing, Quintin L. Quinn, Robert H. Powell Jr., David T. Zimms. Back Row: Marion V. Long, James Meagher, Donald S. Bryan, Francis W. Horne. Squeezed up in the engine housing is Bob Fry who shot down four enemy aircraft.

(Powell Jr.)

Above: An interesting shot of the art work on Col. Joe Mason's P-47 PZ-M, 42-8466. Rt. Joe Mason was the 352nd's first commander.

dive. We followed, trying hard to close the gap. When he thought he was within range Major Stewart opened fire to try to get the bomber to turn either way so we could cut across him. I saw strikes on the port engine. The HE-177 turned sharply and Major Stewart fired at him, angle off, getting more hits. I then fired a short burst but stopped when Lt. John Coleman Jr., Yellow Three, slipped onto his tail. When Lt. Coleman broke off I again slid in line astern and opened fire at about 300 yards. I observed many strikes along the wing roots and the top of the fuselage. I did not observe the enemy ship returning fire. I then closed to about 200 yards. By this time we were down to about 8,000 feet and I broke sharply to the left.

Looking back, I saw the enemy aircraft about a second after he hit the ground. Flames were belching up as high as 1,000 feet. I then looked around for Yellow Leader. Failing to find him, I got Yellow Four, Lt.

Some 'Big Wheels' of the 352nd Fighter Group pose in front of Joe Mason's aircraft. From left to right are James D. Mayden (later C.O. of the group), Willie O. Jackson (C.O. 486th F-S), George E. Preddy (C.O. 328th F-S), Joe Mason (Group C.O.) and John Meyer (C.O. 487th F-S and later the group).

(Powell Jr.)

Horne, and another Turndown aircraft to join me and we came out together flying cross-cover with two ships of another flight. The action took place in the vicinity of La Ferte Bernard at about 11:43 hours and took from 23,000 feet down to 8,000 feet.

I claim one HE-177 destroyed (shared with Major Everett W. Stewart and Lt. John B. Coleman Jr.).

Major Stewart; PE-G, 42-8437; 976 rounds of API

Lt. John B. Coleman; PE-J, 42-22529; 125 rounds of API

Lt. Robert H. Powell; PE-X, 42-8419; 156 rounds of API

On a later mission Bob was returning as part of an eight ship flight when he and the rest met a real honcho Jerry pilot. He recalls ``At the time I think Jack Thornell was leading when somebody spotted a single German twin-engined fighter down below us. We were about Angles 27 at the time, and one flight was sent down to get him, the other flight holding back just in case it was a decoy ship. What a decoy! What a pilot!

For the next several minutes, all eight of us took a shot at this guy and in return got shot at by him. I still think today that we had taken on one of the best German pilots there was. He was flying what we later decided was a ME-410 and he made his aircraft do almost impossible things — skidding across the sky in a halfturn attitude to make us miss him when we thought we had him cold; seemingly stopping his aircraft so we would overshoot him and then turning on our tails as we went past him; then ducking into a nearby overcast and popping out of it to take a shot at us as we looked for him.

Finally, with all the maneuvering, we were getting lower and lower and he raced among the trees with two of our guys on his tail and the rest of us boxing him in from above. Then, chopping everything, appar-

Above, left: A nice shot of the young Lt. Henry J. Miklajcyk with his P-47 PZ-K, 41-6430. We scanned this so you could, hopefully, read all the tiny writin'.

(Steve Miklajcyk)

Above, right: An interesting shot of Miklajcyk's P-47 and a hardworking Moth, used for a variety of yeoman duties. Apparently Henry only had one assigned P-47 as only one set of P-47 serial #s come up in conjunction with his name and his second P-51 was named Syracusan III. A full starboard shot of his P-47 appears on page 21 "Thunderbolt at War" by Wm. Hess.

ently pulling up into a tight turn, he then dropped that thing into a big open field we had just crossed over and bellied it in. Jumping out, he ran into the woods as we came down and strafed his aircraft setting it ablaze. We all agreed later that we'd encountered a real master of our craft and secretly hoped we'd never have to face him alone.

On another mission Earl Abbott saved Bob from becoming a victory for a 109 pilot, while the 352nd was providing escort for a box of B-17s. Shortly after they met up with their charges, some 109s made a determined attack. The 328th dived in to break up the attack, although they were heavily outnumbered. Turning to get on the tail of one of the ME-109s Bob saw to his horror that an enemy ship was on his tail. Bob pulled every trick he knew but the Jerry stayed on his tail loosing off a short burst every now and then. At that moment Bob heard Earl Abbott call out "Break left, Punchy, and I'll get him." So Bob broke hard and 'Abby' nailed the German fighter.

On 8th April, 1944 Bob and his flight made an attack on Quackenbruck Airfield and he recalled, 'I was flying White Two position on a bomber escort-rhubarb mission. We escorted the bombers through their bomb run and then started our low level attack on the same airdrome the 'Big Friends' had just bombed. On our first pass we came in too high, making our angle of attack rather steep. I picked out a ME-210 in its revetment and opened fire from several hundred yards, observing many strikes on and all round it as my pat-

tern changed in size and shape. I pulled up through the smoke, left by the bursting bombs at the other side of the field, following White Three and Four in a zoom climb.

Noting there was little ground fire, I called White Four to follow me in another attack. We swung around and on this pass I could not line up on any enemy aircraft. I peppered several buildings. As I pulled up I saw many hits on the parked aircraft Lt. Jimmy Laing was firing at.

I zoomed up to about 800 feet and skidded around in a tight turn of almost 180 degrees to make another pass. This time I got another ME-210 in my sights and held the trigger down until I was almost flying through it. My fire was very effective and the enemy aircraft was undoubtedly well riddled. I went past and rejoined Lt. Laing and Lt. Freddie Miller (W-3) and came home. I did not look back to see if this last aircraft was burning, although there were, by now, several fires on the field.

| Lt. Robert H. Powell Jr. | PE-K, 42-8657 |
| Lt. James L. Laing | PE-Y, 42-8486 |

The rest of the month of April 1944 turned out to be one of mixed fortunes for Bob. On the day following the attack on Quackenbruck Airfield his friend Fred Yochim went down to become a prisoner of war. Also lost on 28th April was Lt. James L. Laing who also ended up as a POW. The 328th started to use the North American P-51 Mustang on the 22nd when Earl Abbott, J. B. Coleman Jr., Jack Thornell Jr., Quintin

Below, left: A nice shot of, now, Captain Henry Miklajcyk, his C/C R.H. Sprole, and their first assigned P-51, 42-106430 - also coded PZ-K.

Below, right: The only photo we could find of "SYRACUSAN III," PZ-K, 44-13690 in which Capt. Miklajcyk was downed by enemy fire near Halle, Germany Nov 2, 1944. (MACR #10240). Ace Earnest Bostrom explains to Miklajcyk, center, and other 486th pilots some fine points of aerial combat.

(USAF ARCHIVES, Maxwell AFB)

L. Quinn, Marion V. Long and one other pilot flew a Sweep while the rest of the squadron, flying Thunderbolts, carried out a Penetration mission. On this day Bob flew his last Thunderbolt mission and two days later he was assigned PE-P(bar), 42-106757. At the same time he was assigned a new ground crew which consisted of Crew Chief S/Sgt. Robert W. Lyons, Assistant Crew Chief Cpl. Walter C. Hughes and Armourer Cpl. Edwin L. Kingsbury. While the crew was together they had three different Mustangs assigned to them.

His last claims for the month came on April 28th. The group went out on a Ramrod-Rhubarb mission and Bob's new Mustang was hit by the ever present German flak and he recalls, 'We were attacking a German airfield (St. Avord) which was packed with Jerry fighters and bombers sitting around the perimeter track. We shot up some of them on our downward swoop, and then leveled off as low as possible across the open field, selecting our targets on the other side. As I sped across the field I spotted a large open hangar with a JU-88 sitting inside and I started letting go with short bursts until it started to burn. By that time I was flying right at the hangar and I made a sharp climbing turn to miss the shed and get out of there.

As I pulled up over the edge of the field, something exploded in my tail. I knew I'd been hit hard, the aircraft was skidding and climbing without me being able to control it very much. I just kept hoping it would keep flying until I got enough altitude to go over the side. I threw the canopy back, and prepared to do so, but as it slowed in the climb I realized I still had control so I re-buckled my harness and hooked everything up again.

Some of my flight gathered around to protect me and we headed for home. On the radio, they told me there was a big, washtub-sized, hole through my horizontal stabilizer and the metal was all bent upwards. That explained why I was fighting with all my strength to hold the aircraft level. I had an undesigned trim tab back there wanting to push me up into a climb. As we got over the water, however, and I slowed the aircraft

somewhat, it was easier to hold my attitude and with my escort, I came home. The landing was a little tricky, but I brought it in above normal approach speed and got it safely on the ground.

All this made me realize something about strafing. The skill of the pilot made very little difference! You had to fly through so much ground fire, and those gunners didn't know how skilled you were, or care for that matter, and sooner or later they were likely to get you.'

May was to prove quite a month for Bob. The most noteworthy mission was on the 7th when an estimated 1,000 bombers went out on various missions escorted by over 800 fighters. The 352nd went to Berlin and out of nearly 600 bombers only eight were lost, and four fighters of which none were lost to enemy fighters. At the time Bob flew Earl Abbott's PE-A, 42-106844 'Sandra Lee.' On the 13th the group flew a mission to Poland crossing Denmark and Germany. Of the 5 hours and 45 minutes in the air, Bob spent one hour and forty five minutes flying on instruments! The group claimed sixteen for the loss of one pilot and aircraft. Colonel Joe Mason claimed three and George Preddy knocked down two. Lost was Captain Frank Cutler of the 486th Fighter Squadron. On May 21, 1944 Bob flew his first Chattanooga type mission (train busting). The 328th Squadron claimed a total of 22 enemy aircraft destroyed and another 13 damaged, also six locos were knocked out and another five damaged while claims for various other ground targets were made for no losses. In his Consolidated Encounter Report Captain Earl Abbott wrote 'I was leading the 328th Fighter Squadron on a Chattanooga Plan Mission. Shortly before reaching our designated area we went below the overcast at about 8,000 feet. Breaking through the overcast we spotted an airfield believed to be in the area of Alt Ruppin. My section, consisting of White and Red Flights, divebombed it first with our wingtanks. In addition, Lt. Raymond G. Phillips, White Two, destroyed a FW-190 parked on the airfield. Flames were seen as a result of his fire. En-

Left: Capt. Earl R. Lazear Jr. and his P-51. "Peennie's Earl" in white on dark blue shield. Note 4 black Maltese Cross claims. A/C had yellow rudder and black stencil serial #414877. PZ-L was previously coded PZ-A and, after Earl's tour, changed again to PZ-K "Beautiful Betty."
(Lazear)

Right: Though much beyond the scope of these 2 books, it took myriad ground personnel to keep 'em flyin'. Here Lt. Leo R. Johnson 486th Sq. Graves and Registration Officer, and friends pose in front of Alton Wallace's PZ-W, #42-8477.
(Johnson)

countering strong groundfire we went on, flying at 6,000 feet. Shortly thereafter, we spotted a grass field with 200 plus enemy aircraft of many types on it.

My section went south and hit the deck for a strafing attack. The second section composed of Yellow and Blue flights stayed up and steered us in. First section made one pass and stayed on the deck; the claims for this pass are listed below.

The second section, led by Captain Robert H. Sharp, seeing no groundfire, went down making several passes and observing enemy aircraft on the field and in the dispersal areas with netting over them. Types observed included JU-86s, HE-111s, HE-177s, ME 109s, and many U/I/E/A. These aircraft were parked wing-tip to wing-tip. Every member of the section fired their guns at the enemy aircraft — their claims are listed below. Captain Sharp reported many fires being left on the airfield.

In the meantime the first section, after making their one pass, pulled up and spotted several locomotives. Lt. Edmond Zellner, leading Red Flight of the 1st section, attacked four (4) locos with his flight. The section, working as a unit, attacked an electric loco. Red Flight went on to attack a railroad station in the same area (Alt Ruppin).

A lorry and a truck dispersal area were also strafed. Approximately fifteen (15) military personnel came out as we strafed the lorry and were caught in our fire and some were killed.

The second section (Yellow and Blue Flights), after completion of three passes on the airfield, flew in a westerly direction and attacked locos and trains. Yellow Flight fired at one loco and Blue Flight fired at two (2) freight trains. Blue Flight, led by Jack Thornell, also strafed a factory of some description.

Due to the overcast and unfavorable weather conditions, the definite location of combat cannot be ascertained. However, it is believed that the vicinity of Alt Ruppin was the location of the main attack.

Following are the claims of the 328th Squadron as a result of the strafing of the airfield in the area of Alt Ruppin, Germany and of continued strafing of locos,

'Brutal Lulu' gets ready to knock the spots off the Luftwaffe. The regular pilot was Robert H. Berkshire who took care of 4 1/2 aircraft. Code was HO-U, 42-22515.

(Evans)

trains and other ground targets in the same area.

White Flight:
Cpt. Abbott-1 U/U/E/A Dest; 2 U/I/E/A/ Damaged.
Lt. Rayborn-2 HE-111s Dest.
Lt. Bennette-1 HE-111 Dest, 1 U/I/E/A Dest.
Lt. Phillips-1 FW-190 Dest, 1 JU-52 Dest, 1 U/I/E/A Dest.
　Red Flight:
Lt. Zellner-2 JU-88s Dest.
Lt. Godfrey-No E/A.
Lt. Furr-1 JU-52 Dest.
　Yellow Flight:
Capt. Sharp-2 JU-86s Dest, 1 HE-111 Dam, 1 U/I/E/A Dam.
Lt. Smith-1 HE-111 Dest, 1 U/I/E/A Dam.
Lt. Horne-1 U/I/A/C Dest, 1 HE-111 Dam.
Lt. Fieg-3 U/I/E/A Dam.
　Blue Flight:
Lt. Thornell-2 HE-111s Dest, 1 HE-177 Dam.
Lt. Campbell-1 HE-111 Dest, 1 DO-217 Dam.
Lt. Powell-2 HE-111s Dest, 2 HE-111 Dam.
Lt. Dyke-2 HE-111s Dest.
　Total: 22-0-13 (Ground)

Two photos of ace Glennon T. Moran's P-51 ''Little Ann'' HO-M, 42-103320, in a very definitely used condition.

Above: Lt. Col. Meyer's ``Lambie II'' - a P-51B, HO-M, 42-106471 in which he scored 5 1/2 victories - ``. . . mbie II'' of name just visible on nose.

Right: 24 victory ace Lt. Col. John C. Meyer in his first assigned A/C ``Lambie''

Six locos were destroyed, shared as follows;
Dest: 2-shared by Lts. Zellner, Furr and Godfrey.
       1-shared by Capt. Sharp, Lts. Horne, Dyke and Smith.
       1-Lt. Thornell.
       1-Lt. Bennette.
       1-Electric-shared by Capt. Abbott, Lts. Godfrey, Zellner, Bennette, Horne, Furr and Smith.
Dam. 1-Lt. Rayborn.
      1-Lt. Phillips.
      1-shared by Lts. Zellner and Godfrey.
      1-shared by Lts. Zellner and Furr.
      1-Lt. Thornell.
Other claims:
       1 Box Car, Dam. Lt. Rayborn.
       1 Freight train (oil cars, etc.) Dam. Lts. Powell and Dyke.
       1 Factory Dam. Lt. Powell.
       15 German military personnel killed. Lt. Bennette.
       5 German military personnel killed. Lt. Thornell.
       1 RR Station Dam. Lt. Zellner and Furr.

A close-up of Petie II

1 Truck dest. Capt. Abbott and Lts. Bennette and Phillips.

Pilot	Code	Serial	
Cpt. Earl L. Abbott	PE-A	42-106844	'Sandra Lee'
Lt. Garland Rayborn	PE-C	42-106694	
Lt. Charles J. Bennette	PE-T	42-106717	
Lt. Raymond G. Phillips	PE-P	42-106868	
Lt. Edmond Zellner	PE-U	42-106832	'We Three'
Lt. McDonald Godfrey	PE-X	43-7174	
Lt. William W. Furr	PE-R	42-106466	'Lois'
Cpt. Robert H. Sharp	PE-V	43-7146	
Lt. Elmer L. Smith	PE-G	42-106744	'Candy Lamb'
Lt. Frances W. Horne	PE-S	42-106703	
Lt. Lothar Fieg	PE-F	43-6988	
Lt. John F. Thornell Jr.	PE-J	43-24801	
Lt. John Campbell	PE-Q	42-106663	
Lt. Robert H. Powell Jr.	PE-Y	42-106852	
Lt. Samuel F. Dyke	PE-D	42-106859	

Earl L. Abbott
Cpt. Air Corps.
328th Ftr. Sq.

On D-Day Bob flew two missions which totaled over six hours flying. The first was in the area of Montigny and lasted three hours and forty-five minutes. It was his fifty-seventh mission and involved strafing anything that moved. The group claimed two aerial victories, both of which were claimed by 328th squadron pilots; Lt. Leroy J. Allain Jr. bagged one (PE-R, 42-106460), while Lts. Richard C. Brookins (PE-I, 43-7174) and Francis W. Horne (PE-W, 42-106756) shared in downing one. Losses for the day amounted to three pilots, of whom Lt. Robert K. Butler and Lt. Robert G. O'Nan were lost over the Normandy area. The first loss was Lt. Robert Frascotti who crashed into the control tower on take-off in his Mustang 'Umbriago' (PZ-F, 43-6685). The fire from the wreckage of his aircraft provided a grim light for the rest of the group's pilots as they took off on the pre-dawn mission to the beachhead at Normandy.

A few days later Bob managed to catch a couple dispatch riders and some trucks on a winding Normandy lane and Lt. Elmer Smith was hit by flak. The shell was within an inch of his ammo bay. Flying back to base he had to land his Mustang at about 200 MPH due to the damage he had suffered.

On the 21st Bob was able to damage a ME-410 while on a Ramrod and he recalled, 'I was flying No. 3 position in Yellow Flight, with Jack Thornell leading, when we saw some 'Bogies' (unidentified aircraft) approaching the bombers. We investigated and found them to be ME-410s and as we turned into them to break up their attack, one broke sharply into our flight. I took a short squirt at him at about 60 degree angle but had to hold my fire when I spotted another Mustang on his tail.

I swung back to the attack and as I did so, the rest of the ME-410 formation broke up. We tagged onto one, but he managed to stay away from our fire by using the clouds to his advantage.

We finally forced him to break for the deck and Lt. Thornell hit him with a good burst from dead astern. I observed lots of hits from Lt. Thornell and the enemy aircraft broke sharply, turning inside Thornell.

I dumped my flaps and turned on his tail, opening fire at about 300 yards. Only one of my guns fired and my strikes were scattered. He turned inside me and before I could get back at him, Lt. Thornell and Lt. Dyke were on him again.

The Jerry pilot bellied in at high speed under the raking fire from our three ships. We then strafed the wreckage.

I claim 1 ME-410 damaged in the air.'

Robert H. Powell Jr.
328th Fighter Squadron

This was the day that aircraft of the 486th Fighter Squadron teamed up with the 4th Fighter Group, under the command of Don Blakeslee, for the second Shuttle Mission to Russia. Four days later Bob had a nice long haul to the Swiss Alps which lasted for five and a quarter hours and penetrated as far as Jessern.

On July 1st, Bob made his last claim of the war while on a Fighter Sweep over the Pas de Calais area. Upon his return he wrote the following encounter report, 'I was leading Blue Flight on a sweep over the Calais area when, just south of St. Omer, we bounced some ME-109s already mixing it with some P47s at about 23,000 feet altitude. In the melee, our squadron became split up into flights.

I saw some contrails high above us. We were flying at about 25,000 feet then. We started up after them, going balls out. When I reached 29,000 feet altitude I identified them as ME-109s. There were ten of them. I figured we could handle them if we stayed up-sun and climbed. We managed to do this until we got to 31,500 and one of them spotted us. There were only two of us as my second element (Nos 3 and 4) had become lost in the climb.

Above: Bob Powell with his Mustang PE-P, 42-106914 'The West 'by Gawd' Virginian' which he lost on 18th July 1944 due to engine failure.

(Powell Jr.)

Below: Two nice photos of ace William T. Halton, his P-47, PE-T 42-8439 and his P-51, HO-T, 44-14812. Both A/C named "Slender, Tender and Tall." Bottom photo taken just before a mission from Chievres, Belgium in early 1945.

(Mulron/Coggin)

This one Jerry turned into us, so I took a short burst at about 60 degree deflection at 150 to 200 hundred yards range, letting him fly through my cone of fire. I saw hits, a couple on the wings and one on the fuselage.

Since I was pulled up in a short, steep climbing turn, I stalled out at the end of my burst of fire. The ME-109 did a wing-over and went straight down. I didn't give chase as I didn't want to turn my back on the other nine Jerries.

I gave chase to these but lost them when they went down into some clouds, thin wispy stuff. I signaled my wingman, who had done a swell job of sticking in there, and we made for home — but fast.

PE-P, 42-106914
Ammo Exp. 101 Rds.

Robert H. Powell Jr.
328th Fighter Squadron
352nd Fighter Group.

On the 18th of July, Bob was to have a very lucky escape when he crashed #42-106914. It was immediately after he led his flight off that the trouble started and he recalled: ``We were on a mission from Bodney and in one of our normal four-ship take offs from the grass field there. Shortly after becoming airborne, with my wheels having just tucked in, my Mustang suddenly caught fire. I think I had a couple of hundred feet or so altitude, and I had almost run out of field.

Ahead of me were two rows of trees about 100 yards apart at about a 45 degree angle to my take-off direction. It looked like I was going to have to go into these as I lost power, and the old adage of 'crash straight ahead' and 'don't try to turn in a stall' flashed into my head as I saw those trees. I tried it anyway, however, with more of a skid and only a slight bank to put me between those two rows of trees, and it worked, thank God.

The Mustang landed on its belly slightly turned, however, and the soft dirt evidently knocked down the flames somewhat as it plowed along the cleared

The end of #914 came during take off on a mission on 18th July 1944. The engine caught fire and Bob set it down just off the airfield. A ground crew member saved the engine cowling and it now hangs in Bob's home.

(Powell Jr.)

ground. The same attitude of the aircraft also probably twisted the fuselage slightly, as when I tried to roll the canopy off it jammed! Panicsville! I pulled the Emergency Release (located on the right side of the cockpit) in an attempt to get it off, but it would not budge. Super Panicsville!!

After yanking all the straps and radio and oxygen stuff loose, I scooted down in the seat as far as I could go, and pulled up my legs and kicked the hell out of the canopy — and it came off.

I got out of '914' as quickly as I could because the flames were building up again, jumping to the ground and rolling a couple of times to be sure I wasn't on fire, then running like crazy for the trees.

Now the funny part - as I look back on it. I ran until I came to a road or path that led back to the 328th pilot's hut. Dave Lee, the squadron S-2, was on the phone reporting who it was who had crashed and whom he thought had bought the farm. When he realized it was me and that I was OK, he started hugging me like a long lost son. We got into his jeep, after he reported to the control tower that I was safe, and we drove back to the crash scene.

Meanwhile the whole center section of the Mustang's fuselage had blown away, and everyone who was at the scene of the crash was thrashing around in the nearby shrubbery and trees looking for my body. Stupid with joy by this time, I yelled at Doc Lemon, our Flight Surgeon, 'Who was it, Doc?' Before he realized who he was answering, he said 'It was Punchy' (my nickname). Then realizing I was alive, he said, 'How in hell did you get out of that thing?' Cockily, I shouted back, 'With great difficulty, I bounced out.'

One of our airmen rescued the panel (or what was left of it) which had carried the legend 'The West 'by gawd' Virginian' and I still have it today although I had to smuggle it past our inspectors when I returned to the States!

Bob was assigned a new P-51D (which had the bubble canopy) and flew his last combat mission on 4th August 1944 when he flew a Ramrod to Anklam which lasted for nearly six hours and gave him a total of over 300 hours, the statuary number of hours for a tour of combat duty. He was then assigned to HQ's, 8th Fighter Command as Technical Advisor to Public Relations and on Xmas Eve 1944, he boarded a C-3 Liberty ship for the States. For Bob the war was over, but not his service with the Air Force. He left the Air Force on 10th July 1945 (but remained in the Reserves) and returned to West Virginia University.

After his 'Separation from Service' he spent a couple of years at W.V.U. and got his degree in Journalism in 1947 and after that (as previously stated) he joined *Roanoke World News* as a reporter-feature writer. After a while he joined the Norfolk and Western RR and stayed there until his recall in 1950 (4th January) and he was posted to Wright-Patterson AFB, Ohio in a fly-

Two photos of Lt. James N. Wood Jr. and his HO-Z, "The Fox." This was Lt. Col John Meyer's A/C, Petie III," until his automobile accident prevented further combat flying. C/C was Leonard A. Howe.

Above: This photo was taken after a strafing mission when Jim's target exploded right beneath him. Note oil stains on canopy and damage to tail.

(J. Wood Jr.)

ing/public assignment. When the Korean conflict started, with the invasion of South Korea by the Communists, Bob and a number of ex-World War Two veterans were ordered to go direct to Korea. Many Mustangs were taken out of mothballs and sent to the west coast. Luckily, someone realized that something was wrong and cancelled the orders sending Bob and the other pilots to Korea and they were ordered to Nellis AFB, Nevada for transition and gunnery training. When he arrived there he bumped into John C. Meyer (who was taking the 4th Fighter Group to Korea) and also a number of other Blue Nosers from Bodney.

While going through the training programme Bob was grounded due to the fact that he needed surgery and by the time that was over Meyer and the rest of his wartime buddies were in Korea and he was posted back to Wright Patterson AFB.

During WW 2 Bob flew a total of 93 missions and aborted on only three occasions due to mechanical failure, a truly impressive record by any terms.

Mission List for Lt. Robert H. Powell Jr.

Date	F.O.	Time	Code	Location
11.11.43	177	2:18	PE-M	North Sea
26.11.43	191	2:26	PE-K	Strucklinger
30.11.43	193	2:18	PE-P	Weert
4.12.43	195	2:06		Sliedracht
13.12.43	199	2:30	PE-Q	Dorpen
20.12.43	204	3:06	PE-Z	Friescythe
22.12.43	207	3:00	PE-P	Wietmorschen
24.12.43	209	2:24	PE-K	Lille
30.12.43	210	3:30		Chalons
31.12.43	211	3:18	PE-K	Moelan
4. 1.44	212	2:48	PE-N	Munster
5. 1.44	213	2:48	PE-X	Chateaurenault
7. 1.44	215	3:00	PE-K	Arlon
24. 1.44	222	2:28	PE-R	Liege
25. 1.44	WO-6	2:18	PE-X	Gilze-Rijen
28. 1.44	WO-8	2:30		Harlingen.
30.	1.44	227	2:54		Ruhlertwist
6.	2.44	236	3:30	PE-K	Montmirial
8.	2.44	237	3:15	PE-D	Kruft
10.	2.44	239	2:05	PE-O	
11.	2.44	240	3:25	PE-B	Baulaide
13.	2.44	242	2:50	PE-Y	Doullens
24.	2.44	250	2:50	PE-K	Dummer Lake
25.	2.44	251	2:10	PE-K	
2.	3.44	257	3:25	PE-K	Wettenbach
3.	3.44	259	3:00	PE- I	Rech.
4.	3.44	260	3:00	PE-B	Sebhardshain
8.	3.44	263	3:30	PE-S	Berlin
9.	3.44	264	2:35	PE-X	Berlin
11.	3.44	265	2:20	PE-K	France
13.	3.44	267	3:00	PE-K	France
18.	3.44	273A	2:50	PE-Q	Augsberg
18.	3.44	273B	3:40	PE-Q	Augsberg
20.	3.44	275	1:55	PE-K	Aborted-weather
22.	3.44	277	2:50	PE-K	Berlin
23.	3.44	278	2:45	PE-Q	Pas de Calais
26.	3.44	281	2:40	PE-E	Pas de Calais
5.	4.44	288	0:50	PE-F	Aborted-radio
6.	4.44	289	1:55	PE-K	Watten
8.	4.44	291	3:00	PE-K	Dipholtz A/D
10.	4.44	293	3:00	PE-K	Reims
11.	4.44	295A	2:55	PE-C	Berlin
11.	4.44	295B	3:05	PE-C	Berlin
13.	4.44	298B	2:35	PE-K	Huy
15.	4.44	299	3:05	PE-Q	Dipholtz A/D
18.	4.44	304	2:30	PE-Q	N. Sea
22.	4.44	309B	2:50	PE-X	Hamm

P-51 Mustang Missions

24.	4.44	312	3:40	PE-M	N. Sea
25.	4.44	313	4:30	PE-Q	Neudenan

Date	No.	Time	Code	Location
26. 4.44	W.O. 19	2:45	PE-P	Cormeilles En Vexin A/D, France
26. 4.44	315	1:00	PE-P	Aborted-radio
28. 4.44	318	4:40	PE-P	Avord A/D
29. 4.44	320	5:05	PE-O	Berlin
1. 5.44	323	3:00	PE-O	Sens.
4. 5.44	326	3:10	PE-F	Celle.
7. 5.44	329	5:45	PE-A	Berlin
9. 5.44	333	4:00	PE-A	Juvencourt
12. 5.44	337	4:30	PE-X	N. Sea/Relay
13. 5.44	338	5:45	PE-E	Wustrew
21. 5.44	344	4:30	PE-Y	Stendal
31. 5.44	355	4:00	PE-J	Gutersloh
2. 6.44	359	3:05	PE-P	Paris
6. 6.44	371	3:45	PE-A	Montigny
7. 6.44	376	4:45	PE-P	Varnes
8. 6.44	377-2	3:50	PE-P	Nogent
10. 6.44	379	5:25	PE-D	Chartres
11. 6.44	382-1	4:50	PE-U	St.Florent
12. 6.44	383	5:05	PE-C	St. Aignan
14. 6.44	388	3:50	PE-U	Rethel
15. 6.44	390	2:30	PE-P	Preuilly
17. 6.44	394	3:45	PE-P	Bourron Marlotte
21. 6.44	407	5:15	PE-P	Jessern
24. 6.44	415	4:20	PE-P	Luneburg
25. 6.44	417	4:10	PE-P	Lagnieu
25. 6.44	418	4:30	PE-P	St.Martin
28. 6.44	421	1:40	PE-P	Lebach
29. 6.44	422	5:10	PE-P	Neiden
1. 7.44	425	2:35	PE-P	Beauvais, France
6. 7.44	435	3:15	PE-P	Beauvais, France
7. 7.44	436	5:15	PE-P	Leipzig
11. 7.44	441	4:00	PE-P	Munich
13. 7.44	444	2:00		Seeshaupt
14. 7.44	445	5:20		Queret
23. 7.44	460	4:20		Montreau
28. 7.44	469	5:35		Merseburg
31. 7.44	472	5:15		Freising
2. 8.44	474	4:40		Caborg
3. 8.44	477	4:05		Rouen
4. 8.44	478	5:45		Anklan

Decorations awarded to Robert H. Powell Jr.
Air Medal and 3 OLCs.
DFC and 2 OLCs.
Presidential Unit Citation.
European Theatre Award with 3 Battle Stars.

Claims made by Robert H. Powell Jr.
1 ME-110 Destroyed
1/3 HE-177 Destroyed
2 JU-88s Destroyed
2 HE-111 Destroyed
2 ME-210s Probably Destroyed
1 ME-109 Damaged
1 ME-110 Damaged
1 ME-410 Damaged
2 HE-111s Damaged

Aircraft assigned to Robert H. Powell Jr.

Thunderbolt. PE-K, 42-8657. This aircraft was also assigned to Lt. James L. Laing who named it 'Jamie Mi Boy' on the port side. Bob Powell had the name ''The West 'by Gawd' Virginian'' on the starboard cowling. This aircraft was transferred out in late April 1944 when the 352nd Fighter Group converted to the North American Mustang fighter.

Mustang. PE-P(bar), 42-106757. Assigned to Bob Powell in late April 1944. Legend painted on port lower exhaust stack was ''The West 'by Gawd' Virginian.'' This aircraft was crash-landed in mid-June 1944 and was listed as Salvaged, Non Battle Damage. Pilot or reason why crashed is not known.

Mustang. PE-P, 42-106914. Assigned to Bob Powell about 18th June 1944 and had ''The West 'by Gawd' Virginian'' painted on it. This A/C had Maltese cross victory symbols painted on it by the Armorer, Edwin L. Kingbury. The crosses were a fire engine red base circle with white crosses into which were painted black crosses. This is the A/C crashlanded on July 18, 1944 as related in text. The front half of the cowling is still in Bob's possession.

Mustang. PE-P, 44-13930. Assigned to Bob about the end of July 1944. Outline of West Virginia painted on port side just in front of the cockpit and inside a crossed pick and shovel were painted and the Latin legend 'Montani Semper Liberi' which, roughly translated, means 'Mountaineers Are Always Free.'

Bob's final Mustang in its revetment at Bodney, Norfolk. This aircraft survived the war.

(Powell Jr.)

Bob in the cockpit of his last Mustang PE-P, 44-13930. A new type of painting and his final tally of six kills are included. Later the words 'Montani Semper Liberi' were added.

(Powell Jr.)

JOHN F. THORNELL, JR.

328TH FIGHTER SQUADRON, 352ND FIGHTER GROUP

John Thornell was born in Stoughton, Massachusetts on April 19, 1921, his family later moving to Walpole, Massachusetts. He joined the USAAF on June 11, 1940 and whilst training served at Craig AFB and Mitchell Field - where he was commissioned. In February, 1943, he was assigned to the 328th Squadron of the 352nd Group and on March 9 it moved to Farmingdale, New York to begin training on the P-47 Thunderbolt.

The move to Camp Kilmer, NJ began on June 16 for embarkation on the *Queen Elizabeth.* The 352nd sailed on July 1, taking five days to cross and arrived at Clyde on July 6.

Group personnel were marched to the station at Gourock and for the next 24 hours travelled on to Watton in East Anglia, which was to be home base until they moved to Bodney, some five miles away.

After initial training, the 328th Squadron flew its first mission on September 9, 1943, a patrol over the North Sea, but was recalled after only five minutes over enemy territory. At this time Thornell was assigned his first aircraft, a P-47 coded PE-T, 42-8939, which he named 'Pattie Ann.'

On March 11, 1944, the 352nd Group's three squadrons of 16 Thunderbolts each, under the command of Colonel Joe Mason, were briefed to attack the submarine pens at St Nazaire, France. It was to be low level all the way, to prevent the Germans obtaining a radar fix. The night before, the group flew down to Ford in Sussex and topped up the gas tanks of the P-47s. The next morning it took off for St Nazaire as planned, but its presence had somehow been reported, either by radar or an offshore vessel, for the Thunderbolts met flak as they crossed the coast.

The group attacked the pens and on the way out strafed targets of opportunity and also made an attack on Abbeville. Leading a flight of four Thunderbolts, Thornell had Lt. Bill Schwenke in PE-S 42-8428 'Kathie' as his wingman. Both men attacked some parked aircraft on the airfield, Thornell getting some strikes on a captured B-17 and Lt. Schwenke damaging an engine of an HE 111. After pulling away, Thornell noticed that his colleague's aircraft had been hit and was losing a good deal of oil. The two pilots were over the Channel when Schwenke reported that his engine was quitting and he was bailing out.

Thornell called RAF air sea rescue and orbited. Meanwhile, Schwenke bailed out, although Thornell didn't see him climb into his dinghy, as he was low on fuel and had to break away.

As he crossed the English coast the fuel warning light came on and he decided to land at Hawkinge. On

Above: Jack Thornell of the 328th Fighter Squadron, 352nd Fighter Group. This photo was taken in the summer of 1944.

(via Thornell)

Below: Pilots of the 328th Fighter Squadron discuss the merits of a point fifty for the benefit of the group's photographer in front of Don Bryan's PE-B, 42-8381 'Little One.' From left to right is Fred 'Pappy' Yochim, Freddy Miller, Don S. Bryan and Jack Thornell Jr. All Bryan's aircraft were named 'Little One.'

(Powell Jr.)

Above: Two interesting pictures of Lt. John B. Coleman Jr. and his "Mavourneen," PE-J, 42-22529. He participated in the first 8th A.F. HE-177 kill with Bob Powell and Everett Stewart on Jan. 5, 1944. Even the most conservative estimates credit Coleman with 4.33 aerial victories.

(Mulron)

Below: Jack Thornell and his assigned aircraft PE-T, 42-8939 named 'Pattie Ann' after his niece. He was nicknamed "Direct Line" as he always got to hear 'scuttlebutt' first!

(Thornell)

landing approach the engine cut out and, although Thornell managed to land safely, while rolling down the grass runway he hit a steam roller preparing the turf for some returning Spitfires. The driver was uninjured, but the Thunderbolt's port wing sustained damage and the pitot tube was torn off. Calling Bodney to report his safe return and Lt Schwenke down in the Channel, he was told to return to Bodney as soon as possible. The RAF ground crews patched the wing, but were unable to repair the pitot tube and after refuelling, Thornell took off for Bodney.

As he approached his home base he called the tower to inform them that he had no air speed indicator and a Thunderbolt was sent up to make a formation landing with him. After landing he learned that no trace was found of Lt Schwenke and that the group had lost a total of nine aircraft for the day's mission.

On April 19, 1944, while on a mission to Northeim, Thornell shot down two FW 190s on his 23rd birthday. It was his first mission in a Mustang - coded PE-T, 42-106710 - and he was flying on attachment to the 486th Squadron as his own had not completed the changeover to the Mustang.

The squadron was flying at about 28,000 feet when Thornell saw some FW 190s below and called them in to the Squadron Leader, Lt Colonel W. O. Jackson, who led a diving attack on the enemy aircraft. At that moment Thornell's engine began to malfunction, but he continued on down. Being unfamiliar with the Mustang's trim with a full fuselage gas tank, he went into a spin as soon as he attempted to turn with a FW 190. He finally managed to correct the spin at around 13,000 feet. The dogfight was by now down to his level and in the ensuing combat, Thornell shot down two of the FW 190s, for which he was awarded the Silver Star. The citation read:

'For gallantry in action, while piloting a P-51 fighter aircraft on a bomber escort mission over Germany, April 19, 1944. When the engine of Lt. Thornell's plane developed a malfunction, he was unable to maintain contact with his unit and started the long return journey alone. Shortly thereafter, he observed a straggling B-17 being attacked by seven (7) FW 190s.

'Though out-numbered by the enemy, Lt Thornell made an aggressive head-on attack, heavily damaging one fighter and forcing the others to disperse. In the engagement which followed, he destroyed one FW 190 and then positioned himself on the tail of another, this in spite of the fact that his own aircraft was not operating properly. Pressing the attack tenaciously, he followed the enemy fighter down to tree top level, causing him to hit a tree, cartwheel and explode. The gallantry, aggressive fighting spirit and skill in combat displayed by Lt Thornell resulted in the dispersal of an enemy force which would have been a hazard to other bombers in the vicinity.'

By Command of
Lt Gen Doolittle.

Above, left: Henry 'Hank' White with his Thunderbolt PE-H, 42-8627 which he named 'Dallas Darling.' He flew with the 328th Fighter Squadron.

(Powell Jr.)

Above, right: Colonel James D. Mayden with his Mustang PE-X, 44-14111 'Straw Boss 2' (the name was on both sides). This had also been Joe Mason's Mustang.

(Powell Jr.)

Below: Jack Thornell and Lt. Col. K. L. Williams in front of a blue-nosed Mustang at Bodney, Norfolk, home of the 352nd Fighter Group.

(Thornell)

On May 28, the 352nd was detailed to escort bombers to Magdeburg. Over Brunswick it ran into a large formation of ME 109s and FW 190s making very determined attacks on the bomber stream. In the ensuing battle Carl Luksic shot down three FW 190s and two ME 109s to become the first Eighth Air Force fighter pilot to destroy five enemy aircraft on one mission. Thornell destroyed three ME 109s in the air and Johnny Meyer, Joe Mason and Clayton Davis also claimed victories. For the day, the group claimed 27-2-7 and was awarded a Presidential Citation. Thornell was awarded the DSC for his contribution.

On June 6, 1944, the group went on its first mission at dawn. As the 486th Squadron started to take off, Lt Robert Frascotti, flying his P-51B 'Umbriago', crashed near the Bodney control tower and was killed. The group made no claims against enemy aircraft on D-Day, but destroyed and damaged numerous ground targets; Thornell flew seven missions, totalling 15 hours. The day's work consisted of bombing targets just inland from the beachhead, flying back to base, the pilots waiting in their aircraft while they were re-fuelled and returning to France. The longest trip Thornell made was to St. Malo, a flight lasting six hours.

On June 10 the group gave aerial support to the 1st Canadian Division and British troops at Caen. Thornell was on patrol with a section of Mustangs when he spotted a gaggle of ME 109s carrying two bombs apiece. He gave the order to attack and in the following fight shot down two to be awarded a Cluster in his Silver Star. The citation read:

'For gallantry in action, while leading a flight of P-51 fighter aircraft, furnishing support for bombers on a mission over France June 10, 1944. During a strafing attack on a convoy of trucks, Captain Thornell and two members of his flight became separated from the balance of the squadron. Shortly afterwards, he saw a formation of approximately forty (40) ME 109s preparing to dive-bomb Allied positions near Caen. Completely disregarding the hazards of attacking such a vastly superior force, Captain Thornell led his flight in an aggressive assault.

'The enemy formation was so disrupted by the viciousness of his surprise attack that all except one flight jettisoned their bombs and turned to engage the three attackers. In the encounter which followed, his flight dispersed the enemy force, destroying three aircraft and damaging another, Captain Thornell personally accounting for the destruction of two of them. His gallantry and zeal in leading this daring attack are in keeping with the highest traditions of the Armed Forces of the United States.'

Thornell made what was to be his last claim against the Luftwaffe on June 21, when he helped in the destruction of an ME 410 in the air while on a mission to Jessern. He flew his last combat mission on July 11, which lasted five hours 20 minutes.

His ground crew during his time with the 328th Squadron was S/Sgt J. Walters, and Sgt. H. J. Whiteley. Besides Lt Bill Schwenke, Thornell's wingmen were Lt John Campbell (PE-C) shot down and killed over the Zuider Zee, and Lt Lawrence E. McCarthy (PE-M 44-13983, 'Patty IV') who destroyed three enemy aircraft.

Thornell left for the States on August 4, 1944. In the following year he married and he and his wife were to have six boys and two girls. He returned to Europe in 1946 and was stationed in Germany. From 1949 until 1951 he was in Turkey before returning to the States. In 1956 he again returned to England and lived at Northwood for a time. He went home in 1960 and was stationed at Williams AFB in Arizona until 1964, when

Two photos of Lt. Lawrence McCarthy's PE-M, 44-13983. He acted as Jack Thornell's wingman on many occasions. He had 2 1/2 aerial claims including a double on Feb. 20, 1944.

Decorations awarded to Lt Colonel John Thornell, Jr.

Awards	Authority	Basis of award
Air Medal	GO 51, HQ, 8 FC, 6 Dec 43	10 Sorties
OLC to AM	GO 57, HQ, 8 FC, 27 Dec 43	10 Sorties
OLC to AM	GO 5, HQ, 8 FC, 28 Jan 44	10 Sorties
OLC to AM	GO 12, HQ, 8 FC, 23 Feb 44	10 Sorties
DFC	GO 17, HQ, 8 FC, 7 Mar 44	40 Sorties, 1 E/A Destroyed
OLC to DFC	GO 33, HQ, 8 FC, 19 Apr 44	30 Sorties, 2 E/A Destroyed
OLC to DFC	GO 50, HQ, 8 FC, 17 June 44	30 Sorties, 2 E/A Destroyed
OLC to DFC	GO 59, HQ, 8 FC, 13 Jul 44	5 E/A Destroyed
OLC to DFC	GO 63, HQ, 8 FC, 27 Jul 44	5 E/A Destroyed
OLC to DFC	GO 72, HQ, 8 FC, 15 Aug 44	5 E/A Destroyed
OLC to AM	GO 406, HQ, IBD, 8 Oct 44	40 Hours
OLC to AM	GO 406, HQ, IBD, 8 Oct 44	40 Hours
Silver Star	GO 446, GQ, 8 AF, 5 Jun 44	Gallantry in Action
OLC to Silver Star	GO 467, HQ, 8 AF, 14 Jul 44	Gallantry in Action
DSC	GO 44, HQ, USSTAF, 22 Jul 44	Extraordinary Heroism

he transferred to Randolph AFB, Texas, where he was to stay for the next three years.

Thornell's present base is Norton AFB, California. In early 1970 he had a mild heart attack but has since resumed his duties as Inspector of Aircraft and was due to retire on July 31, 1971, after 31 years' service with the Air Force.

Known aircraft flown by Lt Colonel John Thornell, Jr.

Type	Serial	Code	
P-47D	42-8939	PE-T	'Pattie Ann'
P-51B	42-106710	PE-T	'Pattie Ann'
P-51B	42-106872	PE-T	'Pattie Ann'

Combat mission list of Lt. Colonel John F. Thornell, Jr. 328th Squadron, 352nd Fighter Group.

Date	F/O No	Duration	Location
9, 9, 1943	129	0.05	Recalled
14	130	1.06	Ter Neurzen
15	132	2.00	St Just
10, 8, 1943	151	2.30	Gramsbergen
10	153	2.50	Hamninkein
18	162	1.08	Aborted
11, 5, 1943	170	2.06	Dorstein
7	172	2.50	Zutphen
11	177	2.07	Enschide
25	WO-2	2.01	St Omer
26	191	0.05	Aborted
30	193	2.05	Weert
12, 1, 1943	194	2.06	Rheydt
5	196	2.05	Meulen
11	198	2.05	Winschten
13	199	2.07	Dorpen
22	207	2.06	Wietmorschen
24	209	2.06	Lille
30	210	4.00	Spotter
1, 4, 1944	212	2.08	Munster
7	215	2.09	Arlen
14	217	2.04	Bethune-Lille
28	WO-8	2.06	Harlingen
29	226	3.00	Pelm
30	227	2.07	Ruhlertwist
2, 3, 1944	233	3.15	Assen
4	234	2.45	Aldenhoven
5	235	3.05	St Caane
6	236	3.25	Montmirial
8	237	3.15	Relay
11	240	3.20	Baulaide
20	245	0.15	Relay
24	250	3.00	Dummer Lake
25	251	3.00	Lengay
29	255	3.00	Dummer Lake
3, 2, 1944	257	3.30	Wettenbach
3	259	0.30	Relay
4	260	3.00	Sebhardshain
6	262	1.05	Spotter
11	265	3.15	Pas de Calais

Above: Ace William J. Stangel of the 328th made all 5 of his victories on 2 missions: Nov. 2 and Dec. 25, 1944. Note swastika victory markings as on ''Patty IV,'' pictured on page 102.

Middle: The second P-51 (PE-L, 44-13401) assigned to Charles James Cesky who ended the war with 8.5 confirmed air victories. Frequently A/C scoreboards listed ground victories, probables and other pilot's claims in that A/C.

Below: Cesky and his blue-nosed ''Diann Ruth II.'' The majority of his claims were made in his first P-51, 44-13927, PE-L, the original ''Diann Ruth.''

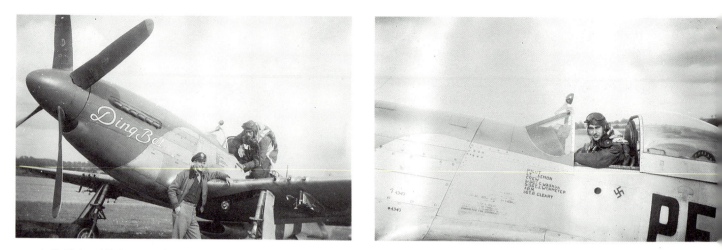

Left: Richard F. Semon with Lt. James F. Lambright on wing of P-51, 44-14343, PE-S, "Dingbat." Although assigned to Semon, both men flew this A/C in combat.

(Semon)

Right: Lt. Lambright off on another mission in the "Dingbat." Buddy Washuh and rest of crew names clearly (we hope!) visible. Note last 4 digits of serial on engine panels done by ground crews to insure proper replacement - Also a subsequent boon to Av-Historians!!

(Semon)

13	267	3.00	Valencienne	4	326	3.00	Celle
15	269	3.05	Urk	7	329	5.45	Berlin
20	275	2.00	Aborted	8	331	4.30	Brunswick
22	277	3.00	Queskenbruck	11	335	3.15	Luplante
26	281	2.40	Valencienne	13	338	5.40	Wustrew
27	282	2.20	Alancon	19	342	0.00	Aborted
28	283	3.15	Reims	2 0	343	3.30	Marne
4, 1, 1944	286	2.45	Weiswempack	21	344	4.35	Stendal
6	289	2.00	Watten	22	346	3.20	Brunswick
10	293	2.40	Reims	25	350	2.50	Marche
11	295A	3.00	Berlin	27	351	4.30	Pforzhein
11	295B	3.10	Spotter	28	352	4.50	Rechlitz
13	298B	2.30	Huy	29	353	5.00	Nord Point
15	299	3.10	Dummer Lake	31st	355	4.00	Gutersloh
19	305A	4.15	Northeim	6, 4, 1944	368B	3.00	Boisville
22	309B	0.45	Returned Early	6	371	6.00	Malo
23	WO-17	4.00	Tours	7	376	4.40	Varnes
5, 1, 1944	322	4.10	Sens	8	377-3	3.00	Nogent
				10	379	5.00	Chartres
				11	382-1	4.50	Nantes
				12	383	5.10	St Aignan
				18	396	4.30	Hildeshein
				20	402	3.45	Ziesar
				20	405	2.45	Soissons
				21	407	5.20	Jessern
				23	413	2.00	Melun
				24	415	4.20	Luneberg
				25	417	2.00	Lagnieu
				25	418	4.30	St Martin
				28	421	4.00	Lebach
				29	422	4.50	Neiden
				7, 5, 1944	430	3.00	Nivelles
				6	433	3.50	Beauvis
				6	435	3.10	Beauvis
				7	436	5.10	Leipzig
				8	437	4.20	Coursen
				11	441	5.20	Glenn

Smile pretty for the camera, John, 17.25 confirmed air vics "ain't too shabby"!

Above: The 328th over Belgium - early '45.

(U.S.A.F.)

Below: Capt. W. Riley, Provost Marshal at Bodney, gives his congratulations to John Thornell who has just successfully completed his last operational mission July 11, 1944.

A beautiful shot of Herb in his office. Note armor plate, radio, K-14 gunsight, maps etc. Small perspec hood over rear view mirror atop canopy was said to add 3 mph.

(Rutland)

HERBERT R. RUTLAND, JR.
360TH FIGHTER SQUADRON,
356TH FIGHTER GROUP

Herbert R. Rutland, Jr. was born March 1, 1922 to Herbert and Dorothy Rutland in Chattanooga, Tennessee. He attended the local grammar school and another later on in Washington, D.C. He graduated from high school in June 1940, continuing his education with one year at the University of Tennessee and a year at George Washington University. In the summer of 1942 he was accepted as an Army Air Force cadet and was posted to Miami Beach, Florida for his basic training February 5, 1943. He was part of the first class at Danville, Kentucky and from there he went to Nashville, Tennessee for his primary training and upon completion he joined the AAF Pilots School, Newport, Arkansas. On February 15 he was posted to Spence Field, Moultrie, Georgia for his Advanced Training and while there flew the AT-6. Upon completion of his training he converted to the P-47 Thunderbolt at Johnson AFB, North Carolina. More training

followed at Dover AAB, Delaware and on December 10 he reported to the Overseas Processing Camp at Richmond, Virginia. Eleven days later he arrived at Camp Kilmer, New Jersey on his way to the ETO. Herb recalls:

"The year was 1944, and it was Christmas Eve. For some twenty-three months the Army Air Force had been preparing me for this moment. They would now put me to work at earning my pay. The troop train from Camp Kilmer, New Jersey had deposited its passengers at the point of embarkation - the west side of New York harbor. I and my fellow pilots felt misplaced as we climbed the gangplank, loaded with battle gear befitting the best of infantryman, down to the steel helmet and laced leggings. At that point few would have guessed that the S.S. Vollendam would be our home for the next twenty-one days, as was the case.

The appearance of this vessel did not inspire a lot of confidence. For several years this converted civilian ship had carried its human cargo between distant points of the globe. We heard a rumor that it had survived several attacks by Jerry U-boats. It was now un-

the English mess attendants carefully polishing the tableware on their dubious looking aprons; this practice was finally discouraged when it became apparent that each attendant was issued but one apron for the entire round trip. By contrast, enlisted personnel stood in line for hours on the open deck to be handed food that, if at all edible, would not stay down for too long.

Except for the pilots on board, it seems that everyone was seasick during the entire voyage. Winter storms in the North Atlantic are unpleasant, even on the finest of luxury liners, and this the Vollendam was not! Due to the rough seas, poor food and a large measure of anxiety, the odor of vomit permeated the entire ship, and you had to watch where you stepped. After a brief visit to the holds where the enlisted men were packed like sardines, it began to make sense to us why the Air Force officers had been elected to stand watch; presumably those who could resist air sickness could likewise fend off sea sickness as well!

In their frantic search for fresh air, many enlisted men found refuge in the lifeboats along the sides of the ship. It was also quickly discovered that each lifeboat contained a store of emergency rations which were far superior to the ship's fare. Thus, those who chose to sleep in sub-freezing ocean air had to routinely be rousted out of the lifeboats - sometimes almost at gunpoint. There was every reason for troop morale to be low at that time. Frustration was vented in various ways. The value of our steel helmets became manifest one dark, miserable night when a heavy steel bolt, dropped from an upper deck, clanged off the helmet of one of the pilots standing watch.

der the command of the British and was crewed by Dutchmen. As our contingent of Air Force officers boarded early, it was immediately assigned 'Ship Police' duty for the duration of the voyage. The pilots were organized to stand four-hour watches throughout the ship, twenty-four hours a day. Later, upon arrival of a vast number of infantry enlisted and officer personnel, the Air Force continued to man the watches, while the infantry officers lounged in the room given the grand title of 'Saloon' and chided us pilots with frequent comments on what a good job we were doing.

In true British fashion, the commissioned officers were afforded better accommodations than the enlisted men. This was not to say a lot, as the food was uniformly terrible, and the 'staterooms' into which the officers were crowded were claustrophobic. Officers' meals were served twice each day in the saloon, with

Above left: Aerial view of Martlesham Heath, wartime home of the 356th.

(Miller)

Left: Captain William C. Brearly and his ship ''Princess Jocelyn'' of the 359th F.S./356 F.G. One of the old hands, he was assigned to the 356th in February 1943 and was still serving V-E Day. He was on the mission to Hagenau when group C.O. Malmstrom went down.

(U.S.A.F.)

Below: Col. Einar Malmstrom, Group C.O. from Nov. '43 until he became a P.O.W. Apr. 23, 1944. Both his P-47s coded QI-R and named ''Kay-J.''

(Mulron)

Some of you may remember the photo on page 295 of the original "Aces and Wingmen," but this is not the same A/C despite vastly similar markings. This one, OC-G, 42-26331, belongs to Lt. Lee F. Richason of the 369th F.S.

(Miller)

Our convoy was gigantic, extending to the horizon in all directions. Escort vessels slashed through the high waves - often disappearing completely from sight in the deep troughs. In line and in front of our ship was a very large U.S. Troop Transport, the 'General Brooke.' During much of the voyage the 'Brooke's' propellor would emerge from the sea as she pitched. She would then list far to port, and then to starboard. Sixteen months later I returned to the States on the 'General Brooke.'

Most of the tankers in our convoy carried at least one fighter aircraft, with wings removed, tied to the deck. After each particularly rough night we would scan the convoy to see if any of the fighters had been swept from the decks. We also counted the ships as best we could. The U-boat activity picked up, and such a large convoy as ours could not fail to attract their attention. As the voyage progressed, we began to hear more and more exploding depth charges set off by our escort. These were both alarming and at the same time reassuring. I never found out if it was true or not, but it was rumoured that several ships belonging to our convoy were hit and had sunk during the long passage to Europe.

L to R: Maj. Mark J. Burke, Lt. James H. Wadlow, and Capt. Richard A. Rann. Rann had 4 different assigned A/C from Nov. '43 until he became a P.O.W. Feb. 25, 45, the last 3 coded OC-R.

(Miller via Blake)

After about fifteen days we sighted land at last, but our journey was not yet over. We lay off the Isle of Wight for a day and then slipped across the Channel in the dead of night to disembark most of the infantry troops at Le Havre. Many of these troops were rushed to the front and were quickly involved in the Battle of the Bulge, all within 48 hours. Having departed our convoy, the Vollendam headed for Scotland with a modest escort of small naval units. The Jerry U-boats were still on the scent, however, and we were forced to take shelter somewhere in the Bristol Channel near Cardiff, Wales. On or about 14th January, 1945 we at last anchored at Gourock, Scotland. There I met up with several of my pilot friends whom I had last seen at Camp Kilmer on Christmas Eve. They had just arrived on a fast luxury liner which had been converted into a troop ship and had taken just six days to cross the Atlantic without an escort. They had also enjoyed a Christmas leave in the process. But, I think, they missed all the fun!

From Gourock we were shipped by train to the 70th Replacement Depot at Stone, Staffordshire. It was from here that all fighter pilots were assigned to units in England and on the Continent. It was here that I witnessed the largest poker game I have ever seen. It went on night and day, with two dealers and a double deck. Some, who had won a big wad on the ship coming over here, lost everything. Here, too, was evidence of wartime shortages not known in the States. A new deck of playing cards went for ten dollars, while American whiskey brought ten pounds sterling (about 40 dollars) a fifth. At this point the Baptist chaplain that had shared our stateroom, along with two other men of the cloth, opened his barracks bag and pulled forth two quarts of 'Old Grand Dad', and sold them both. The Catholic chaplain who had contributed so heavily towards the depletion of the booze in our stateroom walked up to his fellow cleric and was heard to whisper "you Sonovabitch."

It was a well-known fact among the pilots that the Eighth Air Force had, by then, re-equipped with the North American P-51 Mustang. All except the 56th Fighter Group, which kept the Thunderbolt at the insistence of Dave Schilling. And I, like many pilots at the replacement depot, had been trained in the Thunderbolt. It was also well established that over on the Continent the Ninth Air Force and the First Tactical Air Force were using the Jug as their principal weapon in the ground support role. It was also clear to most of us that the war was winding down, and if one was to make his mark in the annals of aerial warfare, there was very little time to do it in. At the depot we were given a questionnaire to complete regarding our choice of assignment by LOCATION! I do not recall any reference to what type of airplane one would prefer to fly in combat. I would guess that most pilots chose the plane they had been trained in and which, by then, had gained their confidence. But a few, for whatever reason, were set on the Mustang - even though transition training would be needed before entering combat. Therefore, most of my friends and I quickly put down the NINTH AIR FORCE hopefully securing for ourselves a very good chance of flying our beloved Jug in combat. Those who were obsessed with the sleek, new Mustang figured the odds (about 13 to 1) and wrote in the EIGHTH AIR FORCE.

That the military works in strange ways was then demonstrated to the dismay of almost everyone. It seems the pilots who chose the Eighth Air Force, in the hopes of flying the Mustang, were given their wish. However, their assignment to the 56th Fighter Group found them in the only Thunderbolt group in the 8th Air Force. Most of those who had opted for the Continent and the Thunderbolt were denied their preference and were also assigned to the Eighth, but they were dispersed among several groups - all flying the Mustang. A few lucky ones managed to end up on the Continent - presumedly in the fighter of their choice. Ironically, none of the pilots I have since spoken to harbor any serious regret at the hand fate dealt them. There were worse alternatives. Some weeks after joining our respective groups the pilots who had trained together at Dover, Delaware in Jugs were shocked to hear that two of their number had perished in a mid-air collision over England. A Thunderbolt from the 56th Fighter Group had engaged a Mustang from the 356th Fighter Group in a simulated dogfight during 'local training.' Somehow neither of the two friends broke away from a head-on pass.

On 24th January, 1945 twenty-two new pilots arrived at Martlesham Heath just outside of Ipswich, Suffolk to join the 356th Fighter Group. These were divided, more or less evenly, among the three fighter squadrons that made-up the group; the 359th, 360th and 361st. The 360th was billeted several miles from the base in Playford Hall. The 359th occupied another stately home, namely Kesgrove Hall. The 361st had to rough it on base.

It's with a degree of guilt that I admit, if one must fight a war, ours was the way to do it! Considering that many of our brethren faced incredibly harsh environments from Attu in the Aleutians to the deserts of North Africa, life at Playford was nothing less than plush. Some thirty officers enjoyed the comforts of home, replete with added amenities even beyond. Several resident enlisted types ran the supply, while a civilian kitchen staff prepared home-style meals in the morning and in the evening. Dick, the bartender, managed the little bar in the living room, and Freddie, the batman, shined shoes and gave wake-up calls each morning. Don, a golden retriever, was a pal to all and loved to jump into the moat for any reason at all.

Above: The first assigned P-47 of Col. Don Baccus, OC-T, 42-8568, "The Bloody Shaft." Below: 2 shots of Don's second P-47, in unhappy circumstances. It is not known whether his A/C carried any personal markings, certainly none were visible at this time.

Above: 2 pictures of Capt. Jack Brown's OC-A #44-11366 before and after an aerial collision with Lt. Fred W. Bruner's OC-O, 44-15403, Feb. 1, 1945. Photos Jim Crow and Kent Miller. Note: Much of the info in this section from Kent's invaluable but O/P work, "Escort, the 356th Ftr. Grp. on operations over Europe 1943-45."

Below: The "Spirit of Aggieland," pride and joy of pilot Lt. Luther E. Bennett Jr. sits on its hardstand.

Social evenings were occasionally arranged - expedited by driving a six-by-six vehicle into the centre of Ipswich and dropping the tailgate. At the mention of 'Playford, Playford' the truck would be quickly filled with the local 'talent' and then return to our quarters. However, reality would return with a rush as we boarded the same trucks for the daily, rattling trip to the base. On these trips it always seemed to be dark and cold . . . and generally very quiet.

On February 3, 1945 I completed my first transitional flight in a P-51B. The changeover from the heavier Thunderbolt caused me no problems. The Mustang did not slow as rapidly as the Jug when the power was cut back, and the Mustang seemed to accelerate much more quickly when the power was added. This would have to be considered by one accustomed to the responses of the Jug when in a combat situation calling for maximum demands on the aircraft.

My first formation flight in the Mustang was a revelation, and an experience that I remember to this day. I took off on the wing of Captain Ed Pleasant, a combat veteran and an exceptional fighter pilot. Ed had no sooner retracted his gear when I noticed that he had unsnapped his oxygen mask and was moving it to one side. The next I knew Ed had stuck a cigar in his mouth

and was calmly proceeding to light it up with his Zippo lighter, using both hands to assist the lighting. At that moment I know we were still under two hundred feet altitude. During this operation his ship was as steady as the proverbial rock. He finally glanced over at me and casually motioned me to move closer to his wing. I was already in the standard close formation, with my wingtip three feet out from and three feet below his wing. I moved in another two feet. After gaining some more altitude, Ed again looked over at me and again motioned me to get closer. This I did, until our wings were overlapping by at least three feet. Ed seemed to be happy as he returned to puffing strongly on his cigar. He had more confidence in me than I had in myself, and I was happy to move out to a more comfortable distance . . . while wondering what there was about the ETO that made smoking in aircraft acceptable!

By February 28, 1945 I had eleven training flights and had accumulated ten hours and forty minutes in the P-51. At last combat ready, and on March 1st, my 23rd birthday, I joined the 360th Fighter Squadron on my first combat mission. The fact was that I was just along for the ride. I concentrated so much on holding a good formation and checking everything that the whole Luftwaffe could have flown by without my noticing. Fortunately, nothing like that happened, and the entire mission was quiet and uneventful (a problem that seemed to plague the 356th for most of the war).

After about the third or fourth mission I began to feel quite comfortable with my new aircraft. And more importantly, I was learning to look out and really see things, while at the same time sensing every move of my element leader. With my increased confidence came a feeling of great impatience. I had yet to see an enemy fighter aloft. It was only years later that I fully came to realize the full implications of the situation. If we were meeting the objectives of our role as fighter pilots there should not be any enemy fighters

Another wounded bird. This time Capt. Louis L. Robertson's #44-15308. U.S.A.F. photo caption lists battle damage - Must have been fun getting it home! Nov 26, 1944.

(USAF via Miller)

in the skies. At full group strength there would be 60 or more fighters on a mission. In maintaining the integrity of this mighty force throughout the escort route, sometimes over a distance of 500 miles, and returning all planes safely to base, we had done our job in the classic sense. But the hopes of a young fighter pilot were not necessarily those of the Wing Command. The fighter pilot wanted action, not just results . . .

It is easy to face the foe bravely when you have him outnumbered, outgunned and psychologically intimidated. It is also likely that men will not give their all in a cause that is perceived as hopeless. Consequently, the air war in Europe took on a different complexion as the Luftwaffe assumed a defensive role. By early 1945 the German Fighter Command had become decimated through the relentless demands imposed on it by its leaders. What remained of the once dreaded Luftwaffe was a small nucleus of wiley old foxes with the instinct to survive in the air — together with a large number of young relatively inexperienced pilots — schooled more in Nazi doctrine than aerial warfare and survival. The tactics involved a few of the old hands leading a gaggle of the inexperienced pilots. This scheme failed to prove effective. More than likely the formation would break-up in confusion and disarray, even if attacked by a much smaller force of Allied fighters and the losses were horrendous.

However, nothing could be taken for granted. As manpower and materials became more and more critical in a shrinking Germany, the old foxes began to enter the fray in the 262 jet fighter. Many an Allied plane fell victim to these old masters, who often attacked singly, or in pairs, employing every tactical advantage that they had learned through many years of combat experience. They were cool, calculating, and deadly - to bomber and fighter alike. As the war drew to a close a squadron of these elite German pilots was formed under the command of Adolf Galland (who had previously held the post of `General of the Fighters' under Goring). This squadron was equipped with

the ME-262 and was a force to be reckoned with. The four top scoring pilots had a total of over 750 kills to their credit up to that time. So, even with the Allied superiority in numbers, our young pilots were ill advised to approach any air encounter in a careless or cavalier manner.

Despite its speed and performance at altitude, the Germans recognized that the ME-262 was not invincible. Its fuel consumption was enormous and that limited its range and endurance. It was particularly vulnerable during takeoff and landing. Allied fighter pilots made full use of this. The German pilots could pick and choose their targets from the smorgasbord so generously laid out by the Allied Air Forces. So, aerial targets of opportunity became the vogue. Thus, operating in small numbers, they would seek unwary victims, strike, and be gone before the alarm could be sounded. But, even so, they had to come down sooner or later. It was at these times they had to run the gauntlet of Mustangs and Thunderbolts that might drop down from the vast umbrella of fighters above. I am sure that many of the German jets shot down by

Below & Bottom: The P-51 of Lt. Col. Wayne E. Rhynard, with artwork Stb. only. Wayne transferred from the 79th in the MTO and flew with the 359 F.G. from Feb. 45 to V.E. Day.

(Miller, Bennett)

piston-engined fighters were 'cut off at the pass' after making their diving attack. If a sweeping turn was required to return to their base, Allied fighters might well intercept the faster plane through speed gained in a long dive and by planning their angle of approach carefully. With a little luck, the Jerry pilot would be low on fuel and without any alternative but to land. As time was running out for Germany, the Luftwaffe was compressed into fewer and fewer airfields. But, these airfields were defended by awesome concentrations of anti-aircraft weapons. While Allied fighter losses had diminished due to aerial combat the ground-fire took its toll.

Such were things as I commenced my short combat tour, which lasted just 51 days, during which I completed 20 combat missions over Germany. In that brief time, I accumulated just over one hundred hours - about one third a tour of duty! The 8th Air Force Fighter Command flew its last mission on May 7, 1945 when my good friend Mike Yannell led thirty Mustangs on a leaflet dropping mission over Germany. A total of fifteen B-17s were escorted. I flew my last mission on April 20.

I was among the many fighter pilots who felt the satisfaction of having been a part of the final victory in Europe, but whose role was that of journeyman rather

3 different A/C of Capt. Raymond R. Withers. He completed 105 missions with the 360th before his transfer to the 359th in Nov 44. All his known assigned A/C carried the name ``Kathleen'' or ``Kathleen Ann.''

(Ivie/Blake/Bennett)

than hero. Collectively, we had done the job that Uncle Sam had trained us for. Personally, I had achieved my lifelong dream of flying. More importantly, I had experienced a period of fellowship and trust rarely equalled in life and had formed friendships that are still strong today. There are countless stories to be told of flying exploits and my story is just one of these; it is a random collection of thoughts relating to my own personal experiences. The astigmatism of time may have obscured certain dates and places but on the other hand, I can bring back other scenes in graphic detail, just as if they had occurred only yesterday!''

Herb's brief combat tour covered just a matter of a few weeks but he, like many others, was living through extremely eventful times and following are some of his recollections:

1st March 1945 through 20th April 1945.
Mission - Escorting B-17s to target:
Our flight weaves back and forth above the bomber formation. I can see faces peering from the gun ports of the Flying Fortresses. Also, movement of the turrets as the nervous gunners track our Mustangs. The gunners are known to be nervous about approaching fighters, and I hope they identify us as friends. Now smoke appears to be blowing back from some of the bombers. Are they firing on us, I wonder? My headset

Above: PI-B, #42-74714 "Gremlin Express" was the assigned A/C of Lt. Norman D. Cota. Above left: shows Norman on an escort mission, while in the photo at right, the "Express" forms the backdrop for an awards ceremony. Below: Capt. Preston W. Easley's "Virginia Squire." A/C previously flown by Capt. Bertrum Ellingson who spent 2 years with the 360th, from Feb. '43 - Mar. '45. (Miller)

explodes as someone yells out "They're firing at us!" The squadron leader cuts in and says "Relax! Thats just chaff they're dumping out."

Mission - Escorting B-17s to the target. Over the Ruhr Valley:

They don't call this place "Flak Alley" for nothing. We are keeping well away from the 'Big Friends,' but within distance to help out if and when needed. Just at this moment there is not much we can do as there are no Jerry fighters because of the flak. The sky ahead of the bombers becomes darkened with bursts, whose black smoke seems to beckon to the oncoming bombers. The Forts plow ahead as though they were aiming for the densest concentration of the black puffs, which now merge with the leading elements of the first squadron. Now the worst is over and the first bombers poke their noses through the murderous flak. Flames emit from two of the bombers which stubbornly hold their position. One of the bombers falters as flames begin to spread, and as we watch several small objects fall from the fuselage. One parachute opens too early and catches alight. To our growing horror the second parachutist suffers the same fate. We are powerless to help and I no longer care to look; all I can do is hope.

Mission - Attack enemy airfield where a previous mission had reported many enemy aircraft:

We drop down and find the field as reported. I can see many aircraft poorly hidden from our position, but I cannot identify by type from this height. Our squadron leader descends gradually as we circle just above the reach of the light ack-ack. I prepare for the expected dive and switch on my guns. Our leader then rocks his wings and heads away from the airfield. I am disgusted at leaving this inviting target and I wonder why? At debriefing the answer is forthcoming. It was a flak trap! The airplanes were dummies, placed there to attract the attention of fighter pilots. Through his binoculars, our squadron leader detected countless gun emplacements all around the field. Too good to be true!

Mission - High altitude fighter sweep deep into Germany:

My altimeter reads over 30,000 feet and I have stomach cramps as the gas expands. I am on full oxygen, but a feeling of light-headedness persists. I am cold, very cold, and it seems to be getting colder still. I grope round for the cockpit heater control, which is low beside the seat and out of sight. I don't know if it's set at maximum heating or if I've set it up wrong. I'm shivering and freezing my butt off. Ego prevents me from switching my radio over to seek advice. The first thing I'll do when I get back to Martlesham Heath is to get my crew chief to show me how the damned heater controls work.

Mission - Strafing attack on an airfield near Schwerin:

I am flying number four in the lead flight of the 360th squadron as our leader dives towards an enemy field below. As I watch, my airspeed indicator climbs toward the 400 MPH mark. I think to myself that this is not at all like the Stateside gunnery patterns that we were taught with their well-defined targets. I concentrate on holding position and trimming PI-R to fly a straight course. I recall a previous mission and the hole shot in my wing by someone who was in a follow-

Mustangs of the 356th complete a turn to port as they head into Germany on bomber escort duties in January 1945. This superb photo was taken by Herb from the cockpit of his A/C.

ing flight when he skidded behind me in a firing pass. As the field approaches, I try to pick out a suitable target. There is very little room for changing direction, so my line of attack will determine what I'll be able to shoot at. As usual, the flight leaders will focus on the most promising targets on the ground. Wingmen will stay with them and take the leftovers, if any. Just as we scream over the edge of the field I glimpse a German aircraft directly in front of me. It seems to have been hit before, as one wing dangles down at an odd angle, presenting me with a large black cross to centre in my gunsight. I decide to give it a good burst just for luck and press the trigger.

Just as my bullets start to strike, my eye catches the ominous flashes of ground-fire pointed at me from a spot on the ground between me and the damaged Jerry aircraft. I dropped the nose of my Mustang down enough to spray the source of the aggravating muzzle flashes. We are so low that this action is regretted immediately, as I fly through a wall of dirt, muck, rocks and debris that my six fifties have sent skywards in a cloud. It is with disbelief that I find myself safely past the field and climbing to join my leader. That we will not make another pass at the field bothers me not in the least.

We are heading west and the clouds now cover all the land below. We have a long way to go when I see that my oil pressure has dropped to about 20 pounds which is *bad news.* I radio this fact to my leader, and he slides over to look at my ship. Aside from several dents in the leading edge of my wings, he finds that everything is still where it ought to be and so we continue on our way. The Packard Merlin continues to churn away without protest while I keep an eye on the gauges. I am cautioned to set in high manifold pressure and low revs so as to lessen the strain on the engine. I'm warned not to try to let down through the overcast if the engine quits altogether, but to bail out. No engine, no gauges. I go over the bail out procedure in my mind; disconnect all hoses and wires that connect me to the cockpit before stepping over the side. Ground control advises us that we are near Bremen, and at that time there is still fighting going on so that was definitely a no-no. Then comes the welcome message that we have crossed the Rhine.

My squadron leader takes us down through a hole in the cloud base that sweet providence has provided and points to a small, flat field below us. I saw a short, temporary runway that had been laid out, and on it were several light reconnaisance planes with US insig-

Above, left: Another great photo by Herb Rutland, this time capturing his fellow 360th squadron mates Lt. James Charleton (PI-B, 44-15189), Lt. George Seanor (PI-O, 44-15300) and Lt. George Schalck (PI-X, 44-63283). Above, right: Lt. Herb Rutland's P-51. Now here's one for you, the serial # is 44-72931! You're looking right at the A/C and it clearly says # 44-72139, right? Wrong! When the serial # was reapplied after painting the rudder, it was done wrong . . . ! Cute Huh? (Rutland) Below, left: Lt. Robert E. Barnhart of the 360th F.S. who claimed an AR-234 on March 14, 1945. Note missing stainless exhaust covers and twin mirrors on his ''Margie Darling.'' Below, right: Mike Yannell's last P-51 ''Audrey 4.'' Name was black outlined in yellow. Pretty A/C - any one know the serial #?

nia in their wings. I thank Mr. Rolls and Mr. Royce and the Merlin, chop the throttle and touch down on the pierced steel planking that had not been fully secured into place. I am on the ground examining the dents in my wings and the scrapes put in the Mustang's belly by the loose PSP when an American jeep arrived. The driver had attached a pair of wire cutters to his bumper and to add insult to injury this hit my wingtip leaving another gash. It just wasn't my day. It happens to be Friday, 13th April! I spent the night in a tent with some US Artillery guys and later hitched a ride back to England. On the way home I visited Paris and I could hear distant booms echoing from across the Rhine in the direction of Dusseldorf.

Mission - Fighter Sweep - Germany.
I lead an element for the first time.

Mustangs are out in force today. The sky is clear with its deep blue outlining the contrails from the Mustangs as we fly out in squadron formation. We are very high, and the enemy has not yet appeared. Well ahead of our formation and several miles to our left, a formation of 18 or 20 Bogies appear at our exact altitude. They do not approach in an unfriendly manner and both formations hold their courses. Now their out-

lines become clear and we see they are Mustangs, but they are on a course that will intersect ours at a ninety degree angle. It is obvious someone will have to turn, and quickly. There is a lot of chatter on the radio, and if our squadron leader calls for a quick break to the left or right it will not be heard over the chatter. A collision of our two formations seems a certainty, and at this precise moment some forty odd aircraft scatter to the four winds. My flight leader breaks so suddenly that I do not attempt to follow, and I concentrate on avoiding other aircraft in the sky. Now I am alone and as I look around I see, to my surprise, that my wingman is still with me. He moves in close and waves.

To reform with the other ships is out of the question, so I take a heading of 270 and head for home. Up ahead and going away I see a bogie. It could be a ME-262 judging from the silhouetted wing pods that I can just barely make out. I push the throttle forward and slowly close on the bogie. He now sees us, and to my disappointment I see the 'wing pods' separate from the aircraft and tumble down towards the earth. The Mustang, for that is what it turned out to be, had dropped his external wing tanks and started to rock his ship violently. I rocked my wings in reply, and the lost pilot slows down and the three of us join up.

Capt. David F. Thwaites, an ace of the 361st F.S., taxis in after a mission over Germany. This was his first P-47. Both were coded QI-L and named "Polly." (D. Thwaites) The crew of "Clarkie" with their A/C, QI-F, 42-74702. L to R: Armorer Elwin D. Phillips, Capt. Sidney Hewett, C/C Bennie Giardiniere and Assnt. C/C Mike Yahwak. Note name "Lanny" on tail under serial and 3 kill markings indicating photo was most probably taken in early April 1944. A later photo of Hewett on the wing of his "Clarkie" showing the markings to advantage. He was shot down and captured May 4, 1944. (S. Hewett)

I see that we now share the sky with another bogie who is angling towards us from behind. I watch him very closely until I can see that it is another Mustang and therefore a friend. He continues our way and I dip my wing as an invitation to join our flight, which now represents three different 8th Air Force fighter groups. Through the haze below I can see the Hook of Holland and feel quite pleased with my navigation. As the coast of England appears ahead, our two friends give a good-bye wave and go their separate ways. I wonder if they would have tagged onto my element if they'd known I'd never led a flight over Germany before!

Mission: High altitude fighter sweep over Germany.

The sky is a deep purple and completely cloudless. We are at our maximum altitude and in battle formation. As usual, no Jerries are to be seen, and I speculate if I will ever get to see one in the air. I remind myself to keep looking around none the less. I scan the sky in all directions and then I happened to glance directly upwards. There, a thousand feet above us are two of the most beautiful aircraft I have ever seen. Under their sky-blue wings I cannot miss the largest black crosses in the world! My surprise and elation is then jarred by the thought that if these two are above us, then how many more are there pouring down on our squadron? By now the radio squawks with belated warnings. I rack my head round trying to see behind, fully expecting to see other jets slashing into our formation. But there are none to be seen. These two above us have decided not to take us on and are content to flaunt themselves in front of us. The speed of the two enemy jets is just terrific as they calmly pull away, just keeping out of firing range. I pull the nose of my Mustang up and let off a short burst in their direction but in doing so I loose flying speed. I have to work damn hard to regain my place within the formation and the lesson is well and truly brought home to me that you must keep your head turning all the time and look into every piece of the sky. Others, too are looking around intently and I hear calls over the radio of "Bogie! Ten o'clock high!" I look but fail to see the bogie at first. Then, there he is, a slender contrail high above — apparently turning very sharply. Another voice breaks in: "Take it easy, stupid; that's the moon." He's right.

Mission: Local flying on a training mission, Martlesham Heath, East Anglia

I enjoy the opportunity to cruise around on a leisurely flight near my home base.

Radio: "Mayday, Mayday"

Tower: "Read you Mustang, what's the problem?"

Mustang: "This darned 'ol dinghy done inflated on me."

Tower: "Can you control your airplane?"

Mustang: ``Yeah, but its hard to reach the pedals.''

Second Mustang in the air: ``Well, just take your knife and puncture the raft.''

Mustang: ``What knife?''

Second Mustang: ``Isn't there a knife taped to the stick?''

Mustang: ``Not in this damned airplane.''

Tower: ``Mustang, how are you doing?''

Mustang: ``This thing is squeezing the shit out of me!''

Third Mustang in the air: ``Why not just bail out of there and be done with it?''

Tower: ``Don't you have a pocket knife?''

Mustang: ``Sure do.''

Tower: ``Then use it.''

Second Mustang: ``Probably left it at home.''

Mustang: ``That's where it is.''

Tower: ``How's your fuel?''

Mustang: ``Twenty minutes, maybe.''

Third Mustang in the air: ``I still say bail out!''

Mustang: ``Screw you, Brother.''

Tower: ``Don't you have a pencil or a pen to stick into the raft?''

Mustang: ``Hell no. Do you think I came up here to write a letter?''

A period of silence . . .

Tower: ``Mustang, are you going to be able to land your aircraft?''

Mustang: ``In a few minutes. I think I've got it now.''

Tower: ``How's that?''

Mustang: ``I managed to put a few holes in it with the fastener of my wrist watch strap. It's starting to go down slowly.''

Tower: ``Mustang, you're cleared to land when ready.''

Mission: Group takeoff at Martlesham Heath

We wait our turn to swing onto the runway and takeoff in pairs. I watch my flight leader to my left as he advances the throttle and begins his takeoff roll. We gain speed and I feel my own ship become airborne as the leader's wheels leave the ground. I grab the retraction lever on the lower left console and pull it inward and upwards and the gear starts to retract. My leader is pulling ahead, and I sense that my ship is sinking towards the runway. I ram the throttle forward in panic and start praying. The sinking stops and my bird starts to gain some altitude and I catch up to my leader and pull in on his wing. I see that the tension nut on the throttle quadrant is loose, which explains how the throttle was able to creep back, thereby reducing power when I definitely did not need it to be reduced. I almost dug up the runway with my prop. We got back from the mission and the debriefing began. The C.O. looked at me and said: ``Lieutenant, I will not have my pilots shine their ass on the runway, you're fined ten pounds ($40.00).'' My first impulse is

Above: Lt. Edward C. Fremaux and his P-47, QI-N. Lt. Fremaux completed 116 missions between Dec. '43 and Sept. '44 with the 361st F.S. Below: Records indicate Captain Reginald C. McDowell's assigned A/C was QI-I, a P-47 named ``Irene.'' Here he stands in front of ``V'' sometime shortly before being shot down during the Arnhem Invasion. (G. Thuring) Bottom: A young Dutch girl sits on the P-47 crashlanded by McDowell, who was able to evade capture and return to the squadron at the end of Sept. In original photo it's just possible to make out the last digit of the serial of this downed P-47, it's a ``4''. McDowell's assigned A/C was 42-76497. (Beynes/Thuring)

Left: "Zombie" was a popular name - this one originally assigned to Maj. Thomas F. Bailey as QI-C, #42-76594. L to R: Assnt. C/C Frank Diorio, C/C Joe G. Weber, Bailey, Armorer Sgt. Ken Miller and Radioman Sgt. John Heise. Right: Same A/C, new pilot: Zombie, now coded QI-U and assigned to Lt. Ronald J. Upp. Note NMF canopy framing on new Malcolm hood.

to explain that I didn't pull the wheels from under the aircraft to show off, but that it was an accident. But, I just reply to the Major: "Yes Sir!" Better he thought me overconfident than careless. I should've checked the throttle tension nut before takeoff.

Mission: Escorting B-17s to bomb Oranienburg.

Smoke from the smoldering fires of the Nazi capital marks our approach to the target, a few miles to the north. The sky is clear and our 'Big Friends' are in good formation. A few Jerry fighters are reported to be in the area but none came near our sector. As we weave near the bombers they encounter heavy and accurate flak. We move out to the side of one squadron of B-17s. One ship is in trouble and, although trailing smoke and fire, holds steadfastly on course with bomb bay doors fully open. While I watch, I see the flak intensify and assume that we must be close to the target. As we pull ahead of our bombers, our squadron leader starts a turn that will allow us to cross under the bomber stream diagonally. Our flight was now the furthest out and therefore the last to cross below the bombers.

We were now almost under them, with most of our fighters already on the other side of the stream. I do not like what I see is happening. Our present track will take us directly under the burning B-17 whose load of bombs I expect to be dropped any second. I call out my concern to my flight leader who at the same time veers to avoid the flaming bomber, whose fate I will never know. Now the radio barks: "Vortex Yellow, take your flight home . . . RIGHT NOW!" I've upset our squadron leader by maybe implying that he would expose us to an unnecessary risk! (Later, I am to have my impression confirmed in very simple and direct terms.) Our flight of four aircraft have a ball on the way back to base - a sightseeing tour no less.

Mission: Escorting B-26 bombers on the Continent

We are deep into eastern Germany and I count a total of 36 Martin Marauders in a neat box to our right. We are at medium-high altitude and there are many reports of enemy fighters in our area coming over the radio. We pass near a Jerry airfield far below, and I am sure I can see signs of activity as occasionally I see glints of light reflecting off moving aircraft on the ground. The sky is clear and we have encountered no flak. With occasional glances at my flight leader, I scour the sky for signs of the Luftwaffe. Suddenly my eye catches a darting streak, appearing from high behind the Marauders and angling down towards them . . . BANDIT! I try to call my flight leader on the radio, but by now the airwaves are filled with RT chatter. My flight leader had not acknowledged my call and I scream into my throat mike as the sleek, shark-like, ME-262 continues past the box of bombers in a gentle diving turn towards us. I am astonished that he is not being chased by a dozen Mustangs, as surely others must have seen his attack on the bombers. As I watch the jet pass below our flight I fight off a frantic urge to split-S from my flight and give chase. Perhaps it was my recent tongue lashing from the Major that stopped me from reacting to my urge. To have left my flight leader in these circumstances would most likely have resulted in yet another verbal blast. If only I had been leading an element, the Jerry might not have been so lucky. My mood changed to anger when I counted the B-26s again and saw there were now only thirty-five.

There was great excitement at Martlesham Heath when we returned as the group had at last had some action. On the way to our debriefing I overheard several accounts of the engagement. One pilot (who had completed a tour in bombers) claimed he had scored quite a number of strikes on the '262 which the flight he was in had claimed as shot down. However, at the debriefing the happy mood changed to shock and disbelief when it was realized that an American A-26 flying alone and full of experimental electronic gear, had been shot down by a flight of Mustangs. Gun camera film later confirmed this. Two of the flight were ex-bomber pilots!

Mission: Fighter Sweep - returning to base

We have completed our mission and are heading back to base. We have flown a long, long mission and as we approach the French border fuel is getting low, so we take the shortest possible route back to England. My element leader reports smoke in his cockpit and I can see him trying to turn round to see just where the smoke is coming from. The squadron leader makes his decision quickly and orders our element to leave the formation and to head for home at a lower altitude. My instructions are to stay with my element leader and to escort him to the nearest landing field if things should get any worse. The other aircraft are now out of sight and we level off while I continue to watch out for a suitable field. My leader calls in that he thinks there is an electrical fire in his radio and he's going to switch it off. I move in closer and watch for his hand signals. I'm relieved when he gives me the OK sign - the fire appears to be out. We stay at low altitude and maintain our course. Suddenly, without warning flak begins to burst dead ahead! Unbelievable! We are supposed to be over friendly territory. We take quick, evasive action and a new heading while I check my maps. There is no doubt that we are over France and on course in what should be friendly skies.

I notice large red lettering on my map which say: RESTRICTED AREA - ALL AIRCRAFT FOLLOWING A WESTERLY COURSE BELOW EIGHT THOUSAND FEET WILL BE FIRED ON . . . Now I understand. We are in the corridor known as buzz-bomb alley, where Allied flak guns defend against the low-flying V-1's (or Doodlebugs as the English call them) launched by the Germans against southern England. As we climb to a safer altitude I am thankful that our airspeed was slower that the V-1's, or the ground gunners would have been dead on target with their first salvo. We made it back to base without any more excitement.

Herb flew his last mission of the war 20th April 1945 and the 356th flew its last mission 7th May 1945 when 12 Mustangs escorted a small force of B-17s on a leaflet dropping mission. The next day the war was over. Herb stayed with the group until September 1945 when he was assigned to the 30th ADG, LeCoulot, Belgium. After serving at various airfields he sailed from Le Havre, France for the States on 1st June 1946. On 12th June he was promoted and the following day was placed on terminal leave and in August he was put on reserve. He is now a Major USAF Retired. Herb and his wife Anne live in Newtown, Pa. and have three offspring, Martha Frances, Louise Anne and William Roger. One of Herb's pursuits has been photography, which he became interested in during his Air Force service and continues to the present day. He is an active member of the 356th Fighter Group Association and the P-51 Mustang Pilots Association.

Mission Summary List
Thursday, 1st March 1945.

F.O. 1679A. Ramrod led by Don Strait to Heilbronn M/Y. Lt. Walter O. Hedrick (PI-F, 44-11156 'Brenda') bails out near Strasburg and is taken POW. One 356th Fighter Group Mustang crashed at Monewdon, Suffolk. (OC-F, 44-14185) The pilot is uninjured. Mission

Left: 356th Ace Don Strait in front of his P-47, QI-T, #42-25844. Both this and his later P-51 carried the name "Jersey Jerk." Below: Major Strait, who finished the war with 13.5 confirmed victories, Lt. Shelby N. Jett in his appropriately named "Jett Job," Lt. Rex R. Burden and two other 361st Squadron P-51s pose for the camera.

Left: Our aptly named cover A/C, Harold Whitmore's "The Lord is my Shepherd." After a number of hair raising escapades, Harold painted the name on himself. Right: The crew of "The Shepherd" with their ship. L to R: C/C Tom Garrity, Whitmore, and Armorer Carl Sproles. (Sproles)

duration was 5:15. Escorted 1st Division B-17s (107 aircraft). 48 Mustangs took part.

Friday, 2nd March 1945.

Ramrod led by Don Baccus to the Chemitz M/Y and Leipzig. Duration 6:05 hours with 57 Mustangs taking part in the mission. Escorted 255 B-17s of the 1st Air Division. F.O.1683A.

Saturday, 3rd March 1945.

Area support led by Phil Tukey under F.O.1690. Fifty-two Mustangs went to Ruhland and the Leipzig area and the mission lasted exactly six hours. Oil installations were the target. A total of 222 Flying Fortresses took part.

Monday, 5th March 1945.

A Ramrod led by Captain Wilbur R. Scheible to the Ruhland area. Fifty-one Mustangs escorted the bombers in the 4 hour 50 minute mission. The primary target (synthetic oil plant) was not bombed due to the bad weather. Secondary targets were bombed using H2X. F.O.1704.

Friday, 9th March 1945.

Bomber escort mission led by Lt. Colonel Don Baccus under F.O.1727A. A total of 52 Mustangs escorted 336 B-17s of the 1st Air Division to the Marshalling Yards at Kassell. Duration 4:40. Herb took photographs.

Monday, 12th March 1945.

Ramrod led by Lt. Colonel James N. Wood to Swinemunde under F.O.1742A. The duration was 5:50 hours. A total of 220 B-17s were escorted.

Wednesday, 14th March 1945.

Major Wayne E. Rhynard led 12 Mustangs on a chaff dropping mission to the Ijmuiden area under F.O.1752A. The mission lasted 2 and one half hours. Robert E. Barnhart in his Mustang 'Margie Darling' of the 360th Fighter Squadron shot down an AR-234.

Thursday, 15th March 1945.

Don Baccus led 'A' group and Wayne Rhynard led 'B' group on a Ramrod to Berlin-Oranienburg. A total of 48 Mustangs took part in escorting 149 B-17s. Roger A. Batie of the 359th Fighter Squadron bailed out over

Winterswij. Duration was 5:30. F.O. 1761A.

Saturday, 24th March 1945.

An Area Patrol was led by Captain Mike Yannell in the Lingen-Metz areas and was the third mission for the 356th that day. F.O. 1828A. Duration 4:40. All missions were part of Operation 'Varsity' the Allied crossing of the Rhine River. Don Baccus led the first mission and Major Rhynard the second. Lt. William C. Jarvis in 44-15139 bailed out over the North Sea and was picked up safe and sound by the ASR.

Friday, 30th March 1945.

A Ramrod led by Mike Yannell escorting B-17s of the 1st Air Division. A total of 61 Mustangs took part under F.O. 1863A. Bremen was the target. Duration was 4:30

Monday, 2nd April 1945.

Mike Yannell led 54 Mustangs on a Ramrod to Skrydstrup, Denmark which took 4:10 hours.

Tuesday, 3rd April 1945.

Under F.O. 1887, 68 Mustangs were led by Major Wayne E. Rhynard on a Ramrod to the Kiel submarine pens. The mission lasted 4:40. A total of 224 B-17s of the 1st Air Division were covered by the 356th Fighter Group.

Wednesday, 4th April 1945.

ASR led by Phil Tukey. Duration 4:45. Lt. John W. Cudd of the 77th Fighter Squadron, 20th Fighter Group bails out into the North Sea. Submarine and aircraft are involved in the search for him. 5th Emergency Rescue Squadron sends out 1 OA-10, 2 B-17s and 22 P-47s. Lt. Nielson leads four Mustangs from the 356th. Lt. Cudd is safely rescued. Earlier on a Ramrod Lt. John E. Pound bails out over Allied lines due to coolant loss.

Friday, 6th April 1945.

Bomber Escort under F.O. 1909A led by Major Donald D. Carlson. The target is Leipzig and the mission lasts for 6 hours. Lt. Raleigh S. Ragsdale of the 360th Fighter Squadron is lost. He is to be the last combat loss for the 356th Fighter Group. A total of 48 aircraft took part in the mission.

Sunday, 8th April 1945.

Ramrod led by Major Wayne E. Rhynard to the Dessau-Magdeburg area. A total of 56 Mustangs flew the 5:50 hour trip. F.O. 1918A.
Tuesday, 10th April 1945.

A Ramrod, under F.O. 1936A, as Colonel Phil Tukey led 56 Mustangs in an attack on the German Army H.Q. at Berlin-Oranienburg. Duration was 5:15. A number of ME-262s were seen and attacked with claims being made by Wayne C. Gatlin and Thurman W. Mauldin, each of whom claimed a 262 destroyed and Edward W. Schrull claiming one more as damaged. All pilots flew with the 359th Fighter Squadron. The last bomber raid on ``Big B.''
Friday, 13th April 1945.

Major Donald R. Carlson led 39 aircraft on a Ramrod to Wismar under F.O. 1962A. The group strafed Schwerin Airfield with the following claims being made:-

Nunzio B. Ceraolo	1 FW-190 Dam. Grd.
Billy D. McNary	2 FW-190s Dam. Grd.
George W. Seanor	1 DO-217 Dam. Grd.
Mike Yannell	1 FW-190 Des. Grd.

The mission lasted 5 hours and 40 minutes. Herb had to land at Munchen Gladbach due to low oil pressure.
Tuesday, 17th April 1945.

A Ramrod was flown under F.O. 2007 led by Don Carlson to the Dresden area. A total of 52 Mustangs acted as escort to 450 B-17s of the 1st Air Division. Duration 5:30.
Wednesday, 18th April 1945.

Major Wayne E. Rhynard led 52 Mustangs on a Ramrod under F.O. 2019A to Burgheim. The bombers were B-26s of the 9th Air Force. One B-26 was shot down by an ME-262 and another by one of the group's pilots. Those who made claims were: Lt. Leon Oliver, who got an AR-234 and Wayne C. Gatlin, L. B. Proctor, Jr. and George W. Seanor, all of the 360th Fighter Squadron, who combined efforts for 1 ME-262 destroyed.
Friday, 20th April 1945.

Mike Yannell led the group on a Ramrod to the M/Y at Brandenburg-Berlin near F.O.2039. Duration 5:15. Nunzio B. Ceraolo was lost in PI-L(bar), 44-63251 'Louise.' A total of 289 B-17s were escorted.

Make no mistake - this was the main reason for fighting in WWII. While at an airfield near Nuremburg, Germany, Herb took these photos of Rudolf Höss ex-commandant of Auschwitz Extermination camp in Poland. Höss is being handed back to Polish authorities after testifying at the Nuremburg war crimes trials. The utter beastiality of his administration, well documented in such works as Time - Life's ``The Nazis,'' is virtually without parallel in the history of western Europe.

Pilots of the 362nd Fighter Squadron, 357th Fighter Group at Leiston Airfield, Suffolk in the fall of 1945. From left to right in the first row is Lt. J.L. Bright, Lt. R.T. Potter, Cpt. H.A. Wyatt, Cpt. R.D. Brown, F/O.A. Schoepke, Cpt. W.W. Gruber, Lt. R.E. Trout, Lt. K.K. Wilson. 2nd Row: - Lt. H.J. Williams, Lt. Ed Hyman, Lt. J. Black, Cpt. C.E. Weaver, Lt. D.W. Cheever, Lt. O.W. Boch, Lt. J.J. Boyne, Lt. F.A. Dellorto, Lt. J.S. Metcalf. 3rd Row: - F/O. R.J. White, Lt. J.F. Duncan Jr., Lt. R. Dunn, Lt. R.H. Bradner, Lt. Brown (I.O.), Lt. E.C. Danner, Cpt. R. Welch, Lt. J.C. McLane, Cpt. D.G. Pickrell (I.O.), Lt. J.H. Bertram, Lt. F.A. Utz. Top: - Lt. M.A. Becraft, Lt. Joseph E. Shea. September 1945. (**Becraft**)

MYRON A. BECRAFT

362ND FIGHTER SQUADRON, 357TH FIGHTER GROUP

Myron A. Becraft was born on October 3, 1923 to Myron and Ann Becraft in Elmira, New York. After the usual American education he graduated from Thomas Edison High School, Elmira Heights, New York. The following year he attended the University of Vermont at Burlington.

In the same year he joined the USAAF and started his training at Maxwell AFB, Alabama. From there he went to Arcadia AFB, Florida where he learned to fly the PT-17. He then transferred to Greenville, Miss. for his Basic Training on BT-13s. Upon completion of this he went to Jackson where he flew the AT-6. He graduated with Class 44-D, on April 5, 1944. He transferred to Eglin Field, Florida for Gunnery Training and later to an OTU in Florida where he flew the P-40. In September, 1944, he was ordered to report to Camp Kilmer and on the 15th he left for England.

Upon arrival he reported to Goxhill for P-51 Transitional Training and on October 3rd, his 21st birthday, he flew the P-51 Mustang for the first time. He had just over 15 hours training when assigned to the 362nd

Fighter Squadron of the 357th Fighter Group, based at Leiston, Suffolk. He was assigned to Blue Flight and his call sign for the duration was 'Dollar 46.'

Along with other pilots at Goxhill he heard the 357th was one of the most outstanding groups in the ETO, with such famous pilots as Leonard 'Kit' Carson, Irwin Dregne and John England. The group, in some 15 months of combat, was to claim the destruction of nearly 700 enemy aircraft (both air and ground). They were the first Mustang group assigned to the 8th Air Force.

On November 21, 1944, Myron flew his first combat mission, a Ramrod to Halle. It lasted four hours and twenty minutes and turned out to be something of an anti-climax with a very uneventful mission being flown.

On December 2nd Myron saw the enemy for the first time. Escorting the Big Friends to Koblenz, between 15-20 E/A were seen. In the ensuing scrap the 364th Fighter Squadron claimed 6 of the 7 German aircraft shot down by the group.

On the first of his four missions to Big B, Myron was assigned a P-51B coded G4-R (bar), 43-6688. Myron recalled: ``I did have a few interesting moments during my tour with the 357th. On my 5th mission, December 5th, 1944, our group went to Berlin. As a junior birdman I got an old P-51B with one of those canopies that looked like it came from a Spit. We were at about 30,000 feet when we encountered about 30 ME-109s and FW-190s. Everybody dropped their wing tanks and started down, but I couldn't get my tanks to release. After several attempts I finally got rid of them, but by then I was sitting up there all by myself.

Being rather excited and wanting to join my flight I just rolled over and split S'd down. The speed built at a terrific rate and as I tried to pull out, I could see that the controls, though they felt normal, were having no effect. I chopped the throttle and as I passed the 18,000 foot mark I noticed the ASI was still showing 450MPH. At about 11,000 feet the controls got real stiff but I was able to start pulling up. At that moment I saw gas coming out of the port wing filler cap. I finally pulled out at about 2000 feet and started to climb for altitude. There were some broken clouds at about 6,000 feet and I headed for them. At that precise moment I heard gunfire. At first I thought it was me pressing the tit, but when I looked down I realized that it was *not* me. I heard the guns again and broke hard left into one of the clouds.

When I came out, I couldn't see any aircraft, either friend or foe. I started to climb again and shortly after leveling off at about 20,000 feet I saw another Mustang. Upon joining up I found it was my own Group leader, Major Joseph E. Broadhead. We then headed for home. During my dive all the fuel in the port tank had been sucked out so I had to juggle the throttle a bit to make sure I got home safely.

When I landed and taxied into the revetment for G4-R, the Crew Chief climbed right up on the wing and asked 'what happened?' I said, 'I don't know. Have my guns been fired?' He replied, 'No, the tape is still on, but *someone* sure must have fired *something* by the looks of the belly of your aircraft.' I didn't even realize I'd been hit! I'd either heard the other guy firing at me, which they say is impossible, or the noise from being hit. One small calibre bullet had gone through the radiator door and into the after-cooler section of the radiator. It's a good thing it's a separate cooling system because I'd lost all my coolant from the after-cooler. Also, what I assume was a cannon shell made a long dent in the radiator air scoop. It must have passed through the spinning prop without exploding! Talk about being lucky!

Meanwhile, the rest of the group had run into approximately 100 FW-190s attacking B-17s of the 3rd Air Division. During the resulting dogfight the group lost Captain Herman R. Zetterquist and Lt. Mathew Martin, who were both shot down and captured. Doubles were claimed by John Kirla, Clarence Anderson, Don Bochkay, Frederick McCall and Dale Karger. Captain Jim Browning knocked down a ME-109 to become the 357th's thirty-first ace. The group shot down 22 enemy aircraft for the two losses previously mentioned.

*Above: S/Sgt. Joe Sewell and his pilot, Myron "Moose" Becraft, with their A/C G4-S, 44-63221. Myron recalls Joe looked after him like a father for his son. The name and moose head were painted on by Jim Gasser, without telling Myron! (**Olmsted**) Middle: It was necessary to run up P-51s every couple days or the plugs would foul with dramatically unpleasant results during take-offs. Here Sgt. Sewell runs up "The Moose." Note post-war underwing "Buzz #s." (**Becraft**) Below: A fine shot of Lt. Jim Gasser's G4-K, 44-11697. Jim later served in the Korean War and is now an active member of the 357th Fighter Group Assn. (**Gasser**)*

On Christmas Eve the 357th Fighter Group hit high gear once again. During an escort mission to Babenhausen, they claimed a total of thirty-one enemy aircraft destroyed. The group flew as two separate units: 'A Group', consisting of 51 P-51s and led by Major Richard A. Peterson, went to Fulda and 'B Group', with 25 Mustangs, led by Colonel Irwin Dregne, went to Koblenz (all the ships of this group were from the 363rd Fighter Squadron).

Both groups ran into heavy enemy opposition but the 363rd still managed to shoot down 8 enemy aircraft. Colonel Dregne knocked down his fifth to become an ace. Meanwhile 'A Group' ran into a mixed bag of ME-109s and FW-190s. A furious battle ensued and 19 E/A bit the dust. Lt. Otto 'Dittie' Jenkins became an ace when he shot down 4 FW-190s. Lt. John Kirla claimed a triple joining Jenkins to become an ace. Claiming doubles were Lt. William T. Gilbert, Ed Hyman and Paul Pelon, all of the 362nd Fighter Squadron. Losses for the group were Lts. Gilbert and Mooney who were shot down in the air battle and killed. Lt. Wendell Helwig collided with Lt. Kenneth J. Mix of the 343rd Fighter Squadron, 55th Fighter Group. Both Mustangs went down.

On January 3, 1945, 'junior birdman' Myron was detailed as part of a section of four Mustangs led by Lt. Charles Weaver. The mission was to escort a PRU Lightning photographing targets near Stuttgart. The five aircraft went in at about 3,000 feet and had no problems until they neared the target when the coolant overheated in Myron's Mustang. He checked his instruments and saw the generator was out. He informed Chuck Weaver, opened the radiator door manually and the temperature soon started to come down. The P-38 pilot had, by this time, completed his runs over the target and started for home. The Mustangs followed and landed safely back at Leiston, Suffolk after some three hours, weary but safe.

Eleven days later the 357th Fighter Group established an all-time record for an Eighth AF Group when they shot down 56 1/2 enemy aircraft in one mission. Bob Foy of the 363rd Fighter Squadron also destroyed a FW-190 on the ground. The Group lost three pilots, Lt. William Dunlop, Lt. James R. Sloan and Lt. George A. Behling. Another seven Mustangs were damaged but were able to return safely to their home base.

The mission began as the 357th was to escort bombers to Derben under Field Order 1515A. 66 Mustangs

*Above left and below left: The two A/C assigned to ace Joe Broadhead, in which he scored most of his 8 confirmed victories while serving as 362nd F.S. Commander. One of the main reasons for high morale in U.S. fighter squadrons was, most assuredly, the fact that their senior officers also led the combat formations. (**Bob Bennett**) Above, right: Major Joe Broadhead, 362nd F.S. Commander in the cockpit of his second assigned A/C "Master Mike." Below, right: This P-51B, in early 357th group markings (white nose and tail stripe) is about to get a new home. It was transfered to the 352nd F.G. during their conversion from P-47s to P-51s. Frequently A/C were exchanged from group to group for various reasons. (**Via Bob Powell Jr.**)*

Mustangs of the 357th began an air battle that lasted for about half an hour from the first clash until Bob Foy got his single FW-190 on the deck. Lt. Colonel Dregne led the 362nd and 364th squadrons against the low gaggle of about 70 FW-190s and the 363rd headed for the top cover of about 70 ME-109s. Very few of the Jerry fighters managed to penetrate the screen set up by the group. The 362nd claimed a total of 23 enemy aircraft destroyed and the 363rd took care of another 12 in the air plus one on the ground. The 364th claimed 21 1/2 FW-190s destroyed *in the air!*

Myron's flight was led by John Duncan who claimed two. John Kirla knocked down four and Harold Wyatt claimed a single. Myron made no claims and later remarked 'I was too damn busy keeping out of the way to get a shot in.' Lt. Colonel Andy Evans also claimed four destroyed. Those in the 362nd who also claimed doubles were: Kit Carson, John Sublett and Charles Weaver. In the 363rd triples were claimed by John Stern and James Browning. A double went to Bob Foy (plus his ground claim). Meanwhile, in the 364th, three pilots scored triples: Chester K. Maxwell, Ray Banks and John Storch. In the double brackets were

took off but ten came back early - several as escorts to aircraft that had to abort. The remaining Mustangs met the 'Big Friends' of the 3rd Air Division near the Frisian Islands, crossing in over Cuxhaven at about 12 noon. It was as the bombers approached Brandenburg (about 40 miles from Berlin) that the group leader, Lt. Colonel Irwin Dregne, spotted about 150 enemy aircraft.

The pilots had been briefed as to what formation the Germans would be flying. And so it turned out that when the enemy came at them in 'company front' formation, Lt. Colonel Dregne acted accordingly. The

Above, left: The A/C and crew of Lt. Ed Hyman. "Whitey" the Armorer, Ed and C/C Ray Morrison with Sgt. Merle Olmsted on wing. Merle, then an assistant crew chief, has written a good deal on the 357th since the war, including the classic "The Yoxford Boys." He also supplied directly or indirectly many of the photos in this section - thanx Merle! Above, right: Ed Hyman and "Rolla U" were on the last wartime mission performed by the 357th. After the war this A/C was sold to Sweden and eventually scrapped in 1958. Below, left: A nice shot of Lt. Joseph Black and the crew of his G4-N, 44-63880 "Mary's Lil Lamb." (Becraft) Below, right: Capt. Gilbert M. O'Brien of the 362nd and his G4-Q, 43-6787. He had a wartime total of 7 confirmed aerial claims, including 2 shared with other pilots. At the time this photo was taken, he'd completed 38 missions which was about ½ a normal tour.

The first Mustang assigned to John B. England of the 362nd FS/ 357th F.G. The impressive scoreboard shows the name is fact not fancy with over 30 missions and 9 A/C to it's credit. See color profile, p. 148. Above, right: A determined looking Capt. John England in the cockpit of his P-51. His final tally of 17.5 confirmed air victories a credit to his aerial aggressiveness. Below, left: John England's final wartime A/C also G4-H, but named ``Missouri Armada'' and serialed 44-14709. (Olmsted) Below, right: Lt. Eldrid C. Danner and Lt. Becraft outside the 362nd OPS room. Note squadron badge on door.

Tommy Adams and Paul R. Hatala. Bob Winks, also of the 364th, was the odd man out in the group with 2 1/2 aerial claims — the other half being claimed by Schuyler Baker of the 20th Fighter Group.

Also making a claim was Lt. Col. William C. Clark, later to become C.O. of the famous 339th Fighter Group. He recalled: ``The lead flight was about three miles ahead of the lead box of bombers at about 27,000 feet. I saw many enemy aircraft pulling white contrails at 1 o'clock to us and at about 30,000 feet. My flight turned into them and while I was still looking at the white contrails we were hit by about 50 FW-190s which I hadn't seen. They flew right through our formation and I think they were intent on hitting the bombers. They came from the right at about our level. I don't know what sort of formation they were flying. All this happened about 15 miles south of Schwern.

One FW-190 flew between myself and the group leader. I was his No. 2 in the lead flight. I gave the enemy aircraft a short burst but did not see any hits at all. For a second I lost sight of my leader, his 51 was

faster than mine and he'd pulled away from me. I saw what I thought to be the group leader and pulled round in trail with him. I saw him get strikes on a 190 and then follow his victim down. Before I could turn and follow him, a FW-190 came up under him and I fired a short burst at the enemy aircraft. His right landing gear came down and this caused him to stall. I overran him and pulled up to make another pass. The 190 was going into a spin with the right leg still hanging down and it looked to me as if the pilot fell out. I saw two chutes but don't know whether either of them belonged to the plane I'd hit. Two more 190s came in on my tail and I turned so sharply I almost spun in. I was able to recover at about 10,000 feet and several ME-109s shot at me as they came down. I counted six chutes at my altitude. I then climbed back to 30,000 feet but saw no more enemy aircraft.'

Lt. Colonel William C. Clark.
364th F/S, 357th F/G.

The pilot that Bill Clark was covering, Lt. Colonel

Dregne, recalled: 'I was leading the 357th Fighter Group providing close support for the first three boxes of bombers. At about 1245 I observed the large gaggle of bandits approaching the lead box of bombers from the 1 o'clock position. I lead Greenhouse squadron (364th) toward the contrails, instructing the other two squadrons to stay close to the bombers. As I got closer to the contrails I noticed a large gaggle coming in at our level, which turned out to be FW-190s flying in company front formation in waves of eight aircraft each. The contrails I had first spotted were ME-109s giving top cover to the 190s. I told Greenhouse squadron to drop their tanks and we turned into the FW-190s. The 190s broke formation and scattered, some of them rolling, some of them split-essing but the majority broke to the right and went into a Lufberry. I got my sights on a 190 and started firing, observing strikes on the fuselage and the tail section. He broke to the left and went into a spin. I broke to the left and continued turning, finding myself in a Lufberry with 8 to 10 FW-190s. I started a tight climbing spiral, the 190s following, but I outclimbed them.

My flight was broken up on the initial attack by the enemy aircraft flying through us. I noticed a bomber box under attack so I started climbing towards it. When I got to the box the fight was over and the Huns gone. I picked up a P-51 and ordered him to cover my

tail. We went to the front of the bombers and started to escort them again. My wingman told me he was low on gas so we headed for home. I spotted a ME-109 below me at about 20,000 feet. I chopped my throttle, slid in behind him and fired. I saw strikes around the cockpit area. The aircraft started to burn, then it spun and crashed.

I claim 1 FW-190 damaged and 1 ME-109 destroyed in the air.

Lt. Colonel Irwin H. Dregne

On a mission to the Munich area the following day Myron recalled: "We were escorting B-17s and it was a beautiful clear day. Our bombers did a great job on the target, a marshalling yard. I was instructed to get some photos of the target with the K-25 camera that had just recently been installed. As I made my run at about 14,000 feet I started a slow climbing turn to the right with the intention of joining my squadron after taking the pictures. I happened to look up and saw, to my great dismay, that some B-24s were almost directly above me and had their bomb bay doors open! From where I was, it looked as though they'd singled

Above left & right: Both the assigned A/C of Capt. Robert H. Becker who made all 7 of his claims in a 5 month period from Feb. to July 44. Below, left: In our copy of this photo of "Lady Ovella" the name of Lt. John Sublett can just be made out on the canopy rail. Note 8 vics registered on side of A/C. Lt. A.W. Bierweiler was killed in this A/C in a training accident May 21, 1945 near the village of Bucklesham, Suffolk. (Olmsted) Below, right: Lt. Becraft leads off in his P-51 followed by Lt. Jesse R. Frey in G4-M, 44-15267 "Ain't Misbehavin." Note post-war under wing codes on the "Moose." (Becraft)

me out for destruction so I poured on the coals and got away as quickly as I could. At our briefing we had *not* been told about any B-24s in our area and to this day I don't know what their target was.''

On March 2, 1945 Myron joined the small select band of fighter aces when he claimed seven enemy aircraft destroyed. The group was led by Captain Donald C. McGee. It was the usual bomber escort mission, this time to Ruhland. A total of 53 Mustangs completed the mission. At about 10 o'clock they intercepted 20 to 30 single-engined enemy aircraft as they neared Magdeburg. Myron recalled: ''I was flying Dollar Blue Three, escorting the bombers. We were near Magdeburg when Dollar Leader, Captain John Sublett, spotted several bandits below. We went down and most of the enemy aircraft tried to escape into the clouds. There were many Mustangs circling around us at about 10,000 feet. A lone ME-109 was in a Lufberry with four 51s. I chased the Jerry, closing to about 500 yards and gave him a couple bursts. His wing came off and he did a snap roll. The aircraft continued breaking up and spinning until he hit the ground.'' Myron's wingman at the time was Lt. Gilbert A. Robinson who supported his claim for the ME-109 in the air.

After the dogfight several elements and flights found themselves over various German airfields. Such was the case for Myron and Lt. Robinson. The airfield they attacked was Kamenz, resulting in the destruction of ten enemy aircraft on the ground — plus another four damaged. In his encounter report Myron stated ''After getting the 109 I saw another two below the clouds and I went below the layer to get at them. I was unsuccessful, however. Again I spotted another Bogie going into the clouds. I chased him but he managed to get away. When I came out of the clouds, I looked down and observed some HE-111s parked in a forest of pine trees. My altitude was about 2,000 feet when I saw Kamenz airdrome. It was just a large grass field with no landing strip at all. My wingman, Lt. Robinson, was still with me at this point.

I made one pass and destroyed one HE-111 and damaged another. The first 111 burned. There was no flak, so I took advantage of the situation and made another six passes, all from different directions. I set fire to two HE-111s with FW-190s on top of them and another plain old HE-111. Lt. Robinson was also having a big time of it, making pass after pass with no opposition. Finally we ran low on fuel and ammunition

Another heavy hitter from the 357th was Maj. Robert W. Foy who confirmed 15 vics only to die in a postwar flying accident. The two photos above show his first P-51, ''Reluctant Rebel,'' while below left is his P-51 D, ''Little Shrimp.'' Below, right: Junior Miss II was the assigned A/C of Lt. G.A. Zarnke. The C/C was Pete Laboranti and the serial was 44-63680. (Laboranti)

A crew chief of the 361st Fighter Group checks out the tonsils of E2-V, 44-14678 which was the only known 'sharkmouthed' Mustang in the 375th Fighter Squadron. Lt. Robert G. Adams was killed in action in this ship when he bailed out and his chute failed to billow out in time 25th January 1945.

(USAF Photo)

Mid June 1945 and the 55th Fighter Group awaits the arrival of the Wing Commander, B/General Murray C. Woodbury. The first Mustang in the front row is the last ship of ace Robert E. Welch, CY-Z, 44-72138. Next is CY-D, 44-14885 first flown by Doug Parker who named it 'Nervous Nell.' It was then taken over by ace Lloyd Boring who renamed it 'Dizzy Jess'. Lt. Boring claimed most of his seven plus victories in it. The first Mustang in the second row is fellow ace Carroll 'Hank' Henry's CL-G, 44-63227, which he named 'Little Trixie'. This was his only assigned aircraft while he flew with the 338th Fighter Squadron.

(Sands)

Fighter ace Brook J. Liles and his wingman of the 343rd Fighter Squadron climb under full power as they start out on a combat mission. Lt. Liles is flying his CY-Q, 44-14175 'Cherry.' Both pilot and aircraft survived the war. Liles went home, 'Cherry' went to Germany with the 55th Fighter Group as part of the Occupation Air Force and was lost in a flying accident in late 45. The nickname was red outlined in black.

(Sands)

A typical early morning mist in North Essex. This P-51D was assigned to the 38th Fighter Squadron, 55th Fighter Group. The code was CG-R, 44-11370. The crew chief was Roger Fraliegh and his assistant was Nick Lapucci. The aircraft was lost on a combat mission 20th February 1945. The number '18' has been painted onto the vertical stab.

(Sands)

Wittering, home of the 55th Fighter Squadron, 20th Fighter Group 1943. The second aircraft from the front is Harry Bisher's KI-N, 42-67823 'Kitty.' On the left is KI-K, 42-67081.

M/Sgt. 'Heine' Ziegler, A Flight Chief, and T/Sgt. Richard O. Bock prepare to change the rudder of a 38th Fighter Squadron, 55th Fighter Group Mustang which was damaged during a close formation practice mission. Sgt. Bob Sand replaced the propeller of the offending Mustang.

(Sand)

A rare color photo of a ME-262, No 111685, coded 9K + FH. This aircraft was built at Schwabisch Hall and was assigned to KG(J) 51. A large letter 'F' was painted aft of the white cross on the fuselage. This particular ship was later taken to Neubiberg, home of the 357th Fighter Group, where it was scrapped. The camouflage was Brown-Violet with Bright Green splotches sprayed on and the undersurfaces were a pale shade of Grey or Blue.

(USAF Photo)

131

One of the 4th Fighter Group's winning teams was Colonel Everett W. Stewart and his ground crew with their last Mustang VF-S, 44-72181 'Sunny V111' of the 336th Fighter Squadron. On the left is Ev, then comes Vervene Young (Arm), Glessner Weckbacher (C/C) and Louis Brown (AC/C). This photo was taken in April 1945.

Colonel Don Blakeslee of the 4th Fighter Group photographed at three minutes to twelve at Debden, Essex, home to his group, the 4th. Note rescue whistle below his left arm.

(USAF)

The grand old lady of the 56th, "Silver Lady" was used by aces Don Smith, Leslie Smith, Francis Gabreski and Witold Lanowski. She went on virtually countless missions without an abort.

(Tabatt)

Fighter ace George E. Bostwick with his last Thunderbolt coded UN-Z, 44-21112, a P-47M. A painting of a duckling was later put on the cowling and the name 'Ugly Duckling' also. The tally represents George's final score. Note K-14 gunsight. The paint job was light and dark blue.

The farm on the airfield at Halesworth, Norfolk was taken over by Dave Schilling and his 62nd Fighter Squadron. In front is fighter ace Leroy A. Schreiber's LM-T, 42-22537. Schreiber was killed in action on 15th April 1944 over Flensburg airfield.

Ground personnel of the 339th Fighter Group based at Fowlmere pose with Jim Starnes' last Mustang 6N-X, 44-72152 'Tar Heel' of the 505th Fighter Squadron. From left to right is Leslie Harbold, Carl Hicks, Joe Per and Fred Nessler. Note K-25 camera attached to the armour plate. Jim was assigned this aircraft on 9th March 1945.

(via Starnes)

Fighter ace Aldwin Max Jucheim of the 83rd Fighter Squadron, 78th Fighter Group talks to his crew chief S/Sgt. Robert H. McCord about their Thunderbolt HL-J(bar), 42-26020. Note designator code under nose, not a common practice but helpful to crew chiefs looking to guide their charges in. Jucheim was taken POW when his P-47 HL-J(bar), 42-26016 was in a collision with a Mustang of the 363rd Fighter Group on 28th May 1944. The Mustang pilot was killed.

(USAF Photo)

Crew Chief Bennie Kennedy and his 'boss', Colonel William C. Clark, C.O. of the 339th Fighter Group. Both men were with the 504th Fighter Squadron and this was their last Mustang. The code was 5Q-C, 44-11175 'Happy IV'-'Dolly'. Note the in field mod over Clark's head, an improvised sun shade to combat the high temps in the blown bubble canopy. Behind is 5Q-B, 44-72582 'Hillbilly' the mount of Lt. Lyle Carter. 7th April 1945.

(Clark)

Mustangs of the 361st Fighter Group line up on the North-South runway at Bottisham, Cambs sometime in July 1944. The second aircraft from the right is E2-V, 44-14678 'Pat' of the 375th Fighter Squadron. This ship led a checkered history. On 18th October 1944 it crashlanded with Caleb J. Layton at the controls. After being repaired it was lost due to enemy action on 25th January 1945 when Robert G. Adams was killed. The Crew Chief was Alvin Walther.

(USAF)

D-Day and the Mustangs of the 361st Fighter Group get ready to roll out again. On the left is Clarence Sullivan Jr. in his E9-S, 42-106707 'Sleepytime Gal'. Next is E9-E, 42-106802 which was later Robert J. Bains 'Blue Eyes'. Following 'Blue Eyes' is Vic Bocquin in his 'Impatient Virgin?' E9-R, 42-106638. In front is B7-E, 42-106839 'Bald Eagle 111' flown by Bob Eckfeldt and just behind him is ace fighter pilot Joe Kruzel's E9-K, 44-13391 'Vi'.

(USAF)

One for RAF buffs. Herb Rutland photographed this Spitfire which visited his base at Martlesham Heath, Suffolk in 1945. The code is MX-T(bar), AB-981 or AS-981. This MK V has the clipped wings.

(Rutland)

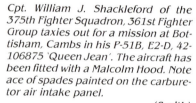

Cpt. William J. Shackleford of the 375th Fighter Squadron, 361st Fighter Group taxies out for a mission at Bottisham, Cambs in his P-51B, E2-D, 42-106875 'Queen Jean'. The aircraft has been fitted with a Malcolm Hood. Note ace of spades painted on the carburetor air intake panel.

(Smith)

A crew chief of the 375th Fighter Squadron, 361st Fighter Group runs up the engine of his Langley Field, Virginia Thunderbolt in July 1943. The group arrived at Bottisham, Cambs in December 1943 and as such was the last Thunderbolt group to be assigned to the 8th Air Force.

(USAF)

Herb Rutland shot this remarkable photo of the rest of his formation while they were on the way to Germany in early 1945. Flying as No. 1 is Jack 'Wild Bill' Crump in PI-W, 44-15056 'Jackie', next is Nunzio B. Ceraolo (No. 3) in his 'Louise' PI-L(bar), 44-63251 and flying his wing in the No. 4 position is Don Jones in his Mustang PI-O, 44-15300 'Milly'. All four pilots flew with the 360th Fighter Squadron, 356th Fighter Group.

(Rutland)

Another shot taken by Herb Rutland on the same mission as in the photo directly above. The painting on Jack Crump's "Jackie" was in memory of his unusual pet, a real live coyote, that he managed to smuggle into England. "Jeep Coyote" had to have been the only one of its kind to fly strafing missions over Arnhem, sharing the driving with Jack in their P-47, PI-W, 42-26322. When "Jeep" was accidently run over, he was buried at Playford Hall with full military honors including a missing man formation fly by.

(Rutland)

Mustangs of the 352nd Fighter Group carry out close escort while on a practice mission with B-24 Liberators of the 753rd Bomb Squadron, 458th Bomb Group (Heavy). The bombers were based at Horsham St. Faiths, the old base for the 56th Fighter Group.

(USAF Photo)

The 'Moose' has her engine run-up after the war. Note anti-buzzing codes under the port wing of G4-S(bar), 44-63221. The aircraft also has tail warning radar which most pilots switched off as it was not too reliable. One pilot even reported that it showed up heavy clouds as enemy aircraft. Originally a black and white photo, this was color washed by Jim Gasser who was also responsible for the nickname of the aircraft. The pilot was Myron A. Becraft of the 362nd Fighter Squadron, 357th Fighter Group.

(Becraft)

The finished job (see black and white photo page). Fred Hayner painted this on Berkeley Hollister's L2-V, 44-14651. When Hollister completed his tour 2nd January 1945 the aircraft may have been assigned to Lt. John Donnell. Lt. Donnell was lost in this aircraft 14th February 1945.

(Hayner)

Harold Bellman (left) pays a visit to his brother at Fowlmere, Cambs, home of the famous 339th Fighter Group. His brother Ray is on the ground while crew chief Bob Burns is on the wing with his pilot Lt. Jeff French. Their Mustang was coded D7-A, 44-11623 and was assigned to the 503rd Fighter Squadron.

(French)

A line up of group commander's aircraft taken at Debden, Essex, home of the 4th Fighter Group. All the C.O.s were at a conference to learn about 'Operation Varsity,' the crossing of the Rhine on 23rd March 1945. From left to right is CV-Q, 44-15717 (Col. John P. Randolph), LC-D, 44-72519 'Gumpy' (Col. Robert P. Montgomery), LH-V, 44-11646 (Col. Ben Rimermann), C5-Q, 44-11678 (Col. Irwin Dregne).

(Richie)

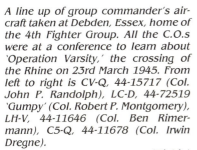

The starboard side of Jeff French's 'Rusty' D7-A, 44-11623 of the 503rd Fighter Squadron, 339th Fighter Group based at Fowlmere, Cambridgeshire.

(French)

John Hudgens served with the 20th Fighter Groiup during the war. He was one of the leading lights of the 20th Fighter Group Association before his untimely death in 1988.

(Hudgens)

A very smart Edward Richie prior to his joining the famous 4th Fighter Group at Debden, Essex. Ed had the foresight to obtain colour film of scenes in and around Debden and proved an invaluable source to the author and many other air historians.

(Richie)

June 2nd 1945 and from the back seat of the group's two seat Mustang Cal Sloan took a series of photographs. In this one are P-51s of the 354th Fighter Squadron. From the front are Stan Silva in his WR-B, 44-11667 'My Catherine S'., WR-V, 44-72462, WR-S(bar), 44-15626 (ex-WR-A Clay Kinnard's 'Man O' War')., a War Weary P-51B coded WR-T(bar)., WR-A(bar)., Lt. Glenn D. Beeler in WR-L(bar), 44-72253., Lt. Don Langley in WR-C, 'Lil Curly Top'. Not in the photo are Jimmy Jabara in WR-P(bar), 44-14346 and Lt. James O'Neill. Shortly after this photo was taken Jabara and Beeler collided and both pilots later thanked the squadron parachute packer for a job well done.

(Sloan)

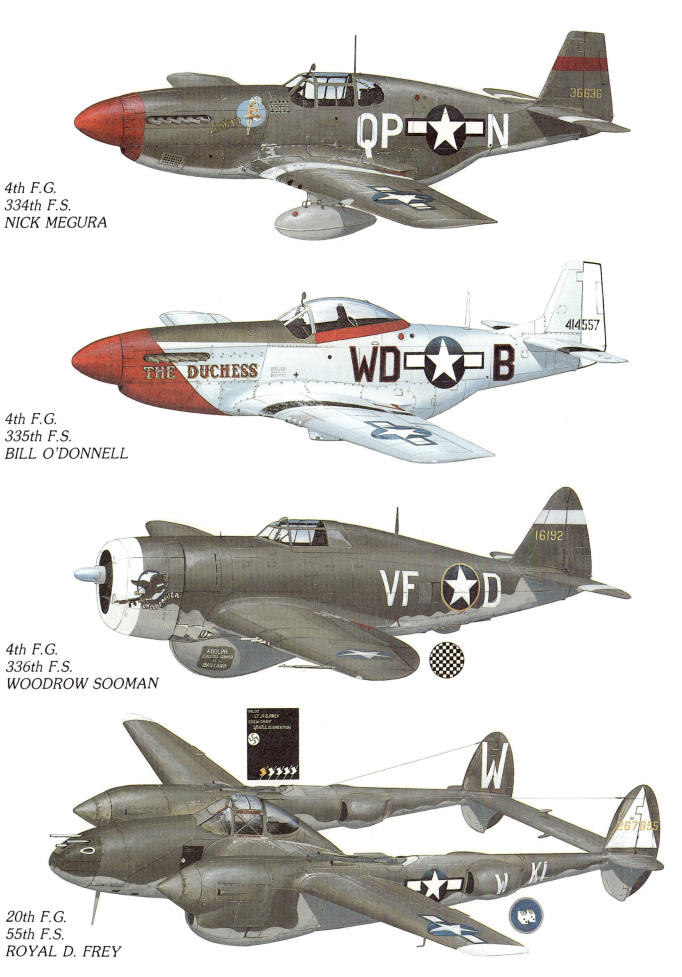

4th F.G.
334th F.S.
NICK MEGURA

4th F.G.
335th F.S.
BILL O'DONNELL

4th F.G.
336th F.S.
WOODROW SOOMAN

20th F.G.
55th F.S.
ROYAL D. FREY

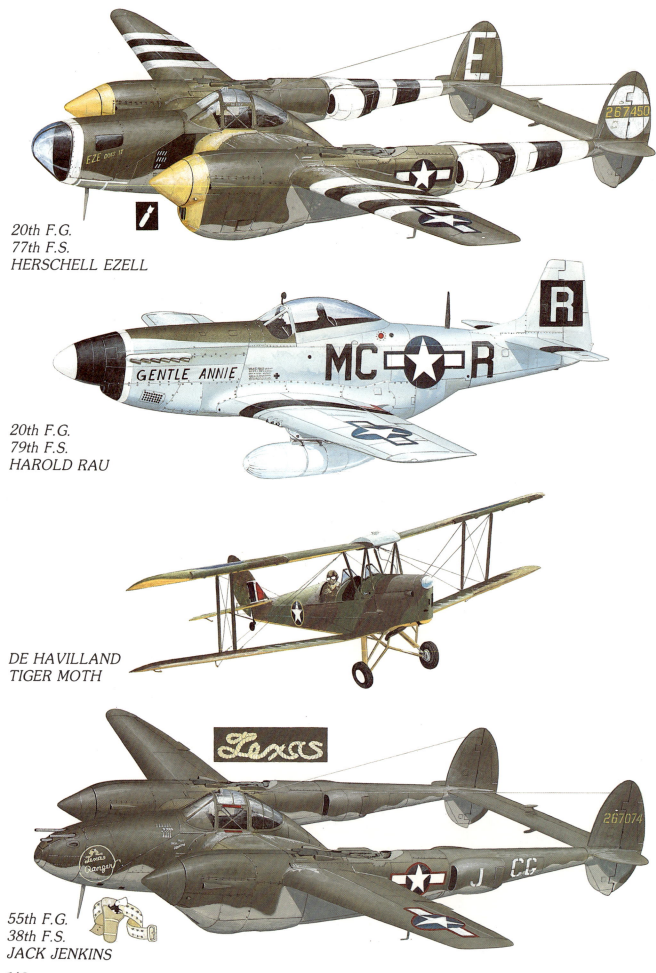

20th F.G.
77th F.S.
HERSCHELL EZELL

20th F.G.
79th F.S.
HAROLD RAU

DE HAVILLAND
TIGER MOTH

55th F.G.
38th F.S.
JACK JENKINS

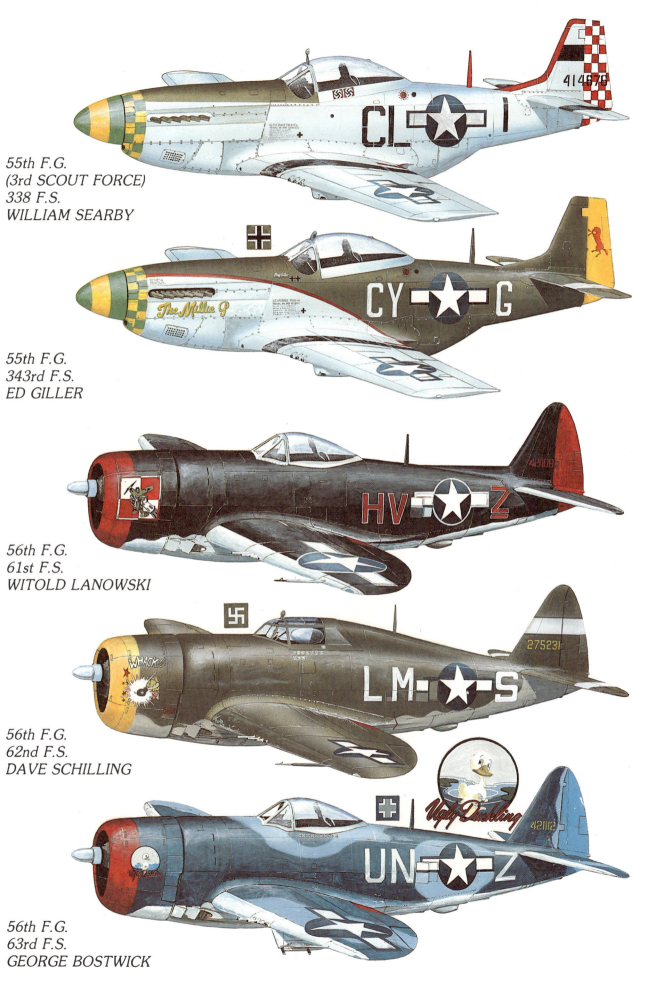

55th F.G.
(3rd SCOUT FORCE)
338 F.S.
WILLIAM SEARBY

55th F.G.
343rd F.S.
ED GILLER

56th F.G.
61st F.S.
WITOLD LANOWSKI

56th F.G.
62nd F.S.
DAVE SCHILLING

56th F.G.
63rd F.S.
GEORGE BOSTWICK

143

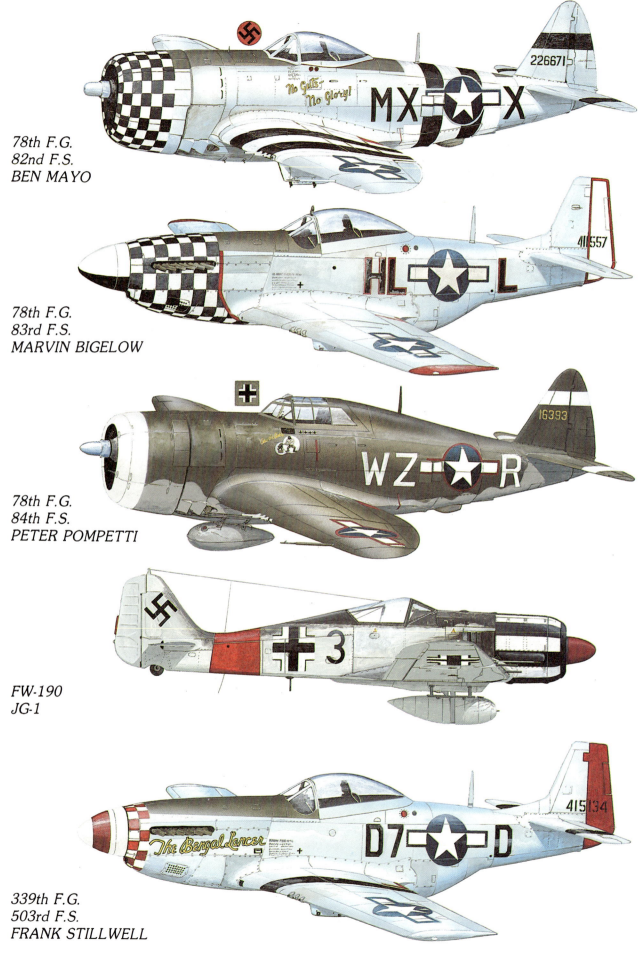

78th F.G.
82nd F.S.
BEN MAYO

78th F.G.
83rd F.S.
MARVIN BIGELOW

78th F.G.
84th F.S.
PETER POMPETTI

FW-190
JG-1

339th F.G.
503rd F.S.
FRANK STILLWELL

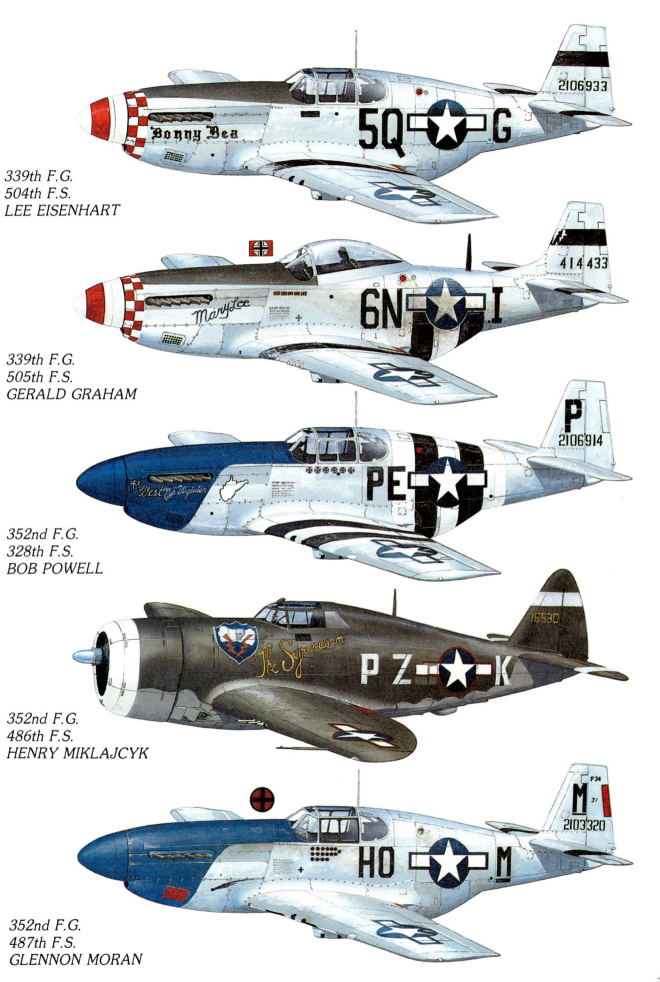

339th F.G.
504th F.S.
LEE EISENHART

339th F.G.
505th F.S.
GERALD GRAHAM

352nd F.G.
328th F.S.
BOB POWELL

352nd F.G.
486th F.S.
HENRY MIKLAJCYK

352nd F.G.
487th F.S.
GLENNON MORAN

145

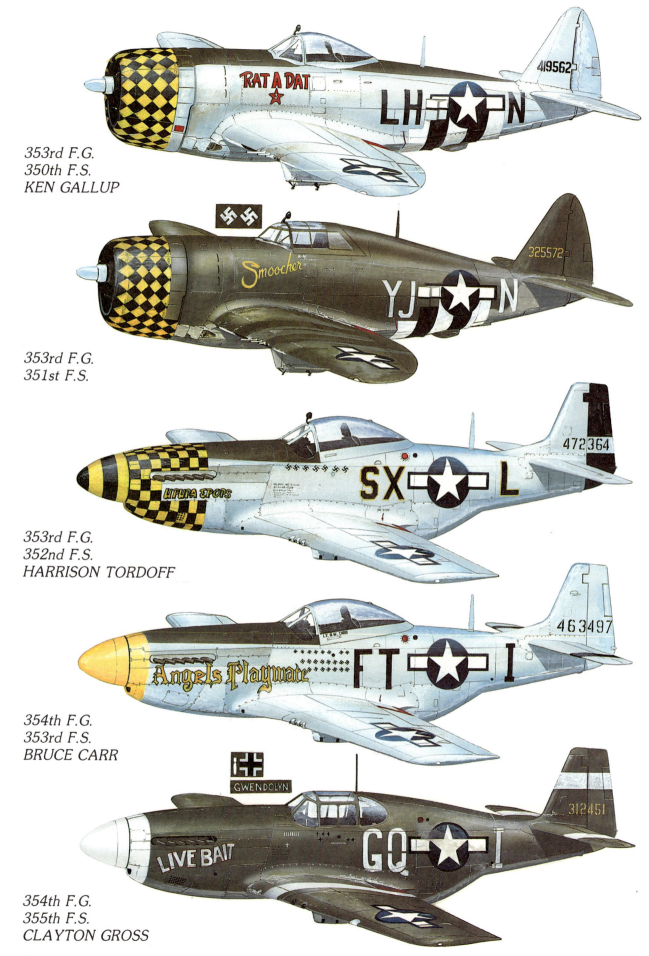

353rd F.G.
350th F.S.
KEN GALLUP

353rd F.G.
351st F.S.

353rd F.G.
352nd F.S.
HARRISON TORDOFF

354th F.G.
353rd F.S.
BRUCE CARR

354th F.G.
355th F.S.
CLAYTON GROSS

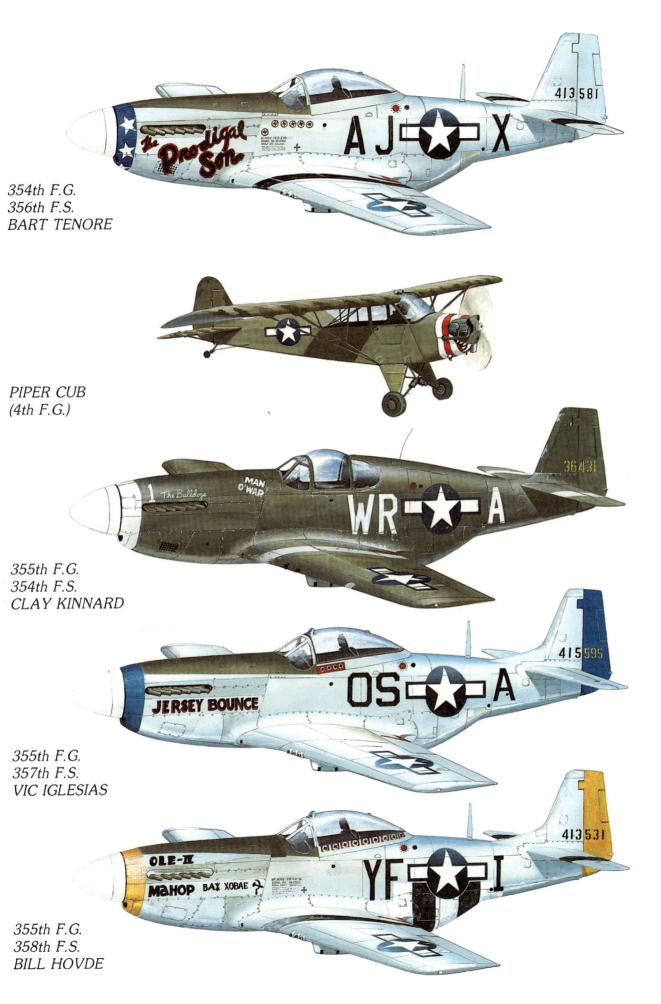

354th F.G.
356th F.S.
BART TENORE

PIPER CUB
(4th F.G.)

355th F.G.
354th F.S.
CLAY KINNARD

355th F.G.
357th F.S.
VIC IGLESIAS

355th F.G.
358th F.S.
BILL HOVDE

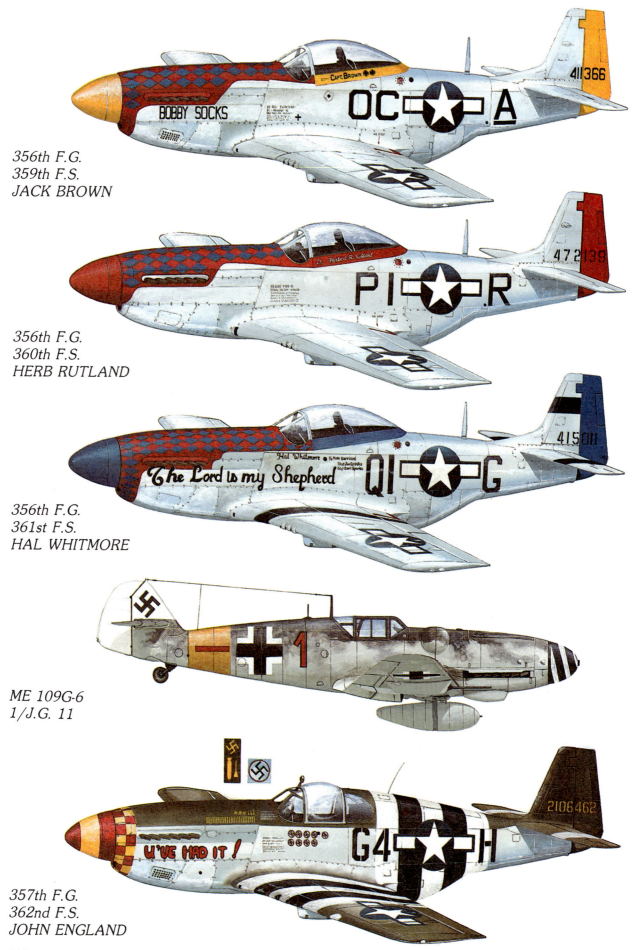

356th F.G.
359th F.S.
JACK BROWN

356th F.G.
360th F.S.
HERB RUTLAND

356th F.G.
361st F.S.
HAL WHITMORE

ME 109G-6
1/J.G. 11

357th F.G.
362nd F.S.
JOHN ENGLAND

148

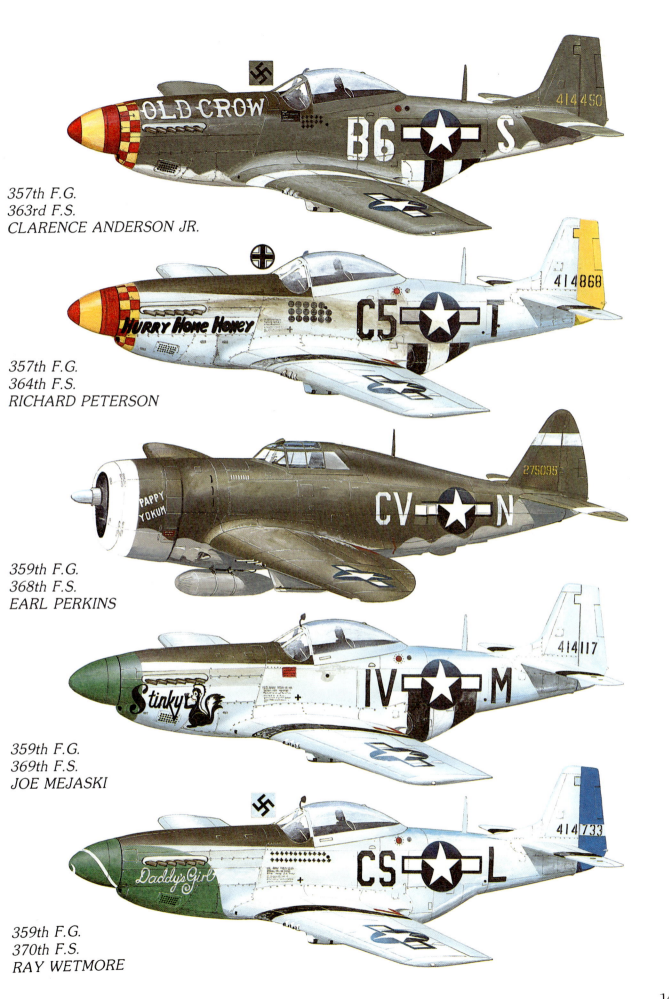

357th F.G.
363rd F.S.
CLARENCE ANDERSON JR.

357th F.G.
364th F.S.
RICHARD PETERSON

359th F.G.
368th F.S.
EARL PERKINS

359th F.G.
369th F.S.
JOE MEJASKI

359th F.G.
370th F.S.
RAY WETMORE

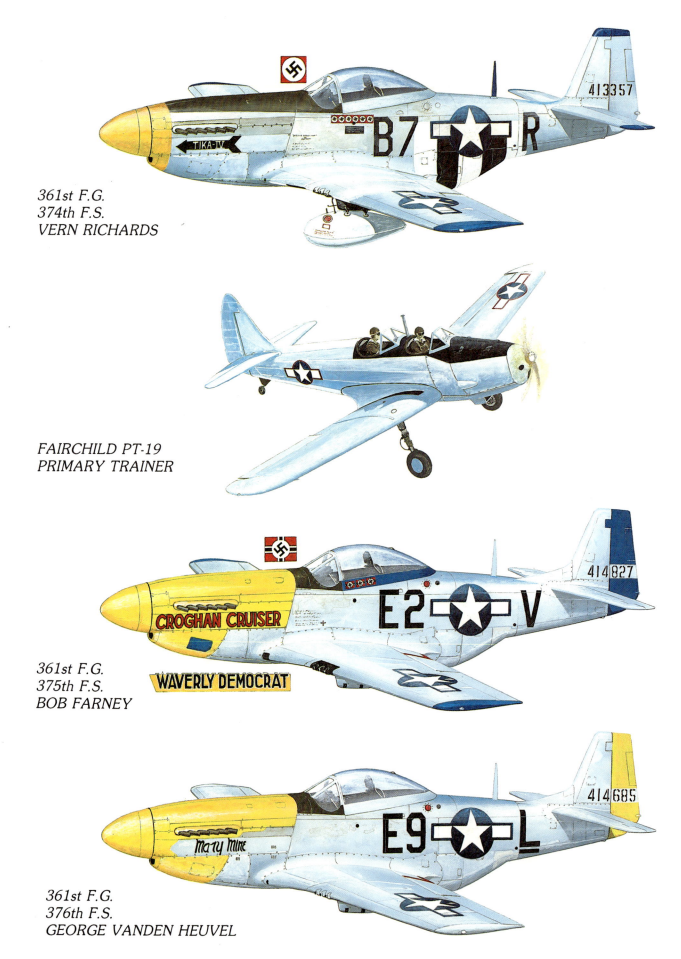

361st F.G.
374th F.S.
VERN RICHARDS

FAIRCHILD PT-19
PRIMARY TRAINER

361st F.G.
375th F.S.
BOB FARNEY

361st F.G.
376th F.S.
GEORGE VANDEN HEUVEL

TIKA-IV

413357

CROGHAN CRUISER

WAVERLY DEMOCRAT

414827

Mary Mine

414685

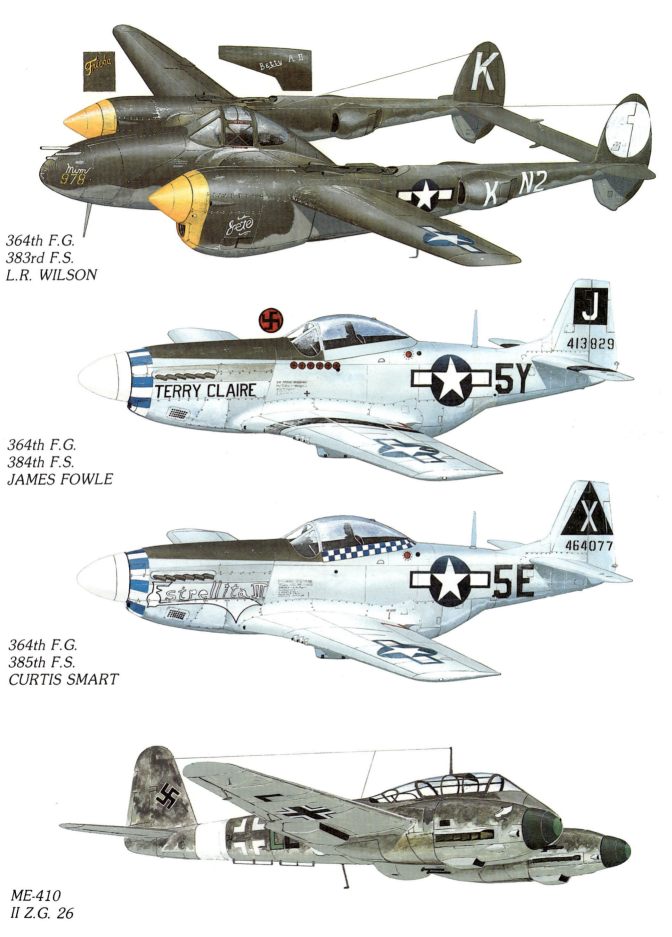

364th F.G.
383rd F.S.
L.R. WILSON

364th F.G.
384th F.S.
JAMES FOWLE

364th F.G.
385th F.S.
CURTIS SMART

ME-410
II Z.G. 26

151

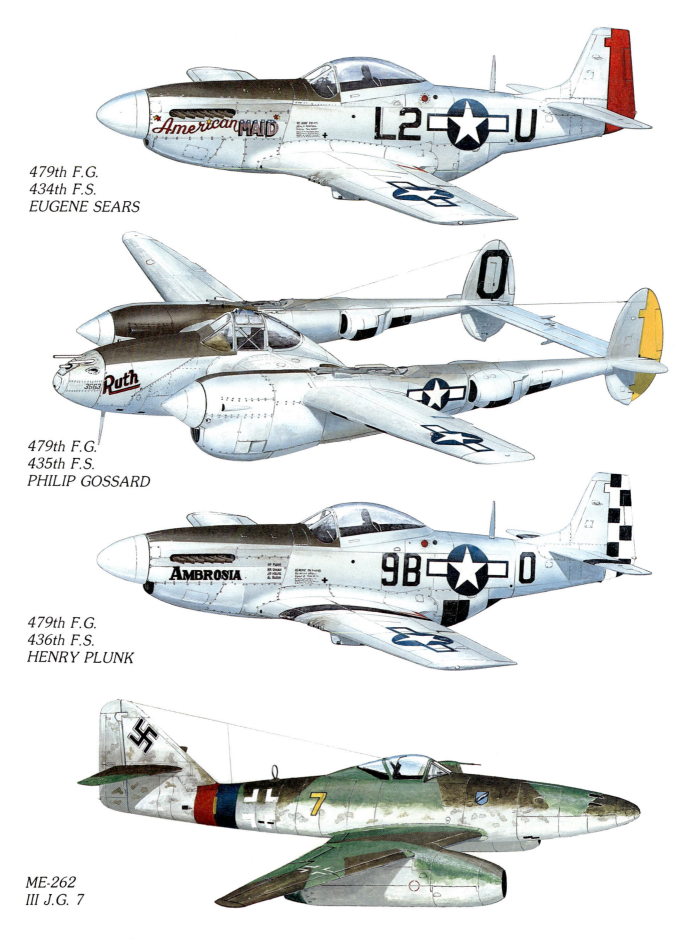

479th F.G.
434th F.S.
EUGENE SEARS

479th F.G.
435th F.S.
PHILIP GOSSARD

479th F.G.
436th F.S.
HENRY PLUNK

ME-262
III J.G. 7

Above: An aerial shot of Leiston Airfield, wartime home of the 357th: 362nd were located top left, the 363rd to the rt. and the 364th were parked near the control tower. (Becraft) Below, left: Two interesting pictures of "Blackpool Bat," the assigned A/C of Lt. G.G. George. Photo at left shows "The Bat" in NMF with coveted Spitfire rear view mirror and mission markers below original issue canopy. (Bennett) Below, right: "The Bat" at some later date w/ Malcolm Hood (the semi-bubble clear canopy type referred to by Myron in his story), O.D. paint, mission marks on the engine cowl, invasion stripes and some sort of artwork(?) after the name. It was group policy for A/C to be NMF in winter and O.D. as soon as the snow disappeared - this totally changing the look of the A/C.

Top, left: A fine late-war photo of Anderson's "Old Crow" with final scoreboard. Besides his 16¼ confirmed vics, Clarence also had 2 damaged and 2 probables. He had a big day on Nov. 27, 1944 when he tangled with a bunch of FW-190s, claiming 2 confirmed and one probable. Top, right: A late war shot of ace Clarence Anderson with his final P-51, #44-14450. Compare style of victory marks to those on A/C when flown by Guy Bender (Vol. II). Note clearly legible last 4 digits of serial on panels to Anderson's rt. Above: At first glance this looks just like Clarence's earlier assigned "B" Model (#43-24823) with all the same markings, O.D. paint, "Old Crow" name, white wall tires, squadron code, drop tanks and even virtually identical camera angles! But its obvious bubble canopy and serial # give it away as just an earlier shot of '4450 pictured above. However, it's fun to compare the 2 shots - the "B" is on page 48 "Aces of the Eighth" by Stafford & Hess.

and pulled off. There were at least a dozen fires when we left."

Lt. Robinson stated that "After trying to catch other enemy aircraft, which eluded us by dodging into the clouds, we found ourselves over an airdrome. There were no runways, but plenty of HE-111s and HE-111s with FW-190s on top of them. They were parked on the edge of a pine forest. On our first pass I destroyed a HE-111, which burned fiercely. Lt. Becraft and I made six more passes on the field. I destroyed a total of four HE-111s which burned. I also damaged two others, one of which had a FW-190 on top of it. The enemy planes were pretty well camouflaged with pine boughs piled all over them. Some of the ships we claimed as HE-111s may have had FW-190s on top; it was almost impossible to distinguish the piggybacks from the regular 111s until we were directly over them.

Our passes were made from different directions and at about a 30 degree dive. When we left, having run low on gas and ammo, there were twelve fires. I saw no activity on the field at any time during our attack and only one building could be seen on the edge of the woods."

Lt., Gilbert A. Robinson

Left: An interesting caption to a similar photo of Jim Browning appeared in Airfoil #2: "He was lost on February 9, 1945, in a tangle with Me262s. The February 9 operation was a major effort with some 1200 bombers striking oil targets. Out in force also were all fighter groups of the 8th, and it was about 1140 hours, at 26,000 ft. when Cement Squadron (363rd) spotted nine Me262s approaching the bombers in the Fulda area (NE of Frankfurt). The squadron dropped tanks and dived on the 262s, which broke formation and scattered. The 262 leader, however, turned into the bomber formation with at least one Cement element following. The mission report does not say what happened to Jim Browning, but it does give a clue: "While pursuing Me262 through Vinegrove 2-6 formation, our element flew through bomber fire, which was, we believe intended for the jet aircraft. The mission leader reported that the jets made wide sweeping turns, allowing the slower Mustangs to cut them off, and two were shot down, one to Don Bochkay, and one to Johnnie Carter. Major Bob Foy was one of those who followed the 262 leader through the bomber formation, and he reported repeated strikes on the jet, but lost it, so claimed only a probable. The final casualty report some 4 months later listed Jim Browning as a K.I.A."

Freeman: This is Lt. Larry Freeman in London bringing you another edition of Combat Thrills . . . the most exciting moments of aerial warfare experienced by the fighter pilots of the U.S. Eighth Air Force. Though the thrills and chills of these fighting men of the sky are many and varied there is always one which tops the rest . . . one which they will forever remember as their biggest Combat Thrill. Today we have the story of First Lieutenant Myron A. Becraft, 21 year old P-51 Mustang fighter pilot with the 357th Fighter Group, whose

home is on Fairview Road, Horseheads, New York. Lieutenant Becraft is here to tell you of the experience in aerial combat that stands out above all others in his mind.

Several days later Myron went to London to be interviewed by Lt. Larry Freeman in a broadcast that was transmitted back to the States. Following is a transcript of the broadcast:

Becraft: When a fighter pilot shoots down his first plane it is undoubtedly one of the greatest thrills of his life . . . except that I was lucky to score not one but seven victories all in one day . . . my first victories over the Luftwaffe.

Freeman: Seven in one mission . . . that's some shooting . . . tell us more about it?

Becraft: Well, one was in the air, and I clobbered the other six planes on the ground. We were on a bomber escort mission over Magdeburg when I happened to get the one in the air . . . I sighted a ME-109 in a Luffberry circle with three Mustangs, so I decided to join in also.

Freeman: A Luffberry circle . . . will you explain that term?

Becraft: Yes. It means to fly in a tight circle . . . each plane trying to get on the plane in front's tail . . . I guess the others in the group thought the Jerry was a Mustang . . . but I closed to within 300 yards of the blue-grey camouflaged German plane and fired two short bursts. I was sort of stunned when I saw my machine gun fire tear into the cockpit and cut off the right wing . . . just like a knife cutting butter. I moved to the side, 'chopped' my throttle and watched the Messerschmitt catch on fire, wiggle violently, and suddenly start to come apart as it spun into the ground.

Freeman: and that's one destroyed.

Becraft: Yes, and then I chased a couple of enemy aircraft through a hole in the clouds, but they disappeared. Then I spotted a fire on the ground where a plane had crashed. I took my wingman down for a look . . . we discovered that we were over a German airfield and there were some Jerry planes on the ground, camouflaged with tree branches.

Freeman: So you decided to strafe those planes?

Becraft: That's right . . . those German airfields are usually pretty well defended with flak guns, I called my buddies on the radio . . . but they were upstairs and couldn't locate the place . . . anyway, I made a pass over the field and to my surprise there was no flak bursting around me . . . then I just took my time and made seven passes over that field. I saw that the planes were twin-engined Heinkel 111 bombers, two of them with FW-190s perched on top of them . . . what we call 'pick-a-backs'. It was really a pleasant feeling, sweeping over that field with no flak and strafing those

On this page are four 357th pilots who had some success against the vastly superior German jet A/C. First is none other than Capt. Chuck Yeager who made the first confirmed victory for the group against 262s on Nov. 6, 1944. He also had 2 more damaged claims on that date. Above, right: Lt. Joe Cannon (an appropriate name for a fighter pilot!) had to settle for a probable when his K-14 gunsight went out at a critical moment near Leipzig, March 19, 1945. Below, left: Lt. Paul Bowles caught a 262 taking off from Ruzyne A/D, near Prague, Czechoslovakia, on Apr. 19. It was the 357th's best day against the Jets with claims for six 262s confirmed. Below right: Another victor on the same mission was fellow 363rd pilot Carroll Ofsthun. Both Bowles and Ofsthun reported that, even with such a great tactical advantage, they had to open fire at maximum range. (Bennett)

planes. On two of my passes I saw two of the big German bombers explode when my machine gun bullets hit. And when I finally left, being low on ammunition, there were four other planes that I had strafed burning. My wingman (Lt. Robinson) only had one gun firing so we took off for home. Knocking down that ME-109 and destroying six more planes on the ground certainly gave me my greatest combat thrill.

Freeman: And that was really taking full advantage of a good opportunity to destroy those German planes. Thanks a lot for the story, Lieutenant Becraft, and the best of luck to you in future missions. Today's Combat Thrill has been told to you by 1st Lieutenant Myron A. Becraft, of the Eighth Air Force and Fairview Road, Horseheads Road, New York. This is Lt. Larry Freeman speaking from London.''

Returning from an escort mission to Hamburg on March 30th, 1945 the coolant system on Lt. Daniel Myers' P-51 'popped' and he bailed out just a few miles from the Dutch coast. Two flights of the 363rd

Fighter Squadron which were with him orbited the downed pilot as he climbed into his dinghy and a call was sent out for ASR. The controller at Leiston dispatched four Mustangs, led by Captain John 'Pappy' Stern, to relieve the orbiting fighters who by this time were getting low on fuel. Just before Pappy Stern arrived, two other Mustangs also began orbiting the 357th pilot. One of the pilots was George 'Pop' Doersch, an ace with the 359th Fighter Group.

Halfway across the North Sea Cpt. Stern joined up with a Catalina which was on its way to the downed pilot. Soon the five aircraft arrived on the scene — about 4 miles off the northeast tip of Schiermonikogg Island. The Catalina landed at about 20.00 hours but due to the bad weather and approaching darkness the pilots didn't know if they were successful in picking up Lt. Myers. It was later found out that the PBY lost an engine while landing due to an oil line breaking. The crew started to repair the line but German shore batteries opened fire. So the pilot taxied the stricken

Above, left: Li'l Red's Rocket C5-S, #43-6653 was the assigned A/C of Captain Thomas L. Harris. Things happened fast in wartime - Tom made Captain just shortly before he was involved in a big dog fight near Strasbourg, France on May 27, 1944. Two victories and one probable were confirmed by eye witnesses before he was, himself, shot down by a 109 (MACR #5108) Note early white markings and only 1 vic tallied below canopy. (Bennett) Above, right: Two 364th Sq. P-51s landed in Sweden Aug. 25, '44. Lt. Charles E. Burtner made a wheels up landing in P51 B, 42-106854. Lt. Walter Baron brought #44-13345 in with a rough engine. This A/C, C5-I "Mary Ann" was later put in service with the Swedish A/F as J-26 #26003. (Olausson) Below, left: Capt. Glendon V. Davis with A/C and crew. The 364th F.S. code, C5, is identifiable above the wing, the serial number is 43-6878, but the individual A/C letter is not known. (Bennett) Below, right: Captain Davis went down in France, April 28, 1944 due to engine failure according to MACR # 4410. He evaded capture and, after several months, returned to England and went home - a 7½ victory ace.

Left: This photo of "Moose" on a rare two-seat 109 was taken at the 354th Fighter Group's Base at Neubiberg, Germany in early '46. Note '354' on windsock. (Becraft) Right: S/Sgt. Joe Sewell with his G4-S. In the background is G4-S 44-15607, 'Ticket to Loraine.' (Olmsted)

aircraft away from the shore, and Lt. Myers, on its one good engine. At one time the aircraft was only some 200 yards away from the shore. The next morning another flight of Mustangs sent to patrol the area saw the PBY listing and damaged by gunfire. The crew had taken to their dinghies. Major Kit Carson led a flight of three Mustangs later in the day to act as top cover.

Flying as his number two was Myron in G4-S(bar), 44-63221 and Myron recalls: "On March 30th one of our pilots bailed out off the Dutch coast. The pilot, Lt. Myers, made a successful landing in the water and got into his dinghy. A PBY, air sea rescue aircraft landed to pick him up, but it broke an oil line and lost one engine. Major Leonard Carson, our operations officer, flew as Combat Air Patrol (CAP) to cover the PBY crew and Lt. Myers until a B-17 could arrive and drop a life-boat. The weather that day was broken clouds at about 4 or 5,000 feet and fairly heavy over the target.

Major Carson was circling above the clouds and I underneath. I don't recall being briefed about enemy aircraft in the rescue area so we kept our drop tanks to stretch out our time over the men. While circling, fat, dumb and happy, I noticed the PBY crew were firing a lot of flares for some reason or other. I glanced up to see an aircraft coming almost directly at me. We'd just been briefed about a new British twin-engined fighter and this looked just like it. I saw that it was firing — what I'd thought were flares were his cannon shells bounding off the sea! I guess he hadn't seen me as he was so intent on shooting up the PBY. He passed me so close I could see his yellow Mae West and the big black crosses on his fuselage stood out

plainly. By this time I started to wake up, switched over to the main tank and turned left, back towards the PBY. After making his pass the ME-262 broke to the right and I was able to cut him off as he turned towards land. I saw many hits from my bullets. He made a hard turn to the left, entered the low clouds and was gone. Evidently there were two 262s, because Carson saw one above the cloud layer at about the same time as I saw mine. But we could not determine if we got either of them. I was awarded a damage claim against the one I fired on." Things got quiet after this and Carson and Myron carried on with their patrol and returned to Leiston after some 5:30 hours.

During their patrol a Wellington bomber dropped a lifeboat. The airmen climbed in but after a short while they took to their dinghies again as the lifeboat was sinking. Another boat was dropped too far away. Shortly after this a B-17 dropped a third lifeboat and this time it was spot on - it landed just 50 yards away and the crew were seen to get aboard safely. After Myron and Carson left another flight of Mustangs was sent out, but due to poor visibility was unable to locate the lifeboat so they headed for home after a search.

On April 1st Captain Ivan McGuire led the last patrol and although the PBY crew were saved, no sign was seen of Lt. Myers. It was later learned he had drifted ashore and was taken prisoner. All told, over 90 Mustangs, 38 Thunderbolts, 25 Warwicks, 6 Mosquitos, 8 Beaufighters, and 3 Flying Fortresses had taken part in the rescue operation. Besides the PBY, a Beaufighter and its crew were also lost!

The claim against the 262 was to be Myron's last for the war. After May 8, 1945 he was involved in the shipment of a number of Mustangs to the Continent as part of the Occupation Forces. July 7, 1945 the 357th transferred to a base just outside of Munich. Myron stayed with his group until late September when he was transferred to an anti-aircraft unit stationed at Augsburg that was rotating its personel back to the States. The unit was formed of troops from many different organizations as a speedy method of getting them home.

At the time Myron had his mind on many things, but most of all it was on the girl he was to marry. A few days after his arrival back in the States on November 16, 1945 he was inactivated. On June 23rd the following year he married his lovely wife Lillian (Osbourne). They have two daughters, Barbara and Bonnie.

After World War Two Myron was recalled to active service in October 1947 and during the Korean conflict flew with the 18th Fighter Bomb Squadron and flew 13 combat missions with them during 1952. Myron and Lillian now live at Warner Robins AFB in Georgia.

Claims made by Lt. Myron A. Becraft

20.12.44	Strafed ground targets . . . trains and railroad station. G4-S(bar), 44-63221
1.1.45	Strafed ground targets . . . 1 train, 3 canal boats and one factory. G4-U, 44-13334.
2.3.45	1 ME-109 Destroyed, Air. 2 HE-111 Destroyed, Ground. Also 2 HE-111s with FW-190s as 'piggybacks' Destroyed. Ground. Kamenz Airfield, Germany. G4-S (bar), 44-63221.
31.3.45	1 ME-262 Damaged, Air. North Sea. G4-S(bar), 44-63211.

24.12.44	Ramrod	5:05	G4-Z	Frankfurt
29.12.44	Ramrod	4:50	G4-Q	Frankfurt
30.12.44	Ramrod	4:50	G4-D	Kassel
31.12.44	Ramrod	4:30	G4-U	Eupen
1.1.45	Patrol	4:40	G4-U	Oldenburg
2.1.45	Patrol	3:20	G4-U	Aachen
3.1.45	PRU	3:05	G4-H	Stuttgart

Above, left: During Gerald Tyler's operational tour he was assigned at least these two P-51s, both carrying the rather strange name LITTLE DUCKFOOT. The first, a B model, was serial number 43-6376 and carried unit code C5-J. This photo shows it undergoing modification by the 469th Service Sqdn., for installation of a Malcolm Hood. Tyler finished the war with 7 victories, and in later years was General Manager of Cavalier Aviation, a Florida company which did extensive P-51 modifications. In 1969 Tyler flew his own Mustang to Europe, including 1750 miles, Gander to Shannon, nonstop! (Olmsted) Above, right: The second "Duckfoot" P-51 D, #44-14660. Clean appearing A/C carries Tyler's final tally. Below, left: Group Commander for the last 5 months of the war, Lt. Col. Irwin Dregne made certain he and his group were in the thick of the action. He flew this "D" and a later "K" to 5 confirmed and 3 probables. His C/C picked the starboard side name, but his later "K" carried "Bobby Jeanne" to port as well. He died in 1967. (Bennett) Below, right: "Geechee Gal" was the assigned A/C of Lt. Joe M. Jenkins. If he was involved in this take-off accident, that wrote off his P-51, he wasn't hurt very badly as he was assigned another P-51 which he named "Geechee Girl." C/C was Cyril Brech. We are grateful to Steve Blake and Steve Sheflin of the sorely-missed Airfoil magazine for this information: Vol. II p. 7.

Date	Mission	Time	A/C	Location	Date	Mission	Time	A/C	Location
5.1.45	Ramrod	2.25	G4-S(bar)	Frankfurt	11.3.45	Ramrod	4:15	G4-S(bar)	Hamburg
7.1.45	Sweep	4:05	G4-S(bar)	Altenkirchen	15.3.45	Ramrod	5:45	G4-S(bar)	Aranien
10.1.45	Patrol	5:25	G4-S(bar)	Kassel	18.3.45	Ramrod	5:25	G4-S(bar)	Berlin
13.1.45	Ramrod	4:15	G4-S(bar)	Mainz	24.3.45	Patrol	5:10	G4-S(bar)	Osnabruck
14.1.45	Ramrod	4:25	G4-S(bar)	Derben	30.3.45	Ramrod	5:40	G4-S(bar)	Hamburg
15.1.45	Ramrod	5:25	G4-S(bar)	Leipheim	31.3.45	ASR	3:55	G4-S(bar)	Borden Island
20.1.45	Ramrod	2:00	G4-S(bar)	Heilbron					
21.1.45	Ramrod	5:40	G4-S(bar)	Aschaffenburg	4.4.45	Ramrod	4:20	G4-S(bar)	Kiel
29.1.45	Ramrod	4:25	G4-S(bar)	Kassel	6.4.45	Ramrod	5:40	G4-S(bar)	Gera
					7.4.45	Ramrod	5:55	G4-S(bar)	Grafenwohr
3.2.45	PRU	4:15	G4-S(bar)	Hanover	20.4.45	Ramrod	5:05	G4-S(bar)	Naver
6.2.45	Ramrod	5:30	G4-S(bar)	Leipzig	21.4.45	Ramrod	5:50	G4-S(bar)	Halzkirchen
9.2.45	Ramrod	5:35	G4-S(bar)	Bohlen	24.4.45	Roving Sup.	6:10	G4-S(bar)	Pilzen
11.2.45	Ramrod	2:55	G4-S(bar)	Wesel					
14.2.45	Ramrod	5:50	G4-S(bar)	Chemnitz					
15.2.45	Ramrod	6:20	G4-S(bar)	Ruhland					
20.2.45	Ramrod	4:40	G4-S(bar)	Nurmberg					
22.2.45	Radio Rel.	5:15	G4-S(bar)	Zwickau					
23.2.45	Ramrod	5:05	G4-S(bar)	Naumberg					
25.2.45	Ramrod	6:10	G4-S(bar)	Munich					
2.3.45	Ramrod	4:20	G4-S(bar)	Ruhland					
3.3.45	Ramrod	0:10*	G4-S(bar)	Brunswick					
9.3.45	Sweep	5:20	G4-S(bar)	Frankfurt					

*Aborted mission, engine cutout on take-off.
Aircraft flown by Lt. Myron A. Becraft while with the 357th Fighter Group
G4-Y, 44-14680 'Duchess'
G4-U, 44-13334 'Wee Willie 11'
G4-S(Bar), 44-63221 'Moose'
G4-X, 44-11198 'Libby'
G4-A, 44-13691 'Passion Wagon'
G4-Q, 44-11190 'Lady Ovella'
94-H, 44-14820 'Spook'
94-R(bar), 43-6688

Above: Two photos of Capt. Robert G. Schimanski and his A/C. Besides his 6 confirmed victories, Bob had a damaged claim as well. All his victories were while serving with the 364th F.S. His P-51, C5-O, 44-14334 carried no personal markings. (Schimanski) Below, left: 364th Squadron Commander, Lt. Col. Tom Hayes and C/C Bob Krull with their first ''Frenesi'' (Free and Easy). One of the real spark plugs in the 357th, Tom served in the Pacific before joining the 357th. He went on to command the 364th Fighter Group and eventually retired as an A.F. General. He led by example, having aced with the hard hitting Yoxford Boys. (Olmsted) Below, right: A nice shot of Tom's ''D'' Model # 44-13318. (Bennett)

ROBERT MILES YORK

370TH FIGHTER SQUADRON, 359TH FIGHTER GROUP

Robert M. York was born on 11th September 1921 in Portland, Maine and after attending several schools he graduated from the Coburn Classical Institute, Waterville in 1940. For the next two years he studied at Portland Jr. College.

While there he joined a flight training programme and obtained his Private Pilot's License in May 1942. Later that month, on the 27th, he enlisted in the USAAC and spent the next three months at Montgomery, Alabama completing his Preflight Training. From there he transferred to Lakeland, Florida for three months of Primary Flying. Upon completion he left for Sumter, South Carolina for nine weeks of Basic Training. He was then transferred to Spence Field near Moultrie, Georgia where he graduated as a pilot on 28th May 1943 in Class 43-E, a year after enlistment. During July and August he was at Matagorda Peninsula, Texas where he took part in an Aerial Gunnery Course and upon completion he returned to Spence Field as an Advanced Flying Instructor. He later became an instructor at Eglin Field, Florida teaching gunnery (this was to pay dividends later). After that

Above: Robert M. York "Last & Forever." Left: A line up of early 368th Squadron P-47s, including Capt. Earl P. Perkins 42-75095 "Pappy Yokum," our choice for the 368th's color profile on page 149. Note "Marryin' Sam" and "Daisy Mae" - two other characters from Al Capp's popular comic strip. "Daisy Mae" was the personal A/C of Major William C. Forehand. Left, bottom: "Geronimo," an early P-47 D-2-RA of the 368th, coded CV-S, down near Burtonwood in May '44. It carried the name and art work on both sides. A starboard shot is on page 21 of Kent Miller's fine 359th history. (Mulron)

he served at Sarasota, Florida flying P-40s and while there met a number of fighter pilots with whom he was to serve in England.

In June 1944, along with his friends, he was ordered to report to Camp Kilmer prior to going overseas. He sailed for England on the 'SS Mauritania' (The author's father served as a stoker on this ship before the war.) and upon arriving in England was posted to the 496th Fighter Training Group at Goxhill, Lincolnshire for Transitional Training on the P-51 Mustang. After he completed his training he was posted to the 359th Fighter Group based at East Wretham, Norfolk.

Posted with him on 2nd August 1944 were his friends, Cy Jones, William F. Collins, George F. Baker and David B. Archibald (all these pilots later became aces). Also assigned were John W. McAlister, who was transferred from the 359th Group prior to completing his combat tour, and Lawrence A. Beardon who was killed on a training mission while with the 359th Fighter Group. Of the fourteen pilots posted that fateful day in 1944, Cy Jones, Benjamin J. Vos, John E. Hughes and Carl M. Anderson were killed in action and Dave Archibald was taken prisoner of war on 18th December 1944. Those who completed their tours of duty

160

Glen Bach in his assigned Mustang 'Pegelin' flies on the wing of Emory Cook in CV-P, 43-12478 and Billy D. Kasper follows in CV-H, 42-106809, ''Little Liquidator.'' All three pilots served with the 368th Fighter Squadron, 359th Fighter Group which was based at East Wretham Norfolk. The date was the 28th August 1944. Right: A tired but happy Billy D. Kasper has just returned from a six hour plus mission to Munich, Germany. Note the faded number 16 under the cockpit. The reason for this is unknown. The aircraft also has no squadron code. (Kasper)

were Bob York, Bob Gaines, Frank O. Lux, Emory C. Johnson, William F. Collins, Rene L. Burtner Jr., and George F. Baker. Burtner was shot down and was able to evade capture and finished his tour upon returning to England.

On 8th August Bob flew his first mission, Area Support, to the Dijon area which lasted for a butt numbing 5 hours. He was in Blue Flight, led by Lt. Warren R. Newberg (Blue 1), and the remainder of the flight consisted of Lt. Elbert W. Tilton (Blue 2), Robert M. York (Blue 3) and Lt. Milton S. Merry as Tail End Charlie. After giving cover to the bombers they, along with Red and Yellow Flights, looked for targets of opportunity. Red Flight soon became separated and at about 1430 hours they saw a truck which Yellow Flight attacked but only damaged. Blue Flight climbed back to about 2,000 feet and continued searching for targets. Some 10 minutes later they found a string of goods cars near Cambrai which they strafed and later claimed 20 damaged. At the end of his encounter report Lt. Newberg remarked that he had never seen an area with ''less in it for targets of opportunity.'' At the time Bob was flying a P-51C coded CS-E , 42-103893.

The following day Bob shot down his first enemy aircraft near Gunsberg and he recalled ''While on an Escort mission my high blower went out so I tied it up in the manual position with my neck-tie. At the Group Leader's order to climb for altitude and make a hundred degree turn to the left my neck-tie slipped and my blower went out. When I had it fixed again Blue Leader was far ahead of me. A flight of about twenty (20) ME-109s came down out of the sun, turned towards me, and then changed their course and went after the bombers. I cleared myself and saw below me, at 20,000 feet, an ME-109 make a pass at a P-51 and then dive away. I rolled down and got in a burst at 60

degrees. The ME-109 split-essed and dove down. I followed, and gave him two more bursts and saw strikes all over the fuselage with a greater concentration in the canopy section and pieces of his plane flew back at me. I followed him down and pulled up level at 800 feet indicating 500 MPH and when I last saw the enemy aircraft he was still going straight down about 500 feet below me. From the speed of his dive he couldn't have pulled out in time.

I claim one, (1) ME-109 destroyed in the air.

At the time Bob used just 367 rounds of API from the guns of CS-U(bar), 42-106862. The claim was confirmed.

On his third mission in as many days (10th August) he was with White Flight led by Lt. Robert Callahan (CS-K, 44-13966), Lt. Cy Jones, White 2 (CS-D, 44-13529), Bob York, White 3 (CS-P, 42-106894) and F/O. James J. O'Shea, White 4 (CS-H, 42-106704) on a dive bombing mission. They attacked a marshalling yard at Lahr and White and Blue Flights claimed the destruction of some rolling stock (including one loco) plus one round bridge demolished and several railway sheds. On this mission the aircraft were using 250lb bombs and Bob also fired 200 rounds of API. On the way home Cy Jones attacked and damaged a loco and four wagons.

On 13th August, Bob led Blue Flight on a Fighter Bomber and Strafing mission near Nogent Le Rotrou. His flight attacked a bridge that passed over a railway track with Lt. Robert G. Oakley scoring a direct hit. The track was cut in one place and the bridge was damaged. The flight was carrying 500 lb. bombs and all pilots returned safely. Four days later, on the 17th, the group was carrying out a dive-bombing mission near Nogent sur Oise-Compiegne. Bob was in Yellow Flight as the number two man covering his flight leader, Ben-

jamin J. Vos. Yellow Three was Lt. John F. McAlister and Yellow Four Lt. Harvey C. Williams. Upon his return Lt. Vos wrote: 'I was leading Yellow Flight on a dive-bombing and strafing mission on the 17th August. There was a 9/10 overcast with a base at about 2,500 feet. Upon going below the overcast, the sections broke up into individual flights. We found four locomotives standing on a siding near an intersection. The entire flight made strafing passes and damaged all four locos. Very concentrated flak from the intersection was noticed; so we left. We then found three military trucks moving on a highway. The whole flight strafed these, setting two of them on fire and damaging the third one. We then found a marshalling yard with approximately 50 cars in it. We dive-bombed the yards, doing most damage to the tracks, on which there were 6 direct hits. Lt. Bob York sighted a truck (a large trailer type) and destroyed it with a bomb.

We then found about ten box cars standing still. The whole flight strafed these, causing damage to all of the cars. After leaving this target, we found another train which contained a loco and three cars. The flight strafed it, but could not get it to burn. I was out of ammo on this pass.

The flight became separated at this point, as Lts. McAlister and Harvey C. Williams sighted a large trailer truck and made two strafing passes on it, but failed to set it alight. They then found about 30 oil cars which they also strafed. These also failed to burn even after several passes.

Lt. York and I went straight from the train on the deck. I sighted a camouflaged group of about 12 box cars on a siding in the woods. I called them in to Lt. York and he made a pass at them, causing either 5 or 7 of them to explode, and from the intensity of the explosion it was believed to be an ammunition train.

I claim in cooperation with Lts. York, McAlister and H. Williams four (4) locomotives damaged, three (3) trains damaged, two (2) trucks destroyed, one (1) truck damaged and tracks in marshalling yard destroyed.

Lt. York claims five (5) or seven (7) ammo RR cars destroyed and one (1) truck destroyed.

Lt. Vos	CS-H, 42-106704	2 250 lb. bombs; 1,260 rds API.
Lt. York	CS-K, 42-103966	2 250 lb. bombs; 1,260 rds API.

Above, left: CV-Z in decidedly different D-Day Livery. Note fuselage bands cover Sq. codes and even extend over canopy framing. Rudder trim tab is in red for flight color. A/C was flown at various times by aces Ben King and Dave Archibald. Note 2 RAF Vultee Vengeance A/C in background - one coded LS-F. (York) Above, right: Group Commander and ace Lt. Col. Don Baccus's A/C. Formerly with the 356th, Don was assigned to the 359th from April to Sept. 45. (Mulron) Below, left: A post V.E. Day line up of 368 F S A/C: CV-Y, 44-13776 ''Kitten''/ CV-N, 44-14965 ''Lady''/CV-T, 44-11758 ''Silky'' - The A/C of Capt. John A. Denman/ and CV-Z, 44-72281 ''Happy II'' - assigned to Lt. James L. Way Jr. Below, right: CV-P at East Wretham in the ''early spring'' of '45. This photo comes to us from Lt. Robert Guggemos, who served as a pilot in both the 368th and 369th F.S. from Oct. '44 to Sept. '45. (Via Jim Crow)

Lt. McAlister	CS-G, 44-14039	2 250 lb. bombs; 932 rds API.	
Lt. Williams	CS-C, 42-106902	2 250 lb. bombs; 652 rds. API.	

At the end of August Bob was on an escort mission when the bombers aborted prior to making R/V. On the return journey Yellow Flight, which consisted of Lts. Vos, York, Welch and Sundheim, dropped down looking for targets of opportunity to shoot up. Near Munster the first chance came when a tug was spotted and the flight made several passes but failed to sink the tug. Lt. Paul E. Sundheim was lost during the attack and was still listed as MIA after the war. After the attack on the tug Vos, York and Welch shot up a loco and some goods cars and also knocked out a switch house.

It was not until 7th October 1944 that Bob claimed his next aircraft, a BV-140 moored on a lake near Dievenow. Although he asked for it to be allowed as destroyed it was reduced to a damaged. He had to share it with Lt. Emory G. Johnson, who claimed an AR-196, and both pilots ended up with a shared BV-140.

On the 27th November on an Escort Mission, Bob was acting as Ray S. Wetmore's wingman in Red Flight when 'Nuthouse' reported many 'Bandits' in the Munster area. Along with Jimmy Shoffit and Robert McInnes they went 'for a look see' and found approximately 200 ME-109s and FW-190s just southeast of Hanover. The time was about 1300 hours and Wetmore recalled:

'I was leading Red Flight when 'Nuthouse' vectored the group to the north of Munster where Bandits were reported. The squadron got split up due to intense flak. I took my flight to the vicinity of our strafing target in the hope of rejoining them. The bandits were in two gaggles of about 100 planes each, one bunch was ME-109s and the other FW-190s.

I immediately started calling our group and notifying 'Nuthouse' their position, altitude and direction. I continued to follow them, remaining high and to the rear of their formation. A few minutes later my second element (Shoffit and McInnes) had to return home due to engine trouble. By this time the Jerries found out I was there and started sending out several four ship flights after us. I continued to call in the Jerries' position until we had to bounce them to save our own

Above, left: Lt. Lawrence Bouchard and Lt. Alma R. Smith, two old hands with the 369th, compare notes. Both completed their operational tours in Aug. '44 after more than a year with the group. (Coleman) Above, right: Mary, with a hugh mission scoreboard just below left of canopy, in the twilight of her career, June '44. She had been the A/C of Larry Bouchard and her crew could well be proud of her: C/C Floyd Myers, Assnt. C/C Bill Wall and Armorer Jim Foley. She was a colorful gal too, with her apple green cowl, bright yellow name and white scoreboard on O.D. Also note classy segmented star on inboard side of wheels. (Bouchard) Below, left: Tiny but nice flying shot of 369th and 370th F.S. A/C on a training mission. Note mixture of early and late P-51s. Below, right: A highly decorative late war P-51. Note checkerboard pattern on top of stabilizer as well as canopy frame and fin strake. (Jim Crow)

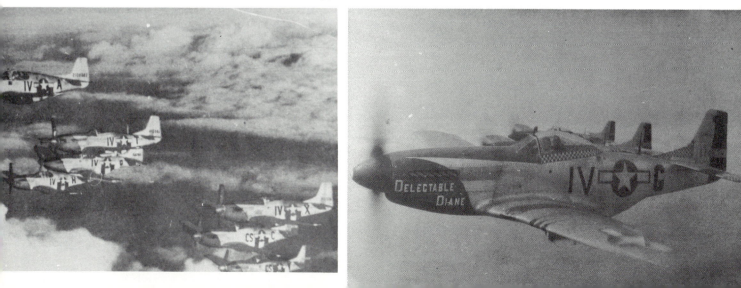

smoke. The last time I saw the ME-109 it was in flames and spinning. I claim this enemy aircraft as destroyed.

I saw another Jerry making a pass on me so I turned into him. We went round and round from about 30,000 feet right on down to the deck. He seemed very aggressive and was darn good with his ME-109. Although I could out turn him he was on my tail a lot of times. He seemed to make good use of his fowler flaps. I finally ran out of ammo but by this time I had hit him several times. I made another pass at him and he bailed out. I then took a picture of him in his chute. Then for the next ten minutes I was attacked repeatedly by FW-190s but managed to out maneuver them. They finally broke off and I headed for home.

I claim three (3) ME-109s destroyed in the air.
CS-H, 44-14979. Cpt. Ray S. Wetmore.
1,243 rds of API.

I saw Capt. Wetmore fire at an ME-109 and saw the ship start to smoke and then go down spinning.
ROBERT M. YORK

necks as they started to bounce us. I closed in on a ME-109 to approximately 600 yards before firing. I was using a K-14 gunsight and as soon as I started firing the ME-109 burst into flames and went down spinning. I claim this enemy aircraft as destroyed.

At the same time I saw my wingman, Lt. Robert York, hit another ME-109 and it went down spinning, pouring out black smoke. I then broke into the Jerries that were attempting to bounce us. I got in a good burst at one from about 300 yards with 20 degrees deflection. The enemy aircraft lit up with my bullets pouring into him and he went into a tumble pouring out black

I was leading the 2nd element in the flight commanded by Capt. Wetmore with Lt. York flying on his wing and Lt. McInnes flying on my wing. We spotted two large gaggles of enemy aircraft and climbed to a position above and to the rear of them while calling to the rest of the squadron. At this time my wingman

Above: Major Fred Hodges' IV-E, 44-14313 parked in its revetment at East Wretham, Norfolk. This is the only known example of a shark-mouthed Mustang in the 359th Fighter Group. Below: Men of the 359th Fighter Group's Communication Section pose with a Mustang of the 369th Fighter Squadron. From left to right in the front row are S/Sgt. Frank Giarratano, Cpl. John Serra, T/Sgt. Stanley Repecki, 'Squelch' the dog, Sgt. Frank Chowanic, unknown, Steve Chowanic. 2nd Row, Sgt. Peter Tetradis, Arnold Coleman, Sgt. Milton Mehlberg, Cpl. Micheal Fabrizio, S/Sgt. Ralph Moe, M/Sgt. George Brownstein, Sgt. Jim Devine, PFC Issac Deutsch, unknown, S/Sgt. Joe Zitterelli. Third Row Sgt. Howard Malloy, S/Sgt. Henry Audisirk, Cpl. Paul Ellis, Cpl. Henry Rather, Sgt. Harry Edgerton and S/Sgt. Frank Sumski. On the cowling are S/Sgt. Max Bundy, Cpl. Irving Silverman, Sgt. Arthur Fritsche, T/Sgt. Aubrey DeBower, Sgt. George Maloof and Sgt. Edward Szymanski.
(Coleman)

said that he couldn't possibly keep up with us and that he must leave immediately. Capt. Wetmore told him to go ahead and that I should escort him. We were about 3 miles away when he heard someone say he was attacking and immediately thereafter I observed two enemy aircraft going down in flames.

JIMMY C. SHOFFIT.

While covering Wetmore's tail Bob managed to shoot down 3 ME-109s and also got another as probably destroyed and his encounter report read,

"I was flying Red Two and with Red Leader we were calling in the position of the gaggle of Jerries to the rest of the squadron. There seemed to be about 200 enemy aircraft in all, 100 ME-109s and an equal number of FW-190s. The enemy top cover spotted us and started to bounce but we turned into them. I came up behind one ME-109 and clobbered him from about 15 to 0 degree deflection. I saw strikes all over him and he started flaming as he went down. I claim this ME-109 destroyed. I then saw Capt. Wetmore, Red Leader, fire at a ME-109 and I saw the ship start to smoke and it went down spinning. I then came up behind another ME-109 and gave him a long burst. My K-14 sight was working perfectly. I saw hits all over the airplane and the ship started to tumble with smoke pouring out and pieces of the aircraft falling off. I claim this ME-109 destroyed (It was in fact reduced to a Probable.)

The third enemy aircraft flew directly in front of me at about 800 yards and he apparently did not see me, but I closed fast as he was in a slight dive. Once again the K-14 gunsight aided me in a long burst and I saw strikes on the canopy and the wing roots. It snapped over and as I passed him the aircraft exploded. I claim this ME-109 destroyed. At that moment and slightly above me I spotted another enemy aircraft. He also saw me and started to turn into me. I cut him off in the turn and held my fire until I was about 500 yards and 90 degrees to him. I pulled my nose through until it blacked the enemy ship out as I continued to fire all the time. I dropped my nose and saw a few strikes on the leading edge of his wing, near the fuselage and on the fuselage itself. I then looked back as I saw tracers going past my wing.

I saw a ME-109 on my tail and did a quarter snap and spin and almost ran into the enemy aircraft that I had just fired on. The pilot bailed out as I went past him. I claim this enemy as destroyed. I continued down in a high speed diving spiral so the enemy aircraft on my tail couldn't draw any deflection. When I hit the cloud layer I leveled out and cleared my tail and saw that the Jerry was gone. I then returned to base.

I claim four (4) ME-109s destroyed in the air.
CS-R, 44-14630
725 rds of API.

ROBERT M. YORK

Above: The crew of "Deviless 3rd," IV-N, 44-13390 pose with their A/C, L to R: C/C Ernie Behm, Assnt. C/C Tony Castelano, Armorer Tony Chardella and Maj. Cranfill on the wing. The name was red and yellow with black background. Middle: Two aces of the 359th. In the background is Claude Crenshaw's "Louisiana Heat Wave." Just enough of the serial is visible above the horizontal stab to determine this was his second A/C #44-13306. Name was in red and yellow outlined in black. "Louisiana" was written above exhaust pipes but does not show in this pic. Crenshaw finished the war with 7 confirmed, Cranfill with 5. Below: After Major Cranfill finished his tour, his A/C was assigned to F/O Thomas G. Bur who renamed it "Big Noise From Winnetka." Tom shared in the destruction of a 109 on Sept. 18 '44 in this A/C, still coded IV-N. (Chardella)

At the same time I saw my wingman, Lt. York, hit another ME-109 and it went down spinning, pouring out black smoke.

Of the above action the PRO officer wrote: Lt. Robert M. York, who shot down 4 of the enemy aircraft, said he and Wetmore split those Jerries like flies and their belly-tanks tumbled down through the sky like rain. They had to drop their extra fuel to be in battle shape.

'After we both got our first ones', he went on, 'I then came up behind another one and gave him a long burst from almost dead astern. Strikes appeared all over his ship, smoke flew out and pieces began falling away. He went down spinning. I must have been doing some spinning about then myself — although I had my eyes glued on the man ahead of me I didn't know where the ground was.

'The third one I got flew directly in front of me. He was about 500 yards away and could not have seen me. I closed fast and I was in a diving turn. I pressed the trigger and saw hits on the canopy and on the wing roots. The ME-109 snapped over and as I passed him he exploded — just like the first one I'd hit — with a flash of red flame. 'I flipped up and got on the tail of number four and was firing away at him, dumb and happy, until I saw the tracers — like little baseballs of fire — scooting past me from a Jerry perched on

Above: Two photos of Captain Joseph W. Mejaski's ''Stinky,'' featured in color on page 149. The nose art went through a whole series of changes before arriving at its final configuration. On photo at right, note last four digits of the serial below the ''S'' in ''Stinky.'' Mejaski served with the 369th Fighter Squadron from June 1944 to February 1945. By the completion of his tour he had claimed 2 confirmed and 3 probables, all ground claims, on 75 combat missions. (Mejaski) Below, left: Early ''D'' models, note absence of fin strake, of the 370 F.S. (Mulron) Below, right: Lt. Jack R. Shulte managed to bring his crippled ''Blondie II,'' CS-S, 44-14192, back to East Wretham but it flipped over, due to damage, upon landing. It was almost 30 minutes before he was rescued, none the worse for his ordeal, March 22, 1945. (Chardella)

my tail. I did a snap-over and barely missed the Jerry in front of me, who was busily climbing out of his cockpit.

'I went into a sharp dive to keep the one behind me from getting any hits, but he stuck right on my tail, firing away. I headed for a cloud and once I was in it I levelled out and headed for home.'

Bob's jubilation that night was tempered by the fact that after knocking down the Jerry aircraft, he had been involved in a bounce on two strange aircraft. They turned out to be Mustangs, but Bob in the heat of combat, had fired before he established the fact. The Mustang pilot whom Bob hit was Major Wilbert 'Weep' Juntilla, who was leading the 353rd Fighter Group that day, and although the Mustang was damaged he made a wheels-up landing back in England.

On 1st January 1945 Bob made his final claim when in a scrap near Luneberg he shot down his fifth aerial victim, a FW-190. At the time he was leading Green Flight in his assigned P-51 CS-Y, 44-14159 which he named 'Rudy.' At about 1130 hours while on an escort mission he recalled "Two FW-190s dove down so close to us that I could plainly see the crosses on their wings and some contrails ahead of us started to split up in all directions. We made a 180 degree turn to the right but my flight had to break to port as four aircraft were coming in on us from about 5 o'clock. These were identified as L/Fs but high above them were two contrails which at that moment started to turn to the east. Green Flight started climbing to intercept them. We climbed to 39,000 feet and came in on one of the contrails and I saw that it was a FW-190.

I closed to about 50 feet above him into the sun. The range was about 350 yards and I could clearly see the belly-tanks and the crosses on his wings. I then fired a long burst and saw strikes on his wings and fuselage. I mushed into his contrail and gave him another burst of fire. He closed his throttle and dumped his flaps. I immediately did the same and slid directly underneath and about 25 feet below him. I had ice on my canopy from his gas and oil. He snap rolled, out of control. I did the same as I tried to get another burst of fire off. He started to spin and at about 30,000 feet he bailed out. I then rejoined my flight and returned to Base."

In his supporting statement Bob's number two man, Lt. Jack E. McCoskey said "I was in Green Flight on Lt. York's wing when Bandits were called in. Less than 200 yards behind a FW-190 Lt. York opened fire and immediately scored strikes on the enemy aircraft. The FW-190 started to smoke and burn but kept going straight ahead. Lt. York opened fire again. This second round of clobbering knocked off the belly-tank and various other bits and pieces. Still smoking badly he made a nose high turn that ended in a wing-over. He went straight down and the pilot bailed out in the dive. The enemy aircraft was destroyed."

Above: Vincent Ambrose admires the newly painted name on his Mustang. He was Operations Officer for the 370th F.S. and used a total of 5 A/C during his combat career. All carried the same name. (Ambrose) Middle: A photo of "Hot Pants," CS-Q, 43-6461 which was landed in Sweden, August 4, '44 by Lt. Wilson K. Baker Jr. Two other 370th F.S. A/C also landed there the same day; Lt. Richard O. Rabb, CS-F, 43-12463. "Some Joke" and Capt. Ray Lancaster in 44-13939. Below: Two Swedish mechanics check out CS-Q. Note fancy outlined letters - a somewhat unusual feature and 12 odd white rectangles below cockpit. Note also A/C is now "Hot" as someone removed its "Pants." (Olausson)

Above: Ray S. Wetmore in his room at Wretham Hall, Thetford on 14th May 1944. When the war in Europe ended he was the highest scoring 8th Air Force fighter pilot still flying operations. His fellow pilots nicknamed him X-Ray Eyes because of his remarkable ability to see enemy aircraft at extreme distances. Ray was killed in a flying accident in the States on 14th February 1951. (USAF) Middle: The last Thunderbolt assigned to ace Ray S. Wetmore. The code is CS-P, 42-75068. Eight kill markings are just below the canopy and just in front of that are about fifty mission symbols. Below: ''Daddy's Girl'' was Ray Wetmore's final wartime A/C and the subject of a color profile on page 149.

Bob flew his last combat mission on 25th February 1945 for a total of 60 missions and about 280 combat hours. He left the 359th Fighter Group and arrived back in the States on 3rd June 1945 and was put on the inactive list although he was to remain in the USAF'ES until 1969.

After the war he attended Portland University Law School and received an LLB in 1950. Two years later, in February 1952, he was admitted to the Maine Bar Law Society. While studying law he ran the York Bus Company and, during the summer months, he also ran a hotel. As a lawyer he carried out work for a construction company, a land development company and became a corporation counselor for Old Orchard Beach, Maine. From 1953 until 1969 his ties with the USAF continued and most of his duty was with the 173rd Med. Bn, Maine. He has four children; Barbara Jane Aker, Caryl A. Seel, Miles S. York and Mark L. York.

At the time of this writing he and Barbara E. are still living in Old Orchard Beach, Maine and he is still practicing law. Bob is a member of The American Fighter Aces Association and is also a member of the 369th Fighter Squadron Association of the 359th Fighter Group. He holds the following decorations and awards; Silver Star, Air Medal with 7 Oak Leaf Clusters, European, African and Middle Eastern Theatre Ribbon with 3 Bronze Stars.

Claims made by Robert M. York.

8th August 1944. CS-E, 42-103893. 453 rounds API. Shared in damaging a truck and 20 goods wagons.

9th August 1944. CS-U(bar), 42-106862. 367 rounds API. 1 ME-109 Destroyed in the air. Confirmed.

10th August 1944. CS-P, 42-106894. 199 rounds API., 2 250 lb. bombs. Shared in the destruction of one Road bridge, one RR shed. Damaged one loco, 4 goods cars damaged and 1 RR shed also damaged.

13th August 1944. CS-U, 42-103604. 2 500 lb. bombs. Shared in damaging a bridge.

17th August 1944. CS-K, 44-13966. 1,620 rounds API. 2 250 lb. bombs. Destroyed either 5 or 7 ammunition cars and one truck. Shared in damaging a train.

27th August 1944. CS-E, 42-103893. 833 rounds of API. Shared in damaging a tug, one loco, fourteen goods cars and one switch house also damaged.

28th August 1944. CS-K, 44-13966. 1,620 rounds of API. Shared in damaging two locos, thirty goods cars, one truck and trailer and one switch tower. Also destroyed ten goods cars.

7th October 1944. CS-Y, 44-14159. 'RUDY' (his assigned aircraft) 447 rounds of API. 1 BV-HA 140 Destroyed, water.

27th November 1944. CS-R, 44-14630. 725 rounds of API. Three ME-109s destroyed air. One ME-109 Probably Destroyed air. Confirmed.

1st January 1945. CS-Y, 44-14159. 'RUDY'. 265 rounds of API. One FW-190 Destroyed in the air. Confirmed.

Mission List of Robert M. York.

No.	Date	Type	Time	Target	F.O. No
1	8.8.44	Area Supp.	5.00	Caen	495
2	9.8.44	Escort	4.35		496
3	10.8.44	Bomb/Strafe	4.35	Bar-le Due	498
4	12.8.44	Escort	6.35	Metz	506
5	12.8.44	Bomb/Strafe	3.20	Pacy-Sur-Eure	511
6	15.8.44	Escort	5.10	Frankfurt	516
7	16.8.44	Escort	4.10	Erfurt	518
8	17.8.44	Bomb/Strafe	3.25	Abancourt	519
9	18.8.44	Escort	6.10	St. Dizier	522
10	24.8.44	Escort	5.10	Kolleda	527
11	27.8.44	Escort	5.35	Berlin	535
12	28.8.44	Strafing	4.00	Nancy-Matz	538
13	1.9.44	Escort	4.00	Paris	543
14	3.9.44	Escort	3.30	Ludwigshaven	547
15	8.9.44	Area Supp.	4.05	Koblenz	557
16	12.9.44	Escort	5.00	Brux	566
17	16.9.44	Escort	3.30	Arnham	573
18	18.9.44	Area Supp.	5.30	Arnham	578
19	20.9.44	Area Supp.	4.10	Arnham	580
20	22.9.44	Escort	5.00	Kassel	583
21	7.10.44	Escort	6.15	Politz	600
22	9.10.44	Escort	5.30	Schweinturt	603
23	15.10.44	Escort	3.35	Cologne	1240A
24	22.10.44	Escort	4.30	Hanover	1254A
25	26.10.44	Escort	3.10	Gelsenkirchen	1264A
26	30.10.44	Escort	4.10	Merseburg	1273A
27	2.11.44	Escort	5.10	Merseburg	1281A
28	6.11.44	Escort	4.50	Hamburg	1291A
29	8.11.44	Escort	5.00	Merseburg	1296A
30	9.11.44	Escort	4.35	Metz	1299A
31	20.11.44	Escort	3.00	Eudenbeck	1320A
32	21.11.44	Escort	5.00	Merseburg	1323A
33	25.11.44	Escort	5.30	Merseburg	1333A
34	26.11.44	Escort	5.00	Leipzig	564A
35	27.11.44	Strafing	5.30	Munster	1343A
36	30.11.44	Escort	5.40	Zeitz	1354A
37	4.12.44	Escort	2.15	Kassel	1370A
38	5.12.44	Escort	5.40	Berlin	1374A
39	6.12.44	Escort	5.05	Merseburg	1383A
40	10.12.44	Escort	4.20	Bingen	1404A
41	11.12.44	Escort	4.50	Frankfurt	1408A
42	12.12.44	Escort	4.40	Merseburg	1412A
43	18.12.44	Escort	4.30	Cologne	1430A
44	23.12.44	Escort	4.15	Hamburg	1443A
45	24.12.44	Escort	5.05	Hattanrod A/F	1446A
46	26.12.44	Escort	4.40	Koblenz	1452A
47	27.12.44	Escort	4.40	Kaiserlautern	1456A
48	28.12.44	Escort	4.20	Siegburg	1458A
49	31.12.44	Escort	2.05	Wesendorf	1471A
50	1.1.45	Escort	5.20	Magdeburg	1478A
51	6.1.45	Escort	3.35	Euskirchen A/D	1496A
52	7.1.45	Escort	4.00	Euskirchen A/D	1499A
53	14.1.45	Escort	5.00	Cologne	1515A
54	16.1.45	Escort	5.00	Ruhland	1521A
55	1.2.45	Escort	5.00	Mannheim	1575A
56	3.2.45	Escort	5.15	Berlin	1586A
57	9.2.45	Escort/Strafe	3.00	Lutzkendurf	1605A
58	23.2.45	Strafe	6.15	Zwickau	1654A
59	24.2.45	Bomb/Strafe	4.15	Wesel Bridge	1658A
60	25.2.45	Escort	5.35	Munich	1662A

Lt. Emory G. Johnson of Centre, Alabama covered Rudy York's tail on many missions. He managed to shoot down two enemy aircraft. Below: Robert M. York and Frank Lux outside Wretham Hall where they were billeted during their tour of duty with the 370th Fighter Squadron, 359th Fighter Group. The group was one of five that made up the 67th Fighter Wing of the 8th Air Force. (York)

A sight sure to gladden the heart of any WWII aviation cadet . . . those sweet little PT-19s. Cadets Farney, Mundorff and Klein check their maps before a flight from Chickasha, Oklahoma. (Farney)

ROBERT J. FARNEY

375TH FIGHTER SQUADRON
361ST FIGHTER GROUP

Robert J. Farney was born on September 25th, 1921 in Croghan, New York. He was educated from 1935 to 1939 at Beaver Falls High School, Beaver Falls, New York. When he finished school he worked on his father's dairy farm as a farm hand. He enlisted in the USAAF on 27th November 1942 at Syracuse, New York and some months later, on January 31, 1943, he was called to active duty. During the next five months he did his Basic Training at college and managed to get 10 hours of flying time in a Piper Cub. In June he went through his Classification and Pre-flight Training at San Antonio Aviation Cadet Center, from there he did 3 months primary training at Chickasha, Oklahoma

where he flew Fairchild PT-19s (175 H.P.) followed at Garden City, Kansas flying BT-13s (450 H.P.). His advanced training was done at Aloe Army Air Field flying in At-6 (650 H.P.). He graduated as a 2nd Lieutenant on April 15, 1944. It was estimated that it cost approximately $40,000.00 to train a fighter pilot over a 32 week period. On September 25, 1944 he boarded a ship at Manhatten Island and sailed the next day for England.

Farney finished his tour in England and returned to the USA in October, 1945. He got home in November and went hunting for 3 days but "got tired of sitting around" and got a job in a paper mill. His discharge came through on December 23. He started work at the paper mill on December 26, where he stayed for six months. He served a Maintainance Apprenticeship for 2 years and 3 months and became the Master Mechanic at 27 years of age. He held that position until January 1, 1984 when he retired. He married Theresa Bush on May 5, 1948. They have four children, Mrs. Mary Frances Baker, Charles Robert Farney, James Nelson Farney, and John Anthony Farney. He now keeps himself busy cutting wood and making Maple Syrup on his 47 acres of land. He and his brother-in-law own a tract of woods (767 acres). He is chairman of the Fire Commission and belongs to the VFW Legion.

Following is the day-to-day diary that was kept by Lt. Robert J. Farney from September 1944 until August 1945. It has been extended slightly in regards to combat reports and some other material which has been added by the author.

17th September 1944. Got on boat at 9.00 P.M. Boat was docked on Manhatten Island.

18th September 1944. Took off promptly at 0700 hours.

19th September 1944. Well out to sea and having a good time.

20th September 1944. 20th, 21st and 22nd fair weather and lots of fun.

23rd September 1944. Saw a whale.

24th September 1944. Sunday, went to Church and ship's captain conducted service. About 1700 hours we sighted land.

25th September 1944. My birthday, I am 23 years old, it seems queer to have a birthday at sea. Boat anchored in bay and waited for high tide. Got a new pilot and at 1900 hours we docked at Liverpool. 2100 hours, British General welcomed all of us.

26th September 1944. Got off boat at 0500 hours, got on train and went to Stone, Staffordshire.

27th September 1944. Processed on 26th and 27th.

28th September 1944. Prepare to leave.

29th September 1944. At 0700 hours took a train ride to Goxhill, Lincolnshire.

30th September 1944. Checked in.

1st October 1944. 1st and 2nd. Checked in and got orientation lectures.

3rd October 1944. Went to Ground School. Had a look at P-51 Mustang.

4th October 1944. Went to Ground School, had nice weather and went to a show in the evening.

5th October 1944. Flew 2 hours 45 minutes in P-51, flew formation with a Spitfire. Went to Ground School and in the evening wrote letters.

6th October 1944. 1 hour link, Ground School, nice weather.

7th October 1944. Rainy day. Went to Ground School. Had dance in evening at club.

8th October 1944. Rained. Went to Ground School and wrote letters.

9th October 1944. Low ceiling, taxied but couldn't take off. Went to Ground School.

10th October 1944. Flew 1 hour 30 minutes formation over the Wash, went to Ground School.

11th October 1944. Went to Ground School, it rained,

Lt. James D. Hastin on the wing of his nicely decorated Jug. The kill mark represents a victory shared with Lt. Henry B. Lederer over a 109G on Jan. 30, '44.

went to Grimsby Town, Humberside. 1300 hours Link Trainer.

12th October 1944. Went to Ground School, it rained, wrote five letters.

13th October 1944. "Friday 13th" Flew 2 hours 30 minutes made two good landings. It rained and I went to Ground School. Going to show at 1830 hours.

14th October 1944. Went to Ground School. Flew 1 hour 15 minutes & blew tire on tail wheel and had a cheerful little fire. Went to show.

15th October 1944. Commissioned six months today. Slept late for the first time since I arrived over here. Had 1 hour link. Went to Grimsby Town, Humberside with Leo Gendron and stayed all night, slept at Red Cross Annex.

16th October 1944. It rained, I went to Ground School then I wrote four letters.

17th October 1944. Visited Hull, Humberside this morning on ferry and had wet dingy drill, had a good look at town which is leveled by the bomb blasts. It rained, went to Ground School. I went into Scunthorpe, Humberside in the evening with Andy and Ford.

This photo was taken when Bob Farney got back to Little Walden, Essex after his first combat mission. He is one of very few fighter pilots who had the distinction of shooting down an enemy aircraft on his first combat mission. This was on the 26th November 1944 and he got a ME-109 in the air. His Crew Chief, Alvin Walther, helps him to start unstrapping the Mustang from his rear end. (Farney)

Lt. Col. George R. Rew, C.O. of the 374th Sq., on the wing of his P-47 "Scarlet Kate." Note the umbrella-bomb symbols for escort missions. A/C was coded B7-R.

18th October 1944. 1½ hours flying time with K-14 computing sight, K-14 does all of the thinking and all I do is squeeze the trigger. Took in Ground School, also received a letter from Corporal Farney (brother).

19th October 1944. Went to Ground School, used Edmonds Trainer, rain and fog today, went to Scunthorpe, Humberside.

20th October 1944. Went to Ground School. Rain and fog.

21st October 1944. Went to Ground School. Rain and fog. Dance at club from 2000-2400 hours-had a good time. Won one pound and ten shillings in a little Blackjack game and played and won two rubbers of Bridge.

22nd October 1944. Sunday. Went to Grimsby Town, Humberside, there was no flying.

23rd October 1944. Went to Ground School, weather is fair. 1 hour 5 minutes camera gunnery.

24th October 1944. Went to Ground School. Poor flying weather. Captain Cox killed himself in a P-51 Mustang, he had 1600 hours in B-17s but this was his first ride in a fighter.

25th October 1944. Today I found out I'm going to the 361st Fighter Group near Cambridge.

26th October 1944. Flew 2.00 hours in haze. Got packed ready to join the 361st.

27th October 1944. Took train ride to Cambridge.

28th October 1944. Had a look at the field, it was a pretty nasty day.

29th October 1944. Met my fellow pilots, had a very good day.

30th October 1944. Went to Ground School. Watched fellow pilots take off for mission, to Hamburg, 1 missing on return. Went to a show. (Lt. Francis Christensen. KIA. B7-L, 43-25032.)

31st October 1944. Just hung around. Lt. Urban L. Drew buzzed the field for excitement. So far he has gotten seven kills.

1st November 1944. Fair day. The boys had a mission to the Ruhr valley via the Zuider Zee and Nijmegen, Holland. Lt. James Eason did a slow roll in celebration of completing his tour and spun in and was killed.

2nd November 1944. A mission to Nurnberg by the group today. Lt. Charles E. Moore and Lt. Chuck Narvis were lost. The group got about ten ME-109s today. I had two hours in the Link Trainer. The result of the raid yesterday by the 8th Fighter Command was the loss of 31 bombers and 14 fighters. Claims were for 206 enemy aircraft shot down.

3rd November 1944. Terrible nasty day. The mission was scrubbed. Got a letter from Clare. Now 2000 hours.

4th November 1944. Nice day. The boys had a mission to Hanover and all was quiet. I got two hours of link. (flew pattern of star and a P-51) I later flew two hours in a P-51D, and was all over East Anglia. The P-51D is a swell ship and I made a very good landing. Did some hedge hopping at 400 MPH and it was really fun. One fellow, Lt. John Havey, got mud in his air scoop so we were really hedge hopping. Time 1935 hours.

5th November 1944. Sunday - the boys had a mission to Strasburg, France today and everything was quiet. I went to Wing H.Q. and watched the proceedings from there - saw five Generals including Doolittle and Spaatz. Rained this afternoon.

6th November 1944. Boys had a mission near Hanover to blow up a bridge. 374th Squadron got a ME-262. This afternoon we saw some combat film and now I'm going to chow. Very nice day and lots of sunshine.

An unpleasant little pile of twisted, smoldering wreckage remind us that combat A/C are very temperamental and unforgiving creatures. As the A/F took copious amounts of pictures of any and a events, most historian/collectors have many of these tragic re minders in their collections. We have, in general, tried to avoid thi genre, however, in the interests of historical accuracy a few of thes seem to be unavoidable. Therefore, this photo records the loss c Lt. Glenn T. Berge and 42-75152 in a take-off accident March ! 1944.

Welcome to the Vernon Richards page! In photo above left he's just returned from a combat mission and parked his original 'Tika,' B7-R, 42-75452 in its revetment near the west end of the runway at Bottisham, Cambridgeshire. *(Bland)* Above, right: An often used, but rarely identified picture of Vern in "Tika." Serial is clearly visible in original A/F print taken from very close B-24. *(U.S.A.F.)* Below: This photo is also no stranger to 8th A/F buffs, but still a great one of Vern in his P-51. Scoreboard records both air and ground claims including a FW-190 and a ME-109 confirmed air vics for June 25, 1944 in another P-51 (43-24830).

7th November 1944. Election Day. The boys had a strafing mission but it was scrubbed. An interesting speaker was here this morning and talked on secret subjects. I flew at 1500 hours this afternoon with the flight and had a real lot of fun. I got a letter from home and one from Clare today. Time is 2030 hours and I am about to write home.

8th November 1944. We heard Roosevelt was re-elected. The boys had another mission (escort) to Nurnburg today and one of our boys got a jet. One fellow cartwheeled on take off and was hurt slightly. Yesterday a P-47 ran into the ground and the pilot was killed. All I did today was sit around and take it easy. Hope to fly tomorrow.

9th November 1944. The boys had a mission to Metz, France and had no air activity. Two fellows crashed on take off but were only shaken up. When the fellows came back a Captain made a poor landing and after giving the plane full throttle it veared off to the left in a half roll and he was killed. The plane struck a shack and three enlisted men were hurt (Richard M. Durbin, was the pilot). I would have gotten three hours this afternoon but my engine got hot, my coolant popped and the brakes froze just before take off so naturally I didn't fly. Got up before breakfast this morning and I mean before breakfast.

10th November 1944. Boys had a mission to Frankfurt but never found the bombers, no activity. I didn't fly today. We had snow last night and it was terrible cold all day.

11th November 1944. Boys had a mission to the Ruhr Valley and all was quiet. In the afternoon I flew 3.00 hours, went to club dance in the evening. By the way, I made a good landing.

12th November 1944. No mission today. We flew in soup for 2.30 hours. Control tower sent up about 200 flares and several rockets to guide our landing.

Couldn't see the field until I was 1,000 feet from the runway and even then could only see the flares and not the ground. I made field on the first pass. A hazardous approach but a very good landing. Some fellows made three and four passes before they got down. Got two letters from home today.

13th November 1944. No mission today. I flew Camera Gunnery with Captain Eugene Cole. We were up 2.30 hours and had a very good time. We flew all over East Anglia from the Thames Estuary up to Norwich and over to Cambridge. Had to get one homing to find the field, the weather was terrible. You couldn't see the ground, but I made a very good landing. I am now going to write home, 2000 hours. Capt. Black (Intelligence) is going to locate Gladys Farney for me.

18th November 1944. Went in hospital with a fever and got out Sunday, was in 3½ days. Lots of buzz bombs were over us. A V-2 landed three miles away and made a hole 50 feet deep. Buildings shake every day from bombs dropping.

19th November 1944. All was quiet. Got out of hospital and was just hanging around. I'm grounded for a week from having taken sulphur pills.

20th November 1944. Boys had a mission but nothing

happened. It's raining and nasty today (When I was in hospital Irene Manning visited the post and she came up to see us fellows in the hospital ''she ain't bad''). We got about nine new fellows in our squadron about two days ago, some are old friends from the States.

21st November 1944. Got two letters from Francis today. They were mailed on 28th October. He is still driving a tank in the U.S. First Army. Boys had a mission to Merseburg today. All is well. I'm still grounded so I got a haircut. Got a letter from Eunice. Cigarettes are frozen but we pilots still get them, all personel get one tin of tobacco a week or five cigars.

22nd November 1944. Wednesday, poor weather and the mission was called off. Today I got my rations of five packs of cigarettes and signed my pay voucher. I also got a wonderful compass and some ammunition for my Colt .45. I will start flying again on Friday.

23rd November 1944. The mission was scrubbed today and after the briefing all we did was sit around waiting for supper. Today was Thanksgiving and we had turkey. They had everything that goes with Thanksgiving up to and including white tablecloths. I got four letters from home today and one from Francis. Time 1900 hours.

24th November 1944. Today I flew all alone in the rain for two hours. I had a good time and made a good landing. I did a little buzzing such as football fields, trains and a golf course. I also made a few farmers duck, but not too many. Saw a rowing race on a canal in Cambridge.

25th November 1944. All was quiet. I'm scheduled to fly my first mission tomorrow. I'm looking forward to it!

26th November 1944. Sunday I went on my first mission to Hanover. It lasted 4:20 minutes. I shot down a FW-190 west of Steinhuder Lake. Pilot never got out. My Flight Leader Leonard A. Wood also got a FW-190. Captain Neely got two 190s and element leader Walter R. Stevens also got one. Altitude 25,000 feet. Landed at St. Trond, Belgium short of gas. To end an exciting day I slept in some German built barracks. Our group destroyed 24 aircraft and our flight in the 375th got 11 of them.

27th November 1944. Found out my brakes were out and had to stay another day.

28th November 1944. Helped mechanics fix my plane. In the evening I listened to a wonderful Belgian orchestra. Heard and saw a lot of Buzz Bombs (V-1's). A Thunderbolt went in and the pilot was killed.

29th November 1944. I got clearance and went to Brussels. Again I landed without any brakes and nearly killed myself. Narrowly missed a B-24 Liberator parked just off the runway. Got my dinner and also got my brakes fixed and took off for home. British flak shot at me near mainland south of Flushing. Got back 'OK' and had my picture taken. Made a hair-raising landing but 'OK' and happy. Found lots of accumulated mail and three Christmas packages. This ends the tale of my first combat mission.

Following is a copy of his Encounter Report:

I was flying Decoy Red Two when we sighted other members of Decoy squadron engaged in a fight with approximately forty plus FW-190s. Decoy Red Flight joined the engagement. Decoy Red One closed on a FW-190 and overshot. When Decoy Red One broke away, I commenced to track him and gave a short burst at 400 yards, 0 degree deflection, but observed

Major Roy A. Webb of the 374th in front of one of his assigned A/C - a P-47, 42-75512 . . . and, in a conveniently dated photo, in front of his last P-47 with Sgt. Hood's elaborately done artwork. In the six month period from Jan. to June '44, Roy shot down 4 confirmed enemy A/C, 2 each 109s and 190s. (Mrs. R. Webb Jr.)

no strikes. The FW-190 started a climbing turn to the left and I, still closing, shot two second bursts at 200 yards, 20 degrees deflection. I observed many strikes from the wing roots to the top of the canopy. The FW-190 slowly rolled over on it's back and went down. Pilot did not bail out and the plane went down flaming. I claim one FW-190 destroyed.

E2-C 44-14662

P-51

735 rounds expended.

SUPPORTING STATEMENT

I was leading Decoy Red Flight when I saw approximately 40 FW-190s flying in three bunches of 10 to 15 each. I bounced one FW-190 but overshot him. Lt. Farney, who was flying Decoy Red Two, was able to stay behind him. The FW broke and went into a steep climbing left turn into the sun. Lt. Farney got strikes on him. He rolled over, jettisoned the canopy and went into a dive. The FW-190 caught fire at the wing roots. I did not see the pilot get out.

Leonard A. Wood.

E2-G (bar), 44-14085

30th November 1944. I went to Leipzig and flew 5 hours and 40 minutes. There were approximately 1,250 B-17s and B-24s. No air activity and all I got was a very tired rear end. Heard that Henry Virkler was killed in a plane accident. Got two letters from home and two from Clare. Time is 18:15 hours. Made a wheel landing.

1st December 1944. Got paid and wrote up my encounter report for 26th November and did a little other business. Today is my day off. While the boys are in a card game I got two hours of link. Later went to Cambridge and went dancing to the ``Dorothy''. No mission today.

2nd December 1944. Saturday, the boys had a mission to Frankfurt and got a couple FW-190s. George Hedge and I went to Cambridge at 1:00 PM, returned this evening at 20:00 hours. Got 20 Christmas cards. Also saw a soccer game. Time is 22:00 hours and I'm going to write home and go to bed. Had a very nice day and **sunshine!**

3rd December 1944. The mission was scrubbed and I went to church instead. Had a rather quiet day and in the evening I wrote five letters.

4th December 1944. We had a mission to a section of Germany, about 150 miles northeast of Frankfurt. Saw no Enemy Aircraft and only got a sore seat. I flew 5.00 hours. Made a wheel landing.

5th December 1944. We had a mission to Berlin today and I flew 5.40 hours, had to sweat my gas a bit. I was rather low but got back O.K. No enemy were seen by us, but one bunch got 14 in another group. One fellow bailed out and I guess is a POW. A few fellows got hit by flak. Had pork chops for supper and am now going to write a letter home and go to bed. Time 1931 hours.

Above: Lt. Colonel Wally Hopkins and Major Jack Pearce about to go for a flight in the two seat Mustang of the 374th Fighter Squadron coded B7-F, 44-14055. (Hopkins) Middle: Later the hood was modified to allow the passenger head room. This was a one piece hood and as such was the only one of its type. (Kozicki) Below: The assigned A/C of Lt. Wayne Moore, C/C was Sgt. Bob Bland. On August 13, 1944, Lt. L.L. Montgomery was KIA in it.

175

6th December 1944. I went on a mission to escort B-24s which bombed a rail center southwest of Hanover and southeast of Dummer Lake. No Enemy Aircraft were seen and I flew 4.00 hours. Went to Cambridge in the evening, missed the bus and got in at 2.00 AM. Took off in fog 200 feet thick.

7th December 1944. No mission today so I got dressed up and was just hanging around. Got a letter from Francis and one from home. This has been a dull day. Time 16.55 hours.

8th December 1944. No mission today. Went to a lecture. New boys flew. Wrote some letters home. Had burned beans for dinner.

9th December 1944. No mission today, nasty weather. Went to Cambridge in the evening and got back at 04.00 A.M. Had a good time.

10th December 1944. We went on a mission to Coblenz. Escorted B-24s who bombed the city and railroad center on the hook of the Rhine River, west of Frankfurt. No Enemy Aircraft. Watched the flak, which tried to catch us and the bombers, but no one got shot down.

11th December 1944. We had a mission to Frankfurt and Coblenz today and all was quiet. The flak was real accurate and plenty of it, but no one got shot down. I'm not ashamed to say it was close enough to me that I gave it a lot of respect. I flew 5.30 hours and made a good landing. I had 30 gallons of gas left. The weather was pretty bad but we all got back O.K. I flew 10 hours in the last two days and am plenty tired. I'm on tomorrow's mission so I'm ready to get some sleep. Time 19.30 hours. Will write home.

12th December 1944. Went on another mission today to the same place we went to yesterday - just west of Frankfurt. They bombed visually and lost one bomber. No chutes were seen, the place bombed was Darrow. I flew 4.50 hours and am tired. Nasty weather coming back - and also going. Lt. Joseph Wolfe made a crash landing.

13th December 1944. Wednesday, after briefing, fog was so terrible we couldn't fly. Had a few lectures and that's all.

14th December 1944. Thursday, "44", some more fog today and we didn't fly. Went to Cambridge in the evening and stayed at the Red Cross.

15th December 1944. Friday. Went to London and bought a new blouse and different things. Ate at the

Above, left: Wally Hopkins signifies (although the wrong way round) two victories. This was his Thunderbolt B7-H(bar). He completed 27 missions in this aircraft before converting to the North American Mustang in early May of 1944. (Hopkins) Above, right: Cockpit area detail of Wally Hopkin's first Mustang B7-H(bar), 42-106655 'Ferocious Frankie.' Note centre of gravity cross on fuselage. This cross moved back on the later model Mustangs. Below: Another fine USAF photo - this of Wallace Hopkin's last wartime P-51. Wally was officially credited with 4 aerial victories. We have a photo of this A/C belly-down in a field after a fuel mixup (using 130/150 octane) caused its new assigned "owner" Lt. Collins J. Mayeux, some serious problems on take off, but let's remember ol' "Ferocious" this way instead.

Grovener House and slept at the Jewell's Club (annex). London is a real nice place.

16th December 1944. Saturday, went by subway to London Bridge and took pictures. Had a lot of fun, especially on the subway getting from one place to another. Met two ballet dancers who were in my estimation pretty nice. Alma Jones and June Frain.

17th December 1944. Went back to camp and no mission. Flew a test hop in E2-M(bar), 44-13339 and was up 1 hour and twenty-five minutes, made a good landing and that's that. Had Southern Fried Chicken for supper.

18th December 1944. Monday, the boys had a mission today but the bombers turned back and the mission was a flop. I helped my Crew Chief, Alvin Walther, work on my plane. He put on a new generator and took off the 'D-Day' markings with acetone. I played a few games of pool tonight and that's all. Time 23:00 hours.

19th December 1944. Tuesday, mission was to strafe an aerodrome near Frankfurt but the fog didn't lift and it was scrubbed. Did a little painting and shot 19s in skeet. Got a letter from Eunice which had been mailed on 12th November. Time 19:00 hours. Will write a letter home and go to bed. Am scheduled to fly a mission tomorrow.

20th December 1944. Fog!! Went to a dance on 21st. We are now figuring on going to the continent to fly missions.

23rd December 1944. Saturday, 08:35 hours. We're packing to go to the continent. I was bounced and only 60 pilots (out of about 120) went and of course that left me out. They went to St. Dizier, France and will fly from there.

24th December 1944. Sunday, boys had a mission and Lt. Caleb J. Layton went down (375th, E2-E, 44-14064), also we lost Billy Sykes of the 376th. Before he was shot down Layton got 2 ME-109s and Lt. William R. Street (375th) also shot down a ME-109.

25th December 1944. Christmas.

26th December 1944. I went to St. Dizier, and flew a mission which lasted 1 hour 55 minutes.

27th December 1944. I was on the alert crew. The boys flew two missions today and one pilot was lost.

28th December 1944. Thursday, fog and no mission was flown.

29th December 1944. I was on a mission and flew 4:18 hours. We escorted B-17s but no action. Flew from here (St. Dizier) to Trier and east. From there we went to Ostend and escorted B-17s to the target and back. Made a sweep and then came home.

30th December 1944. I was on a mission but my coolant switch broke and I didn't take off. My Crew Chief, Sgt. Walther, fixed it and I polished up my plane. I polished for two hours. The boys were on a sweep but didn't have any luck.

31st December 1944. Was on a sweep and flew 2:05 hours. We saw nothing but 'Little Friends' and

clouds. Had a little party tonight and now I'm going to bed. We had an inch of snow last night. Today is the first time I've flown in a snowstorm. I'm on the mission for tomorrow, so Cheerio!

1st January 1945. Monday, Had a mission to Coblenz. Picked up some B-24s and escorted them to the target. The weather was clear. We flew over the Moselle River most of the time. I flew 3:15 hours and made a good landing. In the afternoon we went on a sweep back to Coblenz. Nothing happened and I flew 1:55 hours. 'Ripsaw' and 'Nuthouse' gave us a New Year greeting over the radio. (Radar Control)

Above: The artwork on the nose of Lt. Col. Tommy Christian Jr.'s first P-47: E2-C, 42-75494. It represented his baby daughter whom he would never see. The baby was pink on a white cloud and firing a silver pea-shooter w/black peas. (Kruzel) Below: The P-47 of ace George Merritt of the 375th also was decorated by Art Minor. George and other 361st F.G. pilots reported FW-190s with yellow crosses. George bagged 2 of them on Feb. 22, 1944. (Tyrell)

3 nice shots of Lt. Robert T. Eckfeldt's "Bald Eagle III." The striping on the cowl (also on wing tips and rudder trim tabs) was blue and yellow. This was Bob's last assigned A/C. It's next driver was Thomas "Red" Moore. Bob passed away Dec. 12, 1972.

2nd January 1945. Tuesday, I flew a mission of 3 hours escorting A-26s and B-26s. We went from here to Strasbourg and then to Coblenz where the A-26s bombed. We then escorted the B-26s to their target and came home. 8th A.A.F bombed near same place. This afternoon I flew Colonel Junius Dennison's E2-D, 44-15597 and logged 2:45 hours. In the afternoon I flew on a sweep to Cologne, Frankfurt and back to base. I shot down a ME-109 and he exploded in the air after the left wing was shot off. The poor fellow never had a chance. I later saw it burning on the ground, it was just a mass of red flames and black smoke. We were only at 2,000 feet and it didn't take long for him to get to the ground. He put his wheels down before I got him. I sign off to close another exciting day in my life. The flak was terrific but no one got hit. Today our squadron (375th) got 5 ME-109s in all. Got the report on my guns and I only shot 90 rounds at the E/A. Good Shootin!

ENCOUNTER REPORT
I was flying Decoy White Four when eight bogies were seen flying east. We took after them and closed west of Stuttgart. After identifying them as ME-109s, I followed White Three (Lt. Street) on two of them. Pulling up behind I opened fire at 500 yards with a short burst at 0 degree deflection. I observed strikes on the wing roots. The ME-109 banked sharply to the left and I gave him another short burst from 150 yards with 15 degrees deflection. The E/A blew up as I pulled up in a steep left turn. I claim this ME-109 destroyed. The K-14 gunsight was used.

SUPPORTING STATEMENT
I was flying Decoy White Three with White Four right behind me when we bounced two ME-109s. After shooting one down I made a steep left turn and saw White Four (Farney) get strikes all over the other ME-109. Immediately after Farney's second burst the left wing of the E/A exploded and flew off. He then flipped over on his back and went in, exploding when he hit the ground.

William H. Street. 1st Lt.

3rd January 1945. It rained, snowed and hailed today so we didn't fly. We were scheduled for a dive-bombing mission but didn't get off the ground. I walked a mile tonight and got a shower which I needed badly. Time 21:15 hours.

4th January 1945. We didn't fly today for it was foggy, but we're still scheduled for a divebombing mission. Snowing again.

5th January 1945. Our mission was scrubbed after 2.00 P.M. I made a stand to put beside my bed. We got three inches of snow. We spent some time shooting off German flares. We went to a show tonight "My Kingdom For A Cook". Time 21.00 hours.

6th January 1945. Foggy today. C-47 spun in on approach and the crew was killed. 2 new boys in 376th were killed in training mission. Went to town today and had fun buying stuff. Two of our fellows speak French quite well. Mail came in today and I got ten letters. We got five of the boys from Little Walden tonight. Still got the snow.

7th January 1945. Today we had an overcast so we couldn't fly. At 1300 hours I got paid 7,056 Francs. The Chaplain came in yesterday so this afternoon I went to church. It wasn't much of a church but we were there. Tonight it's snowing and blowing.

8th January 1945. More snow and it really blew. I chopped wood to keep warm. C-47 brought supplies and very few P-47s flew.

9th January 1945. They wouldn't let us fly today but it's quite nice. Went to town and had a few beers.

10th January 1945. I went on my first divebombing mission. We carried two 250 lb. fragmentation bombs each. I flew 2:20 hours. We hit a marshalling yard at Neustadt and had a lot of fun. 15 aircraft of the 375th took part and destroyed 4 goods wagons - later another 25 were knocked out. This afternoon I took E2-M (bar), 44-13339 up for a test hop and flew 1:15 hours but made a poor landing. The boys of the 375th had a mission this afternoon and strafed a train at Stuttgart. 20 goods wagons destroyed.

11th January 1945. Snow and a low ceiling so no missions flown.

12th January 1945. Friday, a little snow and a low ceiling. So I took a bath and watched a movie.

13th January 1945. Had a divebombing mission today and we hit a marshalling yard and a big factory. I went way, way, way down and picked my target, a factory. It was just north of Frankfurt. I logged 2.35 hours and made a wheel landing.

14th January 1945. We escorted B-17s and B-24s. We went from here to Durban - 390 miles; from there to Steinhuder Lake, Dummer Lake, Antwerp and home. Flew 4.40 hours. Made a good landing. Got a lot of mail.

15th January 1945. I was on one mission today and got a good taste of skip bombing. We bombed four tunnels on a railroad south of the Moselle River. I got both of my 500 pound Demolition Bombs in the tunnel and I really hope it plugged her up. I flew 2.20 hours. The 500 pounders really do the business - and I like skip bombing.

"We were trained in glide bombing and when we went to St. Dizier were to act as top cover for the 9th Air Force. We did manage to shoot up a few trains and some aircraft but generally things were pretty dull. I feel that a suggestion I made at the time, that we should start to carry bombs, was favourably received. They put through a technical order and we got a delivery of 250 lb. Fragmentation Bombs. We attacked several factories and I was a bit disappointed at the results. They did not seem to do much damage. They

Above: If you didn't know it before, you certainly do by now. Many A/C had 2, or more names. Bob Farney's A/C, pictured in color on page 150, was named by himself and his C/C. Below: S/Sgt. Alvin Walthers side of E2-V, 44-14827, named after his home town. On the wing is armourer Oscar Pauley, next is the 375th painter Art Minor, whose artwork was exceptional and last is Alvin - a great crew chief! (Farney)

were all colors when they detonated; white, green and red just like a rainbow. I got them to put through another tech order and we got 500lb HE bombs. It was then that we really did some good. We did a real good job bombing the railroad tunnels along the Moselle River. They gave us a primary and a secondary target to bomb. After that we were picked up by radar (Nuthouse) and directed to enemy aircraft locations and top escort. The bombing made the trips a little more interesting."

16th January 1945. Tuesday - Had a mission of 4:35 hours escorting 8th Air Force B-17s and B-24s - a really long ride. We flew from St. Dizier to Koblenz, Dummer Lake, Steinhuder Lake, Berlin, Magdeburg, Leipzig, Frankfurt, Strasburg and then home! We picked up the 'Big Friends' near Steinhuder Lake and took them nearly to home. The bombs hit oil plants and really did a good job. Plenty of black smoke. I made a good three point landing.

17th January 1945. We had a bad day with no one flying. Paul Dougherty and I walked around the airfield and it took 2½ hours. Went to town in the evening and got back about 21:00 hours.

18th January 1945. Bad weather and we did not fly.

Above: Another aesthetically pleasing and historically significant photo. E2-I, 43-24761, "Jacqueline" (Port), "Parvela" (STBD), and crew - L to R: Radioman Cpl. Theron P. Morris, C/C Sgt. Jesse R. Harris, driver Lt. Dean R. Morehouse, and Assnt. C/C Sgt. Weldon J. Bauer. Morehouse downed a ME-109 on July 7, 1944, in this A/C, for his only confirmed air vic of the war. Only slightly over a month later Lt. Sherman Armsby was lost in it. (Harris) Middle: Capt. Howard A. Euler, Sgt. Ben Tyrell, Lt. Leo Gendron and C/C Martin Strickler with E2-C 44-14662 in Belgium 1945. Background A/C is E2-N, 44-14903 "Dusty" flown by Paul Dougherty. Below: Sgt. Strickler's E2-C, named "Christine," on STBD, for his wife, lies in a field after Leo Gendron and another pilot collided in midair. June 18, 1945. (Pearce)

20th January 1945. Snow - so we couldn't fly. I'm disappointed and waiting for nice weather.

22nd January 1945. Monday, we had some snow today but I finally got to fly. Major Charles Keppler and I flew in a snowstorm for 15 minutes so we returned to base. Later we tried again and this time we didn't get back until 18:00 hours. I made two landings, the first one was perfect but not the next one. I flew 2:30 hours. Captain Alton B. Snyder went down when he was hit by flak. He bellied in O.K. and called on the radio that he was safe. He'd just started his second combat tour.

25th January 1945. Pretty good day and we flew two missions. This morning we got a ME-110. I shot numerous rounds at him (1,200) but my sight was gone and Lt. Paul Daugherty and Lt. Wesley Hart claimed him. The rear gunner managed to shoot down Lt. Robert G. Adams who bailed out but his chute did not deploy in time and he was killed. I'd fired my guns for so long that I burned one of them out. I flew 2:45 hours. This afternoon we had another mission and I got a ME-109 about 10 miles east of Speyer. I never saw so much flak in my life. They were firing 20mm and 40mm and small flak. I flew 2:10 hours. I got the 109 on the deck and it was a pretty rough deal. The pilot didn't get out. I will find out how many rounds I fired later (361 rounds). Flew White two on Maj. Charles Keppler's wing both missions.

ENCOUNTER REPORT

"I was flying Decoy White Two when a lone ME-109 was spotted down near the deck. White Leader called for the flight to follow him and went down on the enemy aircraft from 10,000 feet. As he overshot I lined up on the enemy aircraft and opened fire with a short burst from 400 yards, 20 degrees deflection but did not observe any strikes. Increasing my lead to 1 radii at the same angle off I let another short burst from 300 yards and observed many strikes to the fuselage and wing roots as the enemy aircraft broke sharply to the left. I did not see the enemy aircraft go in as I had my hands full evading flak. I was using the K-14 gunsight. I claim one ME-109 destroyed."
E2-L (bar) 44-14411
P-51
361 rounds.

SUPPORTING STATEMENT

"While flying Decoy Blue Leader, I saw Lt. Robert Farney get several strikes on a ME-109. Immediately after White Two pulled up to avoid light flak, the enemy aircraft dove into the deck and exploded."

Lt. Richard D. Anderson.

26th January 1945. Pretty bad day. Started up the plane and was ready to go but flying control wouldn't let us go.

Above, left: L to R: Earnest H. Tidwell, Walter F. Johnson, Bob Wright and Chuck Upwright with their "Toby," E2-K, 42-106631. Above, right: "Toby," sporting 8 vics awaits another crack at the axis. Bob Wright had a confirmed 109 and a shared (with Sherman Armsby) June 29, 1944. (R.C. Wright) Below: Herb Boelter, intelligence officer for the 375th and the group's Tiger Moth at Bottisham A/D. (Mrs. Boelter)

27th January 1945. Six more inches of snow and naturally no flying. P-47 broke in half on take off yesterday and the pilot didn't even get hurt!

28th January 1945. Sunday, we escorted B-26s and A-20s to Bonn on the Rhine. We flew on instruments and didn't break out of the clouds until we reached 7,500 feet. It was really nasty weather and on the way back we were in snowstorms and everything. I was glad to get back on the ground. I flew 2:20 hours. it's still snowing.

29th January 1945. We had an 8th Air Force mission and we flew from here to Koblenz and Hanover and just stooged about and then came home. We took off in fog but had nice weather to land in. We missed the field and went 60 miles west before locating ourselves. I led the Red element today and it was the first time I had a little authority. I flew 4:30 hours and made a poor landing. It was, and still is, terribly cold today and everything squeaks. No mail.

30th January 1945. Rain, sleet, hail and snow. Getting ready to move to Belgium. It is very nasty.

1st February 1945. It's raining this morning but we're about ready to take off for Chievres, which is about 30 miles southwest of Brussels. We flew to our new field in the rain. I flew all the way with one wheel down. Flew 1:20 hours and made a poor landing. We will be billeted in a Chateau. We got some mail today.

2nd February 1945. No flying so the group got ready for the next day. Climbed the big tower which is about 200 foot high.

3rd February 1945. Boys had an 8th Air Force mission to Magdeburg. I was spare and came back because my engine was playing up. Flew 20 minutes.

4th February 1945. Sunday, no mission today so I test hopped Carl Carlson's P-51D Mustang coded E2-A (bar) and gave the base a little buzz job, flew 30

minutes and made a good landing. Rest of the boys came over from England. Attended a lecture on the war situation in the evening.

5th February 1945. It rained all day and we had nothing to do so we swept our room with shoe brushes.

6th February 1945. Fairly good day and we escorted B-24s to Madgeburg. I went as far as Hanover and came back with Woody (Lt. L. A. Wood). Flew 3:25 hours and saw some flak. Helped my crew chief put in new plugs (in the rain).

8th February 1945. Helped to direct a convoy and drove a six-by-six truck. Boys had a mission and

181

shot up a train. One of the other squadrons got a HE-111.

10th February 1945. Flew an 8th Air Force mission and was up 4:15 hours. We went to Frankfurt, north to Dummer Lake and then out. Saw the bombers drop their loads.

11th February 1945. Sunday, went to Dummer Lake to strafe but didn't have any luck. Flew for 3:00 hours and made a wheel landing. I was spare and filled in. Got some mail.

13th February 1945. Helped camera man put a K-25 camera in my plane, just behind the pilot's seat. Was a mission scheduled for today but it was cancelled due to rain. Dresden was to have been the target.

14th February 1945. Boys had a long mission and Lt. Kneifel ran out of gas and had to bail out. I flew a training mission for two hours and upon landing I blew the tail wheel tire. Lt. Street bellied in Major Chuck Keppler's ship E2-L 'Miss Margie' but he's O.K.

15th February 1945. Was scheduled for a long mission but fog kept us on the ground. Got some mail today and had a haircut.

21st February 1945. After several days of not flying due to bad weather flew an escort mission of 4:15 hours. Very quiet.

22nd February 1945. Flew an 8th Air Force bomber escort mission. They bombed from 10,000 feet. Lt. Richard Chandler (374th Sq.) bailed out and became a POW. I flew 5.05 hours and made a bouncy landing.

23rd February 1945. No mission due to ground fog so I painted my plane and did some work on the pilot's room.

24th February 1945. Flew 4.35 hours on an escort mission to Hanover and back. I felt sick most of the trip but managed to pull off a near perfect landing.

25th February 1945. Sick - but ended up going to Mainz and danced from 3 o'clock to 10:00 PM and had a heck of a good time.

26th February 1945. Group flew a mission to Berlin.

27th February 1945. Went to Leipzig today and flew 5:10 hours. Saw a bomber go down. I made a very good landing.

28th February 1945. Pay Day! Flew a bomber escort mission to the Ruhr area via Frankfurt. Duration of the mission was 3:45 hours and I made another ace landing.

1st March 1945. Flew a mission to Munich and saw some of the German jets. I flew 4:45 hours and made a good landing. Flew through 10,000 feet of overcast. Nasty day. I was made 1st Lt. today and we had a little blow out.

2nd March 1945. Had a little enjoyable trip to Magdeberg today. Saw a 109 hit a bomber and later saw a bomber go down. We got plenty of flak over Osnabruck. I flew 4:45 hours and made a perfect landing. We really had a swell mission. Sun is shining now, 15:00 hours.

3rd March 1945. I was scrubbed from the mission. The boys went to Magdeberg. I took a bath and got a hair cut. Fairly nice day.

4th March 1945. We were down for a long mission but after we were ready to take off it was scrubbed. Went to church. We had a formation and we all got Air Medal presentations and had our pictures taken.

5th March 1945. Was on a 9th A.A.F. mission today and we escorted A-20s while some of the boys dive-bombed. I flew 3:10 hours. Flew 1:00 hours in St. Dizier area and it was counted as a mission so I got

The first Mustang of ace Billy Kemp, E2-X, 42-103749. John Lougheed was lost in this A/C when he collided with a B-24 of the 467th Bomb Group. But prior to this, Billy downed 3 109s on one mission in it - Sept. 12, 1944.

36 missions. Boys had another mission this afternoon. I got two shots today.

6th March 1945. Bad weather.

7th March 1945. Bad weather. I flew Maj. Charles Keppler's ship on 1:15 hours of slow time. Flew formation with P-38 and had a lot of fun and also did a little buzzing. Made a good landing.

8th March 1945. Bad weather. This afternoon I flew Major Charles Keppler's ship for 30 minutes and when the engine practically quit I made a forced landing down wind. The aircraft was badly damaged and it was later found out that an intake valve broke causing the engine to backfire and finally the butterfly in the carb broke and that was the end of that lump and aircraft.

9th March 1945. I didn't fly today but the 374th got two FW-190s. Tony Maurice (375th) had a half share in one of them.

10th March 1945. I led Black Flight today but after a little while we got recalled. Will Fly tomorrow.

11th March 1945. Flew a mission to Kiel. We flew north of Denmark over some cold looking water. I was up 4:45 hours and made a very good landing. Going to church.

12th March 1945. The boys flew a mission to Stettin just 20 miles from the Russian front lines. Lt. Paul Daugherty and I escorted a lone Flying Fortress to check out radio control. We flew 3:15 hours and both of us made a good landing.

15th March 1945. Group went to Berlin today and we lost Cpt. Gene Cole, 'Pappa Cole' as we called him. He went down and was taken POW. A couple days later our ground forces overran the area.

16th March 1945. Group went to Berlin today but all was quiet.

17th March 1945. I've been overseas for six months now. Boys flew a sweep to Leipzig and Berlin. I'm cleared to fly again after an ear infection cleared itself up.

18th March 1945. Boys went back to Berlin today. Jets were active.

19th March 1945. Monday, we went to Munich and saw about 100 enemy aircraft on a field. Flew up to 29,000 feet. Beautiful day and flew 4:45 hours and upon my return made a good landing.

20th March 1945. Sunshiny day and no mission. I took up a training flight and flew 1:30 hours and made a good landing. Flew to Charleroi, Brussels, Antwerp, Lorraine, St. Trond and then home. Had a little fun on the way.

21st March 1945. We went on a mission to Dresden and were attacked by 15 ME-262s. They hacked down three bombers but got two of them. I flew 4:45 hours and made a good landing. Fairly nice day.

22nd March 1945. Escorted 300 British Lancasters to just southeast of Hanover and they bombed visually. Two were shot down by flak. I flew 3:45 and made a poor landing.

The next two photos show what happened when Bob Farney test hopped Major Keppler's new Mustang. After a short while the engine started to backfire, then quit altogether and the crashlanding depicted followed. This was on 8th March 1945 in Belgium. The cause was later traced to a broken intake valve which caused the backfiring. This in turn led to the butterfly in the carb breaking and 'Miss Margie' ran out of pep! (Farney)

23rd March 1945. Flew an area support type mission in the Ruhr area and made a very good landing. We landed at 19:25 and it was nearly dark. I had two close calls from flak over the Rhine. One going in and the other on the way out. Germans are still about.

24th March 1945. Day of airborne crossing of the Rhine River. Major Milton Glessner and I shot up three trains. Used up all my ammunition. Lt. Travis had a 20mm go through his tail and Cpt. Russell 'Jake' Wade was killed in his P-51D (E2-T, 44-13568, 'Talley's Hoosier Hobo') when he was hit by flak. Flew 4:40 and made a good landing.

25th March 1945. Sunday, flew an escort mission and some bombers were hit by flak just east of Hanover. I flew 4:50 and made a good landing. Took a bath.

26th March 1945. Flew an escort mission to Leipzig in clouds and landed after 4:45 hours.

28th March 1945. Went to Mons and bought $25.00 worth of perfume. Boys flew a mission to Berlin.

Left: U.S. Army Signal Corps photo with an interesting caption: "PFC Elmer Bickham of 407 E. 5th St. Texarkana, Ark., looks over the wreckage of a U.S. P-51 fighter plane that was hit by flak over East Rossbach, Germany. The pilot escaped injury but was captured by the Germans. Later the area was occupied by 1st Army troops, the Germans captured and the pilot liberated." Photo is dated 27 March '45. Lt. Howard A. Spaulding damaged, but did not confirm, 2 FW-190s in this A/C way back in Nov. (Via Crow) Right: Lt. William T. Shackleford certainly picked a unique way to acquire battle damage. He flew E2-D, 42-106875 "Queen Jean" across a German A/D, on a strafing pass, while U.S. B-24s were bombing it from high altitude. (Castro)

30th March 1945. Took off for a mission but had to abort when my engine quit on take-off.

31st March 1945. Flew a training mission which lasted 2:05 hours.

3rd April 1945. Went to Kiel and flew 5:15 hours. Made a good landing at 20:00 hours. F/O Jared M. Lundin crashed but is O.K.

4th April 1945. Flew an early mission escorting bombers to Kiel and got in a fight with 12 jets. I damaged one and the 375th damaged seven more. The jets shot down 3 bombers. I flew 4:40 hours and made a poor landing.

ENCOUNTER REPORT

"I was flying Decoy White Three when eight ME-262s were sighted coming in at 7 O'clock to the bombers. White Flight bounced the jets and I took chase after two of them in a turn to the left. I was indicating 360 MPH at 20,000 feet and not closing on the jets. I fired three 2 second bursts at 15 degrees deflection and at 600 to 800 yards. I observed a few hits and the plane momentarily appeared to stream gas. Jet gradually pulled out of range and I quit firing. I claim one ME-262 damaged. A K-14 gun sight was used."
E2-V, 44-14827
P-51
724 rounds

SUPPORTING STATEMENT

"I was flying Decoy White 4 when Lt. Robert Farney engaged two ME-262s. I observed a few strikes on one of the ME-262s at a range of approximately 600 to 800 yards."

F/O Stephen C. Kovach.

6th April 1945. I flew Lt. John Havey's E2-J, 44-14556. 'Libby' on a test-hop for 1 hour. I had been scrubbed from the mission today.

7th April 1945. I lead Blue Flight today and I was really king. We were on an escort mission past Hanover and the B-17s bombed from 15,000 feet. The targets were airfields. We were in a little fight and I shot 500 rounds at a jet. I had color film in my gun camera. Mission lasted 4:45 hours and I made a good landing.

8th April 1945. Flew 5:00 hours on a mission to Leipzig and Berlin. Escorted a lone B-17 home.

9th April 1945. I flew four transitional flights which totaled 4:10 hours. I felt quite sick and so did not fly a combat mission. Flew E2-V, 44-14827 back to Little Walden, Essex.

16th April 1945. Flew to Munich and flew 5:40 hours. The group lost two pilots today, Lt. Russell E. Kenoye and Lt. Delmar A. Ford of the 376th Sq.

17th April 1945. Flew my longest mission today to Pilzen on a strafing mission, it lasted 6:40 hours. Lt. Joseph B. Wolfe was listed as KIA when he was flying E2-L (bar), 44-14411. I led Black Flight and we used 108 gallon wing tanks.

18th April 1945. Flew to Prague on a 6:00 mission and made a good landing at home base. Went to a show in the evening.

19th April 1945. No mission today and the boys flew a practice strafing mission on the field and 30 of us fellows who were not flying shot Very pistols at the attacking Mustangs to represent flak. The result was 3 haystacks burnt to the ground. All in all a very nice day.

20th April 1945. The group flew its last mission of the war and it lasted 5:40 hours. No losses and no claims.

23rd April 1945. Got up at 04:20 but we didn't fly. Will try our luck tomorrow. Had a softball game with the Enlisted Men and we won, 6-7.

24th April 1945. Went to Warton in a B-26 - no mission. It was cold but a nice day.

27th April 1945. Turned in my Colt .45 pistol, everything is quiet.

30th April 1945. Got paid. Went by train to Derby, Derbyshire to attend the school at Rolls Royce Engine Division. Heavy snowstorm.

1st May 1945. Going to school. Later I went to a dance and a show (quite a time) got in at 12:30 AM.

3rd May 1945. Thursday, going to school to study about props. Cloudy, foggy day.

7th May 1945. Back at Little Walden and we have all been confined to base. Flew for 2:00 hours and did some ground gunnery.

8th May 1945. VE-DAY, the C.O., Roy B. Caviness, made a speech at 10:00 hours. Everything is quiet and we are still restricted to base. I developed some negs today.

16th May 1945. Very good day and I led a flight for 2:30 hours and made a good landing.

18th May 1945. Flew a mission to train Major O'Dwyer.

19th May 1945. Saturday, went to school and in the evening went to Bottisham for a 375th Squadron dance.

20th May 1945. Got a 6-4 and passed. Went to see a compulsary movie. Had chicken and ice cream for supper.

21st May 1945. Monday lead two training flights today and made two good landings. Showers today and tonight. We are to go through the 'gas' chambers tomorrow.

22nd May 1945. Lead two training flights today. Went to town in the evening and made arrangements to have a new battledress jacket made.

23rd May 1945. Went to gas chamber today. Lead one flight and in the next the lead was taken by Major Glessner, Lt. Charles Willis flew number 2 and I was the third one in the flight. I was sweating my oxygen for the indicator read 'empty' and Maj. Glessner took us up to 15,000 feet. When we got down I told him my situation. He laughed and said not to worry as he was out too!

24th May 1945. Lead a flight again today and flew in overcast for instrument practice. Went to ground school after landing. Got a letter from Francis and home.

4th June 1945. Checked out in a P-47 Thunderbolt. Quite a plane. Flew tow target practice in the afternoon. One of the pilots shot the target right off.

17th June 1945. Lt. J. Warren Geron, an ex-bomber pilot who recently joined the group, took me up in the group's B-17 hack aircraft and we shot eight landings. I made two myself in the co-pilot's seat and the second one was quite good. Flew 1:30 hours. We did alright. Got clearance to go and see Robby C. Farney. Went to church in the evening.

20th June 1945. Got back from seeing Robby C. and I had a nice time. He's fine and getting along OK.

23rd June 1945. Lt. Leo Gendron had the tail of his Mustang cut off while dogfighting with a 339th

Dreary gutted ruins form the backdrop for Chuck Keppler's E2-D, 44-14164, "Phyll." This A/C formerly Urban Drew's "Detroit Miss." (Tyrell)

Left: Photos of the two A/C involved in the terrible training accident of July 23, 1945. "Libby," the A/C of Lt. John Havey, was named for his fiance, Miss Libby Wolfe. (Photo submitted by C/C Eugene Berry) Right: L to R: Leonard A. Wood, Tony Maurice, and Leonard Mottis of the 375th F.S. in front of Maurice's "Tony," E2-M, 44-15028. By coincidence A/C in background is "Libby." (Wood)

Fighter Group Mustang. The pilot of the other ship bailed out too low and was killed. His name was Lt. George W. Porter. One fellow, F/O Wade C. Ross (376th Sq), ran into a haystack and plugged the radiator scoop on his aircraft and the engine overheated and he had to bail out.

25th June 1945. Flew a three hour navigation flight and later had one hour in the Link trainer. Attended a lecture on the Far East.

14th July 1945. Flew to Northern Ireland and was weathered in for three days.

18th July 1945. Had a parade and was decorated with the DFC by B/General Jesse Auton. Maj. General Larson was also present.

20th July 145. Fifty of the group's pilots left for the States today.

23rd July 1945. Monday, Lt. John E. Havey and Lt. J. Warren Geron were killed while on a dive-bombing practice mission today. Havey was flying E2-I, 44-14556 and Geron was in E2-M, 44-15038. They were trying out wing line bombing and probably hit compressibility which caused one of the planes to break up and the other mushed in on pull out. A third Mustang flown by Lt. Charles K. Willis was scrapped after landing due to the rear fuselage being wrinkled.

24th July 1945. I attended the funerals of Havey and Geron at the American Military Cemetery, Madingley, Cambridge.

3rd August 1945. I lead two flights on a divebombing mission and everyone did quite well.

5th August 1945. The group was to give an airshow over Paris, France and as we took off Lt. Curtis Harris crashed on take-off and I had to fly through the black billowing smoke. Lt. Harris was killed.

Mission List for Lt. Robert J. Farney.

Date	Type	Duration	Destination
26.11.44.	Escort	4:20	Hanover
30.11.44.	Escort	5:40	Leipzig
4.12.44.	Escort	5:00	Frankfurt
5.12.44.	Escort	5:40	Berlin
6.12.44.	Escort	4:00	Hanover
10.12.44.	Escort	5:00	Coblenz
11.12.44.	Escort	5:30	Coblenz
12.12.44.	Escort	4:50	Coblenz
26.12.44.	Transfer	1:55	St. Diziel, Fr.
29.12.44.	Freelance	4:18	Trier
31.12.44.	Patrol	2:05	Coblenz
1.1.45.	Sweep	3:15	Coblenz
1.1.45.	Sweep	1:55	Coblenz
2.1.45.	Escort	3:00	Coblenz
2.1.45.	Sweep	2:45	Coblenz
10.1.45.	Fgtrbombr.	2:20	Neustadt M/Y
13.1.45.	Fgtrbombr.	2:35	Frankfurt
14.1.45.	Escort	4:40	Durban
15.1.45.	Fgtrbombr.	2:20	Moselle River
16.1.45.	Escort	4:35	Steinhuder Lk.
22.1.45.	Sweep	2:30	Karlsruhe
25.1.45.	Patrol	2:45	Coblenz Area
25.1.45.	Patrol	2:10	Speyer
28.1.45.	Escort	2:20	Bonn
29.1.45.	Area Sup.	4:30	Hanover
1.2.45.	Transfer	1:50	Chievres, Bel.
6.2.45.	Escort	3:25	Hanover
10.2.45.	Escort	4:15	Frankfurt
11.2.45.	Ground Attk.	3:00	Dummer Lake
14.2.45.	Training	2:00	Chievres Area

16.2.45.	Escort	3:00	Ruhr		7.4.45.	Escort	4:45	Hanover
21.2.45.	Escort	4:15	Dessau		8.4.45.	Freelance	5:00	Leipzig
22.2.45.	Escort	5:05	Nordhausen		16.4.45.	Escort	5:40	Munich
24.2.45.	Escort	4:35	Hanover		17.4.45.	Escort	6:40	Pilzen
27.2.45.	Escort	5:10	Leipzig		18.4.45.	Escort	6:00	Prague
28.2.45.	Escort	3:45	Ruhr					
1.3.45.	Escort	4:45	Munich					
2.3.45.	Escort	4:45	Madgeburg					
5.3.45.	Patrol	3:10	Rhine River					
8.3.45.	Test-Hop	0.30	X-Country					
11.3.45.	Escort	4:45	Kiel					
12.3.45.	Radio-B-17	3:15	Bel.-Fr.					
19.3.45.	Escort	4:45	Munich					
20.3.45.	Training	1:30	X-Country					
21.3.45.	Escort	4:45	Dresden					
22.3.45.	Escort	3:35	Hanover					
23.3.45.	Area Sup.	4:35	Ruhr					
24.3.45.	Area Patr.	4:40	Rhine Area					
25.3.45.	Area Patr.	4:50	Hanover					
26.3.45.	Escort	4:35	Leipzig					
30.3.45.	Escort	Abtd.	Schleswig					
31.3.45.	Training	2:05	X-Country					
3.4.45.	Sweep	5:15	Kiel					
4.4.45.	Escort	4:40	Kiel					

All types of mission including training, cross country and test flights counted as combat time while the 361st Fighter Group was based on the continent due to the proximity of the enemy.

Aircraft flown by Lt. Robert J. Farney.

E2-C, 44-14662.

E2-D, 44-15597.

E2-L, 44-63173. 'Miss Margie'

E2-L (bar), 44-14411.

E2-M (bar), 44-13339.

E2-V, 44-14827. 'Croghan Cruiser-Waverley Democrat'

Bob was assigned 44-14827 on about the 24th January 1945 and it was given the designator code 'V' as the previous coded 'V' aircraft was lost a few days earlier when Lt. Robert Adams was KIA.

Crew Chief: - Alvin Walther. (picked name 'Waverley Democrat').

The war in Europe is over but the training continues. Major Milton Glessner in E2-G, 44-14085 leads Chuck Willis in E2-T (bar), 44-13579 'Vicky Belle' and Robert Farney in E2-V, 44-14827 'Croghan Cruiser.' The date was 23rd May 1945. Note underwing anti-buzzing codes. (Boelter)

George in the cockpit of his "Mary Mine," E9-L, 44-14685. Compare flying gear to that worn today! (Van Heuval)

GEORGE RENZO VANDEN HEUVEL

376TH FIGHTER SQUADRON, 361ST FIGHTER GROUP

George R. Vanden Heuvel was born on July 27, 1917 at Mount Vernon, New York. He was educated at Curtis High School, Staten Island. From 1935 until 1939 he was a student at the School of Technology in Atlanta, Georgia where he obtained a Bachelor of Science Degree in Mechanical Engineering. On May 30, 1939, he was inducted into the Army as a 2nd Lieutenant in the Coast Artillery Reserve Corps. The following January he was ordered to report for active duty with his unit.

At about this time he applied for flying training and the following year he joined Class 42K at Douglas, Georgia where he completed his Primary Training in July. From there he went to Cochran Field, Georgia for Basic Training and Mariana Field Florida for his Advanced Training, graduating on December 12, 1942. He was one of a number of pilots selected to be assigned to Maxwell Field, Alabama for a Basic Training Course for instructors. Upon completion he was reassigned to Cochran Field, Georgia where he trained RAF pilots as well as USAAF pilots.

He recalled the day he and the others got their long awaited overseas orders to take part in the shooting war: "On May 18th, and unknown to each other, five of us were ordered to report to Base Operations at 1300 hours. We assembled in the outer office wondering where, when or how we'd goofed and as to what disciplinary action was to be taken against us. At 1315 hours the Operations Officer called us in and without hesitation said, 'Well, you five asked for it and now you're going to get it.' There was a long pause as we looked at each other. 'You're on your way to combat as fighter pilots and you leave for Spence Field, Georgia tomorrow.' We all let out a rousing cheer while the officer just shook his head."

On the 19th our various friends who were staying behind flew us from Cochran to Spence in BT-13s. We were part of a special class of over 200 pilots selected because we all had over 1000 hours of flight time. From the 20th until the 28th we were checked out on gunnery training in AT-6s and from June 1st we went on to P-40s for three days. From June 4th until the 22nd we were at Dale Mabry in Florida. Gordon M. Graham joined us there. Next came two weeks of Link Training, Classroom and High Altitude Training. It was here that we got news about the landings in Normandy.

'Late in June we all transferred to Venice, Florida and survived 34 hours of flying training in P-40s, including two hours of night formation flying. From there we went back to Dale Mabry and then to Camp Kilmer, New Jersey, ready to go overseas. In mid August we boarded the 'Ile de France'. With us were about 400 bomber pilots and navigators, 10,000 doughboys and one crooner, Bing Crosby.

'Seven days later we arrived at Gourock, Scotland and we fighter jocks entrained for Goxhill, Lincolnshire for P-51 transitional training. The five of us got orders to report to the 361st Fighter Group. 'Ace' Graham was sent to the 355th at Steeple Morden. On the day we joined our new group they moved from their former station at Bottisham, Cambridge to Station 165, Little Walden, Essex.

'I flew a P-51 for the first time at Walden on October 1, 1944 and by a strange coincidence my last flight at Little Walden was on October 1, 1945, also in a Mustang. The three of us who survived left Little Walden to return to the States on October 26, 1945."

Lt. Vanden Heuvel was assigned to 'D' Flight in the 376th Fighter Squadron under the command of Major Jim Cheney, who was shot down 2 days later to become a POW. In mid October 1944 George flew his first combat mission and on November 2nd he made his first claim against the GAF: "I was flying Yorkshire Yellow Two. We were on the left side of the B-17s after they had hit the target and were heading west. Our flight was with the 3rd box from the rear when someone called out that the last box was being hit by enemy fighters. We headed back and followed some ME-109s down, but lost them in the overcast. We went right through the clouds and levelled off. At that moment a FW-190 turned on Lt. Gene Czapla and myself. Lt. Harold Mitchell closed on him and fired, scoring numerous hits. The FW-190 hit the ground and burned. I became separated and as I was turning around, I saw another FW-190 making a steep turn head-on into me. I fired a short burst, but saw no hits, but the E/A did a snap out of the steep turn he was in. As we were about 100 feet off the ground he had no time to recover and hit upside down and burned. I claim one FW-190 destroyed." At the time George was flying E9-D 44-14217.

Soon afterwards he was assigned to his first Mustang coded E9-L (bar), 44-14685 which he named 'Mary Mine'. His crew chief was Eugene Sullivan of Hartford, Connecticut.

On November 26 George got his second and third claims with a show of coolness which belied the fact that he had only flown a few missions. Upon his return to Little Walden the following day he wrote out his report as follows, ``I was flying Yorkshire White Four - escorting B-24s.

We were about 15 miles south of Ulzen when 50 plus FW-190s approached the bombers from the east. We broke into them and I got into a dive at about 500 mph plus and could not pull out until about 10,000 feet. I was all alone then and climbed up southwest along the bombers' track looking for someone to join up with. I was at about 20,000 feet when I saw 10 plus FW-190s ahead and they broke into me.

I turned into them and maneuvered onto a FW-190's tail. I fired a burst but after a few rounds only one gun was firing. I saw no hits. While I was on this FW-190's tail several other 190s were making side passes at me but scored no hits. Two FW-190s, coming from opposite sides, were closing in and shot at me from about an 80 degree deflection angle. I dumped the stick and made a steep diving turn. The two FW-190s collided almost head on and exploded. They fell in a flaming mass. I then continued on out of that area. I claim 2 FW-190s destroyed. At the time I was flying E9-L (bar), 44-14685.''

In a supporting statement Captain John D. Duncan of the 376th Fighter Squadron wrote, ``I was leading the 361st Fighter Group, escorting the first box of 2nd Air Division bombers on the target (which was Misburg). Just as the Big Friends were turning on the I.P., I observed numerous FW-190s coming in at 9 o'clock about three miles away. Advising the group of the situation, I made a 270 degree turn to port. Attacking with my squadron from behind, I found myself flying wingtip to wingtip with a FW-190, which dropped his tank and his flaps and cut his throttle. I did the same, and started to force him into a left turn when I observed Lt. Walter Kozicki, my element leader, closing from 6 o'clock with all guns blazing. I observed hits on the canopy and pieces flying from the left side of the FW-190. The E/A slid off on his left wing doing vicious snap rolls straight for the deck. The last I saw he was in an uncontrolled spin at about 8,000 feet. I believed that the pilot of this aircraft was clobbered.

I climbed back to about 22,000 feet and observed a lone P-51 at my 2 o'clock in a battle royal with 12 to 15 FW-109s which were making passes at the Mus-

Joe Kruzel gives the yellowjackets a time check during the briefing prior to their first D-Day sortie. (Kruzel)

Above, left: 8th FTR Command was certainly blessed with an abundance of able leadership and Joe Kruzel was typical of what was found in most squadrons. He didn't just synchronize watches and point to the flightline, but led many missions and scored at least 3½ aerial vics himself. Above left is a picture of the artwork on his P-47, E9-K, 42-75333 - named for his wife. Bathing suit was white, "Vi" was red and white with black outlines. (Kruzel) Above, right: Lt. Col. Kruzel used a variety of A/C to bring down his 3½ confirmed air vics. This one, 44-13391, photographed at Bottisham, he used for his last claim on June 25, 1944 over a FW-190. (Drew)

tang from all sides. As I was going over to join him, I saw two FW-190s bearing down on him, one from his port side, the other starboard, at about 90 degrees. I called him to break, but he just sat there until the very last second. Then he kicked his stick forward and went into a steep turn to the left. The two FW-190s crashed head-on. I believe the pilot caused the destruction of the 2 FW-190s by his coolness of head and split second timing. Also, I think that any pilot with guts enough to pull a maneuver like that should have full credit for the destruction of both enemy planes".

Writing to his brother Sandy on 27th November, George said 'Dear Sandy, Hi ole pal. Here is my latest report. I can't mention names, dates or places but you can get just as much out of this without them. On a recent mission we were escorting B-24s. Just before they hit the target about 50 ME-109s and FW-190s attacked. We went after them and I got into a dive and into compressibility because I was going too fast. When I finally pulled out I was alone, and lonely. I

The Thunderbolt of Sam C. Wilkerson of the 376th Fighter Squadron at Bottisham airfield. The code was E9-O, 42-75449 and he named it 'Shopworn Angel.' In the background is Bottisham Church. (Johnston)

started climbing back up towards the bombers and also looking for some friendly fighters to team up with. I saw about 12 fighters but as my recognition isn't as good as yours I was pretty close to them when I saw they were FW-190s.

They saw me about the same time and came after me. I didn't have time to be scared so I went after them. We got all tangled up in a dogfight and I guess they got into each other's way in their enthusiasm to get me. At the time though, I was enjoying myself and really felt that old fighting spirit and I destroyed two of them. They exploded. Then all but one of my guns jammed or I would have tried to get them all. So I dove full throttle and everything, outran the rest, and got away. I then flew down the bomber track - still alone - and came near a group of bombers under attack by 50 FW-190's. With only one gun working there wasn't anything I could do but watch until I got so mad that I went hell-bent full throttle after one of them and took a shot at him. I got a couple of hits on his tail with no effect. A few left the bombers and came after me so I left that area in a hurry. I was still alone when I left Germany and when over Holland I finally met up with my squadron commander. As we were low on gas we landed in Belgium. I think I'd have gotten more of the Jerries if the guns hadn't jammed. It really made me mad. I have gotten one each for Mary, Georgie and Terry so the next one I get will have your name on the swastika. I hope it's soon. I must sign off now. WRITE. My love to all.

Your Pal GEORGE.

In a letter to Sandy, George gave a good description of a typical fighter pilot's time while on escort duty., England December 7th 1944.

Dear Sandy: Hi' ole Pal: Just received your letter and

Above: Major Roy Caviness in his P-47, "Goona." We scanned this photo in hopes you could read the spunky message on the bomb: "To whom it may concern, from Goona." If Goona would have moved her big rt. foot, that would have been a nice shot of E9-E, 42-7909 "Carol" as well. (Johnston) Below, left: Ground crewmen stand retreat on the southern perimeter of Bottisham, Cambs. The A/C was Maj. Roy Caviness's "B". We have a later pic of this A/C in a heap after its new owner, Robert Hobb, bailed out successfully April 24, 1945 due to mechanical failure. The A/C was then coded E9-T and named "Lil Larry." (May) Below, right: The Last of the Goonas. Lt. Col. Caviness took this one with him when he went to command the 78th F.G. It then became one of the most photogenic P-51s in the 8th as "Contrary Mary," WZ-I. Left to Right standing: Fredericks, C/C Henry Socha, Armorer Murfe O'Neil, C/C Al La Pierre and Radioman Emerson Nicol.

I must say you ask more questions than Prof. Quiz but I'll be glad to answer all I can. How does that model of yours fly? I'd like to see it. Be sure to save it until I get home. - When I see an enemy plane it's like no other feeling in the world. I become strangely tense and get a funny feeling in my stomach. It doesn't matter what the altitude is either. When the first one I got came at me right off the ground and headed straight at me I just started shooting. It's a great feeling to hear those guns firing. It gives me quite a sense of power - and I didn't have my eyes shut. I saw him flick over on his back and he dove in upside down and crashed,

exploded and burned.

When we fly low we fly lower than you would believe. We fly behind trees, hedges, in between the banks of canals so low we can look up and see people along the banks. We can look up and see trees and stuff, and that is low. We fly at about 300 mph and a mistake would be something. When strafing we stay right on the ground behind trees and stuff until we are near our target then bounce up to about 100 feet and dive down shooting, then hit the deck and make our get-a-way.

We see V-2 rockets take off and climb just about straight up and disappear from sight. The robot

Above: "Hilma Lee," the aircraft of ace William J. Sykes. Black serials and codes (also underwing), red breather and name. As we see from the text, Lt. Sykes was shot down by a 109. MACR#4173 records he was flying E9-F, 44-11203 at the time. He was brutalized by his captors but managed to survive, returning home after repatriation. (Kozicki) Below: Lt. C.E. Sullivan & crew with their A/C E9-S, 42-106707, "Sleepytime Gal."

bombs don't go very high. When I was in Belgium I saw about thirty go over the place I was at, at about 2000 feet. The anti-aircraft guns shot down several of them. One reason we have motor trouble is because the engine is tuned up so fine and the fuel is so powerful. In an emergency we can really travel but it's hard on the engine. The highest speed I ever made was in a dive in which I was going over 600 mph. I couldn't pull out until I got down to 10,000 feet where the air was heavier. This plane is really a dream ship and I sure wish you could see me fly it. I'd love to be back and fly it over our house.

I now have a little more than 1600 hours flying time. I add about 40 to 50 hours a month over here. - Often we take off at dawn, especially if the mission is to be a long one. The other day we took off at dawn on the way to Berlin. It was a six hour trip and I was plenty tired when I got back. We didn't see any Jerries. When going on missions we take candy and gum along but usually fly so high we need to wear our oxygen masks and cannot eat. I was up to 40,000 feet once but most of our escort missions are flown between 25,000 and 30,000 feet. At 30,000 feet we would remain conscious

about 30 seconds to one minute without oxygen.

About making good Germans, you can count on me to make as many as I can. - We have a lot of pilots in my squadron so that I don't get to fly every mission even though I would like to. I'm an element leader now, which means I have a wingman to protect my tail when we get into a scrap while I do the shooting. It is a tough job and when we get to milling around it's hard to stay with anybody. That sky is a big place when we're deep in the heart of Germany and it sure takes a long time to fly out when we're low on gas or have engine trouble. However, we have the best planes in the world and the Mustang P-51 is the best of all. I love hearing from you Sandy. I'll answer any letters you write and any questions you ask, if I can. My love to all and keep Georgie and Terry up-to-date on airplanes,

Your ole pal and 'ace' GEORGE.

On December 23, after completing a mission, the group landed at its new airfield St. Dizier, France with the knowledge that for a time they could forget the feared flight across the North Sea (in which a downed airman was given a matter of a few minutes to survive unless he could get into his dinghy and out of the extremely cold water). While there the group was to operate under control of the 9th Air Force. On December 24, 1944 the group was on a mission with Van flying as wingman to Clarence E. Sullivan Jr. in Yellow Section of the 376th Fighter Squadron when a dogfight developed near Wengerohr, Germany. During this air battle the group shot down four enemy aircraft for the loss of Billy Sykes of the 376th Fighter Squadron. Lt. Sullivan took care of the e/a that shot Sykes down and Van shot down the ME-109 that was chasing Lt. Sullivan.

Van recalled: "I was Yellow Two, flying on Lt. Clarence Sullivan's wing, on a fighter patrol between Bonn and Trier. We were in the vicinity of Wengerohr when White Leader called out bogies below. Lt. Sullivan followed White Flight down. White Leader, Lt. William J. Sykes, called out they were ME-109s and almost immediately after I saw a yellow nose P-51, which I am sure was Lt. Sykes, clobber a ME-109 which began to smoke, fall out of control and explode on the ground. Lt. Sullivan turned towards Lt. Sykes and some more ME-109s, when I saw a ME-109 approaching Lt. Sullivan from the right. I started towards the ME-109 and he turned into me. I got my pipper on him and began firing head-on at extreme range, but the rate of closing was so great only a short burst was possible. There were a few hits on his canopy. He made no effort to dodge so I broke under him and turned to the left to get after him. He made no turn, but continued straight ahead in a gradually increasing dive and dove into the ground where he exploded and burned. I believe the pilot was killed by one of my strikes.

Left: A proud Lt. Kenneth J. Scott Jr. beside his ferocious P-51D, E9-J, 44-13872, Sept. 44. Just a few days later, the A/C was lost over France with another pilot. (Scott Jr.) Above: Ken Scott's first P-51 was E9-Z "Curiosity Betty" - a "C" model. This photo was taken at Botisham in early Sept. '44 before the group's transfer to Little Walden, Essex. Below: A post war 376th F.S. training flight with - back to front: Jay Ruch in E9-A, 42-106944 (is that a fin strake on a "C"?), E9-Y, 44-14514 "Daisy Mae III," Ken Scott Jr.'s E9-V, 44-14600, "Curiosity Betty II," and E9-S, 44-14520 "Hilma Lee" of ace Capt. Wm. Sykes. Note: Sun must be almost directly overhead, judging from the length of the shadows cast by the engine exhaust pipes.

I then turned to rejoin Lt. Sullivan and heard Lt. Sykes call for "someone to get this guy off my tail." Down at my ten o'clock I saw a ME-109 firing at Lt. Syke's plane - from which pieces started flying off. Lt. Sykes called out that they got him, then jettisoned his canopy and bailed out the left side. His chute opened almost immediately. Meanwhile, Lt. Sullivan was closing on the ME-109 and registered numerous hits on his first burst. Lt. Sullivan pulled up right off the trees and the ME-109 went into a steep dive and crashed into the ground.

As I made a turn I flew past Lt. Sykes in his chute and he seemed to be alive and kicking. I claim one ME-109 destroyed and I claim one ME-109 destroyed for Lt. Sykes. I also support Lt. Sullivan's claim for the destruction of a ME-109. Lt. William J. Sykes, 0-793027 was flying E9-F, 44-11203 "HIYA HONEY III". Lt. Clarence E. Sullivan Jr. was flying E9-S (bar), 44-14663 "BABY DOLL".

Just two days later, on December 24, Van knocked down two Jerry aircraft (sharing one with Jay Ruch) to become an ace. The combat took place near Merzig and some 40 years later the author managed to bring one of the 'Victims' into contact with the ace fighter pilot.

At the time Van recalled: "I was flying Yorkshire Red Four and we were on a fighter sweep in the vicinity of Trier when ten plus FW-109s crossed in front of us from left to right. We turned on them and they broke into us. Lt. Claire P. Chennault (E9-C, 44-14251) turned onto one and another turned toward him. I got on the FW's tail and he headed for the deck in a series of steep diving turns. I shot short bursts at him from about 300 yards on the way down, registering occasional hits. He levelled off at about 100 feet and started a turn to the right. I set the K-14 gunsight on

him and fired a long burst, opening fire at 250 yards, 20 degree deflection. Closing to 200 yards, I registered numerous hits on his fuselage, canopy and wing roots. He fell off on one wing and dove into the ground, exploding upon impact. The pilot did not bail out. I then took a picture of the wreck.

I started climbing up and about five miles east of me I saw two planes on the deck. I finally identified them as a FW-190 being chased by Captain Jay Ruch (E9-J, 44-15372). I told Captain Ruch I was covering him and he said he was out of ammunition and for me to shoot the FW-190 down. The FW-190 was smoking slightly and taking weak evasive action on the deck. As he pulled up out of a gully, I clobbered him from about 300 yards, 15 degrees deflection, firing several bursts. He started a turn to the left and I clobbered him again from 200 yards and several pieces flew off the plane. He rolled over on his back and bailed out. I claim one

FW-190 destroyed and one FW-190 destroyed shared with Captain Jay Ruch.
E9-L (bar), 44-14685.

In his combat report Jay Ruch wrote, ``I was flying southwest in the vicinity of Trier at 17,000 feet, leading Red Section. I spotted approximately eleven bandits at my one o'clock low, and proceeded to make a pass on the rear aircraft. As I closed in, the lead planes broke and I definitely identified them as FW-190s. I singled out one of them and started firing at approximately five hundred yards with about sixty degree deflection, no hits observed. I closed to four hundred yards in a tight series of turns and gave him another burst with about 40 degree deflection. I observed strikes on the left wing root and noticed pieces of the plane breaking off. Closing to about 350 yards, I gave him a third burst at the same deflection and observed more hits on the left wing root. I continued firing in tight turns with no more hits observed until I ran out of ammunition. I followed him down to the deck with him trailing heavy black smoke. I followed him for several minutes trying to force him into the ground without results.

Lt. Vanden Huevel took up as my wingman as he saw me following the e/a to the deck. I told him to pull up and start shooting because all my ammunition was gone. He closed to about 200 yards and gave him a short burst with no deflection and I observed many hits all over the plane. The e/a took very little evasive action and Lt. Vandel Huevel gave him a second burst and more hits were observed as the e/a pulled up and the pilot bailed out. The plane crashed into the woods below and burned. I claim one FW-190 destroyed shared with Lt. George Vanden Huevel.

After landing from the mission it was reported in the group records that Lt. Jack Mitenbuler (374th Fighter Squadron) had been compelled to land at an airfield due to battle damage. He met a Jerry pilot captured

Right: Lt. Robert R. Volkman of Wilmington, Delaware. He served with the 376th Fighter Squadron. (Johnston) Below: While test flying his Mustang (E9-H, 44-14197) on 29th October 1944, Bob had to set it down due to a thrown rod. He landed in a field owned by farmer Fred Harrison-Smith and a friendship developed which lasted until Fred's death several years ago. Bob named all his Mustangs 'Mary Jane' after his sister. (Volkman)

by U.S. ground forces after bailing out of his FW-190 after being shot up by two 'yellow nosed Mustangs'. It was reported that the enemy pilot had been flying for about seven years with the Luftwaffe. In early 1979 Van received a letter from the German pilot after research by the author in which he told of his part in the combat on December 26:
Dear Friend,

First of all the question which is probably the most interesting for you, whether I am the German 'Bandit' whom you shot down over Luxembourg, near Florenne-Villes. According to the situation, it should be me. I was at the time a First Lieutenant and Squadron Leader and on that day was leading the 2nd Group of Schlageter squadron (2-JG 26) with our FW-190s. Since I was taken prisoner after that by the Americans, I no longer remember at the moment certain details, such as the exact time of being shot down (12.00 hours. Author) and our starting time from the aerodrome in Furstenau, near Rheine. But I shall try to reconstruct this and I am hoping for your assistance in this.

We had instructions at the time to protect the advance tanks of the von Rundstedt offensive, which had already penetrated deeply into Belgium, from your fighter-bombers and bomber attacks (the 'Indians',

Above: Hans Hartig climbs out of his FW-190 after a sortie against the 'Indianers' as the Luftwaffe pilots called American fighter aircraft. Below: A photo of George's old opponent, now new friend, taken a few years ago. (Hartig)

our name for enemy fighter pilots). I found the tanks, which had been buried and deserted having been put out of action, lacking ammunition and petrol.

Actually I had carried out my instructions but there had been an order not to return from a sortie under any circumstances without contact with the enemy. I was therefore looking for a ground target by flying low, but unfortunately I did not find anything suitable and decided to gain height and join my group going south. I realized I would be quickly discovered by your radar and the enemy air command would send its Indians against us. It was a sunny morning with hardly any clouds, the best weather for you and your Yellow-Jackets to chase after 'German Bandits'.

You proceeded to do this thoroughly, however, I still shot down a Thunderbolt but then I was shot down by a yellow-nosed Mustang. I was able to save myself with a parachute, but that meant the end of the war for me. I am hoping this letter finds you in good health.

Hans Hartig

In a letter to his brother telling him about how he made acedom Van wrote:

``Sandy - this is 'ACE' Van, and I really mean it. I got one and a half planes today. That gives me five and one-half. Here's the story:

We were cruising along and spotted ten FW-190s and bounced them. I was flying Lt. Chennault's wing (one of the General's boys) and he got on a 190's tail. Another turned on him so I went after that 190. I chased him from 15,000 feet down to the ground. I was firing bursts all the way down. When he levelled off over the trees he started a turn to the right and I got my sights on him and really hit him. Pieces started flying off and he dove into the ground.

I started climbing up and saw one of our boys chasing a FW-190. I went to cover his tail. He called me saying he was out of ammunition and told me to shoot him down. I chased the Jerry down gullys and valleys and finally when he pulled up over a little hill he started to turn to the right and I shot hell out of him. He then turned to the left and I shot hell out of him again. His plane started to fall apart and he rolled over and bailed out. Since the first pilot (Ruch) had already damaged him somewhat we shared the victory between us. That's all for now. My regards to all. 'ACE VAN'

The group was at St. Dizier during the winter. When the snow finally started to melt, they encountered serious problems with the slush and mud. Due to the narrow perimeter track, the Mustangs had to taxi out in single file. This was fine for the leader, but for the rest it was a nightmare as the props threw junk everywhere. A pilot could lean forward and clean the two side panels, but the center panel couldn't be reached. So the crew chiefs rode on the wing and at the last possible minute would give the screen a final wipe, but this was considered to be unsafe and was discontinued.

Van and his crew chief, Gene Sullivan, devised a system. They inserted a T-junction in the oil dilution line and ran a small copper tube from it along the base of the windscreen. Next they bored small holes into the tubing, so that when the pilot threw the switch for

Above: George in the cockpit and C/C Gene Sullivan on the wing await the start of another mission from their muddy airfield. Middle: George in his aircraft at St. Dizier, France. The field was coded A-64. Note the 'No-Missum' K-14 gunsight. This was a development of the British gunsight. Below: George's Crew Chief Gene Sullivan has his head down and rearend up as he looks into the cockpit. Lt. Duane Grounds looks over the cowling and Lt. Clarence Sullivan is wheel balancing. Normal yellow nose with a white panel and black lettering. (Vanden Heuval)

the oil dilution pump, gas was forced out onto the windscreen. The next day after taking off with the usual dirty windscreen, Van threw the switch. The flow of gas and the pressure of the wind cleaned the windshield. This went on for several missions and when it was proved to be working safely, Van informed the group engineering officer who threw a fit, saying it was a potential fire hazard and could even cause engine failure on take-off! Although Van disagreed with the E.O. he had to remove the device. But as most of the snow and slush had gone in the week he'd used it, he and Gene figured it had proved itself.

On February 15th, Van moved from St. Dizier to Chievres, Belgium. Only the air echelon moved at that time, non-flying personnel followed later. On February 24, 1945 they went on a trip to Germany, Van recalled:

"Around mid-day we left our base in a two and one-half ton truck in high spirits. We drove across Belgium and viewed the sights of Charleroi, Namur, and Liege. Next we headed north and crossed over into Holland. The people all along the way were very friendly. We stopped for supper in Maastricht. It was a beautiful, up-to-date little city. It hadn't been damaged by the war, and except for the sights, I thought we were back in some town in the USA. We ate at the Red Cross, then went into a little cafe and had some strawberry ice-cream, which tasted very much like home.

At about eight o'clock in the evening, we started out again. It was pretty dark as we drove eastward towards Aachen, then headed North and drove up to Sittart just inside Holland. Just to make the picture complete it started to drizzle. From Sittart we headed east towards Geilenkirchen but took a wrong turn and got lost. We were somewhere out in open country on a little muddy road - and it was really muddy. We crept along for what seemed like hours. On the horizon ahead of us we could see tremendous flashes and pretty soon we could see them behind us too and even hear the explosions. We figured that was our artillery firing behind us - we hoped so anyway. Finally we came to a little bombed and shelled town where an M.P. stopped us and directed us to where we wanted to go. (one of the boys with us was looking for his brother who was in the Medics).

The M.P. told us we were about a half mile from the Roer River and the town had been taken only that morning. It was about midnight then and cold too. So we resumed our journey driving south through more ruined villages, through Geilenkirchen and finally reached our destination. We shouted, "Hello" but not a soul stirred nor could we see a light anywhere. At last we found someone and located the looked-for brother. They gave us some cold C-rations and we talked for a couple of hours. Then with plenty of blankets for cover we picked out a house with a roof and fixed us some beds in the cellar. It was easily the dirtiest, darkest place I ever slept in. Right behind our

*Above: Two photos of Lt. Robert J. Bain and his A/C, ``Blue Eyes,'' taken at Little Walden in the fall of 44. Again note last 4 digits of serial stenciled on engine panels. Aerial warfare could be very frustrating - Bob made 3 ``damaged'' claims, but was unable to have any of them confirmed. (**Bain**) Below: Lt. Delmar A. Ford is waiting to be flagged at Chievres A/F, Belgium. He went down in this A/C on April 16, 45 and became a POW for the last few weeks of the war. (**Kozicki**)*

house was a battery of Long Toms, and they kept banging away all night. Every time they fired, plaster and dust would fall down on us from the ceiling. In spite of that and 'other' explosions I got a good night's sleep.

In the morning we arose at eight-thirty and when I came through the doorway I looked upon a scene of utter desolation. The place was completely in ruins. There wasn't a whole house in sight. We roamed around through that and other towns, and they were all in the same state of ruin. Except for our troops there wasn't a sign of life anywhere. We looked for souvenirs, but there just weren't any. Everything was just total wreckage. We tried to get closer to the Roer River but were told the Germans were shelling the next cross-roads and town, so we decided not to go. We just wandered around staying on beaten paths, because of mines, and talked to a good many of our soldiers. The sun came out in the afternoon, and it turned out to be a beautiful day after all. After supper we headed towards our base, and it was one of the longest and coldest rides I've ever had. We lost our way many times but finally arrived home at four that morning.

Our journey was really an experience. The atmosphere in Holland was so cheerful and friendly, and was such a contrast to what we found after crossing the border into Germany, where there was only desolation and silence. It really did my heart good to know Germany was at last getting some of its own, long delayed, medicine. I was also glad to see that that part of Holland, at least, hadn't suffered too much physically, and I surely hoped the present push would go clear to Berlin.''

On March 14, 1945 most of the group was out on a mission when an urgent call was received for all available pilots of the 361st Fighter Group to scramble. An air patrol was needed over the Remagen Bridge! While the pilots were being briefed, the ground crews were able to get together 31 Mustangs. Van was lucky as his assigned aircraft 'Mary Mine' was O.K.'d. The cloud base over the bridge was about 1200 feet and visibility was about half a mile. The mission was led by Gene Cole (E2-G, 44-14792, 'Margene'). Take off was at about 13:00 hours. As soon as a flight of four aircraft were fueled and armed they took off and headed for the bridge at about 1500 feet altitude, hoping to find the target by dead reckoning. As they arrived over the bridge heavy ground-fire came up from friend and foe alike. Gene Cole made radio contact with the American ground control and was immediately directed to climb through the overcast to check out some unidentified aircraft. The Mustangs broke through the clouds but there was no sign of any aircraft, friendly or otherwise.

At that moment the controller called in again saying that Jerry aircraft were reported at about 1000 feet attacking the bridge, so the Mustangs dropped down through the clouds, but again no bogies. This game of cat and mouse was to be repeated again and again with the same results. This carried on until dusk started to settle and the pilots turned for home base as there were no night landing facilities at Chievres.

*The 361st had it's own private B-17 late in the war, which they used for a variety of things - including runs to France for champagne! (**Kozicki**) An earlier pic of the 361st's WW B-17, before paint was removed, with Howard Johnston. (**Johnston**)*

However, at this time the group lost Gene Cole as they flew near Wetzler, Germany when his engine quit. He crashlanded his ship and was captured by a German Sergeant and a couple of privates but not before he had radioed that he was safe. Also flying on this mission (although it was not officially recorded) was the group Intelligence Officer in the group's two-seater Mustang coded B7-F, 44-14005. The group landed safely at its home base with no further losses.

Van was to make his final claims of the war in his new Mustang coded E9-Z, 44-64005. 'Mary Mine.' On April 16, 1945, in an attack on Reicherberg landing ground, the group claimed 13 destroyed and 2 damaged. Also, at other airfields, they claimed a further 2 aircraft destroyed and another 4 damaged on the ground for a total of 15 destroyed and 6 damaged. Field Order 1997A was a strafing mission and the group was led by Lt. Colonel Roy B. Caviness as 'Glowbright' (the C.O.'s callsign). In his combat report Van reported,

At 1550 GLOWBRIGHT made a pass at Reichersberg landing ground followed by the rest of Yorkshire Squadron. The pass was made NE to SW, with a small left turn off the field, breaking into a right turn to go over and investigate Kircham landing ground. White 3, Lt Chapman, fired on a twin engine airplane in the open at the south corner of the field which caught fire and burned. This was the only undamaged aircraft in the open, all others were already burning, or under the trees.

Yellow Leader, Lt Vanden Huevel, began firing at 800 yards to the SW. As he got the range he saw two a/c parked together. One blew up at 300 yards and the other began to burn as Yellow Leader pulled over them, and identified them as FW-190s. Yellow 2, Lt. Jones, began firing into the same woods until he saw the glint of an a/c parked behind a tree. He fired at it until it exploded. Yellow 3 and Yellow 4 did not fire, but as they pulled up they saw several a/c in a wood SW of the field and went back for them.

Red 3 (leading Red flight), Lt. Allen Chalmers, saw a FW-190 at the SW edge of the woods too late to fire.

So he made a circle to the left and made a west to east pass across the field, pulling his strikes up into the cockpit and seeing the airplane burn as he passed over it.

Blue flight did not fire on this pass, but turned around to the left for another NE-SW pass. This time, Blue Leader, Lt. Eisenhut, found a FW-190 on the north edge of the field and fired from 400 yards until the a/c burned as he passed over it. Blue 2, Lt. Kelly, fired at a Fiesler Storch, but it would not burn, Blue 3, Lt. Duane Grounds, shot up a JU-52 which also would not burn. Meanwhile, Yellow 3 and Yellow 4, Lt. Spencer and Lt. Chadwick, set up a gunnery pattern of their own on several JU-52s parked along the west edge of a woods about 500 yards SW of the field, making passes from west to east. In about five passes they each caused three JU-52s to burn. After his first pass on Kircham NF Yellow Leader, Lt. Vanden Huevel, came back and made a pass at another JU-52 in this same woods, but, though it was clobbered, the a/c refused to burn.

Lt. George R. Vanden Huevel, Yellow Leader, E9-Z, 44-64005. 1575 rounds expended. 2 FW-109s destroyed. 1 JU-52 damaged.
Lt. Van C. Eisenhut, Blue Leader, E9-L, 44-15352. 900 rounds expended. 1 FW-190 destroyed.
Lt. Herbert G. Spencer, Yellow Three, E9-U, 44-14806. 1400 rounds expended. 3 JU-52s destroyed.
Lt. Lewis P. Chadwick, Yellow Four, E9-H, 44-11369. 1600 rounds expended. 3 JU-52s destroyed.
Lt. Allen J. Chalmers, Red Three, E9-P (bar), 44-15752. 600 rounds expended. 1 FW-190 destroyed.
Lt. Harry M. Chapman, White Three, E9-X, 44-13391. 600 rounds expended. 1 T/E U/I destroyed.
Lt. Duane Grounds, Blue Three, E9-G, 44-14251. 300 rounds expended. 1 JU-52 damaged.
Lt. Donald W. Jones, Yellow Two, E9-L (bar) 44-14686. 800 rounds expended. 1 U/I destroyed.
Lt. Marion C. Kelly, Blue Two, E9-C, 44-15040. 336 rounds expended. 1 Fiseler Storch destroyed.

At Kircham airfield Van also claimed a ME-410 destroyed but it was not allowed because it didn't burn or blow up.

Van wrote to his brother Sandy on 18th April 1945, saying,

Dear Sandy, I got three more and you'll probably say it's about time. All on the ground, but what fun. It is some job strafing an airdrome because they are usually well defended. We have to make one pass on the 'deck' while somebody watches from above to see where the guns are located, then we silence them. I led the second flight across this field and there wasn't too much flak but they got one of the first flight and chipped some paint off my new plane. I shot up two FW-190s and they both burned. The leader decided there was too much flak so we went to another field. There we repeated the procedure and this time I thought it was the Fourth of July. I swear my propellor was cutting the grass. I was as low as I could go. I saw one ME-410 under some trees at the edge of the field, gave it the works and it was burning when I pulled up to fly over it. They didn't hit me but damaged several others. It was fun but dangerous. I tried to get a JU-52 parked in the woods but couldn't. 'Bye'. GEORGE.

On 20th April Van flew his last combat mission (which was also the last for the group), it lasted six hours and fifteen minutes. A few days later the war in Europe was over and the group was ordered to start an intensive training programme which involved 'wing line bombing' and strafing practice out over the Wash.

On July 23, 1945 the 375th Fighter Squadron lost two pilots during a 'wing line' practice mission and Van recalled "On this particular day all three squadrons were up practicing and had completed dives from 10,000 and 12,000 feet and it was decided the next flight should start from 18,000. It was a typical July day, warm and very sunny, with visibility at about 10 miles. The rest of the off duty pilots were lounging around the Group's Operational building listening to a radio speaker rigged up outside tuned to the pilot's radio chatter. Those in the flight were Captain William H. Street, Charles K. Willis (now a retired Brigadier General) John E. Havey and an ex-bomber pilot who had recently joined the group J. Warren Geron. The lead aircraft peeled off followed closely by the No. 2. After a few seconds the other two followed and at that moment Cpt. Street called out that he'd hit compressibility and for the others to pull out. Lt. Willis did right away (the Mustang he was flying was scraped due to the fuselage buckling) but Lt. Havey, flying his ship E2-I, 44-14556, 'Libby,' crashed near Ravenstock Green Farm and Geron flying E2-M, 44-15038, 'Tony' crashed near Mitchell's farm. Both pilots are buried in Madingley Cemetery, Cambridgeshire.

After the war was over Van worked at Wright Field, Ohio in the Power Plant Laboratory. From July 1946 until June 1947 he was at Cal-Tec, in California. In 1947 he was at Wright-Patterson Air Force Base working on Drones and Missiles and in 1953 he went to Staff Command School at Montgomery, Alabama. When the Thor missile programme was started in England, Van was on the Checkout and Acceptance Board. Van and his wife Barbara now live in Ealing, London.

199

A really fine looking P-51, Lt. Homer G. Powell's ''Gay Crusader'' at Chievres, Belgium. Red name on yellow 361st nose and black canopy frame. 3 victories on rail were all FW-190s - 2 on Sept. 27, 44 and the other Dec. 26. **(Vulgamore)** The crew of E9-Y, 44-14042 'Heaven Sent - Hell Bent' on a sunny day at Little Walden, Essex. From left to right are D. Jones (Arm), Bob Gallego (A/C/C), Bob Stenger (C/C), Lehman Hollinger (Radio Flight Chief) and pilot Captain Robert D. Schirmer of New Haven, Conn. **(Stenger)**

Mission list for Lt. George R. Vanden Huevel.

Date	Field Order No.	Type	Duration
14.10.44.	F.O.1239A	Escort	1.50
15.10.44.	F.O.12401A	Sweep	3.15
17.10.44.	F.O.1245A	Area Sup.	5.00
18.10.44.	F.O.1246A	Escort	2.20
19.10.44.	F.O.1249A	Escort	4.35
22.10.44.	F.O.1254A	Escort	1.00
26.10.44.	F.O.1264A	Escort	4.00
30.10.44.	F.O.1273A	Escort	4.00
2.11.44.	F.O.1281	Escort	5.30
4.11.44.	F.O.1284	Escort	5.10
8.11.44.	F.O.1288A	Escort	5.10
10.11.44.	F.O.1301A	Escort	4.00
11.11.44.	F.O.1306A	Escort	1.40
16.11.44.	F.O.1314A	Patrol	4.00
18.11.44.	F.O.1317A	Strafing	5.15
20.11.44.	F.O.1320A	Patrol	3.30
21.11.44.	F.O.1323A	Escort	1.45
26.11.44.	F.O.529B	Escort	4.15
29.11.44.	F.O.1384A	Escort	3.20

30.11.44.	F.O.1354A	Escort	2.00		2.3.45.	F.O.1683A	Escort	5.00
412.44.	F.O.1370A	Escort	5.10		3.3.45.	F.O.1698A	Escort	5.00
5.12.44.	F.O.1374A	Escort	2.30		9.3.45.	F.O.4A	Freelance	4.15
9.12.44.	F.O.1397A	Escort	5.00		10.3.45.	F.O.5A	Area Sup.	2.45
12.12.44.	F.O.1412A	Escort	Abort		12.3.45.	F.O.1742A	Escort	2.00
18.12.44.	F.O.1440A	Escort	4.00		15.3.45.	F.O.1761A	Escort	5.00
23.12.44.	F .O.1443A	Escort	3.00		22.3.45.	F.O.1810A	Escort	2.30
24.12.44.	F.O.1446A	Escort	3.30		25.3.45.	F.O.10A	Escort	2.45
25.12.44.	F.O.147	Escort	3.15		26.3.45.	F.O.1843A	Close Sup.	4.30
26.12.44.	F.O.148	Sweep	5.00		30.3.45.	F.O.1863A	Patrol	4.15
27.12.44.	F.O.149	Escort	4.30		31.3.45.	F.O.1874A	Escort	4.00
29.12.44.	F.O.151	Freelance	1.45		3.4.45.	F.O.1887A	Sweep	3.00
30.12.44.	F.O.152	Sweep	2.00		6.4.45.	F.O.1909A	Escort	4.30
31.12.44.	F.O.153	Patrol	2.00		9.4.45.	F.O.1929A	Escort	3.00
1.1.45.	F.O.154	Sweep	4.30		11.4.45.	F.O.1944A	Escort	6.00
2.1.45.	F.O.155	Area Sup.	4.50		16.4.45.	F.O.1997A	Escort	6.00
10.1.45.	F.O.163	Area Sup.	2.30		17.4.45.	F.O.2006A	Escort	6.45
13.1.45.	F.O.166	Fgtrbombr.	4.30		20.4.45.	F.O.2039A	Escort	6.15
14.1.45.	F.O.167	Escort	4.15					
15.1.45.	F.O.168	Fgtrbombr.	3.30					
16.1.45.	F.O.169	Escort	4.45					
22.1.45.	F.O.176	Sweep	4.45					
25.1.45.	F.O.179	Sweep	2.45					
26.1.45.	F.O.180	Patrol	3.00					
28.1.45.	F.O.182	Area Patr.	1.15					
29.1.45.	F.O.183	Area Sup.	4.45					
3.2.45.	F.O.1586A	Escort	4.45					
9.2.45.	F.O.1605A	Escort	3.30					
11.2.45.	F.O.1612A	Strafing	3.00					
14.2.45.	F.O.1622A	Sweep	2.00					
16.2.45.	F.O.1631A	Escort	3.45					
22.2.45.	F.O.1650A	Escort	5.00					
26.2.45.	F.O.1665A	Escort	5.30					
27.2.45.	F.O.1670A	Escort	5.00					
28.2.45.	F.O.1675A	Escort	3.45					

Claims made by Lt. George R. Vanden Huevel.
2.11.44. F.O.1281 N. of Erfurt, Germany. 1 FW-190 Destroyed Air E9-D, 44-14217. 66 rounds.
26.11.44. F.O.529B South of Ulzen, Germany. 2 FW-190s Destroyed Air E9-L (bar), 44-14685. 'Mary Mine' 410 rounds.
24.12.44. F.O.1446A Wengerohr, Germany. 1 ME-109 Destroyed Air E9-L (bar), 44-14685. 'Mary Mine' 400 rounds.
26.12.44. F.O. 148 Merzig, Germany. 1½ FW-190s Destroyed Air E9-L (bar), 44-14685. 'Mary Mine' 1000 rounds.
16.4.45. F.O.1997A Reichersberg NF, Germany. 2 FW-190s Destroyed Ground. 1 JU-52 Damaged Ground. 1 ME-410 Destroyed Ground. Kircham A/F, Germany. E9-Z, 44-64005. 'Mary Mine' 1575 rounds.

Liberators of the 44th and 491st bomb groups were used to ferry personnel of the 361st back to England from Belgium in April 1945.
(Vulgamore)

BRIEF GROUP HISTORIES

4th FIGHTER GROUP

The three RAF Eagle Squadrons, 71, 121 and 133, became respectively the 334th, 335th and 336th F.S of the 4th Fighter Group on September 12, 1942. By the close of hostilities, the group had produced 78 aces, including pilots who claimed the distinction while serving in the RAF. Its score of 1,016 was the highest for the Eighth Air Force. Don Blakeslee destroyed the first aircraft claimed by a P-47 in Europe on April 15, 1943. The group's top P-47 ace was Duane Beeson, with 14. Changing over to P-51s, the group claimed 2 E/A on March 2, 1944, for their first Mustang victories. They lost one of their top aces when Jim Goodson (VF-B) was shot down by flak and taken POW on April 20, 1944. The 4th, along with the 486th Squadron, took part in the first FRANTIC shuttle run to Russia, June 21, 1944. By the end of March, 1945, the group had a total of 867 destroyed and, with another 100 added on April 16, it passed the 1,000 mark. Last mission flown on April 20, 1945. Among top aces were Godfrey, Gentile, Anderson, Montgomery, Norley and Hofer.

They were awarded a DUC for their participation in the pre-invasion softening up of "Fortress Europe", particularly for their aggressiveness in attacking enemy airfields.

Group Commanders

Col. Edward W. Anderson	12.9.42	20.8.43
Col. Chesley G. Peterson	20.8.43	31.12.43
Col. Donald J. M. Blakeslee	1.1.44	6.9.44
Lt. Col. James A. Clark Jr.	7.9.44	20.10.44
Col. Donald J. M. Blakeslee	21.10.44	1.11.44
Lt. Claiborne H. Kinnard	1.11.44	6.12.44
Lt. Col. Harry J. Dayhuff	7.12.44	21.2.45
Col. Everett W. Stewart	21.2.45	21.9.45
Lt. Col. William F. Becker	21.9.45	10.11.45

*Above: Two photos of an interesting bird: Lt. Dewey Newhart's double - named P-47. Newhart was KIA June 12, 1944 when the 350th F.S. was strafing a convoy and they were bounced by 30 109s. The squadron lost 6 pilots that day. Lt. Newhart was flying Wayne Blickenstaff's P-47. In picture #2, Lt. Chauncey Rowan stands in front of Ol' Mud N' Mules/Ark. Trav. (**Jim Crow**) Below, left: P-47 of Lt. Marvin Bledsoe. (**Mulron**) Below, right: Thunderbolts of the 350th F.S. wait to be flagged off on another mission. Behind "Elizabeth" is James Ruscitto in his "Natalie Ann II," LH-R, 42-28357, which was lost on Sept. 18, 1944 (**Glover**)*

20th FIGHTER GROUP

The 20th was assigned to the 8th A.F. on August 24, 1943. By late December their P-38s were escorting bombers over the Continent. By the spring of '44 they had expanded their mission to include fighter-bomber sorties as well. They soon earned a reputation, a unit citation and a nickname (``the loco group'') for their outstanding efforts. They supported the Normandy invasion. July found them re-equipped with P-51s, with which they played their part in the airborne attack on Holland and subsequent crossing of the Rhine. The group produced 25 aces including Jack Ilfrey, James M. Morris, Ernest Fiebelkorn and Jack C. Price. The 20th also had the best P-51 maintenance record in the 8th A.F.

Group Commanders

Col. Barton M. Russell	20.8.43	2.3.44
Lt. Col. Mark E. Hubbard	2.3.44	18.3.44
Maj. Herbert E. Johnson Jr.	19.3.44	20.3.44
Lt. Col. Harold J. Rau	20.3.44	25.6.44
Lt. Col. Cy Wilson	25.6.44	27.8.44
Col. Harold J. Rau	27.8.44	18.12.44
Col. Robert P. Montgomery	18.12.44	3.10.45

Four photos of Glenn Duncan and his A/C virtually surround our mini-history of the 20th F.G. Above left is a shot of his first P-47, 42-8634, carrying 24, 30lb. frag bombs - a present for some unhappy German air field. Glenn was leader of ``Bill's Buzz Boys'' - the first unit in the 8th whose primary mission was the harassment of enemy airfields. Note huge underwing star/bar. (Gallup)

Above: A crewmember services Group Commander Duncan's P-47 while 16 tiny swasticas stand at attention below canopy. (Jim Crow)
Below: Only about 2 years, or a million - depending on the perspective - separate these 2 photos of the young Lt. Col., left, and the seasoned ace, evader, fighter tactician and group leader. (Jim Crow photos)

55th FIGHTER GROUP

The 55th Fighter Group was formed at Hamilton Field, California, on January 15, 1941. Its final base in the States was McCord Field, Washington. First stationed at Nuthampstead, Hertfordshire, from September 14, 1943, it moved to Wormingford, Essex, on April 16, 1944, staying there until July 21, 1945, when it became part of the Allied Occupation Forces stationed at Kaufbueren, Germany. On October 15, 1943, the first group mission was flown and by the end of the month eight had been completed. On April 10, 1944, the first 'Droopsnoot' P-38 mission was flown, two squadrons bombing, with the third acting as escort. In May, a pilot reported 'two ME 109s destroyed and one high tension cable captured'. The pilots had a good day on July 7, 1944, with claims of three ME 109s, eight FW 190s and three ME 410s destroyed. The group changed over to P-51s in July and in that month lost three P-38s and six Mustangs. Nineteen aircraft were lost in August, but September made up for the loss with claims of 84 destroyed. On February 25, 1944, pilots claimed seven ME 262s destroyed in the air plus five FW 190s and two ME 109s on the ground. During April 1945 nearly 150 aircraft were destroyed by the three squadrons. Last mission for the group came on April 21, 1945. Among the 34 aces of the group were Elwyn Righetti, Bob Welch and Ed Giller.

Nine victory ace Capt. Ken Gallup with one of his earlier P-47s. A color profile of his last wartime P-47 is on page 146. *(Gallup)*

Group Commanders

Lt. Col. Frank B. James	15.3.43	3.2.44
Col. Jack S. Jenkins	6.3.44	10.4.44
Col. George T. Crowell	10.4.44	22.2.45
Lt. Col. Elwyn G. Righetti	22.2.45	17.4.45
Col. Ben Rimermann	17.4.45	20.5.45
Lt. Col. Jack W. Hayes Jr.	21.5.45	

Sheep's eye view of the wolf . . . a shot sure to send chills up the spines of ex-bomber boys. The ME-410, though no match for single-seat fighters, was a deadly opponent of the 17s and 24s with its potent cannon armament. (Gallup)

56th FIGHTER GROUP

The 56th Fighter Group was formed at Savannah AFB, Georgia from the 27th Bomb Group on January 1, 1941. This group would later produce some of the top 'sharpshooters' of the Eighth Air Force. Transferred to England, the group served at several bases including Kingscliffe, Horsham St Faith, Halesworth and finally Boxted, on April 18, 1944. The 61st Squadron was the first in the Eighth Air Force to reach 100 victories, on February 22, 1944. The 56th Fighter Group used P-47s right through the war, but some pilots did fly one or two missions in P-51s when the group was experiencing trouble with the P-47M (Colonel George E. Bostwick flew one P-51 mission with the 479th Fighter Group.) On April 13, 1945 the group destroyed 90 and damaged 81 at Eggebek A/D; high scorers were Russ Kyler (five destroyed), Phillip Fleming (4), Lloyd Geren (4), Randel Murphy (10) and Phillip Kuhn (4). The group had 61 aces, air and ground, including Mike Gladych and Witold Lanowski.

Group Commanders

Col. Hubert A. Zemke	1.9.42	30.10.43
Col. Robert B. Landry	30.10.43	11.44
Lt. Col. Dave C. Schilling	11.1.44	18.1.44
Col. Hubert A. Zemke	19.1.44	12.8.44
Col. Dave C. Schilling	12.8.44	27.1.45
Lt. Col. Lucian A. Dade Jr.	27.1.45	8.45
Lt. Donald D. Renwick	8.45	10.45

Top: The camera catches Capt. Vic Byers' ''Hawkeye'' 42-7958 shortly after take-off. Note gear not yet fully retracted. While with the 351st, Vic claimed 2½ confirmed, one damaged and one probable. (Lahke Via Ivie) Above: We thought you might like to see the flip side of ''Smoocher,'' our color profile choice for the 351st. (Lahke Via Ivie) Below left: We weren't going to run this often-published photo again until we discovered the one below rt. Notice extensive damage to ''Smoocher'' must have been repaired and A/C put back on OPS as the number of swasticas below cockpit has jumped from two to four. (Via Ivie)

78th FIGHTER GROUP

The 78th Fighter Group was the only Eighth Air Force formation to be assigned all three US fighters assigned to the ETO. Its first base was Goxhill and subsequently Duxford, until the end of the war. Among notable 'firsts' for the group were the first ace of the Eighth Air Force and the first aerial jet kill by a P-47. They also claimed the highest number of ground kills in one mission - on which several Mustangs carried colour gun camera film! The 78th Fighter Group had a total of 50 aces, some of whom had served with other groups, including John Landers, Tony Colletti, Joe Bennett, Jack Oberhansley and Joe Myers. The group's final mission was flown with the RAF when it escorted bombers to Berchtesgaden on April 25, 1945.

Group Commanders

Col. Arman Peterson	5.42	1.7.43
Lt. Col. Melvin F. McNickle	12.7.43	30.7.43
Col. James J. Stone	31.7.43	22.5.44
Col. Frederick C. Gray	22.5.44	1.2.45
Lt. Col. Olin E. Gilbert	1.2.45	21.2.45
Col. John D. Landers	22.2.45	1.7.45
Lt. Col. Roy B. Caviness	1.7.45	11.45

Above, right: Capt. William K. Lahke, C/C and P-47 #42-75676, "Janny M," YJ-K. Existing records show only 1 confirmed victory, but he was awarded the silver star for his actions on Dec. 25, 1944 when he shot down 2 E/A, escorting a crippled B-24 back to England. Right: A full shot of the same aircraft. Below: Two photos of Bill's later P-51, also "Janny M" but coded YJ-U, 44-14781. Glenn Duncan and Bill were great friends and Bill later named his boy after him. (All photos Lahke Via Ivie)

339th FIGHTER GROUP

The 339th Fighter Group was assigned to the Eighth Air Force on April 4th, 1944 and its first mission was on the 30th of that month. In less than 13 months it claimed 480 victories and had 48 aces. It was also the only fighter group to claim over 100 victories on two occasions, April 4 and April 10, 1945. It flew to eastern Germany on May 29, 1944, a distance of 1,400 miles. The group claimed 15 aerial victories on September 15, 1944. Lt. Jack Daniel had the rare distinction of destroying five FW 190s on his first mission on November 26, 1944, his contribution to the 29 aircraft destroyed by the group on that day. The group flew its last mission on April 21, 1945. Top aces were Joe Thury, Archie Tower and K. B. Everson.

Group Commanders

Col. John B. Henry Jr.	17.8.43	1.10.44
Lt. Col. Harold W. Scruggs	1.10.44	24.12.44
Lt. Col. Carl T. Goldenburg	24.12.44	28.12.44
Col. John B. Henry Jr.	28.12.44	13.4.45
Lt. Col. William C. Clark	13.4.45	10.45

Left and right side photos of Lt. Jack Terzian's ''Marty,'' YJ-Z, 42-22469. A nice b/w profile of which is on P62 ''Slybird'' by Wm. Hess and Ken Rust. Terzian, hit by flak near Brussels May 22, 1944, safely crash landed. Pilot pictured is thought to be Lt. William T. Thistlethwaite, 353rd Grp. photo officer. (Jim Crow) Below, left: Major Frederick H. Le Febre has just returned from an escort mission in his Mustang YJ-L, 44-14771, 'Willit Run?'. Note K-25 camera on the armor plate behind his head. This photo was taken about November '44 as the A/C still has the early 3-row black and yellow group mks. The circle between the nose and the question mark is the 351st Sq. emblem: A skull w/a swastica on its forehead clutched by an eagle's claw. Below, right: Slightly later photo of same A/C. Note 5 new rows of checks on nose. Fred served with the 351st for over a year, his final contribution to the war effort being 2½ confirmed and 1 probable.

352nd FIGHTER GROUP

The 352nd Fighter Group was activated at Bradley Field, Connecticut on September 30, 1942 and eventually assigned to Bodney, Norfolk on July 8, 1943. It flew its first mission with P-47s on September 11, 1943, a patrol over the North Sea. They broke into the scoring November 26, when John C. Meyer claimed one of three ME 109s. George Preddy's first kill came on December 1, 1943 and John Thornell Jr's on January 1, 1944. Bill Whisner claimed an ME 109 on January 29, the same day that Preddy bailed out into the North Sea. April 8 saw Virgil Meroney, the group's top ace with ten victories, go down to become a POW. Mustangs arrived on April 20, 1944, and the group destroyed seven E/A on the ground only four days later. By May 30, the group had 350-5 victories and 486-5 by September 30. On December 30, 175 personnel transferred to Y29 Asch, Belgium. In the German attack of January 1, 1945, Meyer and the 487th Squadron destroyed 23 - Whisner and Moats getting four each. Lt. Bruno Grabovski destroyed 12 locomotives on January 3, to bring his score to 47. On April 16, the group destroyed 40 on the ground and another 68, also on the ground, on the 17th. Ray Littge claimed five for a final score of 23-5 on the same day. May 13 saw the 420th mission - the last for the group. Nicknamed 'The Blue Nosed Bastards from Bodney', the 352nd Fighter Group had 51 aces at the end of the war.

Group Commanders

Co. Joe L. Mason	18.5.43	24.7.44
Col. James D. Mayden	24.7.44	1.9.44
Col. Joe L. Mason	1.9.44	15.11.44
Col. James D. Mayden	16.11.44	9.45
Lt. Col. William T. Halton	9.45	11.45

Top: The last P-47 assigned to Crew Chief Ralph Morrow. It was later named "Buzz Bunny." (*Morrow*) Above: The A/C of Lt. Horace Q. Waggoner of the 352nd Fighter Squadron. C/C Edgar C. Welborn Jr. has just finished his pre-mission inspection. Four kills are stencilled on Miss Illini III at this time. (*Waggoner*) Below, right: Pilot Frank H. Bouldin Jr., C/C Sgt. Frye and Armorer Sgt. Gibbs were the team responsible for the pretty "Dallas Doll." The Luftwaffe probably didn't find it so attractive - Frank confirmed 2 aerial vics in it! (*U.S.A.F. Photo*) Below, left: Lt. Tom Jones poses in front of Bob Abernathy's "Lady Queen II." Burn scars are still prominent on his nose and forehead from "accident" on June 13, 1944. He was making an emergency landing on a short Normandy A.L.S. (advanced landing strip) when his squadron's P-47s were bounced by about 12 other P-47s, believed in Luftwaffe hands, and his A/C burst into flames. (*Morrow*)

353rd FIGHTER GROUP

The 353rd Fighter Group's bases were Goxhill, Metfield and finally Raydon. The first mission by the group was to Holland on August 9th, 1943, under the leadership of Col. 'Hub' Zemke. The group's first confirmed kill came on August 17, falling to Loren G. McCollom on his first mission as Commanding Officer, after transfer from the 56th. The first Mustang mission was flown on October 2, 1944 - 20 P-51s accompanied by 42 P-47s. The group made its greatest killing on April 16, 1945 - 110 destroyed on the ground, mostly at Pocking A/D. The group pioneered ground attack with a special flight with pilots from the 359th and 361st Fighter Groups acting in support. The last mission was flown on April 25, 1945 to the 'Wolf's Lair' at Berchtesgaden, Germany. Total number of aces serving with the group was 56.

Group Commanders

Lt. Col. Joseph A. Morris	15.10.42	16.8.43
Lt. Col. Loren G. McCollom	18.8.43	25.11.43
Col. Glenn E. Duncan	25.11.43	7.7.44
Col. Ben Rimermann	7.7.44	21.4.45
Col. Glen E. Duncan	22.4.45	9.9.45
Lt. Col. William B. Bailey	9.9.45	24.9.45
Lt. Col. Robert A. Elder	24.9.45	10.45

Top: Crew Chief Ralph Morrow's last Mustang to be assigned was SX-R, 44-14804 which his pilot Maurice Morrison named 'El Gato' (note 'gator drawing below name). Morrison shot down a ME-110 on 3rd November 1943 during his first tour and at that time his Thunderbolt SX-R, 42-8687 had been named 'Highlander.' Above: Nose details of Miller's 'Honey Bee.' Note where the alligator painting has been removed. Right: A happy Harold Miller with his "Honey Bee II," still coded SX-R as when he took it over from Morrison. He shot down 2 109s - one on June 12, 1944, the day the 353rd lost 8 P-47s in combat. (Morrow) Below: An element (2 A/C) from the 352nd F.S. start their take-off run down the main runway at Raydon. At left is SX-G, 44-14720 soon to be named "My Galveston Gal." (U.S.A.F. Photo)

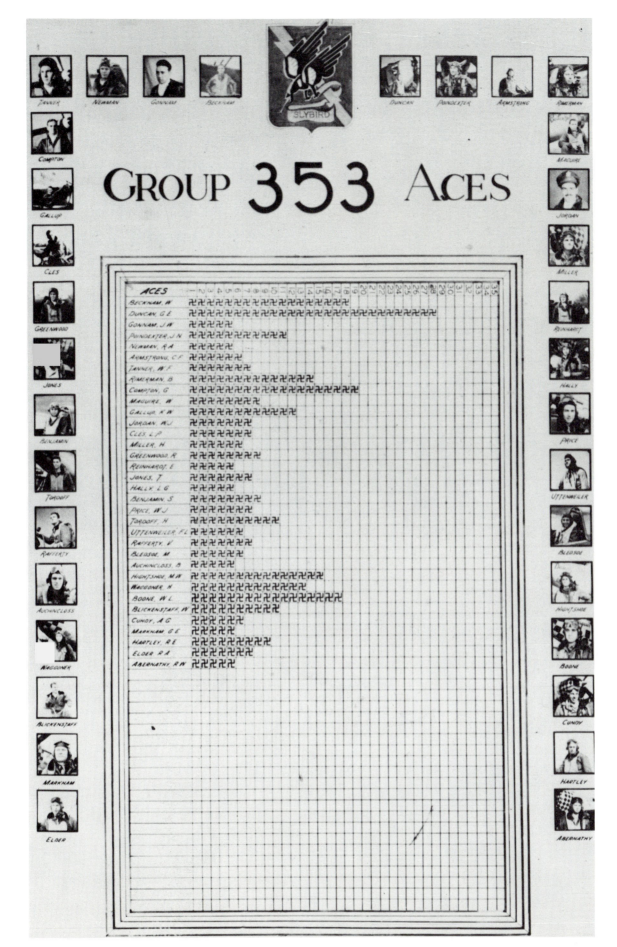

The proud record of the 353rd Fighter Group. This photo was taken about the 10th April 1945 and within a short while would be extended to include another 17 aces before the group flew it's last mission on 27th April 1945. (Duncan)

Top L and R: Two photos of Lt. Wilbert ''Weep'' Juntilla's P-51 after sustaining damage from ''friendly fire.'' Although he managed to fly the A/C back to his home base at Raydon, Suffolk, it was stated at the time that this was the most severely damaged P-51 ever to return from a mission. Accidents of this type were fairly common in WWII as A/C were so similar in appearance. *(Juntilla)* Above, left: The first Mustang assigned to Harrison 'Bud' Tordoff of the 352nd Fighter Squadron. Bud devised the name 'Upupa Epops' from the Hoopoe bird which is noted for its ungainly flying manner. The scientific name for this bird is Upupaepops. He flew this aircraft from sometime in October until the end of his first tour in November 1944. *(Tordoff)* Above, right: Upon his return to the 353rd Fighter Group Bud was assigned 44-72364 SX-L, at the beginning of March 1945, and flew it until the end of the war in Europe. On March 31st he shot down a ME-262 and seven days later he knocked down a ME-109. Ten days later on 17th April he claimed a ME-109, and a DO-217 as destroyed on the ground. He also shared in the destruction of a JU-88 with Lt. Jim Bartley on the same day. *(Tordoff)* Below, left: Another photo of SX-L, 44-72364 and crew. After the war this aircraft was transferred to Germany with the Occupation Forces and on April 24th, 1947, was delivered to the Swedish Air Force and given the number FvNr 26001. On 30th October 1952 she was sold to the Dominican Air Force where it stayed until purchased by Brian O'Farrell, of Johnson Aviation, Florida. The aircraft is to be painted as 'Upupa Epops' and flown in the States. *(Tordoff)* Below, right: Lt. Leroy C. Pletz brings in his Mustang, SX-M, 44-11624 ''Donna Mite.'' This was a P-51 K equipped with an Aeroproducts prop. *(U.S.A.F.)*

354th FIGHTER GROUP

The 354th Fighter Group was assigned to the 9th A.F., but spent much of its operational career under the command of the 8th A.F. It was the top scoring aerial outfit of all the USAAF fighter groups and the first to fly the P-51 Mustang in Europe, adopting the name 'Pioneer Mustang Group'. Among some of its most famous personalities were Jim Howard, Kenneth R. Martin, Richard E. Turner, Wah Kau Kong (KIA in 'Chinaman's Chance' 43-12393) and Sgts Daniel Richards, Dennis Johns, John Ferguson and Donald Dempsey - the only non-commissioned USAAF pilots to fly combat in fighters. The 354th destroyed 701 in the air and 256 on the ground with 53 probables and 428 damaged for 42 pilots KIA. Lt. Charles Gumm claimed the first confirmed P-51 victories on December 16, 1943. The group's P-51s were the first in the ETO to strafe ground targets on February 8, 1944. On January 5, 1944, the group destroyed 18 without loss and 21-1-16 for four lost on April 8. Over 200 were destroyed by April 12. It claimed 19.5-0-5 for two on May 28. The group's 500th mission was flown on September 9. It changed its P-51s for P-47s in November, 1944, retaining them until February, 1945, when it reequipped with Mustangs. The group had claims for 532 locomotives destroyed! The greatest number of kills claimed in one day was 51-1-8 on August 25, 1944. Highest claim by a squadron was on September 12, 1944: 31-0-1! Bruce Carr was the only 354th ace to claim five in one mission on April 2, 1945.

Group Commanders

Col. Kenneth R. Martin	15.11.42	26.11.42
Col. James H. Howard	27.11.42	12.2.44
Col. George R. Bickell	14.2.44	4.4.44
Lt. Col. Jack T. Bradley	5.4.44	1.5.45
Maj. Robert A. Ackerly	2.5.45	16.11.45

In just over six months time, from Dec. 30, 1943 to July 7, 1944, Capt. Donald M. Beerbower shot down 15½ A/C and damaged another 10⅓! Two of his A/C are pictured above and below while Don stands proudly in front of "Bonnie B III" in photo directly above.
(Tabatt)

Photo below is a modeler's delight with full invasion stripes, prominent - and unusual style victory markings, prancing horse emblem on tail and 'Malcolm Hood' canopy. (Tabatt)

355th FIGHTER GROUP

The 355th Fighter Group showed its aggression even before leaving the States when it was involved in a grand fight with members of the 352nd Group just before the two formations sailed for England! The group flew its first mission on September 14, 1943, with P-47s from Steeple Morden. Noted for its strafing prowess, the group had a total of 502-5 ground victories, the highest for any Eighth Air Force Group. It formed a close association with the 4th Group at Debden, with which it flew the fourth FRANTIC shuttle mission to Russia. The group was awarded a DUC for an attack on an airdrome during a severe snowstorm on April 5, 1945 and had a total of 56 aces at the end of the war. Among the 355th top aces were Henry Brown, Gordon Graham, Bill Cullerton and Everett Stewart. The last mission was flown on April 25, 1945.

Group Commanders

Col. William J. Cummings	12.11.42	4.11.44
Lt. Col. Everett W. Stewart	4.11.44	21.2.45
Lt. Col. Claiborne H. Kinnard	21.2.45	7.6.45
Lt. Col. William D. Gilchrist	7.6.45	2.9.45
Lt. Col. Bert W. Marshall Jr.	2.9.45	7.10.45

Above: The 353rd Fighter Sq.'s "Easy Rockin' Mama" and crew pose at Colchester, England March 21, 1944. L to Rt.: Armorer Cpl. R. Cole, C/C Sgt. John Szajna, Pilot Lt. James G. Burke and ASSNT C/C J. Bush. (Szajna Via Crow) Left: 3 photos of Lt. Col. Glenn Eagleston and his last wartime P-51. He was the highest scoring ace in the Ninth A.F. with 18.5 confirmed air vics. Below: 353rd F.S. pilots being briefed for a mission in front of Glenn's P-51. Note tents, in background, of a typical front-line tactical airfield in France, fall 1944.

356th FIGHTER GROUP

The 356th was assigned to Goxhill in August 1943 and began operations with its P-47s in October. Their early missions were escorting heavy bombers to German industrial targets but in Jan., 1944 their primary role switched to low level attack. 356th Group P-47s left a trail of destruction as trucks, shipyards, locomotives, factories, radar installations and even flak towers suffered their attentions. The 356th came into their own near the end of the war. When providing support during the battle for Arnhem they were awarded a DUC for their actions on September 17, 18 and 23. Top ace was Donald Strait (QI-T) who named his aircraft 'Jersey Jerk' and had 13.5 victories to his credit. The group had the distinction of flying the last combat mission of the war by Eighth Air Force fighters on May 7, 1945. The total number of aces was 18, including those who transferred into the group.

Group Commanders

Lt. Col. Harold J. Rau	9.2.43	28.11.43
Col. Einar A. Malmstrom	28.11.43	23.4.44
Lt. Col. Philip E. Tukey Jr.	24.4.44	3.11.44
Lt. Col. Donald A. Baccus	3.11.44	10.1.45
Col. Philip E. Tukey Jr.	11.1.45	10.45

Top: C/C Sgt. John Szajna and Lt. Cary Salter Jr. stand in front of their assigned A/C, P-51 D-25-NA, FT-S, ''Ramblin' Randy.'' This is, most likely, the A/C Salter used to shoot down a FW-190 and a ME-109 on April 2, 1945. On our copy of this photo, the last part of the serial # has been cut off (#44-730-) - anybody out there able to help?? (Szajna Via Crow) Right: Lt. Donald McDowell in his ''Hotei II,'' FT-I, 42-106712. An 8½ victory ace, Don was KIA in another A/C on May 28, 1944. Exactly 2 months later, this A/C was lost as well. (Tabatt) Below: Two photos of FT-Z, 43-6365 'Z-Hub' which was the mount of Lt. Richard H. Brown of the 353rd F.S. They were taken at Rinkaby Sweden after Lt. Eldon E. Posey ran short of fuel on an escort mission. The Swedish A.F. gave it the serial #26001 when it became officially theirs in March 1945. (Olausson)

357th FIGHTER GROUP

The 357th Fighter Group arrived at its first base, Raydon, Suffolk, on November 11, 1943 and subsequently transferred to its permanent base at Leiston, Suffolk on January 31, 1944. The 357th was the first P-51 Mustang group to be assigned to the Eighth Air Force and for the first few missions it was led by Col. Don Blakeslee, who scored a victory with it. The group had the highest kill rate for the entire Eighth during the last year of the war. On January 14, 1945, it claimed the highest number of aerial kills for any Eighth fighter group in one day (56) on a mission to Derben, near Berlin - for which it was also awarded a DUC for bomber escort. Among its aces were 'Kit' Carson, Tom Hayes, Otto Jenkins, and Richard A. Peterson. The group flew its final mission April 25, 1945 and was stationed in Germany after the war.

Group Commanders

Lt. Col. Edward S. Chickering	7.7.43	17.2.44
Coo. Henry R. Spicer	17.2.44	5.4.44
Col. Donald W. Graham	7.4.44	10.10.44
Lt. Col. John D. Landers	11.10.44	2.12.44
Col. Irwin H. Dregne	2.12.44	21.7.45
Lt. Col. Andrew J. Evans Jr.	21.7.45	11.45

Top: Pilots of the 354th Fighter Group relax after their mission on March 3, 1944. L to Rt: Capt. Dick Turner, Capt. Wallace Emmer, Lt. Col. Glenn Eagleston, Lt. James G. Burke, Lt. J. Riddel, Capt. Don Beerbower and Lt. Carl Franz. (Turner) Left: The first of four A/C assigned to ace Frank Rose Jr. This one has just been involved in some excitement - as denoted by huge oil streak from crankcase overflow pipe. This A/C was later lost in combat Nov. 4, 1944. Below: Two photos of Capt. Bruce Carr's FT-I, 44-63497 - Below left photo taken in front of Eifel Tower, Paris as part of big USAF A/C victory display. (Jim Crow) Bruce downed 5 of his eventual total of 15 on April 2, 1945 when he bagged 3 FW-190s and 2 ME-109s. He served two tours with the "Pioneer Mustang Group's" 353 F.S.

359th FIGHTER GROUP

The 359th was stationed at East Wretham near Thetford, Norfolk, from October 19, 1943 to November 2, 1945. It flew the P-47 until May, 1944, when it converted to Mustangs. Of note is the code change of the 370th Squadron - CR to CV - the only known instance in the Eighth Air Force. The reason is unknown. The first mission was flown on December 13, 1943. From then until the end of the war it achieved these results: 346 missions, 373 aircraft destroyed, 23 probables, 185 damaged, 364 locomotives and 1,000 box cars destroyed! The group also destroyed more ME 163s than any other Eighth Air Force group. Their greatest day was September 11, 1944 when on a bomber escort in the vicinity of Gissen, Germany it destroyed 35 (air and ground), four probables and 16 damaged. The leading ace still flying with the Eighth Air Force at the end of the war was the group's Ray S. Wetmore, with 24-5 victories. The 359th counted 23 aces at the end of the war, including several who transferred into the group.

Group Commanders

Avelin P. Tacon Jr.	1.43	11.11.44
Col. John P. Randolph	12.11.44	7.4.45
Lt. Col. Donald A. Baccus	8.4.45	9.45

Top: A young Clayton Gross pictured on the wing of his trice-named A/C ("Gwendolyn," "Live Bait," "Peggy") also featured in our color section, p. 146. Right: Same A/C, different angle. Another big help in identifying photos, after all these years, is the thoughtful way the A/F had in making pilots put their names on all issued equipment. (Mulron) Below, right: Gross's last wartime A/C, P-51 GQ-I, 44-63668 was later assigned to Lt. Robert J. Ramer who renamed it "Ensign Babs." Note 355th Ftr. Sq. badge on tail - a somewhat unusual phenomenon. (Smelser) Below, left: A close-up of the emblem, partially obscured by a lump of black fur. (Jim Crow)

361st FIGHTER GROUP

Perhaps one of the most colourful of the groups, the 361st was nicknamed 'The Yellowjackets' by the bomber crews it escorted. Converting to the Mustang in May, 1944 it destroyed 23 locomotives on the first P-51 mission. Lt. Dale F. Spencer knocked down four ME 410s in less than 30 seconds on September 27, 1944. On October 7, Urban L. Drew became first Allied fighter pilot to destroy two ME 262s in the air - over Achmer A/D. The group destroyed 19 E/A on November 26. The 361st was assigned to the Ninth Air Force at St Dezier, France, and returned to the Eighth and the UK on April 9, 1945. The last mission of the war was flown by the group on April 20 and at the end of hostilities in Europe had destroyed 331 E/A. The 361st was one of the few groups to use underwing codes late in the war.

Group Commanders

Col. Thomas J. J. Christian Jr.	10.2.43	12.8.44
Col. Ronald F. Fallows	14.8.44	30.8.44
Lt. Col. Roy B. Caviness	31.8.44	20.9.44
Lt. Col. Joseph J. Kruzel	20.9.44	2.11.44
Lt. Col. Roy B. Caviness	3.11.44	2.12.44
Col. Junius W. Dennison	3.12.44	15.4.45
Lt. Col. Roy B. Caviness	15.4.45	29.6.45
Col. John D. Landers	1.7.45	11.45

*Left: The problem with running a substandard photo like this is that, more than likely, we'll receive 5 or more **great** ones of the same plane as soon as we do! Anyway, here's a photo of Capt. William B. King and his P-51B, GQ-D, 43-6724. (**Tabatt**)*

*Below: Looking for all the world like an angry hornet's nest, 354th F.G. A/C taxi out at Headcorn Airfield, Kent, England for a mission on May 15, 1944. Far left is Capt. King's first "Peach." Far right is Frank Q. O'Conner's AJ-Q, "Verna Q." This "Atlanta Peach" was badly damaged in a forced landing on Dec. 10, 1944. (**U.S.A.F.**)*

*Top: Subtle name on Bob Stephen's Mustang says it all. As with all Bob's assigned A/C, code was GQ-S. (**Turner**)*

364th FIGHTER GROUP

The 364th flew its first mission on March 3, 1944 and also suffered its first combat casualty when Lt. Col. Frederick Grambo crashed in a P-38 and was killed. On April 15, 1944 seven P-38s failed to return and the last P-38 mission was flown on July 29, with more losses than victories. After converting to the Mustang the group fared better and three pilots each claimed an ME 163 destroyed on October 7, 1944. Under the command of Lt. Col. John Lowell, the 364th destroyed 29.5 aircraft in one mission: Lts. Murphy and White shot down an AR 234. After a chase of over 200 miles, George Cueleers (N2-D) claimed an ME 262 in the air. Five aircraft were destroyed on April 19, 1945 and, six days later, the group flew its last mission. The number of aircraft destroyed by the group totalled 390.5. The 364th had 23 aces.

Group Commanders

Lt. Col. Frederick C. Grambo	12.6.43	29.2.44
Col. Roy W. Osborn	29.2.44	9.9.44
Lt. Col. Joseph B. McManus	9.9.44	23.10.44
Lt. Col. John W. Lowell	23.10.44	2.11.44
Col. Roy W. Osborn	2.11.44	3.1.45
Lt. Col. Eugene P. Roberts	3.1.45	11.45

Above: Capt. Lowell K. Brueland's last P-51, GQ-U, 44-63702, of the 355th F.S. also carried a cheerie little message on it's nose. He wasn't kidding, either, as he was officially credited with 12½ air vics - a close look at the area directly behind exhausts will show a picture of "The Reaper" himself. Late war tiny blue-white nose checks. (Turner)

Below: A couple nice 354th F.G. flight line shots featuring Lewis W. Powers' "Sheriff," GQ-M, 44-11445. This plane was lost in action with Lt. Frank Pavelich on Oct. 28, '44. (Tabatt)

Below: Lt. Kenneth E. Meidigh of the 354th Fighter Group holds up a Nazi flag he liberated after escape from a German prison. Captured March 31, 1945, he escaped only a couple weeks later.
(U.S.A.F.)

479th FIGHTER GROUP

The 479th was the last group to be assigned to the Eighth and was also the last of the four P-38 groups in the 8th A.F. The group flew its first mission on May 26, 1944. Capt Arthur Jeffrey claimed an ME 163 on July 27. After the loss of Col Riddle, the group was taken over by 'Hub' Zemke: the first mission under his command resulted in 43 destroyed and 28 damaged. Conversion to the Mustang began on August 13, 1944 and during the next month, on the 29th, it destroyed ME 109s, of which Zemke claimed two and James Herren three. Lt Thompson destroyed an AR 234 for his second jet victory and the last claim by the 15 fighter groups of the Eighth Air Force on April 25, 1945. He was killed a few days later in a flying accident. In 351 missions the group claimed a total of 433 destroyed and was awarded a DUC. It had 27 aces, including those who had transferred from other groups.

Group Commanders

Lt. Col. Kyle L. Riddle	25.12.43	10.8.44
Col. Hubert A. Zemke	12.8.44	30.10.44
Col. Kyle L. Riddle	1.11.44	23.11.45

Top: Lt. Mack Tyner of the 356th Fighter Squadron was killed in this aircraft 10th March 1944 while ratracing with Lt. Charles Simonson. Tyner named 43-12437 'My Pet.' It was found that the engine mounting bolts had failed. Left: Lt. Albert G. Redfern (who must have had some Red Indian blood in him) mounts his Mustang from the wrong side at the 354th's base in France. Below: Lt. Albert D. 'Flaps' Fowler of Washington, D.C. and the 356th Fighter Squadron.

Below: Lt. Bartholomew C. Tenore and his last assigned P-51, the subject of our 356th F.S. color selection. This ship was lost with another pilot on Nov. 21, 1944. Bart finished the war with confirmed claims for 6 A/C - 4 in the air, 2 on the ground - only to die in an unfortunate post war A/C accident. **(Smelser)**

Above: Lt. George W. Hall and his P-51 AJ-H, 43-12199 at Boxted in March, 1944. "Stud," as his 356th Squadron buddies nicknamed him, was listed MIA April 13, 1944. **(Turner)**

Top: "The Pioneer Mustangers" were assigned P-47s in Nov. 44 and were thus equipped during the Battle of the Bulge. Although there were, doubtless, misgivings about their new equipment, the 354th nevertheless distinguished themselves as their jugs became familiar and welcome sights to allied troops as they supplied invaluable ground support. **(Jim Crow)** *Above: An Oddball's Oddball: The 354th was only equipped with jugs for about 3 months, but apparently the 356th Squadron retained this 2 seat conversion as a hack.* **(Mulron)** *Below, left: 2 photos of a very squished 356th F.S. P-51 taken at their E.O.W. Base, Neubiberg, Germany. Just barely discernable on canopy rail: "Lt. M.D.E. Stach"* **(Jim Crow)**

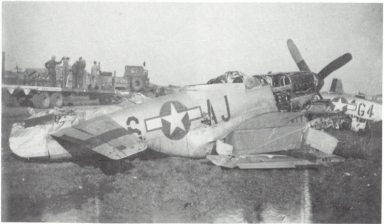

Top left: "The Stars Look Down," was the first 2 seat P-51, a "B" model. It was used to fly General Eisenhower around to the various battlefields. It was coded GQ-♊︎. The "♊︎" is the sign for Gemini, the Twin - seems appropriate enough! A nice color painting of this A/C is on P-16 of Squadron Signal's "P-51 Mustang in Color." Note: our photo shows the addition of the 354th's blue and white nose checkers, probably added later. (Jim Crow) Center left: Frank Q. O'Connor, 10¾ victory ace of the 356th F.S./354th F.G. in the office of his first Verna Q, AJ-O, 43-6322. In case you can't read the crew names in front of the scoreboards, they are: Sgt. C.O. Stopyra, Sgt.

T. Zink. Note nice detail on sliding panel of canopy. (Mulron) Bottom left: A later Verna Q, P-51D, AJ-O, 44-14016. This A/C was assigned to Frank in Feb. '45, after the 354th was re-equipped with P-51s. Above: Frank readies for another mission with his first "Verna Q" in the background. (O'Conner) Below, right: Friends and fellow aces Frank O'Conner and Dick Turner discuss tricks over a warm English beer at the "O" Club at Boxted. Dick recommended Frank as his replacement as 356th F.S. Commander. A full story on Richard Turner follows in Vol. II. (Turner)

ACES LIST

The following list represents the confirmed aerial victories of the included 15 8th A.F. fighter groups and those of the 354th fighter group, 9th A.F. from Oct. 2, 1942 to May 8, 1945. This compilation is the result of serious and ongoing study of existing A.F. records, gun camera films, personal records and official and private Axis sources.

At first glance, it probably seems absurd that almost 50 years after the fact, there is still no one universally agreed upon, definitive aces list, but so it is. The problem lies in the confirmation of the victory: one plane goes down and four claim it, or one pilot scores 3 definite victories but has no witnesses. These are but two of the myriad special cases facing the historian. Even official records are sometimes lost, incomplete or just plain inaccurate - after all, they are also the work of fallible human beings!

But still we present this list with a fair degree of confidence as it represents almost a lifetime of work on the part of its' compilers. Steve Blake has maintained, and constantly updated his list for many years and has kindly consented to let us use his totals. Danny Morris and Dwayne Tabatt have been working on the serials and codes for assigned A/C of the aces for over twenty years.

Notice this list is restricted to A/C actually assigned to the pilot. It does not reflect ground kills (we have a special list of these scheduled for vol. II) and it only includes aces who actually scored at least some of their victories in units covered in these 2 volumes.

And finally, we welcome any verifiable information you can supply us concerning this list, or any other material in these two volumes as we plan to update and correct them for future editions.

Gabreski, Francis A.   28
P-47D   HV-A   42-7871
P-47D   HV-A   42-8458
P-47D   HV-A   42-25510
P-47D   HV-A   42-25864
P-47D   HV-A   42-26418

Johnson, Robert S.   27
P-47C   HV-P   41-6235
  All Hell
P-47D   HV-P   42-8461
  Lucky
P-47D   HV-P   42-76234
  Double Lucky
P-47D   LM-Q   42-25512
  Penrod & Sam

Preddy, George E.   26.83
P-47D   HO-Y   42-8521
P-47D   HO-P   42-8500
  Cripes A Mighty
P-51B   HO-P   42-106451
  Cripes A Mighty 2nd
P-51D   HO-P   44-13321
  Cripes A Mighty 3rd
P-51D   PE-P   44-14906
  Cripes A Mighty

Meyer, John C.   24
P-47D   HO-M   42-8529
  Lambie
P-51B   HO-M   42-1064 71
  Lambie II
P-51D   HO-M   44-14151
  Petie 2nd

P-51D   HO-M   44-15041
  Petie 3rd

Schilling, David C.   22.50
P-47D   HV-S   42-7938
  Hewlett Woodmere Long Island
P-47D   HV-S   42-75237
P-47D   HV-S   42-75388
P-47D   HV-S   42-75231
  Whack
P-47M   HV-S   44-21125

Christensen, Frederick   21.50
P-47D   LM-C   42-75207
  Rozzi Geth
P-47D   LM-C   42-26628
  Miss Fire and Rozzi Geth II

Wetmore, Raymond S.   21.25
P-47D   CS-P   42-75068
P-51B   CS-P   42-106894
P-51D   CS-L   44-14733
  Daddy's Girl

Mahurin, Walker, M.   20.75
P-47C   UN-M   41-6334
P-47D   UN-M   42-8487
  Spirit of Atlantic City New Jersey

Gentile, Donald S.   19.83
P-47D   VF-T   42-8659
  Donnie Boy
P-51B   VF-T   43-6913
  Shangri La

Duncan, Glenn E.   19.50
P-47D   LH-X   42-8634
  Dove of Peace IV
P-47D   LH-X   42-7988
  Dove of Peace V
P-47D   LH-X   42-25506
  Dove of Peace VI
P-47D   LH-X   42-25971
  Dove of Peace VII
P-51D   LH-X   44-73060
  Dove of Peace VIII

Carson, Leonard K.   18.50
P-51D   G4-C   44-13316
  Nooky Booky II
P-51K   G4-C   44-11622
  Nooky Booky IV

Eagleston, Glenn T.   18.50
P-51B   FT-U   43-12308
P-47D   FT-L   44-20473
P-51D   FT-L   44-63607

Beckham, Walter C.   18.00
P-47D   YJ-X   42-8476
  Little Demon

Zemke, Hubert   17.75
P-47C   LM-Z   41-6330
  May Taravish
P-47D   UN-Z   42-75864
P-47D   UN-Z   42-26413
  Oregon's Britannia
P-38J   J2-Z   43-28832
P-51D   9B-Z   44-14351

England, John B.   17.50
P-51B   G4-H   42-106462
  U've Had It
P-51D   G4-H   44-13735
  U've Had It
P-51D   G4-H   44-14709
  Missouri Armada

Beeson, Duane W.   17.33
P-47D   QP-B   42-7890
  Boise Bee
P-51B   QP-B   43-6819
  Bee

Thornell, John F. Jr.   17.25
P-47D   PE-I   42-2474
  Pattie
P-51B   PE-T   42-106872
  Pattie II

Johnson, Gerald W.   16.50
P-47D   HV-D   42-7877
  In The Mood
P-47D   UN-Z   42-75232

Godfrey, John T.   16.33
P-47D   VF-P   42-7884
  Reggie's Reply
P-51B   VF-P   43-6765
P-51B   VF-P   42-106730
  Reggie's Reply
P-51D   VF-F   44-13412

Anderson, Clarence E. Jr.   16.25
P-51B   B6-S   43-24823
  Old Crow
P-51D   B6-S   44-14450
  Old Crow

Beerbower, Donald M.   15.50
P-51B   FT-E   43-12373
  Bonnie B
P-51B   FT-E   43-12375
  Bonnie B II
P-51D   FT-E   44-13628
  Bonnie B III

Peterson, Richard A.   15.50
P-51B   C5-T   43-6935
  Hurry Home Honey
P-51D   C5-T   44-13586
  Hurry Home Honey
P-51D   C5-T   44-14868
  Hurry Home Honey

Whisner, William T.   15.50
P-47D   HO-W   42-8404
  Beverly
P-51B   HO-W   42-106449
  Princess Elizabeth
P-51D   HO-W   44-14237
  Moonbeam McSwine

Bradley, Jack T.   15.00
P-51B   FT-W   43-12102
  Marjie M

Carr, Bruce W.   15.00
P-51D   FT-I   44-13693
  Angel's Playmate
P-51D   FT-I   44-63497
  Angel's Playmate

Foy, Robert W.   15.00
P-51D   B6-V   44-13717
  Reluctant Rebel
P-51D   B6-V   44-63621
  Little Shrimp

Hofer, Ralph K.   15.00
P-47C   QP-L   41-6484
  Missouri Kid/Show Me
P-51B   QP-L   42-106924
  Salem Representative

Landers, John D.   14.50
P-51D   CG-O   44-13823
  Big Beautiful Doll
P-51D   WZ-I   44-72218
  Big Beautiful Doll
P-51D   B6-   44-
  Big Beautiful Doll
P-51D   E2-I   44-72218
  Big Beautiful Doll

Powers, Joseph H. Jr.   14.50
P-47D   HV-P   42-75163
  Power's Girl
P-47D   LM-F   42-76232

Brown, Henry W.   14.20
P-47D   WR-Z   42-74703
  Baby
P-51B   WR-Z   42-106448
  Hun Hunter, Texas
P-51D   WR-Z   44-13305

Dahlberg, Kenneth H.   14.00
P-51B   FT-O   43-7163
  Dahlberg's Dilemma
P-47D   FT-O   42-29336

Emmer, Wallace N.   14.00
P-51D   FT-G   44-13948
  Arson's Reward

Goodson, James A.   14.00
P-47D   VF-W   42-7959
P-51B   VF-B   43-13848
P-51B   VF-B   43-6895
P-51B   VF-B   44-13303

Jeffrey, Arthur F.   14.00
P-38J   L2-O   42-104425
  Boomerang
P-51D   L2-O   44-14423
  Boomerang Jr.
P-51K   L2-O   44-11674
  Boomerang Jr.

Bochkay, Donald H.   13.83
P-51B   B6-F   43-6933
  Alice In Wonderland
P-51D   B6-F   44-15422
  Speedball Alice
P-51D   B6-F   44-72244

Carpenter, George   13.83
P-47C   WD-I   41-6226
P-51B   WD-I   43-6575
  Virginia
P-51B   WD-I   42-106675

Strait, Donald J.   13.50
P-47D   QI-T   42-25844
  Jersey Jerk
P-51D   QI-T   44-15152
  Jersey Jerk

Bryan, Donald S.   13.33
P-47D   PE-B   42-8381
  Little One
P-51B   PE-B   43-6894
  Little One II
P-51D   PE-B   44-14061
  Little One III

Top: What better way to begin this section on the 355th F.G., than with a photo of the 354th F.S. mascot, "Yank", resting atop the squadron commander's A/C. Major Henry B. Kucheman Jr. served briefly as Sq. Commander from June 12 until July 31, 1944 when he completed his tour.   Above: Another shot of Major Kucheman's P-51 "Lil Lo", WR-U, 42-106460. Compare this shot in O.D. with above in NMF. He had a big day on April 24, 1944 when he confirmed three 109s in one aerial combat, defending B-17s on a ramrod to the Munich area.   Below left: One final shot of Major Kucheman, this one with his earlier P-47 decorated by the extremely talented Sgt. DeCosta.   Below right: Another DeCosta decorated P-47. Captain Walter J. Koraleski Jr's "Miss Thunder", WR-L. "Korky" used this A/C to down two 109s and share another on one hot mission, March 6, 1944. (Bennett)

Millikan, Willard W.   13.00
  P-47C VF-U 41-6181
    Missouri Mauler
  P-51B VF-U 43-24769
    Missouri Mauler
  P-51B VF-U 43-6997

Moran, Glennon T.   13.00
  P-47D HO-M 42-2785
  P-51C HO-M 42-103320
    Little Ann
  P-51D HO-M 44-13320

Olds, Robin   13.00
  P-38J L2-W 43-28341
    Scat II
  P-38J L2-W
    Scat III
  P-51D L2-W
    Scat IV
  P-51D L2-W 44-14426
    Scat #5
  P-51D L2-W
    Scat VI
  P-51D L2-W 44-72922
    Scat VII

Stephens, Robert W.   13.00
  P-51B GQ-B 43-12152
    Killer
  P-51B GQ-S 42-12209
    Killer
  P-51B GQ-S 43-6382
    Killer
  P-51B GQ-S 42 -106685
    Killer
  P-51D GQ-S
    Killer

Williamson, Felix D.   13.00
  P-47D LM-I 42-22541
  P-47D LM-M 44-20555

Brueland, Lowell K.   12.50
  P-47D GQ-U
    Wee Speck
  P-51D GQ-U 44-63702
    Grim Reeper/Wee Speck

Brown, Quince L.   12.33
  P-47D WZ-J 42-74573
    Okie

Gleason, George W.   12.00
  P-51D L2-H 44-14740
    Hot Toddy

Hively, Howard D.   12.00
  P-47C PQ-J 41-6576
  P-51B QP-J 43-6898
    Deacon
  P-51D QP-J 44-15347

Schreiber, Leroy A.   12.00
  P-47D LM-T 42-22537
  P-47D LM-T 42-25577

Megura, Nicholas   11.83
  P-51B QP-N 43-6636
    Ill Wind
  P-51B QP-F 43-7158

Blakeslee, Donald J.   11.50
  P-51B WD-C 43-6437
  P-51B WD-C 42-106726
  P-51D WD-C 44-13779

Conger, Paul A.   11.50
  P-47D HV-C 42-75435
    Hollywood High Hatter
  P-47D HV-N 42-7880
    Redondo Beach California
  P-47D HV-G
    Dream Baby
  P-47M UN-P 44-21134
    Bernyce

Kirla, John A.   11.50
  P-51D G4-H 44-14624
    Spook
  P-51D G4-H 44-72180
    Spook

Stewart, James C.   11.50
  P-47D HV-Q 42-74650
  P-47D HV-S 42-75393
  P-47D HV-K 42-75218

Yeager, Charles E.   11.50
  P-51B B6-Y 43-6763
    Glamorous Glen
  P-51D B6-Y 44-13897
    Glamorous Glen II
  P-51D B6-Y 44-14888
    Glamorous Glen III

Frantz, Carl M.   11.00
  P-51B FT-Q 42-106701
    Joy

McKennon, Pierce W.   11.00
  P47C WD-A 41-6582
  P-51B WD-A 42-106911
    Yippi Joe
  P-51B WD-A 43-6896
  P-51D WD-A 44-13883
  P-51D WD-A 44-14221
    Ridge Runner III
  P-51D WD-A 44-14570
    Ridge Runner
  P-51D WD-A 44-63166
  P-51D WD-A 44-72308
    Ridge Runner III

Overfield, Loyd J.   11.00
  P-51C FT-A 42-103683
  P-47D FT-Z 44-20272

Quirk, Michael J.   11.00
  P-47C LM-K 41-6215
  P-47C LM-K 41-6295
  P-47D LM-K 42-74242

Turner, Richard E.   11.00
  P-51B AJ-T 43-12434
    Short Fuse Salle
  P-51D AJ-T 44-13561
    Short Fuse Sallee
  P-51D AJ-T 44-15622
    Short Fuse Sallee

O'Connor, Frank Q.   10.75
  P-51B AJ-O 43-6322
    The Verna Q/Stinky
  P-47D AJ-O 42-26678
    The Verna Q
  P-51D AJ-O 44-14016
    The Verna Q
  P-51D AJ-O 44-63729
    The Verna Q

Above left: A close up on ''Miss Thunder''.   Above right: Captain Koraleski with his later P-51, WR-L, 43-6968. He became the Bulldog's first ace with a variety of confirmed claims on April 5, 1944. Only 10 days later he was lost in this A/C due to mechanical failure. (Bennett) Below Left: April 24, 1944. Only 9 days after the loss of Captain Koraleski, Lt. Robert E. Woody downed 4½ confirmed and one damaged for an 8th A.F. record and a DFC. Below right: Here Lt. Woody and Crew Chief Gertzen, left, and Assistant Crew Chief Bennett celebrate the event on their P-51, WR-W, 43-6520, ''Woody's Maytag.'' (Bennett)

Ceuleers, George F.	10.50		**Glover, Frederick, W.**	10.33
P-38J N2-D 42-68017			P-51B VF-C 43-12214	
Connie & Butch Inc.			Rebel Queen	
P-51D N2-D 44-13971			P-51D VF-B 44-14787	
P-51D N2-D 44-15020			P-51D VF-B 44-64153	
P-51D N2-D 44-72719				
			Norley, Louis H.	10.33
Clark, James A. Jr.	10.50		P-47C VF-O 41-6183	
P-47C QP-W 41-6195			Red Dog	
P-47C QP-W 41-6413			P-51B VF-O 43-12416	
P-47D QP-W 42-75252			P-51B VF-O 43-6666	
P-51B QP-W 42-106650			P-51B VF-O 43-6802	
P-51B QP-W 43-672 6			P-51D WD-O 44-15028	
P-51B QP-W 43-6560			P-51D VF- 44-15350	
P-51D QP-W 44-13372			P-51D QP-O 44-72196	
			P-51D QP-O 44-73108	
Doersch, George A.	10.50		Red Dog XII	
P-47D CS-J 42-8552				
P-51B CS-J 43-24810			**Anderson, Charles F. Jr.**	10.00
P-51D CV-R 44-72067			P-51B VF-N 43-6972	
			Paul	
Halton, William T.	10.50		P-51B WD-L 43-7181	
P-47D PE-T 42-8439				
Slender, Tender and Tall/Bugs			**Blickenstaff, Wayne K.**	10.00
P-51B PE-T 42-106717			P-51D LH-U 44-72374	
Slender, Tender and Tall			Betty E	
P-51D PE-T 44-13966				
Slender, Tender and Tall			**Gladych, Bolek M.**	10.00
P-51D HO-T 44-14812			P-47D HV-M 42-25836	
Slender, Tender and Tall			Pengie III	
Hovde, William J.	10.50		**Lines, Ted E.**	10.00
P-51B YF-I 43-6928			P-51B WD-H 43-7172	
Ole II			P-51D WD-D 44-13555	
P-51D YF-I 44-13531			Thunderbird	
Ole III				
P-51D YF-I			**Rankin, Robert J.**	10.00
Ole IV			P-47D HV-H 42-74662	
P-51D YF-I			Wicked Wackie Weegie	
Ole V				
			Bankey, Ernest E.	9.50
Littge, Raymond H.	10.50		P-51D 5E-B 44-15019	
P-51C HO-M 42-103320			P-51D 5E-B 44-73045	
E Pluribus Unum			Lucky Lady VII	
P-51D HO-M 44-13320				
Silver Dollar			**Spencer, Dale F.**	9.50
P-51D HO-M 44-72216			P-47D E9-D 42-25969	
Helen			P-51B E9-D 43-24808	
			P-51D E9-D 44-14217	
Storch, John A.	10.50			
P-51D C5-R 44-13546			**Adams, Fletcher E.**	9.00
The Shillelagh			P-51B G4-L 43-12468	
P-51D C5-R 44-72164			Southern Belle	
The Shillelagh				

Top: *"Palma"*, the A/C of Lt. Brady C. Williamson. Above: On Sept. 18, 1944, after five days postponement due to bad weather, the 355th put up 72 A/C on *"Frantic 7"*, a shuttle to Russia. *"Palma"* had engine troubles and ended her career off the end of the runway. (Bennett) Below: So ol' Uncle Sam gave Brady a bran' spankin' new P-51. (read and weep, warbird owners!) *"Palma II"* carried Brady's air and ground claims on the canopy rail. Note late use of D-Day markings. (Bennett) Below right: Sometimes it took two wars to make an ace. Lt. James Jabara, standing next to his uniquely personalized P-51, only confirmed 1 ½ air victories in WW II (with the 363rd F.G.) but downed 15 in Korea, to become a <u>triple</u> ace!

Andrew, Stephen W.   9.00
 P-47D   PZ-A   42-6699
  Spirit of Los Angeles City College
 P-51B   PZ-A   42-106467

Beyer, William R.   9.00
 P-51B   E9-N   44-14144

Fiebelkorn, Ernest C.   9.00
 P-38J   LC-N   42-68068
 P-51D   LC-N   44-11161
  June Nite

Gallup, Kenneth W.   9.00
 P-47D   LH-N   42-22275
  Rat A Dat
 P-47D   LH-N   42-26525
  Rat A Dat
 P-47D   LH-N   44-19562
  Rat A Dat 3

Juchheim, Alwin M.   9.00
 P-47D   HL-J   42-74690
 P-47D   HL-J   42-26020

Meroney, Virgil K.   9.00
 P-47D   HO-V   42-8473
  Sweet Louise/Hedy
 P-51B   HO-V   43-7166

Morrill, Stanley B.   9.00
 P-47D   LM-F   41-6387

Roberts, Eugene P.   9.00
 P-47C   WZ-Z   41-6330
  Spokane Chief
 P-51D   5E-O   44-15061
  Jimmie the First

Dalglish, James B.   9.00
 P-51D   FT-P   44-63732
 P-51D   GQ-K   44-72774
  Pvt. Betty Mae

Bennett, Joseph H.   8.50
 P-47D   HV-O   42-75269
 P-51B   VF-N   43-6572
 P-51B   VF-T   43-6838
 P-51B   VF-T   42-106686
  Ann III

Cesky, Charles J.   8.50
 P-51D   PE-L   44-13927
  Diann Ruth
 P-51D   PE-L   44-134-01
  Diann Ruth II

Hayes, Thomas L. Jr.   8.50
 P-51D   C5-N   44-13318
  Frenesi

Jenkins, Otto D.   8.50
 P-51B   G4-P   43-6829
  Joan/Floogie
 P-51D   G4-P   44-14245
  Floogie II
 P-51D   G4-X   44-63189
  Toolin' Fool's Revenge

Luksic, Carl J.   8.50
 P-47D   HO-Z   42-75860
  Lucky Boy
 P-51B   HO-Z   43-7145
  Elly's Lucky Boy
 P-51B   HO-Z   43-7588

McDowell, Donald   8.50
 P-51B   FT-L   43-7136
  Ho Tei
 P-51B   FT-L   42-106712
  Ho Tei II

McGratten, Bernard J.   8.50
 P-51B   WD-W   43-6767

Moats, Sanford K.   8.50
 P-51B   HO-U   42-106751
  Kay
 P-51D   HO-K   44-14848
  Kay III

Schlegel, Albert L.   8.50
 P-51B   WD-O   42-106464
 P-51D   WD-O   44-14066

Booth, Robert J.   8.00
 P-47D   IV-F   42-8695
  Oily Boid
 P-51B   IV-F   43-6757
 P-51B   IV-F   43-7199

Lt. Colonel Claiborne Kinnard led an active and interesting career with the wartime 8th AF. He commanded the Bulldogs from November '43, through the next seven crucial months of combat, participating in many of the key battles waged in the skies over Germany. He was next assigned to the 355th Group headquarters but still led combat missions, earning one of only 7 DSCs awarded the group for his actions on July 7, 1944. Next he was to command the 4th F.G. for a brief period in late '44, before returning to command his own beloved 355th from Feb. '45 until the end of the war.   Top Right: His first P-51 is featured in our color profile section on page 147 and his other 3 A/ C, two with the 355th and one with the 4th are well documented. This A/C was apparently assigned to him sometime during the summer/ early fall of 1944. Note absence of fin strake, 18 victories, invasion stripes and O.D. upper surfaces. Photo on page 56 "Angels, Bulldogs and Dragons" by Bill Marshall confirms this but also doesn't show serial number. Above: Here he leads his 355th F.G. providing cover for "Operation Varsity," the crossing of the Rhine, March 24, 1945. (Marshall) Below right: His final A/C with late war markings, rocket rails, drop tanks and Spitfire mirrors. (Richards) Below left: Crew Chief Albert LaPierre, of the 361st F.G. based at Little Walden, Essex, points to the impresssive scoreboard. This photo was taken shortly after V.E. Day at a group commander's conference. (Molter)

Above: Lt. William Dexon Martin's first score was on the long haul to Poznan, Poland on May 13, 1944, when he bagged a HS-129 on the deck. He claimed 2 ME-109s on June 20 and another of August 6, 1944, to finish the war with a total of 4 confirmed. Note: Much of the information in this section is corroborated with the fine book by Bill Marshall, "Angels, Bulldogs and Dragons", the definitive work on the 355th F.G. (Bennett)   Below: The two assigned A/C of ace Charles D. Hauver.   Left: A Malcolm Hood has been fitted to "Patricia", which carries typical early markings. the "C" on top of rudder is for "C" flight. (Marshall)   Right: Hauver's "Red Raider" touches down at Steeple Morden after another successful mission. Charles scored all his victories in just 3 sorties in November and December 1944.

Bostwick, George E. 8.00 P-47D LM-Z 42-26289 Ugly Duckling P-47M UN-Z 44-21112 Ugly Duckling	**Kinnard, Clairborne, H. Jr.** 8.00 P-51B WR-A 43-6431 Man O War P-51B WR-A 44-15625 P-51D WR-A 44-73144 Man O War P-51D QP-A 44-14292 Man O War	**Stewart, Everett W.** 7.83 P-47D PE-G 42-8437 Sunny IV P-51B WR-S Sunny V P-51D WR-S 44-13540 Sunny VI P-51D WR-S 44-15255 Sunny VII	**Lasko, Charles W.** 7.50 P-51B GQ-L 43-6451 P-51B GQ-E 43-6764 Suga P-51B GQ-E 42-106935 Suga
Broadhead, Joseph E. 8.00 P-51B G4-V 43-12227 Baby Mike P-51D G4-V 44-14798 Master Mike		**Bryan, William E. Jr.** 7.50 P-51D D7-J 44-13601 P-51D D7-J 44-15074 Big Noise	**Lowell, John H.** 7.50 P-51D 5Y-L 44-14992 P-51D 5Y-L 44-63263 Penny 4
Elder, John L. 8.00 P-51B OS-R 42-106732 Moon P-51D OS-R 44-63633	**Schiltz, Glen D. Jr.** 8.00 P-47D UN-Z 42-75232	**Cutler, Frank A.** 7.50 P-47D PZ-P 42-5399 P-51B PZ-P 43-6578 Soldier's Vote	**Ilfrey, Jack M.** 7.50 P-38J MC-O 43-28431 Happy Jack's Go Buggy P-51D MC-I 44-13761 Happy Jack's Go Buggy
Fowle, James M. 8.00 P-51D 5Y-J 44-13829 Terrie Claire P-51D 5Y-Q 44-14184 Terrie Claire III	**Shaw, Robert M.** 8.00 P-51D C5-H 44-13875	**Davis, Glendon V.** 7.50 P-51B C5- 43-6878 Pregnant Polecat	**Miklajcyk, Henry J.** 7.50 P-47C PZ-K 41-6531 The Syracusan P-51B PZ-K 42-106430 The Syracusan P-51D PZ-K 44-13690 Syracusan the 3rd
Gerard, Francis R. 8.00 P-51D D7-U 44-13808 Yi Yi P-51D D7-U 44-15003	**Sublett, John L.** 8.00 P-51D G4-Q 44-11190 Lady Oxella	**Karger, Dale E.** 7.50 P-51D C5-U 44-15026 Cathie Mae/Karger's Dolly P-51D C5-U 44-72313 Cathie Mae II	**Righetti, Elwyn G.** 7.50 P-51D CL-M 44-14223 Katy Did P-51D CL-M 44-72227 Katy Did
Jackson, Michael J. 8.00 P-47D LM-J 44-19780 P-47M LM-J 44-21117 Teddy	**Vogt, John W. Jr.** 8.00 P-47C UN-V 41-6325 P-47D UN-W 42-75109 P-47D PI-V 42-26553 Jersey Mosquito	**Lamb, George M.** 7.50 P-51D AJ-I 44-13882 Uno Who II P-51D AJ-I 44-72513 Uno Who III	**Garrison, Vermont** 7.33 P-47D VF-H 42-74663 P-51B VF-H 43-6871
	Weaver, Charles E. 8.00 P-51D G4-A 44-72199		
	Lang, Joseph L. 7.83 P-51D QP-Z 44-14123		

Top left: Not the best quality, but significant photo of Lt. Lee G. Mendenhall, longtime member of the 354th F.S., in his P-47   Top right: Lee named his A/C "Texas Terror". Here we see "III", a P-51B, in early markings with 4 large swasticas in white circles below canopy. Above right a really pretty shot of Mendenhall's final A/C, "Texas Terror IV," taken during the late summer of 1944. If you look closely, you can see the much abbreviated D-Day stripes and the "I" which makes this A/C definitely "IV" and not "V" as sometimes erroneously reported. (Bennett) Above left: The group's Piper. Below left: Captain Joseph E. Mellon confirmed two aerial and eight ground victories during the winter of '44-'45. In volume II, we intend to publish lists of air/ground claims by squadrons . . . . stay tuned. Below right: Five of these claims painted on Joe's canopy rail were added after the 354th made a total mess of Husam Airfield on April 13, 1945. (Bennett)

Top: Glare hides the name and ''Bulldogs'' above exhaust on Bert Marshall's ''Jane III''. Captain Marshall served as 354th Fighter Squadron C.O. and, later, as a Lt. Colonel, 355th Fighter Group C.O. (Mulron) Above: On their way to becomming the 8th AF's top strafing outfit, the 355th took their lumps from German flak. Here, Bert Marshall limped his damaged ''Jane VI'' back to Steeple Morden and his long-suffering crew chief Gerry Thompson, March 23, 1945. Below: The only ''Jane'' to survive the war. Serials and codes for Bert's assigned aircraft are at the bottom of the first column on your right. The victories recorded on the canopy runner include ground claims, (Marshall)

Morris, James M. 7.33
P-38J LC-E 42-67717
My Dad/Til We Meet Again

Goodnight, Robert E. 7.25
P-51B AJ-G 43-12206
P-51B AJ-G 43-12213
Mary Anne

Anderson, William Y. 7.00
P-51B FT-T 43-12172
Swedes Steed
P-51D FT-T 44-13383
Swedes Steed III

Becker, Robert H. 7.00
P-51B G4-O 42-106783
Sebastian
P-51D G4-O 44-14231
Sebastian Jr.

Browning, James W. 7.00
P-51B B6-P 43-6563
Gentleman Jim
P-51D B6-P 44-14937
Gentleman Jim

Carder, John B. 7.00
P-51B C5-J 42-106777
Taxpayer's Delight

Cramer, Darrell S. 7.00
P-51D CL-Z 44-14121
Mick #5

Crenshaw, Claude J. 7.00
P-51B IV-S 42-106689
P-51D IV-I 44-13306
Louisiana Heatwave
P-51D IV-I 44-15016
Heatwave

Edens, Billy G. 7.00
P-47D LM-F 42-75093

Graham, Gordon M. 7.00
P-51D WR-F 44-14276
Down For Double
P-51D WR-F 44-15255

Hockery, John J. 7.00
P-47D MX-L 44-19950

Jackson, Willie O. Jr. 7.00
P-47D PE-D 42-8452
P-51B PZ-J 42-106661
Hot Stuff
P-51D PZ-J 44-13398
P-51D PZ-J 44-14709

Jamison, Gilbert L. 7.00
P-51D 5E-A 44-14035
Etta Jane

Johnson, Clarence O. 7.00
P-51D HO-C 44-13953
Bula B VI

King, Benjamin H. 7.00
P-51C CV-A 42-103898
Matilda IV

Klibbe, Frank W. 7.00
P-47D HV-K 42-75694
P-47D HV-S 42-75658
Little Chief/Anderson Indian
P-47D HV-V 42-76179
Little Chief

Lamb, Robert A. 7.00
P-47C HV-L 41-6211
Jackie

Lewis, William H. 7.00
P-51D CY-S 44-13907
P-51D CY-S 44-14907

Maguire, William J. 7.00
P-51D YJ-M 44-14569
P-51D YJ-M 44-14893

Marshall, Bert W. Jr. 7.00
P-51D WR-B 44-14440
Jane III
P-51D WR-F 44-14409
P-51D WR-F 44-14276
Down for Double
P-51D WR-B 44-72253
Jane VI
P-51D WR-B 44-72953
Jane VII

O'Brien, Gilbert M. 7.00
P-51B G4-Q 43-6787
Shanty Irish

Pierce, Joseph F. 7.00
P-51B B6-N 43-6644

Poindexter, James N. 7.00
P-51D SX-G 44-14598
Honey III

Reynolds, Robert 7.00
P-51B FT-U 43-6517
50 Calibre Concerto

Rogers, Felix M. 7.00
P-51B FT-C 43-12161
Beantown Banshee
P-51B FT-O 43-6833
Beantown Banshee

Shafer, Dale E. Jr. 7.00
P-51D D7-C 44-14671
P-51D D7-C 44-72147

Smith, Leslie C. 7.00
P-47D HV-Z 42-26044
Silver Lady
P-47D LM-L 44-19925

Starck, Walter E. 7.00
P-47D HO-X 42-8684
Lucia
P-51B HO-X 43-24807
Starck Mad/Even Stevens

Truluck, John H. Jr. 7.00
P-47D UN-L 42-74750
Lady Jane

Tyler, Gerald E. 7.00
P-51B C5-J 43-6376
Little Duckfoot
P-51D C5-J 44-14660
Little Duckfoot

Wicker, Samuel J. 7.00
P-38J N2-W 42-67453
Betty Jo II
P-51D N2-W 44-13936
Betty Jo III
P-51D N2-W 44-14243

Woods, Sidney S. 7.00
P-38J L2-M 43-28465
P-51D L2-M 44-14416
P-51D QP-A 44-72251

Woody, Robert E. 7.00
P-47D WR-W 42-8493
P-51B WR-W 43-6520
Woody's Maytag

Cummings, Donald 6.50
P-51D CG-U 44-15192

Hubbard, Mark E. 6.50
P-38J LC-V 42-67708

Hunt, Edward E. 6.50
P-51B FT-S 42-106597
Smoldering Boulder
P-51D FT-S 44-13559
Ready Eddy

Koenig, Charles W. 6.50
P-51D FT-K
Little Horse (Le Petite Chaval)

Moseley, Mark L. 6.50
P-47D LM-H 42-25522

Riley, Paul S. 6.50
P-47C WD-Y 41-6369
P-51B WD-Y 43-6922

Murphy, John B. 6.75
P-47D CV-A 42-8613
P-51B CV-A 42-106878
P-51D CV-A 44-13513

Kruzel, Ward A. 6.50
P-51C E2-K 43-25286
P-51D E9-K 44-14391
Vi
P-51D E9-K 44-14406
Vi

228

Weldon, Robert D. 6.25
P-51B AJ-W 43-6687
Mackie
P-51B AJ-W 43-12172
Mackie 2nd
P-51B AJ-W 43-12433
Mackie 3rd
P-51D AJ-W 44-63679
Mackie

Bille, Henry S. 6.00
P-51D OS-K 44-14314
Prune Face

Brown, Harley L. 6.00
P-51D KI-N 44-13779
P-51D KI-A 44-11250
Be Good/Brownies Ballroom

Candelaria, Richard G. 6.00
P-51K J2-K 44-11755
My Pride and Joy

Care, Raymond C. 6.00
P-47D QP-R 42-7981

Carlson, Kendall E. 6.00
P-47C VF-E 41-6575

Carter, James R. 6.00
P-472D HV-J 42-7960
P-47D HV-H 42-28834
P-47M HV-C 44-21129

Cook, Walter V. 6.00
P-47C LM-W 41-6343
Little Cookie

Cundy, Arthur C. 6.00
P-51D SX-B 44-15092E
Alabama Rammer Jammer

Drew, Urban L. 6.00
P-51D E2-D 44-14164
Detroit Miss

Emerson, Warren S. 6.00
P-51B GQ-Q 42-106445

Evans, Andrew J. Jr. 6.00
P-51D G4-B 44-64051
Little Sweetie 4

Evans, Roy W. 6.00
P-47D WD-E 42-7863

Gross, Clayton K. 6.00
P-51B GQ-I 43-12451
Live Bait/Peggy
P-47D GQ-I 42-28750
Live Bait
P-51D GQ-I 44-63668
Live Bait

Gumm, Charles F. Jr. 6.00
P-51B GQ-V 43-6320
Toni
P-51B GQ-V 42-106749

Hall, George F. 6.00
P-47D UN-H 42-7896
P-47D UN-F 42-75266

Hart, Cameron M. 6.00
P-47D UN-B 42-26299
P-47D UN-B 44-19937

Haviland, Frederick R. Jr. 6.00
P-51D OS-H 44-14403
Barbara

Howard, James H. 6.00
P-51B AJ-A 43-6375
Ding Hao
P-51B AJ-A 43-6515
Ding Hao

Howe, David W. 6.00
P-51D QP-G 44-13884

Howes, Bernard H. 6.00
P-51K CY-E 44-11370
My Lil' Honey
P-51D CY-E 44-63567
My Lil' Honey
P-51D CY-C 44-63745

Jones, Cyril W. Jr. 6.00
P-51D CS-W 44-14071
Dora Dee

Keen, Robert J. 6.00
P-47D HV-Y 42-74724
P-47D HV-W 42-75509

Top: The young crew chief running up Lt. Reed B. Butler's 357th Fighter Squadron P-47 (OS-H), is now ±70 years old. Before any more time passes by, we need to record as much of this crucial period in our history as we can. Above: Lt. Victor D. Iglesias' "Jersey Bounce". Below right: "P-51D-10 of Captain Leslie D. Minchew, 357th Squadron, 355th Fighter Group. Spinner white, band behind spinner and rudder, red, as is the background for 'kills'. Bar under O indicates that this was the second aircraft so coded in the squadron. 153 on rudder is yellow and panel forward of cockpit reads 'Pilot Capt. Minchew Crew Chief S/Sgt. Liebold'." Page 17 "Markings of the Aces" by Theodore R. Bennett. In a recent letter, Mr. Bennett indicated the nose and rudder colors were blue. Below left: A close up of the same aircraft with Bill Hovde's "My Butch" in the immediate background. Capt. Minchew transferred from the 354th to the 357th F.S. where he made most of his 5.5 claims. Note detail o serial and Crew Chief Sgt. Liebold's name. (Mulron)

Kemp, William T.   6.00
  P-51C E2-X 42-103749
    Betty Lee
  P-51D E2-X 44-14270
    Betty Lee II
  P-51D E2-X 44-15076
    Betty Lee III

Larson, Donald A.   6.00
  P-51B 6N-B
    Mary Queen of Scots
  P-51D 6N-B 44-13609
    Mary Queen of Scots

McGinn, John L.   6.00
  P-51D CL-P 44-14291
    Da Quake

McKeon, Joseph T.   6.00
  P-51D LC-C 44-13992
    Regina Coeli III

Mills, Henry L.   6.00
  P-47C QP-Q 41-6191
  P-47D QP-Q 42-74751
  P-51B QP-Q 43-6690

Murphy, Alva C.   6.00
  P-51D G4-U 44-13334
    Bite Me

Oberhansly, Jack J.   6.00
  P-47D MX-X 42-7883
    Iron Ass
  P-47D MX-X 44-19566
  P-51K QP-X 44-11661
    Iron Ass

Olson, Norman E.   6.00
  P-51B OS-X 43-7176
    Ma Fran 4th

Pugh, John F.   6.00
  P-51B G4-N 42-106473
    Geronimo

Roberson, Arval J.   6.00
  P-51B G4-A 43-6688
    Passion Wagon
  P-51D G4-A 44-13691
    Passion Wagon

Scheible, Wilbur R.   6.00
  P-47D QI-Z 42-75426
  P-51D QI-Z 44-15083

Schimanski, Robert G.   6.00
  P-51D C5-O 44-14334

Simmons, William J.   6.00
  P-51B GQ-W 43-7065

Starnes, James R.   6.00
  P-51B 6N-X 42-106936
    Tar Heel
  P-51D 6N-X 44-14113
    Tar Heel
  P-51D 6N-X 44-14387
    Tar Heel

Thwaites, David F.   6.00
  P-47D QI-L 42-75214
    Polly
  P-47D QI-L 42-76457
    Polly

Turley, Grant M.   6.00
  P-47D MX-S 42-27339

Welch, Robert E.   6.00
  P-51D CY-O 44-14140
    Wings of the Morning
  P-51D CY-Z 44-72138

Whalen, William E.   6.00
  P-51B QP-O 43-6899
  P-51D WR-R 44-1460
    Hi Nell

Wilkinson, James W.   6.00
  P-47D MX-W 42-26387
    Miss Behave

Fortier, Norman J.   5.83
  P-51B WR-N 42-106870
  P-51D WR-N 44-15373
  P-51D WR-N 44-72361

Top: Crew Chief Gale torrey paints another swastica on ``Barbara'' while the pilot, Capptain Fred R. Haviland Jr., looks on. (Haviland)    Above: A side shot of ``Barbara'', OS-H,44-14403. The wing tanks are on, but most likely are empty as the tires don't appear at all compressed as they would be from the full weight of the fuel. Fred became an ace on November 26,1944 when he shot down his 5th and 6th aircraft a 109 and a 190, on a Ramrod to Hanover. He is also credited with 6 ground claims. (Marshall) Below: After V.E. Day, this old P-47 was assigned to the 357th F.S. for familiarization prior to transferring to the Pacific. The square around the R denotes a training aircraft.

Koraleski, Walter J. Jr. 5.53	Compton, Gordon B. 5.50
P-47D WR-L	P-47D YJ-O 42-25702
Miss Thunder	P-51D YJ-O 44-72299
P-51B WR-L 43-6968	Little Bouncer
Amoss, Dudley M. 5.50	Gailer, Frank L. Jr. 5.50
P-51D CG-B 44-13818	P-51D B6-A 44-11331
	Expectant
Bickel, Carl G. 5.50	
P-51B FT-Z 43-6453	Graham, Lindol F. 5.50
Z Hub	P-38J MC-L 42-67491
	P-38J MC-L 42-67926
Bickford, Edward F. 5.50	Susie
P-51D AJ-V 44-73137	
Alice Marie	Hatala, Paul R. 5.50
	P-51B C5-B
Burdick, Clinton D. 5.50	Jeanne
P-51D QI-B 44-15310	P-51D C5-B
DoDo	
	Heller, Edwin L. 5.50
Buttke, Robert L. 5.50	P-51B PZ-H 43-6704
P-38H CY-F 42-67047	Hell er Bust
P-51D CY-F 44-15025	P-51D PZ-H 44-14696
Beautiful Lovenia	Hell er Bust

Above left: All 5 of Lt. William J. Cullerton's aerial victories were in P-51s. His first two claims were 109s on August 16, 1944. He also had 15 ground claims and flew with the 357th until he bailed out over enemy territory on April 8, 1945. (Jim Crow) Top right: Bill wasn't flying "Miss Steve" when he went down. Apparently, another pilot had bellied it in on take off, the ship was repaired and assigned to Lt. Watkins, who renamed it "Fickle Fannie". The aircraft serial number 44-13677, was also recoded OS-X to OS-N. (Bennett) Below: This USAF photo dated March 16, 1944 shows the first P-51 assigned to Lt. Robert L. Garlich, 43-12194, at the end of its career. Below left: Bob and Crew Chief Bill House pose in front of his next aircraft, 44-14966, "Lucious Lu." All Bob's aircraft were coded OS-S (bar). (Garlich) Bottom right: The last few months of the war proved to be good hunting for Garlich, who confirmed 6.5 ground victories before the end of the war in Europe. Here sits the second "Lucious Lu" 44-15512 among friends. (Muldron)

Top: Two 358th Fighter Squadron P-51s on a training flight over England. Foreground is W. H. Douglas' "Baby Buggy", followed by "Lada Dana," 44-13879, later flown as "Clare 2" by C.J. Rosenblatt. Above: Major Emil Sluga's 44-13354 "Slugger." Emil was forced to bail out and become a POW when hit by flak on March 21, 1945. Below: The "Dakota Kid," 42-103317 was the personal mount of Lt. Noble E. Peterson of the 358th Fighter Squadron. 75 gallon tanks in foreground tell a story . . . . another long escort mission is about to begin. (Marshall)

Horne, Francis W.   5.50
P-47D PE-C 42-8580
P-51B PE-O 42-106681

King, William B.   5.50
P-51B GQ-B 42-106424
Atlanta Peach
P-51B GQ-D 43-6724
Atlanta Peach II

Lenfest, Charles W.   5.50
P-47D WR-F 42-22464
Lorie
P-51B WR-F 43-6948
Lorie II
P-51B WR-F 42-106874
Lorie III
P-51D WR-F 44-14409
Lorie IV
P-51D WR-F 44-14275
Lorie V

Long, Maurice G.   5.50
P-51D GQ-L 44-13328
Mary Pat III
P-51D GQ-L 44-63815
Mary Pat

McCauley, Frank E.   5.50
P-47C HV-Z 41-6271

Minchew, Leslie D.   5.50
P-51D OS-O 44-14753

O'Brien, William R.   5.50
P-51D B6-G 44-13622
Billy's Bitch

Pascoe, James J.   5.50
P-38J 5E-Z 42-67453
P-51D 5E-W 44-13890
Green Eyes

Ruder, Leroy A.   5.50
P-51B C5-X 43-6872
Linda Lu

Shoup, Robert L.   5.50
P-51C AJ-S 42-102997
Fer De Lance

Smith, Donovan F.   5.50
P-47C HV-M 41-6319
P. J. & Hun Hunter
P-47D HV-U 42-75272
Ole Cock II
P-47D HV-S 42-75382
Ole Cock III

Tanner, William F.   5.50
P-47D LH-O 42-26472
Prudence V
P-51D LH-O 44-72212
Prudence VII

Vanden Heuvel, George   5.50
P-51D E9-L 44-14685
P-51D E9-Z 44-64004
Mary Mine

Winks, Robert P.   5.50
P-51D C5-
Trusty Rusty

Biel, Hipolitus T.   5.33
P-51B QP-T 43-6941

Duffy, James E. Jr.   5.20
P-47D WR-Y 42-75681
P-51D WR-Y 44-63764
Dragon Wagon
P-51D WR-Y 44-72186
Dragon Wagon

Abernathy, Robert W.   5.00
P-47D LH-Q
Lady Gwen
P-51D LH-Q 44-15589
Lady Gwen II

Allen, William H.   5.00
P-38J CY-J 42-67966
Pretty Patty
P-51D CY-J 44-14049
Pretty Patty II

Ammon, Robert H.   5.00
P-51D D7-A 44-14004
Annie Mae

Asbury, Richard W.   5.00
P-47D AJ-S 44-20208
P-51D AJ-S 44-63782

Baccus, Donald A.   5.00
P-47D OC-T 42-8568
The Bloody Shaft
P-47D OC-G 42-76583
P-51D OC-G 44-14993
P-51D CV-U 44-72746

Bank, Raymond M.   5.00
P-51D C5-Y 44-15266
Fireball

Beavers, Edward H. Jr.   5.00
P-51D D7-Z 44-13980
P-51D D7-Z/P 44-14525
Joanie

Bostrom, Ernest O.   5.00
P-51D PZ-O 44-13929
Little Marjie

Brown, Gerald   5.00
P-38H CG-G 42-67028

Chandler, Van E.   5.00
P-51D VF-U 44-14388
Wheezy

Cole, Charles H. Jr.   5.00
P-51D LC-U 44-11324
P-51D KI-K 44-72160

Comstock, Harold E.   5.00
P-47C UN-Y 41-6320
P-47C UN-Y 41-6326
P-47D UN-Y 42-75870

Coons, Merle M.   5.00
P-51D CG-C 44-14068
The Worry Bird

Cox, Ralph L.   5.00
P-51D CS-H 44-14979
P-51D IV-N 44-72154

Cranfill, Niven K.   5.00
P-47D IV-N 42-74645
Deviless
P-51B IV-N 42-106848
Deviless 2nd
P-51D IV-N 44-13390
Deviless 3rd
P-51D CV-Q 44-15100
P-51D CV-Q 44-15717

Cullerton, William J.   5.00
P-51D OS-X 44-13677
Miss Steve

Daniell, J. S.   5.00
P-51D 6N-K 44-14745
Sweet N Low Down

Davis, Clayton E.   5.00
P-47D HO-F 42-22492
Marjorie
P-51B HO-C 43-6805
Marjorie II
P-51D HO-C 44-13651

Dregne, Irwin H.   5.00
P-51D C5-Q 44-13408
Ah Fung Goo II
P-51K C5-Q 44-11678
Ah Fung Goo/Bobby Jeanne

Egan, Joseph L. Jr.   5.00
P-47C UN-E 41-6584
Holy Joe
P-47D UN-E 42-75069
P-47D UN-E 42-75855

Elder, Robert A.   5.00
P-51D LH-S 44-72736
Miss Gamble

Fisk, Harry E.   5.00
P-51B AJ-F 43-6621
Duration Plus
P-47D AJ-F 44-20464

Gerick, Steven   5.00
P-47D HV-O 42-26024
Tally Ho Chaps

Hanseman, Chris J.   5.00
P-51D 6N-H 44-13556
  Eleanore IV

Harris, Thomas L.   5.00
P-51B C5-S 43-6653
  Lil' Red's Rocket

Hartley, Raymond E.   5.00
P-51D YJ-H 44-15539
  Ku

Hauver, Charles D.   5.00
P-51B WR-R 43-6917
  Patricia
P-51D WR-R 44-14704
  Princess Pat

Haworth, Russell C.   5.00
P-51D CL-K 44-13642
  Krazy Kid

Hiro, Edwin W.   5.00
P-51B B6-
  Horse's Itch
P-51D B6-D 44-13518
  Horse's Itch

Hodges, William R.   5.00
P-47D CS-O 42-74719
P-51D CS-D 44-14427

Icard, Joe W.   5.00
P-47D LM-I 42-75241
P-47D LM-I 42-75040

Johnson, Evan M. V   5.00
P-51D 6N-J 44-13471
  The Comet

Jones, Frank C.   5.00
P-51D WD-P 43-6897
P-51D WD-P 44-13389

Julian, William H.   5.00
P-47C HL-R 41-6328

Lazear, Earl R. Jr.   5.00
P-51D PZ-L 44-14877
  Pennie's Earl

London, Charles P.   5.00
P-47C HL-B 41-6335
  El Jeepo

Markham, Gene E.   5.00
P-51D YJ-Q 44-14929
  Mr. Gray
P-51D YJ-Q 44-14949
  Mr. Gray
P-51D YJ-Q 44-72171
  Mr. Gray II

Marsh, Lester C.   5.00
P-51D D7-P 44-14947

Martin, Kenneth R.   5.00
P-51B GQ-E 43-6359

Mason, Joseph L.   5.00
P-47D PZ-M 42-8466
  Gena/This Is It
P-51B PZ-M 43-6776
P-51B PZ-M 42-106609
P-51D PZ-M 44-13395
P-51D PZ-M 44-14911
  This Is It

Maxwell, Chester K.   5.00
P-51D C5-H 44-63861
  Lady Ester

McElroy, James N.   5.00
P-51B YF-S 43-7023
  Big Stoop/Ridge Runner
P-51D YF-S
  Big Stoop III

McMinn, Evan D.   5.00
P-47D HV-F 42-8458

Merritt, George L. Sr.   5.00
P-47D E2-A 42-75404
  Dr. I. P. Daily
P-51C E2-A 42-103347

Pisanos, Spiros N.   5.00
P-47D QP-D 42-7945
  Miss Plainfield
P-51B QP-D 43-6798

Pompetti, Peter E.   5.00
P-47C WZ-R 41-6393
  Axe the Axis

Price, Jack C.   5.00
P-51D LC-G 44-14693
  Feather Merchant 5th

Priest, Royce W.   5.00
P-51D WR-E
  Weepin Deacon II

Reese, William C.   5.00
P-51B C5-F 43-12313
  Bear River Betsy

Ritchey, Andrew J.   5.00
P-47D FT-E
P-51D FT-E

Rose, Franklin Jr.   5.00
P-51B FT-V 42-106897
P-47D FT-V 42-29188
P-51D FT-V 44-63584
P-51D FT-V 44-63624

Rudolph, Henry S.   5.00
P-47D FT-M 42-29346
P-51D FT-J 44-63685

Schank, Thomas D.   5.00
P-38J CL-T 42-104106
  Stinger
P-51D CL-I 44-13668
  Rocky Mtn. Canary

Schuh, Duerr, H.   5.00
P-51D HO-A 44-13530
  Dutchess

Sears, Alexander F.   5.00
P-51B HO-O 43-6454

Smith, Kenneth G.   5.00
P-51B WD-K 43-6803

Stangel, William J.   5.00
P-51D PE-C 44-14015
  Stinky 2

Stanley, Morris A.   5.00
P-51D C5-V 44-13678

Sykes, William J.   5.00
P-51D E9-S 44-14520
  Hilma Lee

Talbot, Gilbert F.   5.00
P-51B GQ-U 43-6737
  Peggy
P-51D GQ-P 43-63666
  Peggy/Deacon

Tordoff, Harrison B.   5.00
P-47D SX-L
  Upupa Epops
P-51D SX-L 44-14805
  Upupa Epops
P-51D SX-L 44-72364
  Upupa Epops

Waggoner, Horace Q.   5.00
P-47D SX-M 42-2661
  Miss Illini
P-51D SX-X 44-14802
  Miss Illini III

Warner, Jack A.   5.00
P-51D AJ-G 44-14010
  Chicago's Own

Warren, Jack R.   5.00
P-51B C5-F 43-12124

Wilson, William F.   5.00
P-51D 5E-Y 44-14258
P-51D 5E-Y 44-14838

Wise, Kenneth   5.00
P-51D FT-H 44-64104
  Wano

York, Robert M.   5.00
P-51D CS-Y 44-14159
  Rudy

Top and above: Two nice shots of Lt. Russell J. McNally's "Morphine Sue," 43-6815, YF-O. Starboard photo shows serial, abbreviated D-Day markings, drop tanks and name "Bo Mc" above exhaust. Below: McNally's second P-51, "Morphine Sue II," ready and waiting for its next mission. The drop tanks would be filled shortly before take off as the high octane fuel played havoc with the seals if left in too long. (McNally)

233

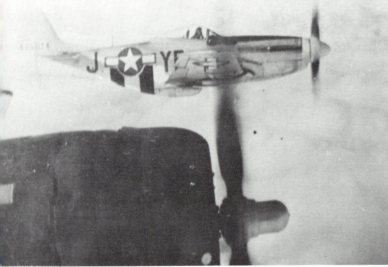

Above right: Crew Chief Downing bids farewell to Major William J. Hovde, 10.5 victory ace of the 358th fighter Squadron, just before operation ``Frantic 7'', the 355th shuttle mission to Russia. The Major believed in being prepared, that's his name and rank in Russian on his aircraft the subject of a color painting on page 147. He served as 358th Squadron Commander from May to August 1945. Top left: After the war Billy transferred to the 354th F.S. This is ``Ole VII'' in postwar Bulldog colors. Above: A 358th F.S. pilot pulls in close to a big friend. Soon after this photo was taken, Lt. Arthur E. Alexander went down in the aircraft when it lost its coolant somewhere just north of Munster. He spent the rest of the war as a POW. (via Glover) Below: 44-14389, YF-N of the 358th Fighter Squadron sits on a rain soaked airfield, late summer/early fall '44. Barely discernable name on cowl: ``Baltimore Joe Joe II.'' (Mulron) Right: Lt. Robert Brown's colorful P-51D. Painted carb cover was unusual for the 358th, but then again, so was the artwork. (Bruno)

SQUADRON CODES

4th Fighter Group
QP .... 334th Squadron
WD .... 335th Squadron
VF .... 336th Squadron

20th Fighter Group
KI .... 55th Squadron
LC .... 77th Squadron
MC .... 79th Squadron

55th Fighter Group
CG .... 38th Squadron
CL .... 338th Squadron
CY .... 343rd Squadron

56th Fighter Group
HV .... 61st Squadron
LM .... 62nd Squadron
UN .... 63rd Squadron

78th Fighter Group
MX .... 82nd Squadron
HL .... 83rd Squadron
WZ .... 84th Squadron

339th Fighter Group
D7 .... 503rd Squadron
5Q .... 504th Squadron
6N .... 505th Squadron

352nd Fighter Group
PE .... 328th Squadron
PZ .... 486th Squadron
HO .... 487th Squadron

353rd Fighter Group
LH .... 350th Squadron
YJ .... 351st Squadron
SX .... 352nd Squadron

354th Fighter Group
FT .... 353rd Squadron
GQ .... 355th Squadron
AJ .... 356th Squadron

355th Fighter Group
WR .... 354th Squadron
OS .... 357th Squadron
YF .... 358th Squadron

356th Fighter Group
OC .... 359th Squadron
PI .... 360th Squadron
QI .... 361st Squadron

357th Fighter Group
G4 .... 362nd Squadron
B6 .... 363rd Squadron
C5 .... 364th Squadron

359th Fighter Group
CV .... 368th Squadron
IV .... 369th Squadron
CS* .... 370th Squadron

361st Fighter Group
B7 .... 374th Squadron
E2 .... 375th Squadron
E9 .... 376th Squadron

364th Fighter Group
N2 .... 383rd Squadron
5Y .... 384th Squadron
5E .... 385th Squadron

479th Fighter Group
L2 .... 434th Squadron
J2 .... 435th Squadron
9B .... 436th Squadron

*Formerly CR-

Above Lt. Loren R. Wilson's flying billboard sported four names: "Mim" on port nose, "Betty A III" starboard, "J'ete" was on out-board side port engine cowling and "Frieda" outboard stbd.

Below: Lt. Kenneth F. Nicholson crashlanded his P-38 at his home base of Honington, Suffolk on March 2, 1944. This A/C was repaired and Ken went on to score 1 confirmed and 1 damaged, both FW-190s, with it.

Above: George F. Ceuleers and crew pose with their P-38, N2-D, 42-68017. The C/C was S/Sgt. Archer, Armorer was Sgt. Simpkins. On March 8, 1944 the 383rd was involved in its first successful dogfight and George recorded his first victory, a FW-190.

Below: Thirteen months later (April 4, 1945) George scored the last of his 10½ vics in an almost 200 mile chase of a ME-262 jet. Records show that this was indeed the A/C: N2-D, 44-72719.

(U.S.A.F. Photo)

ACES IN A DAY

Unlike many air historians, I have always recognized claims for aircraft on the ground or water. In this I have merely reflected the policy of the Fighter Victory Credits board of the Eighth Air Force. The strafing of an airfield was, without any doubt, the most hazardous duty performed by the fighter pilot. Certainly very few of them looked forward to it. Many of America's most talented, most dedicated pilots were lost on these hazardous but vital missions. May the outstanding record of their brave accomplishments never be forgotten.

Pilot	Air	Grd	Date	Grp
Cpt. Don S. Gentile	0	5	5.4.44	4
Cpt. Donald M. Malmsten	0	6	27.2.45	4
Lt. Col. Sidney S. Woods	5	0	22.3.45	4
Lt. William O. Antonides	0	5	16.4.45	4
F/O. Donald P. Baugh	0	5	16.4.45	4
Lt. Kenneth G. Helfrecht	0	5	16.4.45	4
Lt. Douglas P. Pederson	0	6	16.4.45	4
Lt. Joseph L. Mansker	0	6	25.8.44	20
Cpt. Charles H. Cole	0	6	8.2.45	20
Lt. Reps D. Jones	0	5	8.2.45	20
Cpt. Lowell E. Einhaus	0	5	8.2.45	20
F/O. Frederick H. Jurgens	0	8	10.45	20
Lt. Edward L. Kier	0	5	10.4.45	20
Lt. Joseph A. Peterburs	0	5	10.4.45	20
Lt. David Stewart	0	7	10.4.45	20
Lt. William H. Allen	5	0	5.9.44	55
Cpt. William H. Lewis	5	0	5.9.44	55
Cpt. Robert E. Welch	0	6	9.4.45	55
Cpt. Frank E. Birtciel	0	5	9.4.45	55
Col. Elwyn G. Righetti	0	6	9.4.45	55
Col. Elwyn G. Righetti	0	6	16.4.45	55
Col. Elwyn G. Righetti	0	9	17.4.45	55
Cpt. Robert J. Rankin	5	0	12.5.44	56
Cpt. Fred J. Christensen	6	0	7.7.44	56
Lt. Col. Dave Schilling	5	0	23.12.44	56
Cpt. Felix Williamson	5	0	14.1.45	56
Lt. Russell S. Kyler	0	5	13.4.45	56
Lt. Randel Murphy Jr.	0	10	13.4.45	56
Lt. Thomas W. Queen	0	5	13.4.45	56
Col. John D. Landers	0	8	10.4.45	78
Lt. Anthony T. Colletti	0	5	16.4.45	78
Cpt. Donald J. deVilliers	0	5	16.4.45	78
Cpt. Gene C. Doss	0	5	16.4.45	78
Lt. Col. Olin E. Gilbert	0	6.50	16.4.45	78
Lt. Danford E. Josey Jr.	0	5	16.4.45	78
Cpt. Edward R. Kulik	0	7	16.4.45	78
Col. John D. Landers	0	9	16.4.45	78
Lt. Dorian Ledington	0	5	16.4.45	78
Lt. Duncan M. McDuffie	0	5	16.4.45	78
Lt. Dale S. Sweat	0	5	16.4.45	78
Cpt. Edward R. Kulik	0	7	17.4.45	78
Lt. Clyde E. Taylor	0	8	17.4.45	78

Two photos of Col. Roy Osborn's P-51, N2-O, 44-13923, "Billy's Boy" taken when he was C.O. of the 364th. Certainly an unusual fact about Roy was that he has confirmed vics in all 3 8th A.F. Fighters!

Cpt. Archie A. Tower	0	5	11.9.44	339
Cpt. J. S. Daniel	5	0	26.11.44	339
Lt. Hal Burch	0	5	10.4.45	339
Lt. Jerome T. Murphy	0	5	10.4.45	339
Lt. Robert H. Paul	0	5	10.4.45	339
Maj. Archie A. Tower	0	8	10.4.45	339
Lt. John R. Byers	0	5	16.4.45	339
Lt. Steve J. Chetneky	0	6	16.4.45	339
Lt. William C. Clark	0	6	16.4.45	339
Lt. Herbert G. Marsh	0	5	16.4.45	339
Cpt. Robert H. Ammon	0	9	17.4.45	339
Cpt. Philip M. Loveless	0	5	17.4.45	339
Cpt. Kirke B. Everson Jr.	0	7	17.4.45	339
Lt. Leon M. Orcutt Jr.	0	9	17.4.45	339
Lt. Joseph L. Thury	0	5	17.4.45	339
Cpt. Edwin L. Heller	0	5	24.4.44	352
Lt. Carl J. Luksic	5	0	8.5.44	352
Maj. George E. Preddy	6	0	6.8.44	352
Cpt. Clarence O. Johnson	0	5	10.9.44	352
Cpt. Donald S. Bryan	5	0	2.11.44	352
Cpt. William T. Whisner	5	0	21.11.44	352
Cpt. Edwin L. Heller	0	7	16.4.45	352
Lt. Charles C. Pattillo	0	5	16.4.45	352
Lt. Joseph D. Carter	0	5	17.4.45	352
Cpt. Raymond H. Littge	0	5	17.4.45	352
Lt. Karl J. Waldron	0	5	17.4.45	352
Lt. James N. White Jr.	0	5	17.4.45	352
Maj. Walker L. Boone	0	7	27.2.45	353
Cpt. Herbert G. Kolb	0	5	27.2.45	353
Lt. Col. Wayne Blickenstaff	5	0	22.2.45	353
Maj. Robert A. Elder	5	0	22.3.45	353
Cpt. Gordon B. Compton	0	5	16.4.45	353
F/O. Richard N. Gustke	0	5	16.4.45	353
Cpt. Melville Hightshoe	0	5	16.4.45	353
Lt. Herbert G. Kolb	0	9.5	16.4.45	353
Lt. James H. McClure	0	5	16.4.45	353
Lt. Bruce D. McMahan	0	5.5	16.4.45	353
Lt. Joseph D. McMullen	0	5.5	16.4.45	353
Lt. Gerald J. Miller	0	5	16.4.45	353
Col. Ben Rimermann	0	6	16.4.45	353
Maj. Claiborne H. Kinnard	1	4	5.4.44	355
Lt. James N. McElroy	0	5	5.4.44	355
Cpt. Clarence O. Johnson	0	5	10.9.44	355
Lt. William J. Cullerton	2	6	2.11.44	355
Maj. Robert L. Elder	1	6	2.11.44	355
Cpt. Joseph E. Mellen	0	5	13.4.45	355
Lt. Duran Vickery	0	5	13.4.45	355
Cpt. Frank A. Morgan	0	5.5	20.2.45	356
Cpt. Charles E. Yeager	5	0	22.10.44	357
Cpt. Leonard K. Carson	5.5	0	5.12.44	357
Lt. Myron A. Becraft	1	6	2.3.45	357
Lt. Claude J. Crenshaw	5	0	21.11.44	359
Lt. David B. Archibald	5	0	18.12.44	359
Lt. Paul E. Olsen	5	0	18.12.44	359
Lt. Col. Roy A. Webb Jr.	0	5	29.6.44	361
Lt. William R. Beyer	5	0	27.9.2	361
Cpt. Ernest E. Bankey	5.5	0	27.12.44	364
Lt. Richard D. Candelaria	5	0	7.4.45	479
Maj. Robin Olds	0	5	16.4.45	479
Cpt. Donald J. Pierce	0	5	16.4.45	479

Captain John C. Hunter of the 383rd Fighter Squadron in his Mustang, N2-E, 44-13707. The photo was taken with a K-25 camera and the shadow of the photo ship's wing can be seen on Hunter's A/C.
(Smelser)

237

Top: Photos of 364th F.G. P-38s, especially early ones, are relatively rare. We wish we could tell you the complete story of this 384th bird, but we can't. Can one of our readers help? (Mulron) Above: Lt. James Fowle of the 384th F.S. and his Crew Chief with their A/C 'Terry Claire III', 5Y-J, 44-13829. All 8 of his aerial vics were in this A/C, including the 4 ME-109s he blasted out of the air in just 20 minutes on Dec. 23, 1944. (U.S.A.F. Photo) Below: Col. Robert E. Lacy of the 384th and his 5Y-D, 44-14021 ''Jackie Jr.'' During his combat time he damaged one E/A in the air and destroyed 3 on the ground. (U.S.A.F. Photo)

AGAINST THE JETS

The first confirmed jet kill fell to the guns of Colonel John B. Murphy of the 359th Fighter Group in a Mustang coded (S-K, 44-13 966 on 16th August 1944. The jet was the rocket propelled ME-163. Major Joe Myers and Lt. Manford O. Croy (both of the 78th Fighter Group) claimed the destruction of the first ME-262 on 28th August 1944 while flying the P-47 Thunderbolt. Following is a list of claims by the fighter pilots who served with the Eighth Air Force.

NOTE: The asterisks indicate claims not credited by USAF Historical Study #85.

4th Fighter Group

Cpt. Fred W. Glover	1 ME-163	2.11.44.
Cpt. Louis Norley	1 ME-163	2.11.44.
Lt. Franklin W. Young	1 ME-262	1.1.45.
Lt. Carl G. Payne	1 ME-262	25.2.45.
Lt. Raymond A. Dyer	1 ME-262	4.4.45.
Lt. Micheal J. Kennedy	1 ME-262	4.4.45.
Lt. Willmer W. Collins	1 ME-262	10.4.45.

20th Fighter Group

Lt. Ernest C. Fiebelkorn	.5 ME-262	8.11.44
Cpt. John K. Brown	1 ME-262	10.4.45.
F/O. Jerome Rosenblum	.5 ME-262	10.4.45.
Lt. John W. Cudd Jr.	.5 ME-262	10.4.45.
Lt. Albert B. North	1 ME-262	10.4.45.
Lt. Walter T. Drozd	1 ME-262	10.4.45.
Cpt. John K. Hollins	1 ME-262	10.4.45.

55th Fighter Group

*Lt. Phillip Eastman	1 ME-262	13.1.45.
Lt. Walter J. Konantz	1 ME-262	13.1.45.
Lt. Dudley M. Amoss	1 ME-262	15.2.45.
Cpt. Donald M. Cummings	2 ME-262	25.2.45.
Cpt. Donald E. Penn	1 ME-262	25.2.45.
Lt. Millard O. Anderson	1 ME-262	25.2.45.
Lt. Billy Clemmons	1 ME-262	25.2.45.
Lt. Donald T. Menegay	1 ME-262	25.2.45.
*Lt. John F. O'Neil	.5 ME-262	25.2.45.
*Lt. Frank E. Birtciel	.5 ME-262	25.2.45.
Lt. John W. Cunnick III	1 ME-262	22.3.45.
Lt. Patrick L. Moore	1 ME-262	30.3.45.
Maj. Edward B. Giller	1 ME-262	9.4.45.
*Lt. Grady Moore	1 ME-262	9.4.45.
Lt. Keith R. McGinnis	1 ME-262	10.4.45.
Lt. Kenneth Lashbrook	1 ME-262	10.4.45.
Maj. Eugene Ryan	1 ME-262	16.4.45.
Lt. Robert Deloach	1 ME-262	19.4.45.

56th Fighter Group

Lt. Walter R. Groce	.5 ME-262	1.11.44.
*Lt. John W. Keeler	1 ME-262	14.3.45.
Lt. Norman D. Gould	1 AR-234	14.3.45.
Lt. Warren S. Lear	.5 AR-234	14.3.45.
Lt. Sanford N. Ball	.5 AR-234	14.3.45.
Lt. Edwin M. Crosthwait	1 ME-262	25.3.45.
Maj. George E. Bostwick	1 ME-262	25.3.45.
Cpt. John C. Fahringer	1 ME-262	5.4.45.
*Cpt. William F. Wilkerson	1 ME-262	10.4.45.

*Lt. Donald Henley	.5 ME-262	10.4.45.
Lt. Walter J. Sharbo	.5 ME-262	10.4.45.

78th Fighter Group

Maj. Joe Myers	.5 ME-262	28.8.44.
Lt. Manford O. Croy Jr.	.5 ME-262	28.8.44.
Maj. Richard E. Conner	1 ME-262	7.10.44.
Lt. Huie H. Lamb Jr.	1 ME-262	15.10.44.
*Lt. William E. Hydorn	1 ME-262	9.2.45.
*Cpt. Edwin H. Miller	1 ME-262	9.2.45.
Cpt. Winfield H. Brown	.5 AR-234	19.3.45.
Lt. Huie H. Lamb Jr.	.5 AR-234	19.3.45.
Lt. James E. Parker	1 AR-234	19.3.45.
*Lt. Allen A. Rosenblum	.5 AR-234	19.3.45.
*Lt. Richard I. Kuehl	.5 ME-262	19.3.45.
Cpt. Edwin H. Miller	1 ME-262	21.3.45.
Lt. Robert H. Anderson	1 ME-262	21.3.45.
Lt. Walter E. Bourque	1 ME-262	21.3.45.
Lt. John H. Kirk	1 ME-262	21.3.45.
Lt. Allen A. Rosenblum	.5 ME-262	21.3.45.
Cpt. Winfield H. Brown	.5 ME-262	21.3.45.
Lt. Milton B. Stutzman	.5 ME-262	22.3.45.
Lt. Eugene L. Peel	.5 ME-262	22.3.45.
Cpt. Harold T. Barnaby	1 ME-262	22.3.45.
Lt. Col. John D. Landers	.5 ME-262	30.3.45.
Lt. Thomas V. Thain Jr.	.5 ME-262	30.3.45.
Lt. Wayne L. Coleman	1 ME-262	31.3.45.

339th Fighter Group

Lt. Stephen C. Ananian	1 ME-262	9.2.45.
*Lt. Robert C. Havighurst	1 ME-262	2.3.45
Lt. Vernon N. Barto	1 ME-262	20.3.45.
Lt. Robert E. Irion	1 ME-262	20.3.45.
Lt. Nile C. Greer	1 ME-262	21.3.45.
*Lt. Billy E. Langohr	.5 ME-262	21.3.45.
Lt. Carroll W. Bennett	1 ME-262	30.3.45.
Cpt. Robert F. Sargent	1 ME-262	30.3.45.
Cpt. Harry R. Corey	1 ME-262	4.4.45.
Lt. Robert C. Havighurst	1 ME-262	4.4.45.
Lt. Nile C. Greer	1 ME-262	4.4.45.
Cpt. Kirke B. Everson Jr.	.5 ME-262	4.4.45.
Lt. Robert C. Croker	.5 ME-262	4.4.45.
*Lt. Oscar K. Biggs	1 ME-262	7.4.45.
*Lt. Robert V. Blizzard	1 ME-262	7.4.45.
*Cpt. Robert J. Frisch	1 ME-262	17.4.45.
Lt. John C. Campbell Jr.	1 ME-262	17.4.45.
Lt. Col. Dale E. Shafer Jr.	1 AR-234	18.4.45.

352nd Fighter Group

Lt. William G. Gerbe	.5 ME-262	1.11.44
Lt. Harry L. Edwards	1 ME-262	9.12.44.
Lt. Col. John C. Meyer	1 AR-234	31.12.44.
Lt. Charles D. Price	1 ME-262	22.2.45.
Cpt. Donald S. Bryan	1 AR-234	14.3.45.
Cpt. Raymond H. Littge	1 ME-262	25.3.45.
Lt. James C. Hurley	1 ME-262	30.3.45.
*Lt. Col. John C. Meyer	1 ME-262	31.3.45.
Maj. Richard McAuliffe	.5 ME-262	10.4.45.
Lt. Joseph W. Prichard	.5 ME-262	10.4.45.
Lt. Carlo A. Ricci	.5 ME-262	10.4.45.
Lt. Charles C. Pattillo	1 ME-262	10.4.45.

Top: 'Francisco' of the 385th Fighter Squadron was repaired and flown again. On 5th December 1944 Lt. Romoldo Visconte was killed when he crashlanded this aircraft in Allied held territory. Coded 5E-R, 44-14189, this aircraft was assigned to the 1st Group Scout Force of the 364th Fighter Group. Center: A Mustang of the 385th Fighter Squadron lands at Honigton, Suffolk. Lt. Erskine Rivers had to abandon this aircraft on 30th November 1944 due to engine failure. He managed to evade capture and was soon back flying combat missions. The code is 5E-J, 44-13957. Below: Ace James L. McCubbin with his Mustang 5E-F, 44-11242 which he named 'Mary Al.' He served with the 385th Fighter Squadron and claimed a total of five enemy aircraft: 4 in the air, 1 on the ground.

Above: Two views of Col. Eugene Roberts' P-51 at Honington. Roberts scored all 9 of his air vics in P-47s with the 84th F.S., 78th F.G. *(Tabatt)*

353rd Fighter Group

Lt. Billy J. Murray	1 ME-262	14.1.45.
Lt. James W. Rohrs	.5 ME-262	14.1.45.
Lt. George J. Rosen	.5 ME-262	14.1.45.
Maj. Wayne K. Blickenstaff	1 ME-262	22.2.45.
Cpt. Gordon B. Compton	1 ME-262	22.2.45.
Lt. Harrison B. Tordoff	1 ME-262	31.3.45.
Cpt. Gordon B. Compton	1 ME-262	10.4.45.
Cpt Robert W. Abernathy	1 ME-262	10.4.45.
Lt. Jack W. Clark	.5 ME-262	10.4.45.
Lt. Bruce D. McMahan	.5 ME-262	10.4.45.

355th Fighter Group

*Cpt. Henry H. Kirby Jr.	.5 ME-262	22.2.45.
Lt. John K. Wilkins Jr.	1 ME-262	1.3.45.
Lt. Wendell Beaty	1 ME-262	1.3.45.
Cpt. Charles H. Spencer	1 ME-262	19.3.45.
Lt. Elmer H. Riffle	1 AR-234	4.4.45.

356th Fighter Group

Lt. Harold E. Whitmore	1 ME-262	21.2.45.
Lt. Robert E. Barnhart	1 AR-234	14.3.45.
Lt. Wayne C. Gatlin	1 ME-262	10.4.45.

*Lt. Thurman N. Mauldin	1 ME-262	10.4.45.
Lt. Leon Oliver	1 ME-262	18.4.45.

357th Fighter Group

Cpt. Charles E. Yeager	1 ME-262	6.11.44.
Lt. James W. Kenney	1 ME-262	8.11.44.
Lt. Edward R. Haydon	.5 ME-262	8.11.44.
Lt. Robert P. Winks	1 ME-262	15.1.45.
Lt. Dale E. Karger	1 ME-262	20.1.45.
Lt. Roland R. Wright	1 ME-262	20.1.45.
Cpt. Donald H. Bochkay	1 ME-262	9.2.45.
Lt. Johnnie L. Carter	1 ME-262	9.2.45.
Maj. Robert W. Foy	1 ME-262	19.3.45.
Cpt. Robert S. Fifield	1 ME-262	19.3.45.
F/O. James A. Steiger	1 ME-262	17.4.45.
Maj. Donald H. Bochkay	1 ME-262	18.4.45.
Cpt. Charles E. Weaver	1 ME-262	18.4.45.
Lt. Col. Jack W. Hayes Jr.	1 ME-262	19.4.45.
Lt. Paul N. Bowles	1 ME-262	19.4.45.
Lt. Carroll W. Ofthsun	1 ME-262	19.4.45
Cpt. Robert S. Fifield	1 ME-262	19.4.45.
Cpt. Ivan L. McGuire	.5 ME-262	19.4.45.

Below: Lt. Curtis L. Smart's 5E-V, 44-64077, "Estrellita III," the subject of a color profile on page 151. Note, in photo below left, that the name has been printed but not outlined. *(Smart)*

Above: Another ace of the 364th was Maj. Earnest E. Bankey. These two shots are of his last P-51, 5E-B, 44-73045. His previous P-51 was lost with F/O Theodore F. Lasch on April 10, 1945. No stranger to the 364th, he served in various capacities for over a year with them, making his first claims in April '44 while the group was still in P-38s. Note: stripes on inner edge of flap are degree indicators.

Lt. Gilman L. Weber	.5 ME-262	19.4.45.		Lt. Col. George F. Ceuleers	1 ME-262	4.4.45.
Lt. James P. McMullen	1 ME-262	19.4.45.		Cpt. Douglas J. Pick	.5 ME-262	10.4.45.
359th Fighter Group				Lt. Harry C. Schwartz	.5 ME-262	10.4.45.
Lt. Col. John B. Murphy	1 ME-163	16.8.44.		Cpt. Walter L. Goff	1 ME-262	17.4.45.
Lt. Cyril W. Jones Jr.	1 ME-163	16.8.44.		*Lt. William F. Kissell	1 ME-262	17.4.45.
Cpt. Ray S. Wetmore	1 ME-163	15.3.45.		Cpt. Roy W. Orndorff	1 ME-262	17.4.45.
Maj. Niven K. Cranfill	1 ME-262	19.3.45.		**479th Fighter Group**		
Lt. Harold Tenenbaum	1 ME-262	10.4.45.		Lt. Norman R. Benoit	.5 ME-262	7.10.44
Lt. Robert J. Guggemos	1 ME-262	10.4.45.		Col. Hubert Zemke	.5 ME-262	7.10.44.
361st Fighter Group				Lt. Eugene E. Wendt	1 ME-262	25.3.45.
Lt. Urban L. Drew	2 ME-262	7.10.44		Lt. Richard G. Candelaria	1 ME-262	7.4.45.
Lt. William J. Quinn	1 ME-262	6.11.44.		Lt. Hilton O. Thompson	1 ME-262	7.4.45.
Lt. Anthony Maurice	1 ME-262	8.11.44.		Cpt. Verne E. Hooker	1 ME-262	7.4.45.
Lt. Harry M. Chapman	1 ME-262	21.3.45		Lt. Hilton O. Thompson	1 AR-234	25.4.45.
Lt. Richard D. Anderson	1 ME-262	21.3.45.		**2nd Group Scouting Force**		
Lt. Kenneth J. Scott	1 ME-262	30.3.45.		Lt. John K. Wilkins Jr.	1 ME-262	1.3.45.
Lt. James T. Sloan	1 ME-262	9.4.45.		Lt. Charles Rodebaugh	1 ME-262	14.3.45.
364th Fighter Group				Lt. Marvin H. Castleberry	1 ME-262	31.3.45.
Lt. Eugene Murphy	.5 AR-234	25.2.45.				
Lt. Richard White	.5 AR-234	25.2.45.				
Lt. John B. Guy	1 ME-262	30.3.45.				

Below: The result of a landing accident which occured on 22nd February 1945. This was the assigned aircraft of Everett N. Farrell of the 385th Fighter Squadron. He named it 'Sweet Mama II' 5E-P, 44-15576. The assigned ship of Lt. Donald Bloodgood which he named 'Majero 11.' The code was 5E-B (bar), 44-11213. Lt. Bloodgood lost this aircraft 25th April 1945 while on a training flight. (Bloodgood)

Eighth Air Force Fighter Command Wing Call-signs 1944-45

65th Fighter Wing	Colgate
66th Fighter Wing	Oilskin
67th Fighter Wing	Mohair

Airfield Call-signs May 1943-April 1944

4th F. G.	Debden	Carmen
20th F. G.	Kingscliffe	Churchpath
55th F. G.	Nuthampstead	Rockcreek
56th F. G.	Halesworth	Sturdy
78th F. G.	Duxford	Rutley
339th F. G.	Fowlmere	Gaspump
352nd F. G.	Bodney	Speedboat
353rd F. G.	Metfield	Boyhood
355th F. G.	Steeple Morden	Towrope
356th F. G.	Martlesham	Recount
357th F. G.	Leiston	Earlduke
359th F. G.	East Wretham	Woodbrook
361st F. G.	Bottisham	Lakepress
364th F. G.	Honington	Outside

Airfield Call-signs May 1944-May 1945

4th F. G.	Debden	Diction
20th F. G.	Kingscliffe	Churchpath
55th F. G.	Wormingford	Fusspot
56th F. G.	Boxted	Dogday
78th F. G.	Duxford	Rutley
339th F. G.	Fowlmere	Gaspump
352nd F. G.	Bodney	Speedboat*
353rd F. G.	Raydon	Cockle
355th F. G.	Steeple Morden	Tworoom
356th F. G.	Martlesham Heath	Recount
357th F. G.	Leiston	Earlduke
359th F. G.	East Wretham	Woodbrook
361st F. G.	Little Walden	Darkfold
364th F. G.	Honington	Outside
479th F. G.	Wattisham	Heather

*Bodney's Call-sign was changed to Beachhouse in April 1945

Ex-bomber pilots learn about the P-15B from Lt. Myers of the 385th Fighter Squadron who was on Temporary Duty from Honington. From left to right are Myers, Herb Howard, 100th BG., O.V. Lancaster, 385th BG., L. Abendroth, 486th BG., Andrew Fuller, 486th BG., Wes Lundholm, 100th BG., Bill Sandbloom, 486th BG., Don Guthrie, 486th BG., and Stan Gagon, 447th BG. (via McLachlin)

65th Fighter Wing Group Call-signs April 1944 to May 1945

	A Group	B Group	C Group
4th Fighter Group	Horseback	Amber	Mascot
334th Ftr. Sq.	Cobweb	Tiffin	
335th Ftr. Sq.	Caboose	Supreme	
336th Ftr. Sq.	Becky	Ronnie	
56th Fighter Group	Fairbank	Subway	Pantile
61st Ftr. Sq.	Whippet	Household	
62nd Ftr. Sq.	Platform	Icejug	
63rd Ftr. Sq.	Daily	Yorker	
355th Fighter Group	Uncle	Hornpipe	Borax
354th Ftr. Sq.	Falcon	Chieftain	
357th Ftr. Sq.	Custard	Moses	
358th Ftr. Sq.	Bentley	Beehive	

361st Fighter Group	Cheerful	Marble	Maltese
374th Ftr. Sq.	Noggin	Kingdon	
375th Ftr. Sq.	Cadet	Daydream	
376th Ftr. Sq.	Titus	Style	

(at Station 374, Bottisham)

479th Fighter Group	Highway	Snowwhite	Flareup
434th Ftr. Sq.	Newcross	Reflex	
435th Ftr. Sq.	Lakeside	Haddock	
436th Ftr. Sq.	Bison	Springbox	

66th Fighter Wing Group Call-signs April 1944 to May 1945

55th Fighter Group	Windsor	Grahic	Kodak
38th Ftr. Sq.	Hellcat	Program	
338th Ftr. Sq.	Acorn	Richard	
343rd Ftr. Sq.	Tudor	Saucy	
78th Fighter Group	Phoenix	Slapstick	Boycott
82nd Ftr. Sq.	Surtax	Rainbox	
83rd Ftr. Sq.	Cargo	Torquise	
84th Ftr. Sq.	Shampoo	Spotlight	
339th Fighter Group	Armstrong	Student	Pretend
503rd Ftr. Sq.	Beefsteak	Unique	
504th Ftr. Sq.	Cockshy	Gluepot	
505th Ftr. Sq.	Upper	Slapjack	
353rd Fighter Group	Jonah	Keylock	Muffin
350th Ftr. Sq.	Seldom	Persian	
351st Ftr. Sq.	Lawyer	Squirrel	
352nd Ftr. Sq.	Jockey	Bullring	
357th Fighter Group	Dryden	Silas	Eyesight
362nd Ftr. Sq.	Dollar	Rowntree	
363rd Ftr. Sq.	Cement	Diver	
364th Ftr. Sq.	Greenhouse	Hawkeye	

67th Fighter Wing Group Call-signs, April 1944 to May 1945

20th Fighter Group	Walnut	Oatmeal	Katie
55th Ftr. Sq.	Sailor	Paton	
77th Ftr. Sq.	Outcry	Glory	
79th Ftr. Sq.	Primrose	Screwgun	
352nd Fighter Group	Topsy	Bearskin	Cloister
328th Ftr. Sq.	Ditto	Tarmac	
486th Ftr. Sq.	Angus	Rocket	
487th Ftr. Sq.	Transport	Vicar	
356th Fighter Group	Lampshade	Notebook	Seaweed
359th Ftr. Sq.	Farmhouse	Bucket	
360th Ftr. Sq.	Vortex	Deansgate	
361st Ftr. Sq.	Chinwag	Webber	
359th Fighter Group	Chairman	Cavetop	Ragtime
368th Ftr. Sq.	Jigger	Handy	
369th Ftr. Sq.	Tinplate	Earnest	
370th Ftr. Sq.	Redcross	Rollo	
364th Fighter Group	Sunhat	Weekday	Harlop
383rd Ftr. Sq.	Escort	Tantrum	
384th Ftr. Sq.	Goldfish	Zeeta	
385th Ftr. Sq.	Eggflig	Pillow	

SQUADRON CALL SIGNS

SQUADRON CALL SIGNS

At various times during the war these call signs were changed for security or other reasons including that of clarity, ie, to clear bomber and fighter radio channels being jammed by the Germans on a particular mission.

Squadron	Call Sign
38	Hellcat
55	Towntalk
61	Whippet
62	Platform
63	Daily
77	Outcry
79	Primrose
82	Surtax
83	Cargo
84	Bayland

Above left: Lt. Keith Canella, from Santa Ana, California, became MIA June 22, 1944. According to MACR #6108, he and ''Sweet Mary'', #43-28731, L2-K were caught by flak, about 5 miles S.E. of LaFere, France, and crashed.

Below: George Dan Hendrix downed a JU-88 early on the morning of Aug. 12, 1944 to register the 434th Squadron's fourth victory. His A/C was named after his home town in California, also home of Edgar Rice Burroughs - author of ''Tarzan.''

Below: Lt. Arnold G. Helding and his ''Lucky Lady'' pose for the photographer. Lt. Leroy Lutz was lost in this A/C (43-28714) also on June 22, 1944. P-38s were used extensively in the Normandy Beachhead area because of their unmistakable silhouette.

328	Steamboat
334	Greenbelt
335	
336	Shirtblue
338	Acorn
343	Tudor
350	Pipeful
351	Roughman
352	Wakeford
353	Anchor
354	Haywood
355	Youngman
356	Fetlock
357	Custard
358	Bently
359	Farmhouse
360	Vortex
361	Chinwag
362	Dollar
363	Cement
364	Greenhouse
368	Jigger
369	Tinplate
370	Redcross
374	
375	Cadet
376	
383	Escort
384	
385	
434	Newcross
435	Lakeside
436	Bison
486	Angus
487	Transport
503	Beefsteak
504	Codesky
505	Upper

Top: OK, guys, it's cheesecake time! Fred Hayner, of the 479th, who supplied many of the photos in this section (all 3 p. 244 and all but bottom L this pg.), decorated many a plane. The pilots dubbed him "Hayner the Painter." Top photo is an early example of his work on a 434th F.S. P-38.

Above: Another Hayner masterpiece, "Sleepytime Gal" (44-23169, L2-Z) and pilot Lt. James Wallace became flak victims near Steenwijk, Holland August 15, 1944. (MACR #8121) Below, left: Thomas C. Olson, who piled up a very impressive score of ground vics, (see Vol. II), and his first P-38, L2-W. L to R: Assistant C/C Alworth D. Larson, Olson, C/C Loy C. Slaton. All Olson's assigned A/C were named "Lelah May." (Gossard Via Ivie) Below, right: "Hayner the Painter" caught in the very act! Fred gets P-51, 44-14651, of the 434th, ready for our color section (P138). Note lovely lady has yet to make her appearance. This A/C was lost with Lt. J.C. Donnell on Feb. 14, 1945.

Above: Major James Herren returned from a mission and found himself surrounded by 479th "Big Wheels," who promptly awarded him his Silver Oak Leaves. L to R: Lt. Col. Sidney S. Woods, Herren, Lt. Col. Wm. F. Stenton, Major Frank R. Silver, Capt. Claire A.P. Duffie, and Major Wm. T. McElhinney. In the background is Herren's P-38, L2-A, 42-68008, "Touché." Just a few months later, on Oct. 30, Lt. Col. Herron became MIA in his similarly named P-51, L2-F, 44-14396 (MACR #10,922). Below: Frank J. Keller with his first P-38, L2-I, 42-104140. The C/C was Sgt. Norval Baker of Hot Springs, Arkansas. Frank claimed 2 A/C destroyed, one being the first confirmed ground claim for the fledgling 479th fighter group. Bottom: Captain Frank in his next, and last, P-38, L2-I, 43-28377, "Hilo Hattie." Pilot and A/C were lost on August 9 and Keller ended up as a guest of the Luftwaffe until EOW. (Hayner)

Above: Lt. Tom Tipps with his lightning, L2-R, "The Zaniest Wildcat." Tom shot down a 109 on July 6, 1944 and claimed another on the ground. Below: Tom Tipps and C/C Cullie Flynn all re-equipped with a shiny new P-51 including a Spitfire rear view mirror. This A/C, 44-14311, also had the small interior rear view mirror. Wanna stay alive? Watch yer tail!

Left: Fighter ace Arthur Jeffrey named all his A/C "Boomerang" and all were coded L2-O. This A/C, his only assigned P-38, carries serial #42-104425. When the 479th changed over to P-51s, many pilots retained the same name but put "Jr" on the end of it. The Mustang must have felt a bit like a sport plane after the huge '38. Lt. Calvin Murphy was lost in this A/C on Sept. 6, 1944 near Darmstadt, Germany (MACR #8566). Top, right: Art's P-51, 44-11674, with 13 vics on canopy rail. On his way to becoming the 479th's top air ace, Art shot down some really unusual A/C: his first (and also first for the 434th) was a FW-200, a big, lumbering 4 engined giant. His next kill was a genuine rarity, a ME-163, the only rocket propelled A/C to ever reach operational status in any A.F.! Above right: After his tour, Art's P-51 was assigned to Lt. Hilton O. Thompson, who renamed it as shown. Also the code became L2-I. (Mulron/Tabatt)

AIRFIELD CODES

SAAF and RAF Airfield Identification Letters

Code	Airfield	Code	Airfield	Code	Airfield	Code	Airfield
H	Abereth	BA		JM	Bardney		Boreham
B	Abingdon	BJ		BD	Barford St. John		Boscombe Down
M	Acastor Malbis	BH		AQ	Barkston Heath		Bottesford
I	Acklington	BS		BM	Bassingbourn		Boulmer
Y	Alconbury	BQ		AU	Beaulieu		Bourn
N	Aldermaston	BE		BV	Beccles		Bovingdon
E	Angle	BB		BX	Benbecula		Boxted
O	Appledram	EB		RB	Benson		Bradwell
F	Ashford	BI		BW	Bibury		Brawdy
D	Aston Down	BC		AC	Bicester		Breighton
P	Atcham	GI		ZT	Biggin Hill		Brenzett
T	Attlebridge	BK		BN	Binbrock		Brize Norton
R	Ayr	JB		BF	Birch		Bruntingthorpe
		BR		BN	Bircotes		Brunton
		IZ		JO	Bisterne		Bungay
		BT		AZ	Bitteswell		Burn
F	Babdown	AL		BU	Blyton		Bury St Edmunds
G	Baginton	BO		BY	Bodney		Butley
L	Balderton	OG			Bognor		
F	Banff	OH			Bolthead	KY	Calverley

247

Left: "Kraut Knocker," 44-14423, was assigned to Lt. Robert Bromschwig. It was lost on May 5, 1945 when the engine quit on take off. If the serial sounds familiar, it's because this bird was originally assigned to Art Jeffrey as his first P-51 "Boomerang Jr." It's original code was then L2-"O", the pic shows it as L2-"T" and the pictures of it off the end of the runway show it to have been changed again to L2-"L". Right: Air Force Day at Wattisham, home of the 479th fighter group, and thousands of curious English civilians got their first close-up of the famous P-51 Mustang. Capt. Clarence Haynes sits astride the cowling of Lt. Robert Bromschwig's second "Kraut Knocker" L2-T, 44-15381. The engine panels with the name on them were probably salvaged from his earlier ship. C/C was Neil Dornbus and Henry W. Briggs took care of the point fifties. (Hayner)

KA	Clark	CF	Church Fenton	DZ	Dalcross
CC	Castle Camps	CL	Church Lawford	DI	Dallachy
CJ	Castle Coombe	CG	Coleby Grange	DA	Dalton
CD	Castle Donnington	CQ	Colerne	DM	Darley Moor
AX	Castletown	CS	Coltishall	DD	Davistowe
CA	Catfoss	DV	Condover	XD	Deanland
AK	Catterick	CY	Coningsby	DC	Debach
AJ	Chailey	KO	Connel	DB	Debden
CH	Charmy Down	XQ	Coolham	DP	Deenethorpe
KH	Charter Hall	CM	Cottom	DF	Defford
CU	Chedburgh	CT	Cottesmore	DG	Deopham Green
CE	Cheddington	RG	Granage	DS	Desborough
YW	Chedworth	CX	Cranfield	DQ	Detling
CV	Chelveston	CK	Cranswich	DJ	Digby
CI	Chilbolton	CP	Cranwell	DH	Dishforth
CN	Chipping Norton	CR	Croft	DK	Docking
JC	Chipping Ongar	KX	Croxby	DN	Dounreay
OW	Chipping Warden	AW	Croughton	DO	Downham Market
IV	Chivenor	CO	Croydon	DE	Drem
XC	Christchurch	UG	Colmhead	DR	Driffield
CB	Church Broughton			DU	Dumfries

Two photos of the attractive A/C of Lt. Eugene Sears, the subject of a color profile on page 152. As can be clearly seen from the information in this volume, every group had its own style of markings. In the 479th, it was, more or less, standard for an A/C to carry the same name on both sides.

L	Dunholme Lodge
W	Dunkeswell
T	Dunsfold
X	Duxford
Y	Dyce
C	Earls Colne
A	Eastchurch
F	East Fortune
K	East Kirkby
M	East Moor
H	Edge Hill
Z	Edzell
S	Elsham
V	Elvington
L	Ely
N	Enstone
R	Errol
T	Evanton
X	Exeter
Y	Eye
A	Fairford
P	Fairlop
C	Fairwood Common
H	Faldingworth
L	Feltwell
G	Fidnogask
I	Finmere
V	Finningley
N	Fiskerton
O	Folkingham
D	Ford
R	Fordoun
U	Foulsham
W	Fowlmere
M	Framlingham
B	Frazerburgh
X	Friaton
K	Fulbeck
S	Full Sutton
J	Funtingdon
B	Gamsdon
K	Gatwick
P	Gaydon
T	Glatton
F	Gosfield
X	Goxhill
U	Grafton Underwood
W	Grangemouth
L	Gransdon Lodge
H	Grantham
R	Graveley
N	Gravesend
A	Great Ashfield
D	Great Dunmow
M	Great Massingham
E	Great Orton
S	Great Saling
S	Great Sampford
C	Greenham Common
Y	Grimsby

Above: Phillip D. Gossard of Cincinnati, Ohio, his 435th F.S. P-38 (J2-O, 43-23663) "Ruth" and crew. (Ivie) Below: Two photos of Gossard's P-51 #44-14354, "V for Val." The 479th had the irritating habit of removing the serial numbers from the tails of their A/C, making identification difficult. (Ivie/Bennett)

Left: The flight of 4 joins up and heads out. At the far side No. 2 is J2-J, 44-14263, 'Roarin' Rose' flown by John J. Coursey. No. 1 is our previously photographed J2-N, 44-14827 and No. 3 is J2-J, 44-15236. Above: The Mustang of Capt. Ray K. Friend, which he named 'Sweet El II.'' Ray claimed 1½ A/C with this P-51, J2-B, 44-14378. (Gossard via Ivie)

Top: A Mustang of the 435th takes off under the load of 2 110 gallon wing tanks for a deep penetration mission.

GV	Grove				
		HE	Hibaldistow	JY	Jurby
HP	Harrowbeer	HC	High Ercall		
HK	Hawarden	IH	High Halden	KV	Keevil
HA	Halesworth	HI	Hinton-in-the-Hedge	KS	Kelstern
EG	Halpenny Green	HX	Hixon	KM	Kemble
HN	Hampstead Norris	HM	Holme	KE	Kenley
HG	Hardwick	HQ	Honeybourne	KD	Kidlington
HH	Harlaxton	HY	Honeley	KI	Kimbolton
HR	Harrington	HT	Honington	KC	Kingscliffe
XB	Hartford Bridge	JH	Horham	IN	Kingsworth
HW	Harwell	HO	Hornchurch	KB	Kingston
AU	Haverford West	OR	Horne	KW	Kinloss
VK	Hawkinge	HF	Horsham St Faith	KL	Kinnel
ED	Headcorn	HV	Hullavington	KK	Kirknewton
HU	Hells Mouth	HD	Hunsdon	KK	Kirmington
HL	Hemswell	KU	Hurn	KN	Knettishall
ND	Hendon	HZ	Husband's Bosworth		
HP	Hepworth			LK	Lakenheath
HS	Heston	IB	Ibsley	LA	Langer
HJ	Hethel	IA	Isle Abbots	LJ	Langham
				LQ	Lasham

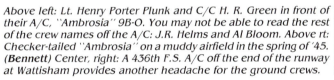

Above left: Lt. Henry Porter Plunk and C/C H. R. Green in front of their A/C, "Ambrosia" 9B-O. You may not be able to read the rest of the crew names off the A/C: J.R. Helms and Al Bloom. Above rt: Checker-tailed "Ambrosia" on a muddy airfield in the spring of '45. (Bennett) Center, right: A 436th F.S. A/C off the end of the runway at Wattisham provides another headache for the ground crews.

XL	Lashenden	LM	Ludford Magna	MT	Metfield
LV	Lavenham	LU	Ludham	MN	Metheringham
LC	Loconfield	LP	Lulsgate Bottom	ML	Methwold
LG	Leeming	YL	Lydd	MG	Middleton St George
LE	Leicester East	LZ	Lymington	MW	Middle Wallop
LI	Leiston	PY	Lympne	MI	Mildenhall
LF	Lichfield	YM	Lyneham	IL	Milfield
LB	Lindholme			MJ	Millom
LY	Leuchars	MY	Manby	IT	Milltown
LO	Linton-on-Ouse	MQ	Manston	MX	Molesworth
LT	Lissett	MR	Marham	MO	Moreton-in-Marsh
LH	Little Horwood	MB	Market Harborough	MV	Moreton Valence
LR	Little Rissington	MA	Marston Moor	MS	Montrose
LS	Little Snoring	MH	Hartlesham Heath	EP	Morpeth
LX	Little Staughton	MC	Matching	MD	Mountford Bridge
LL	Little Waldon	MK	Matlake	MF	Mount Farm
LW	Llandwrog	ME	Melbourne		
JS	Long Marston	MM	Melton Mowbray	NI	Needs Oar Point
LN	Long Newton	MZ	Mendlesham	NE	Netheravon
IO	Longtown	MP	Mepal	NM	Newmarket
OL	Lossiemouth	XM	Merston	NA	Newton

Hans J. Grasshoff of the 436th with his Mustang "Little Zippie," 9B-J, 44-14574. He also had a P-38 named "Zippie." Hans claimed a total of 6½ air/ground vics. The name was written in black and outlined in red. (Plunk)

PR	Pershore		
PT	Perton		
PH	Peterhead		
PO	Pocklington		
PN	Poddington		
PK	Polebrook		
PE	Port Ellen		
PA	Portreath		
PU	Poulton		
PD	Predannick		
PW	Prestwick		
RK	Rac?heath		
RY	Ramsbury		
RS	Rattlesdon		
RA	Raydon		
RI	Redhill		

XN	Newchurch	OV	Overton Health
XR	New Romney	OA	Oakington
NZ	New Zealand Farm	OY	Oakley
NC	North Coates	OI	Odiham
NO	North Creake	OB	Old Buckenham
NK	North Killingholme	OM	Old Sarum
NL	North Luffenham	ON	Ossington
NP	North Pickenham	OU	Oulton
NH	Northolt	OS	Ouston
NQ	North Weald		
NW	North Witham	PS	Penshurst
NU	Nuneaton	PP	Perranporth
NT	Nuthampstead	CE	Peplow

SW	Snailwell
SX	Snaith
SN	Snetterton
KF	Snitterfield
SC	South Carney
KP	Southrop
SL	Spilsby
ZG	Squires Gate
KT	Stanstead
ST	Stanton Harcourt
KZ	Stapleford Tawney
XS	Staplehurst
KR	Steeple Morden
SS	Stoney Cross
NX	Stradishall
ZO	Stacathro
NF	Stratford
NY	Strubby
US	Strugate
SU	Sudbury
UM	Sumbugh
SB	Sutton Bridge
VY	Valley
WA	Waddington
UY	Wakerly
WB	Warboys
XW	Warmwell
OT	Warton
WV	Watchfield
WJ	Waterbeach
WT	Wattisham
WN	Watton
WZ	Welford
WM	Wellesborne Mountfor◄
JW	Wellingore
WU	Wendling
WX	Westcott
EW	West Freugh
WQ	Westhampnett
UE	Westley
UG	West Malling
WG	Weston-on-the-Green
ZW	West Zoyland

Left: On Jan. 13, 1945, Flight Officer Raymond E. King was escorting Lt. Fred Zellman home with a rough engine, when his own engine quit. He ditched his P-51, 9B-J, 44-14574 (ex-"Little Zippie" pictured above) just off the coast at Clacton-On-Sea, Essex. Although rescued quickly, King died of exposure in the local hospital. The A/C was later raised and is now in a local museum. (Stuart) Right: The crew of 44-14613 of the 436th, L to rt: Assistant C/C B.N. Armstrong, C/C Harold E. Virgin Jr., Driver T. E. Myers and Armorer George E. Bozeth. Their appropriately named A/C is the final picture for Vol. I!

256